Wisconsin's
Past and Present
A Historical Atlas

Wisconsin after Statehood, 1849

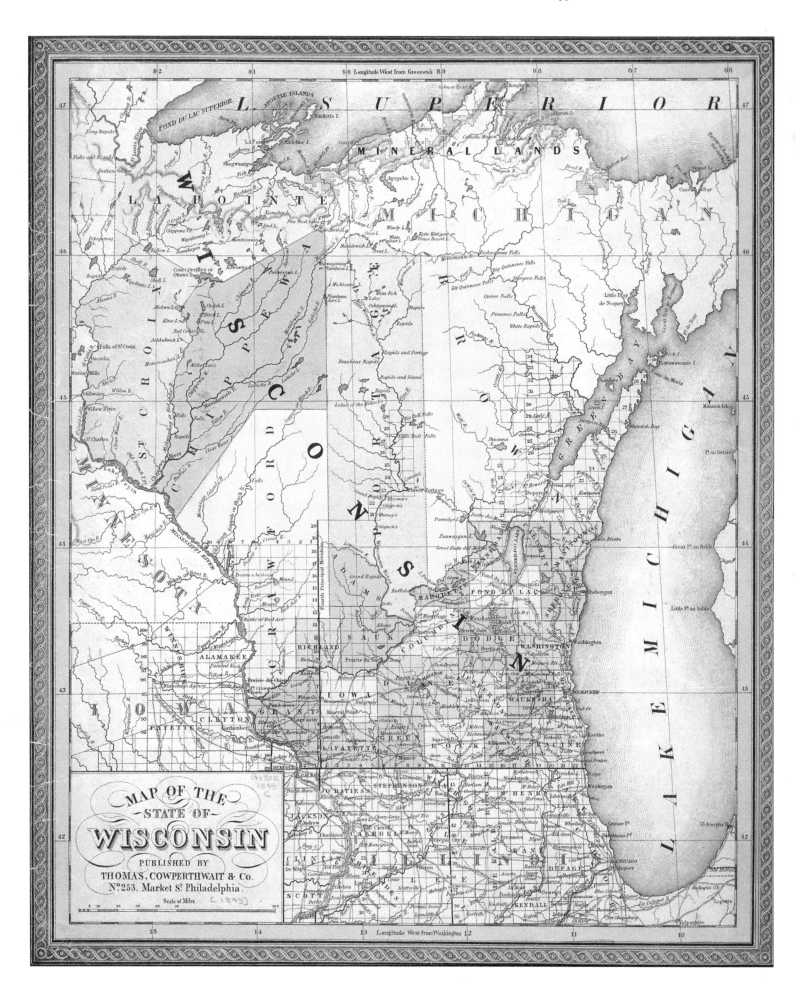

MAP OF THE
—STATE OF—
WISCONSIN
PUBLISHED BY
THOMAS, COWPERTHWAIT & Co.
No. 253, Market St. Philadelphia.

Scale of Miles

WISCONSIN, 2002

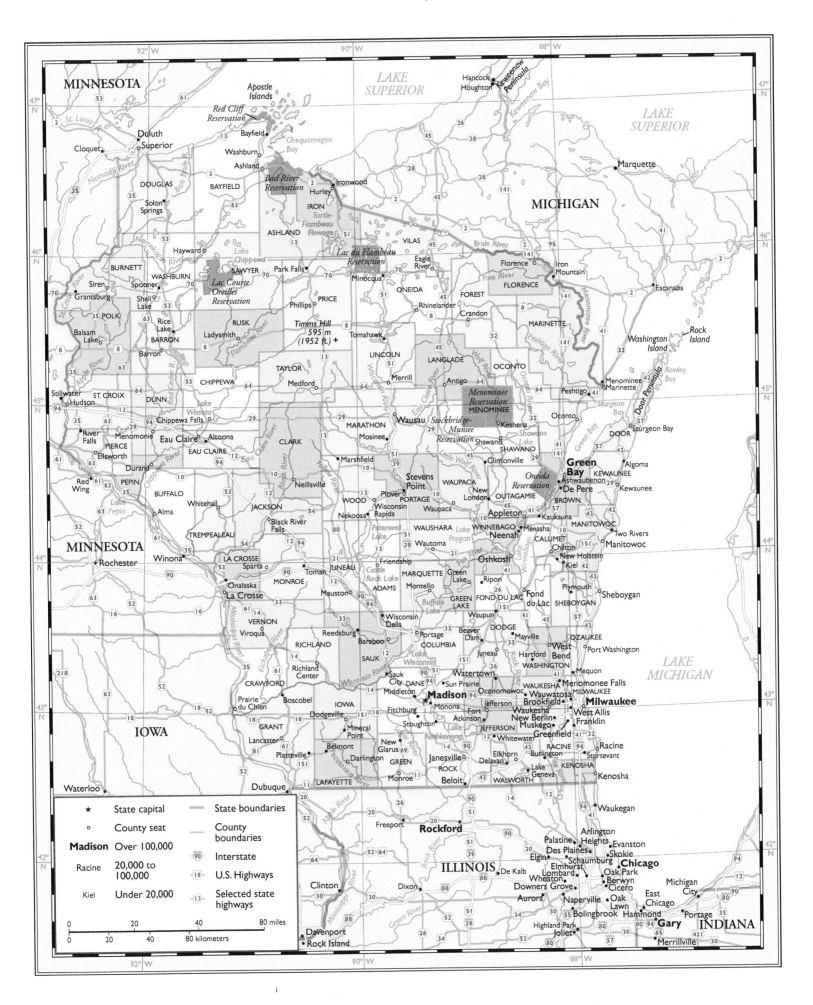

MINNESOTA

LAKE SUPERIOR

LAKE SUPERIOR

MICHIGAN

Apostle Islands

Red Cliff Reservation

Hancock
Houghton
Keweenaw Peninsula

Keweenaw Bay

Duluth
Superior
Cloquet
Bayfield
Washburn
Ashland
Chequamegon Bay

Nemadji River
St. Louis
Bois Brule R.

Marquette

DOUGLAS
BAYFIELD

Bad River Reservation
Hurley
Ironwood

IRON
Turtle-Flambeau Flowage

Solon Springs

Namekagon River

ASHLAND

Montreal R.

Brule River

Florence
Iron Mountain

MICHIGAN

Escanaba

Hayward
Lake Chippewa

Park Falls

Lac du Flambeau Reservation

VILAS

Eagle River

FLORENCE

Pine River

Menominee River

BURNETT
WASHBURN
Spooner
Shell Lake
Siren
Grantsburg

Lac Courte Oreilles Reservation

SAWYER

Minocqua

ONEIDA

Rhinelander

FOREST
Crandon

MARINETTE

Washington Island

Rock Island

POLK
Balsam Lake
Rice Lake
Ladysmith
Phillips
PRICE

Timms Hill
595 m
(1952 ft.) +

Tomahawk

LINCOLN
Merrill

LANGLADE
Antigo

OCONTO

Peshtigo
Marinette

Barron
BARRON

RUSK

Flambeau River

Wisconsin River

Eau Claire River

Wolf River

Oconto River

Peshtigo River

Oconto

Rowley Bay

Stillwater
Hudson
ST. CROIX
Chippewa Falls
Altoona
Eau Claire
EAU CLAIRE

CHIPPEWA
TAYLOR
Medford

CLARK

MARATHON
Mosinee

Wausau

Stockbridge-Munsee Reservation

Menominee Reservation
MENOMINEE
Keshena

Shawano
Shawano Lake

SHAWANO
Clintonville

DOOR
Sturgeon Bay

Sturgeon Bay

Door Peninsula

Green Bay

River Falls
PIERCE
Ellsworth
Durand
Menomonie
DUNN

Marshfield

Little Wolf River

Red Wing
PEPIN
Lake Pepin
Alma
Whitehall
BUFFALO

Neillsville

WOOD
Nekoosa
Wisconsin Rapids

Stevens Point
PORTAGE
Plover

WAUPACA
Waupaca
New London

OUTAGAMIE
Appleton
Kaukauna

Oneida Reservation
Ashwaubenon
De Pere

Green Bay
KEWAUNEE
Algoma
Kewaunee

BROWN

MANITOWOC
Two Rivers
Manitowoc

Black River
Yellow River

TREMPEALEAU
JACKSON
Black River Falls

Winona

LA CROSSE
Sparta
Onalaska
La Crosse

Rochester

MINNESOTA

Castle Rock Lake
Petenwell Lake

WAUSHARA
Wautoma

Friendship

Menasha
Neenah
WINNEBAGO

CALUMET
Chilton
New Holstein
Kiel

Lake Winnebago
Lake Poygan

Oshkosh

MONROE
Tomah

JUNEAU
Mauston

ADAMS

MARQUETTE
Montello

Green Lake
Ripon
GREEN LAKE

FOND DU LAC
Fond du Lac
Waupun

Plymouth
SHEBOYGAN
Sheboygan

Fox River

Viroqua
VERNON

Kickapoo River

Reedsburg
RICHLAND
Richland Center

Wisconsin Dells

Portage
COLUMBIA

Baraboo
SAUK

Buffalo Lake

DODGE
Beaver Dam
Mayville
Juneau
Hartford
WASHINGTON
West Bend

OZAUKEE
Port Washington
Mequon

LAKE MICHIGAN

Prairie du Chien
CRAWFORD

Boscobel
Dodgeville
IOWA

Wisconsin River

Sauk City
Middleton
DANE
Madison
Monona
Sun Prairie

Watertown
Oconomowoc
WAUKESHA
Waukesha
Brookfield
Jefferson
Wauwatosa

Menomonee Falls
MILWAUKEE
Milwaukee
West Allis
Franklin

Rock River

GRANT
Lancaster

Mineral Point

Fitchburg
Stoughton
Fort Atkinson
JEFFERSON
New Berlin
Muskego
Greenfield

Belmont
Platteville

New Glarus
Darlington
GREEN
Monroe

Lake Mendota
Lake Koshkonong

Whitewater
Elkhorn
Delavan

Burlington
RACINE
Racine
Sturtevant

Pecatonica River

LAFAYETTE

Janesville
ROCK
Beloit

WALWORTH
Lake Geneva

KENOSHA
Kenosha

Dubuque

Waterloo

IOWA

ILLINOIS

Freeport

Rockford

Waukegan

Arlington Heights
Palatine
Evanston
Skokie
Des Plaines
Elgin
Schaumburg
Elmhurst
Lombard
Wheaton
Downers Grove
Aurora
Naperville
Bolingbrook
Highland Park

Chicago
Oak Park
Berwyn
Cicero
Oak Lawn
Hammond
East Chicago

Michigan City

De Kalb
Dixon

Clinton

Davenport
Rock Island

Mississippi River

Green River

Rock River

Joliet
Gary
Merrillville
Portage

INDIANA

Legend

★ State capital

○ County seat

Madison Over 100,000

Racine 20,000 to 100,000

Kiel Under 20,000

State boundaries

County boundaries

90 Interstate

18 U.S. Highways

13 Selected state highways

0 ___ 20 ___ 40 ___ 80 miles

0 ___ 20 ___ 40 ___ 80 kilometers

The Wisconsin Cartographers' Guild

Marily B. Crews-Nelson
Laura Exner
Michael Gallagher
Zoltán Grossman
Amelia R. Janes
Jeffry Maas

Wisconsin's Past and Present
A Historical Atlas

The Wisconsin Cartographers' Guild

The University of Wisconsin Press

The University of Wisconsin Press
1930 Monroe Street, 3rd Floor
Madison, Wisconsin 53711-2059
uwpress.wisc.edu

3 Henrietta Street, Covent Garden
London WC2E 8LU, United Kingdom
eurospanbookstore.com

Printed in the United States of America

Map on page ii: **Wisconsin after Statehood, 1849.** From *Mitchell's New Universal Atlas*
(Philadelphia: Thomas, Cowperthwait & Co., 1849)
State Historical Society of Wisconsin
Map on page iii: **Wisconsin, 2002.** Cartographers: production and design, Amelia Janes;
editing and research, Zoltán Grossman; research, Michael Gallagher. 2002.

Meridel Le Sueur, *North Star Country,* ©1945 by the University of Nebraska Press.
Lines from Lorine Niedecker, "My Friend Tree," ©1961 by Cid Corman, are reprinted by permission of Cid Corman.
Robert M. La Follette, *La Follette's Autobiography,* is published by the University of Wisconsin Press.

Library of Congress Cataloging-in-Publication Data
Wisconsin's Past and Present: a historical atlas/
The Wisconsin Cartographers' Guild.
142 pp.   cm.
Includes bibliographical references (p.93) and index.
ISBN 0-299-15940-X (alk. paper)
1. Wisconsin—History.   2. Wisconsin—Historical geography.   3. Wisconsin—History—Maps.
I. Wisconsin Cartographers' Guild.
F581.W57   1998
977.5—dc21   98-24580

ISBN 978-0-299-15940-5 (cloth: alk. paper)

Contents

Names identify coordinators of two-page spreads.
Italic type indicates original map or illustration.

Peoples & Cultures

Land & Economy

Society & Politics

Cartographers / Authors

Marily B. Crews-Nelson was born in Milwaukee, and grew up in Lancaster, Grant County. She received a B.S. in geography with a cartography emphasis from the University of Wisconsin– Platteville in 1991, and spent several years doing highway design. With her husband, Doug, also a cartographer, she is producing maps once again. Marily and Doug live in Verona with daughters Audrey and Sadie.

Laura Exner received a B.A. in geography from the University of Wisconsin–Madison. She works as a cartographer and lives in Middleton with her husband Paul.

Michael Gallagher has worked as a map editor and cartographer for over 10 years. A native of Milwaukee, he received a B.S. from the University of Wisconsin–Madison in history (1979) and a B.S. in cartography (1985). His background includes service in the U.S. Navy and Navy Reserve. He has brought his passions for maps and history together in the atlas project, and is the "technical guru" for the project. Mike lives in Madison with his wife Diane.

Zoltán Grossman is internal editor for the atlas project. He has been making maps since the age of six, and has been a professional map editor since the age of 24. He received a B.A. in history and geography (1984), and an M.S. in geog-

raphy (1998) from the University of Wisconsin–Madison. He has written and developed educational curricula on U.S. and global history and geography, and has a special interest in interethnic relations and indigenous peoples. Zoltán grew up in a Hungarian family in Minnesota and Utah, and lives in Madison with his partner Debi.

Amelia R. Janes came to Wisconsin from Kentucky in 1980. Her first experience in cartography was hiking through the brush of central Wisconsin, field sketching and surveying burial and effigy mounds for archeological research. Since then she has combined her fine arts education, including an M.F.A. in drawing/design from the University of Wisconsin–Madison in 1983, with years of practical cartographic training and production. Amelia lives in Madison with her companion Paul.

Jeffry Maas was born in Superior, and grew up in Solon Springs, Douglas County. He attended the Minneapolis College of Art and Design and the University of Wisconsin–Superior, receiving a B.A. in geography from the University of Wisconsin–Eau Claire in 1993. He has combined his love of art, graphic design, maps, and history into a career in cartography. Jeff lives and works in Madison.

Consulting Editors

Ingolf Vogeler is Professor of Geography at the University of Wisconsin–Eau Claire. He earned a Ph.D. in geography from the University of Minnesota in 1973. His research focuses on rural areas and agriculture in the United States and Western Europe, and cultural landscapes in North America, Latin America, Africa, and Asia.

John O. (Jack) Holzhueter was born and raised in Menomonie, Dunn County. He received bachelor's and master's degrees in journalism and U.S. history at the University of Wisconsin–Madison. Since 1964, he has been employed by the State Historical Society of Wisconsin in editorial and research capabilities. Avocationally, he is a church musician.

Foreword
Learning to see the past
that is all around us

The book you hold in your hands is a great gift, for it can teach you to see this state and its past with fresh eyes.

Although geographers have on occasion produced collections of thematic maps for Wisconsin, there has never been an atlas specifically devoted to tracing the state's history. The only publication ever to call itself a historical atlas for Wisconsin was produced in the 1870s, and although it contained much useful information on the state's early settlers, it was really a series of contemporary maps published in the same volume with biographical sketches and brief historical essays describing the early settlement of the state. A dozen decades have now passed since that pioneering work, so it seems especially appropriate that the Wisconsin Cartographers' Guild has chosen the occasion of the state's Sesquicentennial to produce its first historical atlas. For a group of independent cartographers, working cooperatively on a shoestring budget, to have produced such an original and distinguished volume is a remarkable achievement, and everyone who cares about the history and geography of Wisconsin is in their debt. We will be studying and learning from this book for many years to come.

Geography and history complement each other in endless ways, but the academic past of the two disciplines has frequently left them estranged from each other. Historians too often tell wonderfully compelling stories about past lives and ideas, without quite managing to convey the textured richness of the landscapes within which those stories take place. For their part, geographers too often draw maps that brilliantly reveal the complex spatial and environmental relationships people have with each other and with the land, without always suggesting the intricate and often surprising evolution of those relationships over time. My own view, as an inveterate student and collector of historical atlases from the United States and all over the world, is that historical atlases are among the most potent tools we have for forcing ourselves to confront the full richness of the world we inhabit, a world that is as challenging to understand in space as it is in time. What we discover in such books is the powerful traditions and causal forces that have led people to live how and where they now do, modified in turn by the serendipitous accidents of history that have played no less powerful a role in shaping the lives we now lead.

The wonder of a great historical atlas is its ability to juxta-pose a multitude of different themes in different places and periods so as to suggest the extraordinary interconnectedness of the world around us. The United States as a whole has had surprisingly few such atlases: one thinks of Charles O. Paullin's *Atlas of the Historical Geography of the United States,* published in 1932, still in many ways the most ambitious historical atlas produced in this country; James Truslow Adams' *Atlas of American History,* published in 1943; and the *American Heritage Pictorial Atlas of United States History,* published in 1966. Important and useful as these books may be, none holds a candle to the breathtaking *Historical Atlas of Canada,* published in three volumes between 1987 and 1993, a work that puts to shame its neighbors to the south. Although no historical atlas published on a limited budget for a single state is likely to compete with these path-breaking Canadian volumes, in fact *Wisconsin's Past and Present: A Historical Atlas* begins to point the way toward what a new generation of historical atlases will look like in this country. Employing the powerful new cartographic and compositional tools that are now available on computers, it has become possible to process much more quickly and easily much larger quantities of data about a more diverse array of themes than ever before.

New printing technologies have enabled even a small state atlas like this one to represent its insights and arguments not in the difficult-to-decipher patterns of black ink on white paper, but in all the subtleties that can be expressed when a nearly infinite array of colors is available to the map-maker. The result is not just a feast to the eye, but to the mind as well.

A book like this one should be approached less as a volume to be read cover to cover—though it will certainly reward such a reading—than as an occasion for inspired browsing. Turn from a spread of maps on the distribution of the state's ethnic groups to a comparable spread on state agriculture, and you will almost inevitably find yourself wondering why certain peoples were drawn to certain locations and certain kinds of crops. Study the maps of glaciation in Wisconsin and bear them in mind as you browse through comparable maps of vegetation, watersheds, and industries, and you will not be able to escape the conclusion that events seemingly buried in the deep geological past continue to have a profound influence on landscapes and human lives all around the state. Spend some time comparing Wisconsin's rivers, railroad lines, and roads with maps displaying the state's settlement history and contemporary demographic distribution, and you'll be forced to recognize remarkable continuities in the ways people have moved and made homes around the state. Half the pleasure in such discoveries is in making them oneself, and it is a characteristic of this kind of book that one finds in it more data than argument: here you have the raw materials for almost endless speculation about this remarkable state, its peoples and landscapes.

My own hope is that citizens of Wisconsin will buy this book and keep it close at hand whenever they travel around the state. Although it was surely not written mainly as a tourist guide, I can imagine few more inspired uses to which it might be put. If only we can train our eyes to see it, the landscape around us is one of the richest and most fascinat-

ing historical documents we possess, a source of endless stories and insights if we can unlock its secrets. In trying to understand the landscapes we now inhabit and travel through, one of the most powerful questions we can ask is, "How did this place come to be this way?" That is precisely the question that this new atlas gives us the tools to start answering on our own. I suspect it won't quite fit in my own glove compartment, but I'm planning to figure out some way to leave a copy in my car so I'll never have far to reach when confronting some new puzzle in the places I visit—and I urge you, dear reader, to do the same!

William Cronon
Frederick Jackson Turner Professor of
History, Geography, and Environmental Studies
University of Wisconsin–Madison

Introduction

In this Sesquicentennial year, many Wisconsin citizens are asking what makes their state unique. How did "Wisconsin" evolve from a collection of arbitrary boundary lines on the landscape to a cohesive political and cultural entity—a place unto itself? The answer may lie, at least to some extent, in the state's location at the intersection of natural and cultural regions. Wisconsin has always been a part of North America on the "edge." It was at the edge of great glacial ice sheets, and subsequently on the "tension line" between the Northwoods and the Central Plains. It later became a meeting ground for many different Native American nations, and a new home to diverse groups of immigrant settlers, who introduced new cutting-edge political and economic ideas to the rest of the country. Wisconsin developed between the urban centers of Chicago and the Twin Cities, and parts of the state became a hinterland to both metropolitan areas. The state still serves as a borderland combining the agricultural Midwest, the industrial Great Lakes region, and the Northern forests, and its people reflect this regional diversity. Drawing from its traditions, Wisconsin continues to stand on the forefront of innovative government policies and community-based ethics. It continues to be a unique place where many different aspects of nature and culture clash, interact, and sometimes find a balance.

Wisconsin's Past and Present: A Historical Atlas was born out of a love for our state and for the art of mapmaking. The people of Wisconsin have not had a historical atlas since 1878. Two years ago, the Wisconsin Cartographers' Guild decided that the state's 150th birthday was an ideal time to make the long-held dream of a new historical atlas come true and to provide an educational resource that would last beyond the 1998 celebration.

The Wisconsin Cartographers' Guild was founded in May 1996 by six professional mapmakers in the Madison area. We have a total of about 40 years of experience in the craft, and have complementary backgrounds in thematic cartography, geography, history, art, and science. We have worked together for years on computer graphics production and desktop publishing, and have pooled our skills, resources, and technology to continue this close working relationship.

In a sense, this atlas is itself a product of historical circumstances. The Guild reflects a working environment similar to the artisan craft guilds and rural cooperatives in Wisconsin's past, but different in using modern technology. Advances in computers, and heightened public interest in Wisconsin's history in its Sesquicentennial year, have given impetus to the production of an atlas that we hope provides an exciting look into the state's past.

How to use the atlas

This atlas is organized into sections around three central categories. The first section, *Peoples & Cultures,* looks at indigenous and immigrant groups and the state's religious and cultural diversity. The second section, *Land & Economy,* examines Wisconsin's natural resources, agriculture, and industries. The third section, *Society & Politics,* reviews the development of boundaries, social movements, and government in Wisconsin's history. Within each section, two-page spreads present historical themes in a roughly chronological fashion.

Spreads were coordinated by different cartographers/ authors, and so serve as distinct essays on various historical themes. Since the themes in the atlas are strongly interrelated, however, the spreads are by no means self-contained, for each one contains references to other spreads. In the Weather Hazards spread, for example, the story of the 1871 Peshtigo Fire refers to the discussion of harmful lumbering practices in the Timber spread. The cross-references are abbreviated versions of the spread titles. For example, *Germans* refers to the spread "Becoming German American."

Each spread contains a main body of text giving a basic chronological overview of the theme, a primary map, and secondary maps and columns that tell more in-depth stories related to the central theme. Some graphics help to provide context for the maps and text, while other graphics (such as charts) can themselves be used as reference tools.

Educational uses

The atlas is intended for the general public, and particularly for schools. History and social studies instructors have long needed a concise, visual publication about Wisconsin history to heighten students' interest in the subject, and inspire students to do further research. The *Bibliography & Sources* section provides resources for further study. We hope that instructors in high schools and colleges will incorporate the atlas into the U.S. history curriculum, to supply a local perspective on larger events at the national level. The history of our own backyard can help illuminate and increase the understanding of the history of our country and world. Maps help to bring this history alive, and locate it in particular places, in a way that texts or photographs alone cannot. We are currently working with the Office of School Services of the State Historical Society of Wisconsin on development of an Atlas Teacher's Kit, including overhead transparencies. The Guild is also exploring the possible development of posters, a CD-ROM, and other educational ancillaries.

This atlas is intended not to serve as a comprehensive text

on Wisconsin history, but to be a starting point to stimulate readers' interest in exploring the state's history. Wisconsin is blessed with an abundance of resources to assist that exploration. The State Historical Society of Wisconsin publishes the six-volume *History of Wisconsin* series and numerous readable booklets on different facets of state history. It also maintains a number of educational sites—including Old World Wisconsin in Eagle, the State Historical Museum in Madison, and the nationally renowned State Historical Society Library in Madison. The University of Wisconsin Press publishes many resources, including the *Cultural Map of Wisconsin, Wisconsin Land and Life*, and *The Atlas of Ethnic Diversity in Wisconsin*. Many other books we found useful in our research are listed in the *Bibliography & Sources* section.

An impossible task

Producing a historical atlas is a complex exercise in combining time and space, in the setting of a particular place. Even the title, *Wisconsin's Past and Present: A Historical Atlas*, combines the elements of time (history), space (maps), and place (a single state). There was no possible way to reflect all the events or people that have affected Wisconsin, so certain choices had to be made. We would have liked to cover more themes—such as health, crime, sports, or wildlife—and may be able to do so in future editions of the atlas.

We wanted the atlas not to focus exclusively on important individuals at the top of society, or on singular events. We wanted the atlas to help reveal how the people and landscape of Wisconsin have been transformed over time, especially since statehood in 1848. The atlas spread format allows early historical themes to be brought up to the present day, to make the point that Wisconsin history is still alive. History did not stop in 1890, 1940, or 1990, and current events very much have their roots in the past.

Some choices in atlas development involved ethnic groups. Time, space, and place—rather than raw population numbers—were again the criteria for developing presentations. A small indigenous group that has lived in Wisconsin for centuries (and ceded lands that created the state) may have more coverage than an older indigenous group that moved completely outside Wisconsin. Likewise, an immigrant group that settled in large rural areas early in the state's history may have more coverage than a larger immigrant group that settled later in the cities. These choices certainly do not reflect any relative importance of ethnic groups, but rather indicate how sources "map" them over a larger area and time period in Wisconsin history. It should be noted that ethnic groups are covered on spreads besides the specific presentations in the *Peoples & Cultures* section, and that the *Atlas of Ethnic Diversity in Wisconsin* provides a more detailed view of ethnicity based on modern census numbers and distribution.

Other choices involved which areas of the state to highlight on the spreads. Given the state's geographical diversity, it has been important to represent the different regions of the state in the atlas. Yet since the maps have been selected to represent larger issues or trends in state history, rather than the separate histories of cities, some sizable communities may not be represented. Again, this reflects limitations of space, rather than the relative importance of towns or cities in Wisconsin history.

Any historical atlas is also bound to contain some factual errors, whether resulting from inaccurate sources, conflicting opinions of experts, or weak coffee. Any comments, corrections, or suggestions can be mailed to the Wisconsin Cartographers' Guild (2701 University Avenue, #409, Madison, WI 53705).

Two lifetimes

The 150 years of Wisconsin's history as a state may seem like a long time, given the enormous changes that have taken place in the landscape and society since 1848. Yet the state's existence only encompasses the life spans of two 75-year-olds. There may be an elderly person living in your neighborhood or village who, as a child, knew people who had been born before statehood. Studying Wisconsin history is a way to gain insight on the changes that have transformed the lives of individuals and communities in the course of their lifetimes.

As William Cronon points out in the Foreword, Wisconsin is a wonderful place to make discoveries. It is a state with rich stories and multilayered places that give us insights into the history of our country and our world. While we cannot tell all these stories, or map all these places, we hope that this atlas inspires readers to go and search for these stories and places themselves.

The Wisconsin Cartographers' Guild
Statehood Day
May 29, 1998

Acknowledgments

Our first thanks are to our families, especially to Paul Fetcho, Debi McNutt, Jesse Grassman, Diane Gallagher, Jessica Wendt, Doug Crews-Nelson, Audrey Hoffman, Sadie Crews-Nelson, Paul Exner, and Jennifer Davis. Thank you for your perseverance and your understanding of our long hours, anti-social behavior, and unsolicited lectures on glaciation, land surveys, and Norwegian tobacco farmers. Special thanks to Doug Crews-Nelson and Jon Daugherity for helping with map production.

Thanks to the two consulting editors for the project: to John O. (Jack) Holzhueter, editor at the State Historical Society of Wisconsin, for his invaluable early mini-seminars and later text editing, and to Professor Ingolf Vogeler, at the University of Wisconsin–Eau Claire Department of Geography, for his inspiring cartographic ideas and map editing.

Thanks to the University of Wisconsin Press for endorsing the project in its embryonic form in 1996, and particularly to Director Allen Fitchen, Production Manager Terry Emmrich, Chief Editor Elizabeth Steinberg, Publicists Joan Strasbaugh, Marketing Manager Sheila Leary, Editor Juliet Skuldt, Designers Ben Neff and Rebecca Gimenez, and their colleagues.

Thanks to Associate Director Steve Salemson for initiating this third printing of the atlas in 2002. The Press produced nearly 10,000 copies from 1998 to 2001. The atlas was the number one bestseller to U.S. academic libraries in February 1999 (according to Baker & Taylor listings).

Thanks to all those thematic experts who reviewed or assisted with research on particular atlas pages, and who are more fully acknowledged in the bibliographies for each two-page spread.

Thanks to the State Historical Society of Wisconsin for awarding its 1999 "Book Award of Merit" to the atlas. Thanks also to Office of School Services Director Bobbie Malone for co-producing in 2000 the teacher's guide *Mapping Wisconsin History*, which includes color transparencies and lesson plans based on this atlas.

Thanks also to the State Historical Society Director George L. Vogt, Publications Director Paul Hass, Archivist Sally Jacobs, and past *History of Wisconsin* series authors William Fletcher Thompson, Alice Smith, Robert C. Nesbit, Paul Glad, and Richard Nelson Current. Thanks also to the helpful staff at the Library Desk, Reference, Archives, Government Documents, and Iconographic collections.

Thanks to the Wisconsin Sesquicentennial Commission for funding the project in part, with funds from individual and corporate contributors and the state of Wisconsin. Special thanks to Leroy Lee, director of the Wisconsin Academy of Sciences, Arts and Letters, and Commission chairman Dean Amhaus. Thanks to the Wisconsin Humanities Council for funding the Guild educational tour on the atlas. Also thanks to Anchor Bank and Kohl Charities for funding, and to Anne Katz of the Wisconsin Assembly of Local Arts Agencies for acting as fiscal receiver.

Thanks to current and emeritus U.W.–Madison faculty and staff who supported the project, particularly to Professor William Cronon for helping to shape the project and for writing the Foreword, as well as to Professors Emeritus Arthur Robinson and Francis Hole and Professors Robert Ostergren and David Woodward of the Department of Geography, Cartographic Laboratory Assistant Director Onno Brouwer, Professor Emeritus Margaret Beattie Bogue of the Department of History, and American Indian Studies Program Acting Director Craig Werner.

Thanks to Ellen Goldlust-Gingrich and Jennifer Mader for indexing the atlas.

Thanks to Guild Board members Janice Rice, Steve Cotherman, Randy Gabrys-Alexson, Patty Loew, and J. Michael Harrington, for their encouragement and assistance.

Thanks to all others who offered support and encouragement to the project, including Wisconsin Legislative Reference Bureau senior research analysts Peter Cannon and Richard Roe, former U.S. Senator and Governor of Wisconsin Gaylord A. Nelson, State Senator Fred Risser, Robert Allen, David Mollenhoff, Professor Emeritus Norman Risjord of the U.W.–Madison Department of History, Professor Charles Collins of the U.W.–Platteville Department of Geography, Professor Mark Schug (chair of the Wisconsin Council for the Social Studies), Professor David Wrone of the U.W.–Stevens Point Department of History, and historian Allen Ruff. Thanks also to Professor Michael P. Conzen, Chairman of the University of Chicago Department of Geography, and Milwaukee Public Museum Curator Emerita of Anthropology Nancy O. Lurie for their insightful critiques of the project.

Thanks to those who helped publicize and review the book, including Wisconsin Public Television, Wisconsin Public Radio, *Wisconsin State Journal, Capital Times, Milwaukee Journal-Sentinel, Chicago Tribune, Wisconsin Trails*, WMTV-15, Madison Public Library, Paul G. Hayes, Steven Hoelscher, Michael P. Conzen, Daniel Block, and many others.

Thanks to Wisconsin.com for hosting the Guild website (www.wisconsin.com/wibook), which includes map samples and an account of how the Guild produced the atlas.

Thanks to all the instructors who have used the atlas or teacher's guide in Wisconsin classrooms, and who will continue to inspire students to learn about our state's history and geography in the years ahead.

Finally, thanks to each other, for pulling off what some thought to be an impossible job, and for staying good friends throughout the project.

The people are a story
that never ends,
a river that winds and falls
and gleams erect in many dawns,
lost in deep gulleys,
it turns to dust,
rushes in the spring freshet,
emerges to the sea.
The people are a story
that is a long incessant coming alive
from the earth in better wheat,
Percherons, babies and engines,
persistent and inevitable.
The people always know
that some of the grain will be good,
some of the crop will be saved,
some will return and bear
the strength of the kernel,
that from the bloodiest year
some survive to outfox the frost.

—Meridel Le Sueur
from
North Star Country (1945)

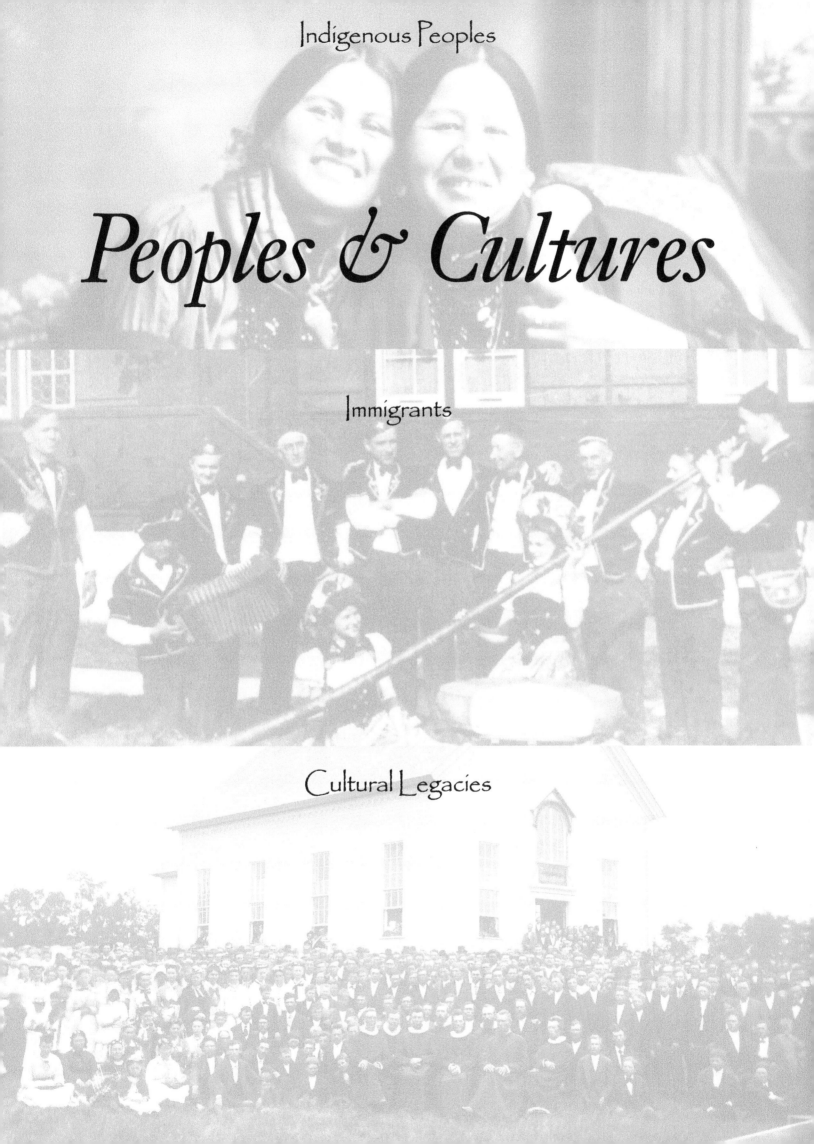

Peoples & Cultures

Indigenous Peoples

Immigrants

Cultural Legacies

Early Cultures

Human beings have lived in Wisconsin for at least 12,000 years. As the glacial ice sheet receded (see *Glacial*), Wisconsin was home to such animals as mammoths and giant beavers. **Paleo-Indians** hunted, fished, and gathered wild plants in the area. Around 6500 BC, the landscape gradually changed to resemble the present-day environment. Native Americans who adapted to these changes developed the **Archaic** culture. Hunting and gathering groups migrated throughout the region, and made tools from stone they excavated from quarries. Although these earliest cultures existed throughout the continent, Wisconsin would later become home to several unique cultures. The map below shows examples of archeological sites left behind by ancient peoples. Some of the sites were inhabited by different cultures in different eras.

About 3000 BC, groups of **Archaic** people began to fashion tools from copper dug from pits in Michigan's Upper Peninsula. The Old Copper culture was one of the first in the world to fabricate metal. The greatest number of Old Copper tools (tens of thousands) have been found in eastern Wisconsin, which some archeologists refer to as the "heart" of the culture.

Around 800 BC, people of the **Early Woodland** culture began to make clay pottery, store food, and build *conical* (round) burial mounds for their dead. They could use a variety of stone tools and needed less land to gain a livelihood. Some people of the **Middle Woodland** culture began around 100 BC to build large groups of burial mounds, and to bury special objects (such as clay masks) with their dead. They also began to interact with the Hopewell culture of the Mississippi and Ohio river valleys (see map at right), which buried the important members of its society in elaborate mounds, and developed new farming and weaving techniques. Hopewell pottery is considered the finest of any made in the region. Hopewell trade networks brought shells from the Gulf Coast and stones from the Rockies and Appalachia.

— Extent of effigy mound culture in Wisconsin

☐ Hopewell culture (*circa* 1 BC–300 AD)

Survival of the Ghost Eagle

European-American society has over time looked at Native American mounds as astronomical observatories, centers of pagan worship, evidence of ancient explorers, profitable sources of plunder, or archeological sites. In the 19th and 20th centuries, the construction of farms and towns destroyed as much as 80 percent of Wisconsin mounds. Some of the mounds were surveyed and mapped before they were flattened. If the soil used in the original moundbuilding is different from the soil in the surrounding farm field, crops on the old mounds sometimes grow at a different rate from adjacent crops. Aerial crop photographs have revealed some of these flattened effigy mounds beneath the farms. One former mound north of the Wisconsin River near Muscoda is in the form of an eagle with a 1,300-foot wingspan—the largest bird mound ever recorded. The Ho-Chunk (formerly Winnebago) have proposed reconstructing this "ghost eagle" on the basis of old surveys and modern photos. The Ho-Chunk believe that their ancestors built the effigy mounds, and see themselves as caretakers of the mounds. Similarly, they have stories and legends that may relate directly to the Woodland-era images in rock art sites (such as the giant Gottschall site figures in the Red Horn panel below).

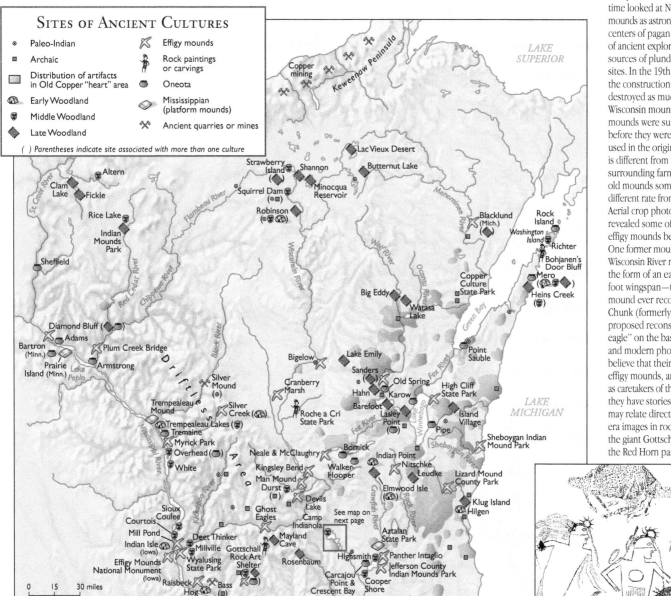

SITES OF ANCIENT CULTURES

⊙ Paleo-Indian
▣ Archaic
▭ Distribution of artifacts in Old Copper "heart" area
Early Woodland
Middle Woodland
◆ Late Woodland

Effigy mounds
Rock paintings or carvings
Oneota
Mississippian (platform mounds)
Ancient quarries or mines

( ) Parentheses indicate site associated with more than one culture

Man
 Bird
 Panther
 Goose
 Bear
 Deer
 Turtle
 Canine

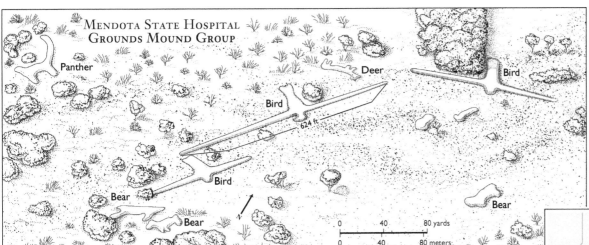

MENDOTA STATE HOSPITAL
GROUNDS MOUND GROUP

Panther

Deer

Bird

Bird

624 ft

Bear

Bird

Bear

Bear

Bear

0   40   80 yards
0   40   80 meters

Surviving Effigy Mounds in Madison Area

1. Burrows Park
2. Elmside Park
3. Hudson Park
4. Edna Taylor Conservancy
5. Mendota State Hospital Grounds
6. Cherokee Park
7. Vilas Circle Park
8. Vilas Park
9. Forest Hill Cemetery
10. Edgewood College
11. Observatory Hill
12. Willow Drive
13. Picnic Point
14. Arboretum
15. Spring Harbor School
16. Governor Nelson State Park
17. Yahara Heights County Park
18. Indian Mound Park
19. Goodland County Park
20. Siggelkow Park

Lake Mendota

Lake Monona

Lake Waubesa

0   2 miles
0   2 kilometers

Late Woodland Indians built more than 1,500 effigy mounds in the Four Lakes region of Dane County (see map at right). Many of them were constructed between 800 and 1100 AD, in groups containing from three to more than 50 mounds. Some of the largest effigy mounds in the world are located on the Mendota State Hospital Grounds in Madison (above). One of the three large bird mounds has a 624-foot wingspan, the largest known surviving effigy mound in the state. The group includes effigies of two panthers (one of which has a rare curved tail), and a rare four-legged deer. At least six mounds in the group no longer exist. In the early 20th century, Madisonians formed one of the earliest mound preservation movements in the country. Recent laws protect these important cultural resources, but incidents of desecration still take place. The mounds are still considered sacred by Wisconsin's Native Americans.

Around 650 AD, peoples of the **Late Woodland** culture began to construct mounds in the *effigy* (image) of animals. Groups of effigy mounds are nearly all found in southern Wisconsin, often in high places overlooking bodies of water. They served as ceremonial centers and often as burial grounds. Some effigies may have symbolized *clans*, or extended family groups. Mound builders also made images by digging an *intaglio* (cut into the earth) effigy form. Effigy building ended around 1200 AD, although conical burial mounds were built or used up to the era of European contact. Since then, four-fifths of all Wisconsin mounds have been destroyed (see column on facing page).

During the final 300 years of the effigy mound culture, people from two other cultures also lived in Wisconsin. The **Middle Mississippian** culture was

based in Cahokia (near present-day East St. Louis, Illinois), which at its height was one of the world's largest cities (see map at lower left). Cahokia contained huge ceremonial platform mounds, one covering 16 acres, and was a center for commercial trade, farming, and artistry. A key river outpost of the culture was the town of Aztalan, near present-day Lake Mills (see illustration). Aztalan had three large platform mounds and a large knoll, or hill. Early European visitors likened the platform mounds to Mexican pyramids. Aztalan remnants today consist of mounds, houses, and a rebuilt fortified log stockade.

The **Oneota** culture resembled Mississippian culture, but its people rarely built mounds. Native Americans of the Woodland, Mississippian, and Oneota civilizations may have fought each other, but they shared some of the same art forms. Large Oneota villages were located in the southern half of present-day Wisconsin, where villagers practiced intensive farming and made a distinctive style of pottery. Some Oneota and Late Woodland peoples etched *pictographs* (paintings) and *petroglyphs* (carvings) on rock walls, mainly in the caves and shelters of the unglaciated Driftless Area. An outstanding example of rock art is found in the Gottschall shelter, which contains more than 40 images, including human and animal figures (see facing page).

Effigy and platform mounds were no longer built after 1200 AD. In the 1500s and 1600s, some cultures moved into or out of the region, and new peoples began to emerge from Wisconsin's cultural mosaic.

Mississippian and Oneota Cultures

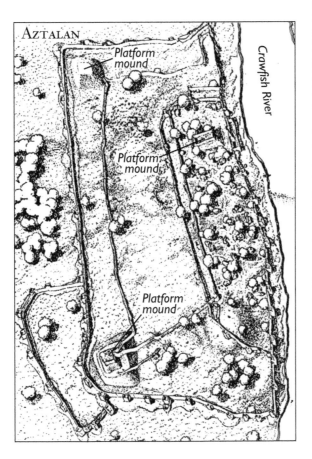

AZTALAN

Platform mound

Platform mound

Crawfish River

Platform mound

Lake Superior

Lake Michigan

Lake Huron

ONEOTA

Aztalan

Cahokia

MIDDLE MISSISSIPPIAN

CADDOAN MISSISSIPPIAN

SOUTH APPALACHIAN MISSISSIPPIAN

PLAQUEMINE MISSISSIPPIAN

— Present-day state boundaries

Native & European Encounters

The Menominee, Ho-Chunk (Winnebago), and Dakota (Sioux) were the chief Native nations in Wisconsin when the first French explorer arrived in 1634; the Potawatomi were probably present as traders. The French had already begun a fur trade around the eastern Great Lakes that had increased competition and conflict among tribes in that region. In 1641, the Iroquois launched a 60-year war to seize control of the fur trade, displacing many tribes and forcing them to flee rapidly westward. Among the tribes that made their way to Wisconsin were the Odawa (Ottawa), Huron, Petun, Sauk, Meskwaki (Fox), Kickapoo, Miami, Mascouten, and Illinois (see column at right). After a series of conflicts with the French, Dakota, and other regional powers, most of them eventually moved southward

first European in Wisconsin. In the 1600s the French explored along water routes (such as the Fox and Wisconsin rivers) connecting the Great Lakes with the Mississippi River. They built forts, missions, and trading posts along the strategic routes, long used by Native peoples for trade.

French fur-trade era, 1634–1763. To expand the fur trade into the western Great Lakes, the French made alliances with Native nations, whose members had the skills to hunt and trap at a commercial level. In Europe, the highly prized fur was the beaver's; its thick, lustrous coat was used for garments, and its hair was felted into hats. Native hunters also collected the pelts and skins of deer, marten, raccoon, fox, otter, and muskrat. They exchanged the furs for metal hatchets, knives, kettles, traps, needles, fish hooks, cloth and blankets,

Refugee Peoples

Many Native peoples fled the eastern Great Lakes after the Iroquois Wars broke out in the 1640s. The wars were fought over control of the fur trade, in which tribes were involved as hunters (below) or middlemen. The Huron (Wyandot) and Petun (Tionontati) spoke Iroquoian languages, but their main Native enemies were the Iroquois, who drove them from the St. Lawrence River valley to Lake Huron. They fled farther to the Green Bay area, joined by Odawa (Ottawa), and moved around northern Wisconsin in the 1650s–1660s, only to be driven out by the Dakota. By the 1760s, the Huron were living along Lake Erie,

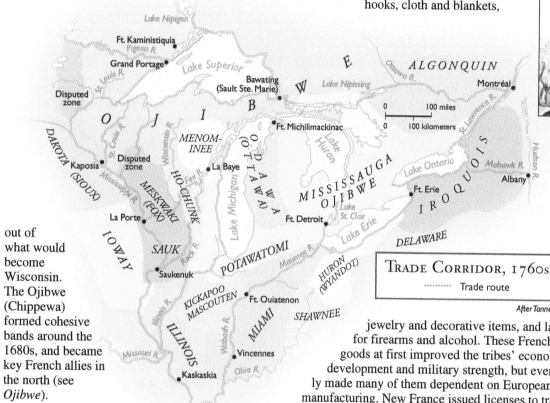

but the U.S. removed them to Kansas and Oklahoma in the 1840s. The Sauk and Meskwaki (Fox), Algonquian-speakers who arrived at Green and Chequamegon bays in the 1650s, had settled along the Fox-Wisconsin waterway by 1700. The Meskwaki formed a barrier to the French fur-trade expansion, and began to fight the French in the 1710s (see *Colonial Boundaries*). In the 1730s, the Sauk joined the Meskwaki in the conflict, but to no avail. By the 1770s the two tribes were living together in large villages along the Mississippi and Wisconsin rivers. They ceded much of southwestern Wisconsin in an 1804 treaty, and withdrew southward along the river (the Ho-Chunk took their place). Their resistance to removal from Illinois sparked the 1832 Black Hawk War (see *Land Conflicts*). Today they have lands in Iowa and Oklahoma. The Kickapoo, Miami, Mascouten, and Illinois were Algonquian-speakers who came into Wisconsin around southern Lake Michigan, and also settled along the Fox-Wisconsin waterway and fought the Dakota. The Kickapoo were renowned across the continent as military fighters. In the late 1600s, as many as 20,000 Mascouten and Miami lived in a town on the Fox River. By the 1760s, the Miami had moved to Indiana, and the Kickapoo had moved to Illinois, where they absorbed the Mascouten. The Miami and Kickapoo were removed to Kansas and Oklahoma in the 1820s–1830s. Some later fled to northern Mexico, where they still guard their traditions today.

out of what would become Wisconsin. The Ojibwe (Chippewa) formed cohesive bands around the 1680s, and became key French allies in the north (see *Ojibwe*).

French explorers. The French colonists of the St. Lawrence River valley were the first Europeans to move into the western Great Lakes, or *pays d'en haut* ("upper country"). Besides expanding the fur trade, they wanted to find a river passage across North America (for a trade route to Asia), explore and secure territory, and establish Christian missions to convert Native peoples. The government of *Nouvelle-France* (New France) in Montreal received permission from the Huron to let young Frenchmen live among them, adopt their language and customs, and become familiar with the landscape and water routes. One such man, Étienne Brûlé, may have explored as far west as Lake Superior in 1621–23.

In 1634, the Huron took Jean Nicolet to meet the Ho-Chunk at Red Banks on Green Bay, making him the

jewelry and decorative items, and later for firearms and alcohol. These French goods at first improved the tribes' economic development and military strength, but eventually made many of them dependent on European manufacturing. New France issued licenses to traders, but many unlicensed traders known as *coureurs du bois* ("woods runners") also infiltrated the region. Members of both groups took Native women as wives, creating the mixed-blood group called *Métis*. The *Métis* played an important role in maintaining relations between Native and colonial traders, and later founded their own European-style villages. In the 1710s, the French built new forts along the Great Lakes and the Fox, Wisconsin, and Mississippi rivers. British encroachment on the fur trade helped lead to the French and Indian War and the French loss of the region to Britain in 1763 (see *Colonial Boundaries*).

British fur-trade era, 1763–1815. As the British took control of the region, many French, Native American, and *Métis* traders east of the Mississippi began working for them. The British decentralized the fur trade, which reduced the tribes' economic

Map labels:
Lake Nipigon · Ft. Kaministiquia · Pigeon R. · Grand Portage · Lake Superior · St. Louis R. · Disputed zone · Bawating (Sault Ste. Marie) · ALGONQUIN · Ottawa R. · Lake Nipissing · Montréal · St. Lawrence R. · OJIBWE · St. Croix R. · Wisconsin R. · MENOMINEE · Ft. Michilimackinac · Lake Huron · ODAWA (OTTAWA) · DAKOTA (SIOUX) · Kaposia · Disputed zone · Fox R. · La Baye · HO-CHUNK · MISSISSAUGA OJIBWE · Lake Ontario · Mohawk R. · Hudson R. · Albany · Mississippi R. · MESKWAKI (FOX) · Lake Michigan · Ft. Erie · IROQUOIS · La Porte · IOWAY · SAUK · Rock R. · Ft. Detroit · Lake St. Clair · Lake Erie · DELAWARE · Saukenuk · POTAWATOMI · Maumee R. · HURON (WYANDOT) · Illinois R. · KICKAPOO · MASCOUTEN · Ft. Ouiatenon · SHAWNEE · Wabash R. · MIAMI · ILLINOIS · Missouri R. · Vincennes · Kaskaskia · Ohio R.

0 100 miles
0 100 kilometers

TRADE CORRIDOR, 1760s
·········· Trade route

After Tanner

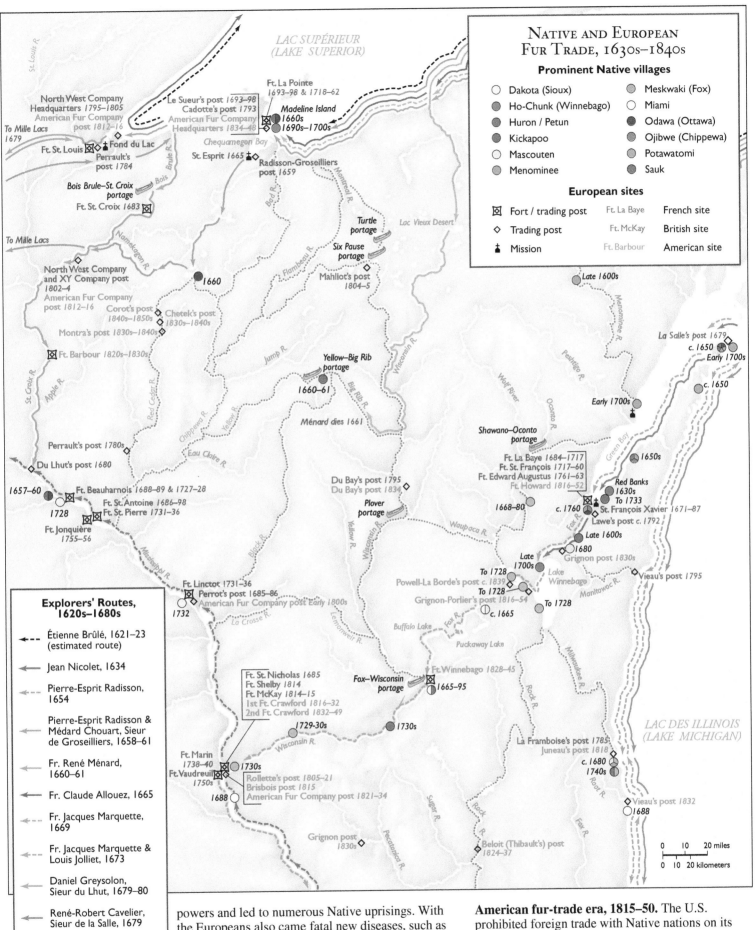

NATIVE AND EUROPEAN FUR TRADE, 1630s–1840s

Prominent Native villages

- ○ Dakota (Sioux)
- ● Ho-Chunk (Winnebago)
- ● Huron / Petun
- ● Kickapoo
- ○ Mascouten
- ◐ Menominee
- ◐ Meskwaki (Fox)
- ○ Miami
- ● Odawa (Ottawa)
- ◐ Ojibwe (Chippewa)
- ◐ Potawatomi
- ◐ Sauk

European sites

- ⊠ Fort / trading post
- ◇ Trading post
- ♦ Mission
- Ft. La Baye — French site
- Ft. McKay — British site
- Ft. Barbour — American site

LAC SUPÉRIEUR (LAKE SUPERIOR)

St. Louis R.

North West Company Headquarters 1795–1805
American Fur Company post 1812–16

To Mille Lacs 1679

Ft. St. Louis
Fond du Lac
Perrault's post 1784

Le Sueur's post 1693–98
Cadotte's post 1793
American Fur Company Headquarters 1834–48

Ft. La Pointe 1693–98 & 1718–62
Madeline Island 1660s
1690s–1700s

Chequamegon Bay

St. Esprit 1665

Radisson-Groseilliers post 1659

Bois Brule–St. Croix portage

Brule R.

Bad R.

Montreal R.

Lac Vieux Desert

Ft. St. Croix 1683

Turtle portage

Six Pause portage

Mahliot's post 1804–5

Flambeau R.

Namekagon R.

To Mille Lacs

North West Company and XY Company post 1802–4
American Fur Company post 1812–16

1660

Corot's post 1840s–1850s
Montra's post 1830s–1840s

Chetek's post 1830s–1840s

Jump R.

Yellow–Big Rib portage

Wisconsin R.

Late 1600s

Menominee R.

Ft. Barbour 1820s–1830s

St. Croix R.

Apple R.

Red Cedar R.

1660–61

Big Rib R.

Ménard dies 1661

Peshtigo R.

La Salle's post 1679
c. 1650
Early 1700s

c. 1650

Perrault's post 1780s

Chippewa R.

Eau Claire R.

Yellow R.

Early 1700s

c. 1650

Du Lhut's post 1680

1657–60

Ft. Beauharnois 1688–89 & 1727–28

1728

Ft. St. Antoine 1686–98
Ft. St. Pierre 1731–36

Ft. Jonquière 1755–56

Black R.

Du Bay's post 1795
Du Bay's post 1834

Plover portage

Yellow R.

Wisconsin R.

Waupaca R.

Shawano–Oconto portage

Oconto R.

Green Bay

1650s

Ft. La Baye 1684–1717
Ft. St. François 1717–60
Ft. Edward Augustus 1761–63
Ft. Howard 1816–52

Red Banks 1630s
To 1733

1668–80

c. 1760

St. François Xavier 1671–87

Lawe's post c. 1792

Fox R.

Late 1600s

1680

Grignon post 1830s

Vieau's post 1795

Mississippi R.

Ft. Linctot 1731–36

Perrot's post 1685–86
American Fur Company post Early 1800s

1732

La Crosse R.

Lemonweir R.

Fox R.

Buffalo Lake

Puckaway Lake

Late 1700s

To 1728

Powell–La Borde's post c. 1839

Grignon-Porlier's post 1816–54

c. 1665

To 1728

To 1728

Lake Winnebago

Manitowoc R.

Rock R.

Milwaukee R.

LAC DES ILLINOIS (LAKE MICHIGAN)

Explorers' Routes, 1620s–1680s

- Étienne Brûlé, 1621–23 (estimated route)
- Jean Nicolet, 1634
- Pierre-Esprit Radisson, 1654
- Pierre-Esprit Radisson & Médard Chouart, Sieur de Groseilliers, 1658–61
- Fr. René Ménard, 1660–61
- Fr. Claude Allouez, 1665
- Fr. Jacques Marquette, 1669
- Fr. Jacques Marquette & Louis Jolliet, 1673
- Daniel Greysolon, Sieur du Lhut, 1679–80
- René-Robert Cavelier, Sieur de la Salle, 1679
- Fr. Louis Hennepin, 1680
- Other major water route
- Major portage

Ft. St. Nicholas 1685
Ft. Shelby 1814
Ft. McKay 1814–15
1st Ft. Crawford 1816–32
2nd Ft. Crawford 1832–49

Fox–Wisconsin portage

Ft. Winnebago 1828–45

1665–95

1729–30s

1730s

Wisconsin R.

Ft. Marin 1738–40
Ft. Vaudreuil 1750s

1730s

Rollette's post 1805–21
Brisbois post 1815
American Fur Company post 1821–34

1688

La Framboise's post 1785
Juneau's post 1818

c. 1680

1740s

Vieau's post 1832

1688

Sugar R.

Rock R.

Pecatonica R.

Grignon post 1830s

Beloit (Thibault's) post 1824–37

Fox R.

| 0 | 10 | 20 miles |
| 0 | 10 | 20 kilometers |

powers and led to numerous Native uprisings. With the Europeans also came fatal new diseases, such as respiratory viruses, smallpox, cholera, and measles, which decimated the Native population and increased the survivors' dependence on colonial trade. Green Bay, La Pointe, and Prairie du Chien emerged as primary Wisconsin sites of the British fur trade, which continued after the new United States of America took control in the 1780s. Growing U.S.-British conflicts led to the War of 1812, after which Britain lost control of the region.

American fur-trade era, 1815–50. The U.S. prohibited foreign trade with Native nations on its territory. The American Fur Company established posts throughout the western Great Lakes to exclude rival British traders, and had developed a trade monopoly by the 1820s. The Great Lakes fur trade declined in the 1830s–1850s because of the depleted beaver population, Native land cessions, and the subsequent removal of Native Americans to reservations.

Native Nations of Eastern Wisconsin

The Menominee, or *Omāeqnominniwuk* ("Wild Rice People"), are Algonquian-speakers who are believed to have lived in Wisconsin for over 5,000 years. A European first saw Menominee villages when the French explorer Jean Nicolet arrived in 1634. The tribe joined the French in fighting against the British, who took control of the region in 1765. The Menominee fought on the British side in the American Revolution and the War of 1812. U.S. military forces arrived in 1816, and built Fort Howard at Green Bay. Over the next three decades, the Menominee lost most of their lands but avoided removal to the West.

After their reservation was founded in 1854, the Menominee built a successful lumber industry. They later resisted "timber barons" who sought to harvest the rich forest (see *Timber*), and avoided the fragmentation of their lands under the 1887 General Indian Allotment Act (see *Land Conflicts*). The Menominee built their own sawmill in 1907. The following year, the U.S. Forest Service began to manage the Menominee forest. Poor federal forest practices left many fallen trees to rot in the 1930s. The tribe sued the government for over $7 million, and finally won the case in 1954. That same year, as part of a policy to absorb economically successful tribes into U.S. society, Congress began the process of terminating tribal status for the Menominee. Though its economy was by then in decline, the reservation became Menominee County in 1961. The Menominee were a test case for "termination," which turned into a disaster. They had to sell their lands to pay property taxes on their forest, leading to deeper poverty and despair. A movement pressured the federal government to restore tribal status in 1973.

Ironically, termination enabled the tribe to avoid the provisions of Public Law 280, which had replaced federal control with state jurisdiction on most other reservations. Today, the tribe again controls many of its own affairs, and its revitalized timber economy has been augmented by gaming and other industries.

Seeing the Forest for the Trees

Chief Oshkosh (above) led the Menominee resistance to removal and secured a Wisconsin reservation in 1854. Before he died two years later, Oshkosh asked his people to harvest their forest gradually from one side of the reservation to the other, giving each timber stand time to revitalize itself before the process of cutting started again. His concept of "sustained yield" forestry stood in sharp contrast to the clear-cutting of virgin timber across the rest of northern Wisconsin in the "timber baron" era (see *Timber*). This knowledge was passed from generation to generation. Today, the legacy left by Oshkosh and other Menominee leaders includes the finest old stands of hardwoods, virgin pine, and hemlock in the Great Lakes region. This legacy can be clearly seen from outer space. Despite having one of the most active timber industries in the region, the reservation now contains more board feet of timber than it did when its reservation was established in 1854. The Menominee have become internationally famous for their sustainable forest harvest practices and environmental ethic. The tribe limits its annual cut to 29 million board-feet of timber, and selects specific trees rather than cutting swaths of forest. Tribal foresters encourage a diversity of timber varieties (46 in all) rather than planting one variety that could become vulnerable to disease or market fluctuations. They also maintain diversity in the species of plant undergrowth and wildlife that benefit tree growth, since each part of the ecosystem has an effect on the forest as a whole. The tribe maintains that its very survival depends on managing and protecting the forest.

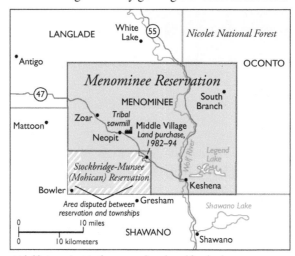

In this 1991 satellite photo, the outline of the heavily forested reservation is unmistakable in contrast to the surrounding cleared farmlands.

THE NEW YORK INDIANS

The Oneida were one of the Six Nations of the Iroquois Confederacy, or *Haudenosaunee,* formed in ancient times under the "Great Law of Peace" (which some scholars believe later served as a possible model for uniting the 13 colonies). Iroquois political unity was shattered when the Oneida sided with the Americans in the Revolution. Because the Oneida were then themselves divided religiously between Christian and traditional factions, they were vulnerable to land theft. By 1788 New York state had taken 5.3 million acres. In 1820–22, Mohawk Episcopal lay preacher Eleazer Williams successfully negotiated with the Menominee for a new land base near the Fox River. A large tract of Menominee land was ceded to the Oneida in an 1832 treaty with the U.S., which in 1838 brought the Oneida reservation to its present-day size of 65,400 acres. Timber interests and farm settlements encroached upon the reservation. The 1887 General Indian Allotment Act divided and privatized tribal lands, which were then nearly all confiscated after taxes went unpaid. Starting in 1937, a federally recognized tribal government began to buy back some lands. Despite these pressures on Oneida land and people, the culture has survived; many Oneida children are learning their language. The only Wisconsin tribe next to a large urban area (see *Land Conflicts*), the Oneida have been successful in gaming and business ventures.

The Stockbridge–Munsee are a blend of the remnants of two great nations. The Stockbridge began in Massachusetts as a Christianized faction of the Mohican Nation. They were joined by the Munsee, themselves part of the Lenni-Lenape (Delaware) Nation. Together, they moved to Oneida lands in New York, and later followed their leader John Metoxin to the Fox River and Lake Winnebago. After an attempt to remove them to Kansas failed, they settled on their present reservation. Some of their land was later claimed by white townships.

The Brotherton (Brothertown) are an amalgamation of Eastern refugee tribes, who came together at a mission on New York Oneida land in 1785. They moved with the Stockbridge–Munsee as far as Lake Winnebago. By taking U.S. citizenship and attempting to exchange their new reservation for better lands, they unwittingly surrendered their tribal status in 1839. Their descendants in the area are trying to regain federal recognition as a tribe.

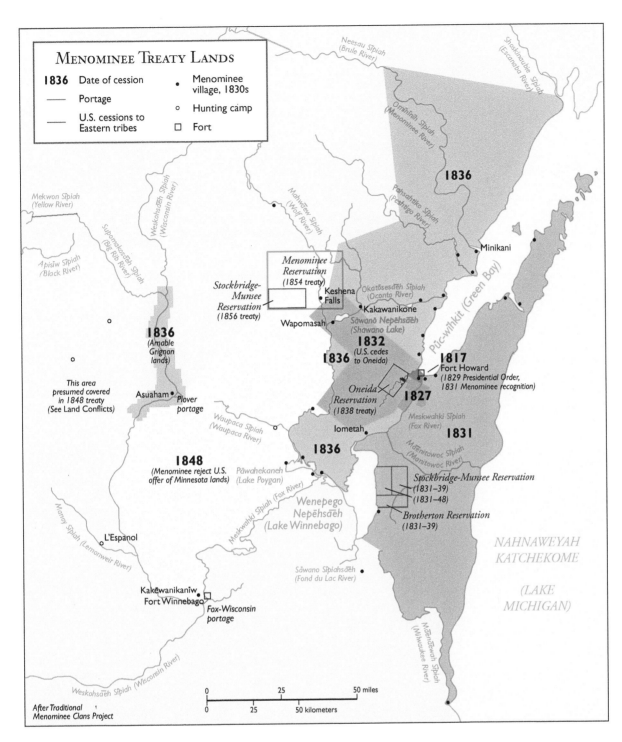

MENOMINEE TREATY LANDS

1836 Date of cession
— Portage
━━ U.S. cessions to Eastern tribes

● Menominee village, 1830s
○ Hunting camp
□ Fort

Neesau Sīpiah (Brule River)

Shokīnauhbe Sīpiah (Escanaba River)

1836

Omīnīnīh Sīpiah (Menominee River)

Minikani

Pahsahtiko Sīpiah (Peshtigo River)

Mekwon Sīpiah (Yellow River)

Mahwaew Sīpiah (Wolf River)

Weskohsāēh Sīpiah (Wisconsin River)

Supomakosdēh Sīpiah (Big Rib River)

A̅pisiw Sīpiah (Black River)

Menominee Reservation (1854 treaty)

Stockbridge-Munsee Reservation (1856 treaty)

Keshena Falls

Okatōsesdēh Sīpiah (Oconto River)

Kakawanikone

Pūc-wihkit (Green Bay)

1836 *(Amable Grignon lands)*

Wapomasah

Sāwanŏ Nepēhsāēh (Shawano Lake)

This area presumed covered in 1848 treaty (See Land Conflicts)

Asuaham ● Plover portage

1832 *(U.S. cedes to Oneida)*

1836

Oneida Reservation (1838 treaty)

1827

1817 Fort Howard *(1829 Presidential Order, 1831 Menominee recognition)*

Waupaca Sīpiah (Waupaca River)

Iometah

Meskwahki Sīpiah (Fox River)

1831

1848 *(Menominee reject U.S. offer of Minnesota lands)*

1836

Pāwahekaneh (Lake Poygan)

Măēnitowoc Sīpiah (Manitowoc River)

Stockbridge-Munsee Reservation (1831–39) (1831–48)

Brotherton Reservation (1831–39)

Wenepego Nepēhsāēh (Lake Winnebago)

L'Espanol

Manoy Sīpiah (Lemanweir River)

Meskwahki Sīpiah (Fox River)

NAHNAWEYAH KATCHEKOME

Sāwano Sīpiahsāēh (Fond du Lac River)

(LAKE MICHIGAN)

Kakewanikanīw
Fort Winnebago

Fox-Wisconsin portage

Măēnāŧawah Sīpiah (Milwaukee River)

Weskohsāēh Sīpiah (Wisconsin River)

| 0 | 25 | 50 miles |
| 0 | 25 | 50 kilometers |

After Traditional Menominee Clans Project

The Menominee lived in villages in an area ranging from present-day Minnesota to Chicago. Their 10-million-acre hunting range extended from Lake Michigan as far west as the Yellow, Chippewa, and Red Cedar rivers—where it overlapped Ho-Chunk, Ojibwe, and Dakota lands (see *Land Conflicts*). The area was rich in wild game, fish, and wild rice, and was on the trade route between the Great Lakes and the Mississippi River. The Menominee were thus ideal fur-trade partners with the French (see *Encounters*). U.S. control began with the 1817 acquisition of land around Fort Howard at Green Bay, on the Fox River in the heart of Menominee territory. In a series of treaties over three decades, the Menominee ceded large chunks of the territory to the U.S. for 7 to 10 cents an acre. The cessions were made first along the strategic Fox River waterway, and later throughout the rich farm lands of eastern Wisconsin, as well as a strip along the Wisconsin River. In the 1825 Treaty of Prairie du Chien, the Menominee agreed with neighboring tribes to delineate exact boundaries for the cessions. In treaties with the U.S., tribes from New York acquired some of the ceded lands in 1831–32 (see map below). The Menominees' land base was finally eliminated in a treaty in 1848, when the U.S. offered them a reservation in the Crow Wing River region of north-central Minnesota. They refused, and six years later were awarded a new reservation, most of which lay within their traditional region. It was centered on the Wolf River, where Chief Oshkosh had set up a village at Keshena Falls. In 1856, the U.S. detached two reservation townships for the new Stockbridge-Munsee Reservation. The Menominee founded new villages within their heavily wooded reservation, covering 10 townships, or over 230,000 acres. Keshena became the official seat of the tribal government in 1937.

To keep their nations together in the face of U.S. removal policy, sections of several tribes migrated from New York to Wisconsin in the 1820s–1830s. Some were guided by missionaries; others by tribal leaders seeking to rebuild their nations on new soil. Together, they gained land along the Fox River from the Menominee and U.S. governments. The Stockbridge-Munsee and Brotherton, who had their roots in the East Coast, followed a land route to Wisconsin. Some Oneida left New York via the Great Lakes, and others settled in Ontario. As the Fox River valley was colonized, the Stockbridge-Munsee were relocated to Lake Winnebago, then to Indian Territory, and finally to Shawano County. The Oneida negotiated for a land base west of Green Bay, but the Brotherton gave up their Lake Winnebago reservation.

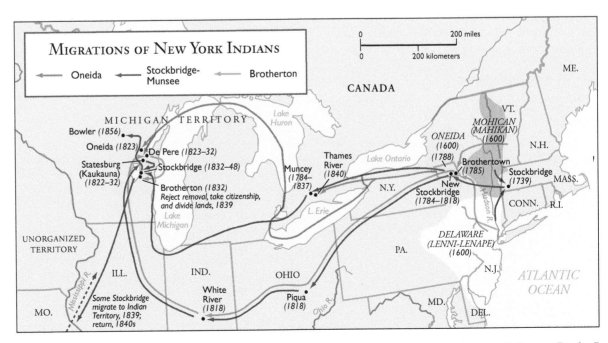

MIGRATIONS OF NEW YORK INDIANS

← Oneida ← Stockbridge-Munsee ← Brotherton

| 0 | 200 miles |
| 0 | 200 kilometers |

CANADA

ME.

Lake Huron

MICHIGAN TERRITORY

Bowler (1856)
Oneida (1823)
De Pere (1823–32)
Statesburg (Kaukauna) (1822–32)
Stockbridge (1832–48)
Brotherton (1832) *Reject removal, take citizenship, and divide lands, 1839*

Muncey (1784–1837)
Thames River (1840)

VT.
MOHICAN (MAHIKAN) (1600)
N.H.
ONEIDA (1600) (1788)
Brothertown (1785)
Stockbridge (1739)
MASS.
New Stockbridge (1784–1818)
CONN. R.I.

Lake Ontario
N.Y.
Hudson R.

UNORGANIZED TERRITORY

Lake Michigan

L. Erie

PA.

ILL. IND. OHIO

Mississippi R.

Some Stockbridge migrate to Indian Territory, 1839; return, 1840s

White River (1818)

Piqua (1818)

Ohio R.

MO.

MD.

DELAWARE (LENNI-LENAPE) (1600)

N.J.
DEL.

ATLANTIC OCEAN

The Ho-Chunk & Dakota Nations

The Ho-Chunk, or *Hocąk* ("People of the Big Voice"), are a Siouan-speaking people formerly known by other people as the *Winnebago* ("People of the Dirty Water"). When Jean Nicolet arrived in 1634 at their Red Banks village on Green Bay (see *Encounters*), the Ho-Chunk already had been ravaged by famine and European diseases. They were further devastated by conflict with other tribes in the mid-1600s Iroquois Wars. After gradually rebuilding their economy by participating in the fur trade, they had moved inland to Lake Winnebago by 1700. They later began to move south, along the Rock and Wisconsin rivers, and cultivated corn, beans, and squash around new villages they built.

Ho-Chunk fighters aided the French against the British and their allied tribes in the 1750s; later they helped the British against the Americans (including attacking Prairie du Chien in the War of 1812). After the British defeat, they adapted to life under U.S. rule, and readjusted their trading relationships. The 1820s lead rush was the beginning of the end for Ho-Chunk control over southwestern Wisconsin. Miners violated U.S. law by driving Ho-Chunk off their lands, which led to the 1827 Red Bird uprising around Prairie du Chien. In retaliation, the tribe was forced to cede the Lead District land in 1829. It had to cede more lands to the east in 1832. In the same year, different Ho-Chunk factions aided opposing sides in the Black Hawk War (see *Land Conflicts*).

A delegation went to Washington in 1837 to plead for the tribe's remaining lands, but its members were not allowed to go home until they ceded them. They finally agreed because they feared for their families' well-being (two years earlier a smallpox epidemic had killed a fourth of the tribe) and believed verbal assurances that they would have eight years to leave Wisconsin, though the treaty allowed eight months. The "Treaty-Abiding Faction" of the Ho-Chunk were moved to the "Neutral Ground" around Iowa's Turkey River. The area was territory contested by the warring Dakota and Sauk, and the Ho-Chunk were often caught in the middle. In 1846, they were moved to a new "buffer zone" on the Long Prairie River in northern Minnesota, where they were caught

Wakąja Zi, or Chief Yellow Thunder (above right), led the Ho-Chunk resistance to removal from Wisconsin, where tribal members had historically formed the largest Native American nation. He signed the treaty of 1829 and, as part of a delegation to Washington, was induced to sign the treaty of 1837. When he discovered that the treaty ordered his people to relocate to Iowa, he refused to go. Three years later, U.S. officials at Fort Winnebago invited him to a meeting, where he was seized and transported westward. Like many other Ho-Chunk, he returned to live along the Wisconsin River, but the government persisted in its attempts to remove the "Disaffected Bands" from Wisconsin, arousing some public opposition. In 1873, for example, Reedsburg citizens physically blocked soldiers from putting a Ho-Chunk family on a westbound train. Such public concern, combined with the tenacity of Yellow Thunder's followers, enabled the Ho-Chunk to remain in Wisconsin. The following year, Yellow Thunder died in his Wisconsin homeland.

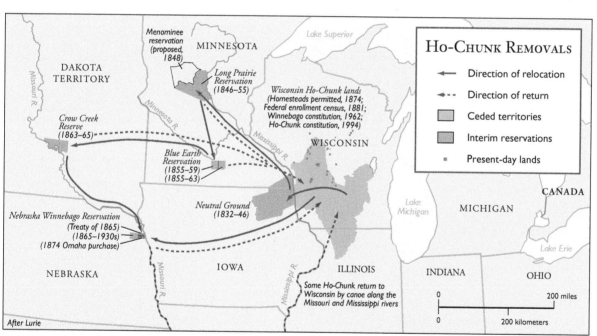

HO-CHUNK REMOVALS

→ Direction of relocation

◄--- Direction of return

Ceded territories

Interim reservations

■ Present-day lands

Menominee reservation (proposed, 1848)

MINNESOTA

Lake Superior

DAKOTA TERRITORY

Long Prairie Reservation (1846–55)

Wisconsin Ho-Chunk lands (Homesteads permitted, 1874; Federal enrollment census, 1881; Winnebago constitution, 1962; Ho-Chunk constitution, 1994)

Crow Creek Reserve (1863–65)

Blue Earth Reservation (1855–59) (1855–63)

WISCONSIN

Missouri R.

Minnesota R.

Mississippi R.

Nebraska Winnebago Reservation (Treaty of 1865) (1865–1930s) (1874 Omaha purchase)

Neutral Ground (1832–46)

Lake Michigan

MICHIGAN

CANADA

Lake Erie

NEBRASKA

IOWA

ILLINOIS

INDIANA

OHIO

Missouri R.

Mississippi R.

Some Ho-Chunk return to Wisconsin by canoe along the Missouri and Mississippi rivers

0   200 miles

0   200 kilometers

After Lurie

The Ho-Chunk Casino in Lake Delton has been one of the most successful Wisconsin gaming establishments in the 1990s. Congress laid the groundwork for Native American casinos in the 1988 Indian Gaming Regulatory Act, which allowed tribes to adopt certain classes of gaming if the state also adopted them. Three years after state voters had approved a lottery, Wisconsin tribes signed their first gaming compacts with the state. Some tribes quickly became the biggest employers in their counties—like the Ho-Chunk in Sauk County—and were able to fund social programs and reduce welfare rolls. Other tribes located farther from cities or tourist centers did not fare as well. Conflicts between and within tribes, as well as between tribal and state officials, have also cast a shadow over the future of tribal casinos in Wisconsin.

THE DAKOTA NATION

The Mdewakanton (Mystery Lake) Dakota, also known as the Santee Sioux, once inhabited much of northern Wisconsin. These Siouan speakers practiced a woodland economy of small-game hunting, fishing, and gathering rice—much different from the later historical image of the buffalo-hunting Plains Sioux.

As the fur trade (see *Encounters*) enabled the Ojibwe to move into Dakota lands, full-scale war broke out between the two tribes in 1736, which lasted (with a few truces) until 1854. The Dakota were outside the French trade network, which supplied the Ojibwe with guns and iron axes. The areas of most intense conflict were the wild rice beds of northern Wisconsin and the rich deer-hunting grounds on the "tension line" between northern forests and southern grasslands (see *Timber*). The Ojibwe gradually pushed westward into northern Minnesota.

At the beginning of the 19th century, the Dakota still owned a swath of western Wisconsin, where they had a few settlements or hunting camps. In 1837, federal Indian Agent Lawrence Taliaferro convinced U.S. officials that the Dakota still used the area, and helped to secure favorable treatment for the tribe in a land cession. The cession—along with an Ojibwe cession the same year—provided Wisconsin with its richest stands of pine. Many Dakota moved to the Minnesota side of the Mississippi River, where Dakota still live on the Prairie Island Reservation. The case of the Dakota was the only successful removal of a tribe from Wisconsin. Some Dakota today are trying to establish a historic site on their ceded lands on the Wisconsin side of the river.

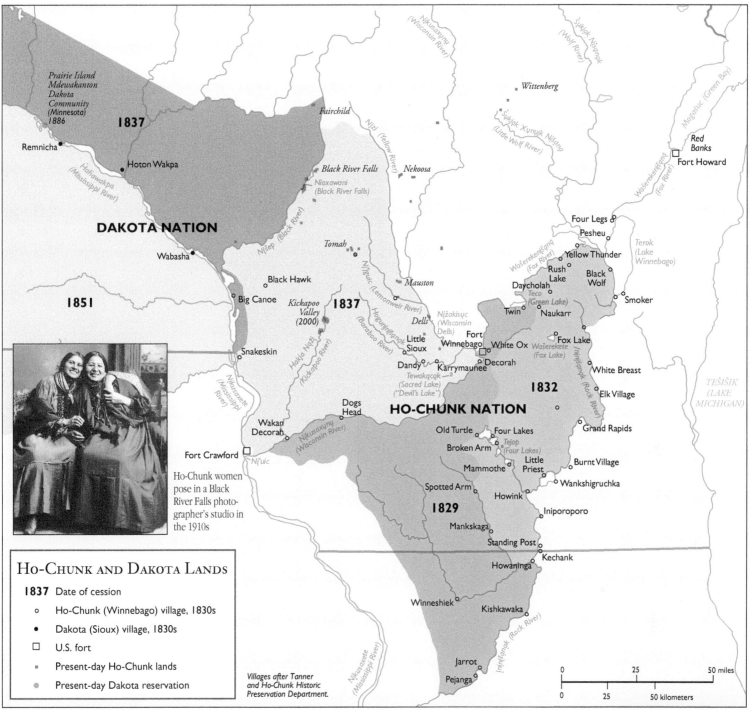

HO-CHUNK AND DAKOTA LANDS

1837 Date of cession

- ○ Ho-Chunk (Winnebago) village, 1830s
- ● Dakota (Sioux) village, 1830s
- □ U.S. fort
- ▪ Present-day Ho-Chunk lands
- ● Present-day Dakota reservation

Villages after Tanner and Ho-Chunk Historic Preservation Department.

Ho-Chunk women pose in a Black River Falls photographer's studio in the 1910s

between the warring Dakota and Ojibwe. They again moved in 1855 to a reservation at Blue Earth in southern Minnesota, where they farmed peacefully until the 1862 Dakota uprising turned vengeful settlers against all Native Americans. The Ho-Chunk were forced to march to the Crow Creek Reserve in Dakota Territory. Over 500 died on this winter version of the Cherokee "Trail of Tears."

Many Ho-Chunk returned home to Wisconsin, while others escaped down the Missouri River to stay with the Omaha tribe. A portion of Omaha lands became the Nebraska Winnebago Reservation, and its inhabitants became known as *Nosajaci* ("Dwellers on the Muddy"). The "Disaffected Bands" who had hidden in Wisconsin were called the *Wazijaci* ("Dwellers among the Pines"). Led by Yellow Thunder and Dandy, the impoverished holdouts were subjected to military roundups until 1874, when they were finally permitted to establish homesteads.

The Wisconsin Ho-Chunk population grew with returnees from the removals. Though they had no

reservation, the Ho-Chunk retained their traditional tribal structures and continued their seasonal economic patterns of hunting, trapping, planting, and gathering. Some kept their Medicine Lodge religion; others attended Christian mission schools (many still retaining their traditional beliefs). The Native American Church—a blend of peyote religion and Christianity—gained many Ho-Chunk adherents after it reached in the state in 1908.

Members of all three religious groups continued the warrior tradition by enlisting in the U.S. military, as did other Native Americans. Ho-Chunk fought on the U.S. side in the Civil War, against other Native Americans on the northern plains, and in World Wars I and II, Korea, Vietnam, and the Persian Gulf. World War II veterans were active in the effort to file a 1949 land claim, and helped establish the Wisconsin Winnebago Business Committee in 1962. The tribe was renamed the Ho-Chunk Nation in 1994. While the Ho-Chunk still uphold their cultural traditions, operating large casinos has made them one of the most economically successful tribes in the state.

By World War I many Ho-Chunk were working in cranberry bogs for as little as 25 cents a day, picking cherries in orchards, or laboring in farm fields. The tourism industry was beginning to offer other sources of livelihood, especially around Kilbourn City (later Wisconsin Dells). Women like Susie Redhorn (above) used their basketry skills to earn income. Other Ho-Chunk performed at the Stand Rock Indian Ceremonial, as they still do today.

The Ojibwe Nation

The Ojibwe (said to mean "Puckered Moccasin People"), also known as the *Chippewa*, are a group of Algonquian-speaking bands who amalgamated as a tribe in the 1600s. They called themselves the *Anishinaabe* ("Original People"), and saw themselves as kin to the Odawa ("Trader People") and the Potawatomi (see *Potawatomi*). Starting about 1640, many Ojibwe moved westward from the Sault Ste. Marie area at the tip of the Upper Peninsula (see map below). Some turned south into Michigan's Lower Peninsula, later joining the Odawa (Ottawa) and Potawatomi in the Three Fires Society confederacy. Others continued west along the Lake Superior shore and settled on Madeline Island about 1680.

The Ojibwe later migrated westward and southward along river systems (see map on facing page). Confronting the Dakota (Sioux) in bitter battles, they gradually displaced them westward. They exchanged furs for firearms and other European implements. Many French fur traders married into and adopted Ojibwe culture, producing a mixed-blood tribal majority and a distinct *Métis* community (see *Encounters*). Although some Ojibwe converted to Catholicism, many continued to follow their own spiritual teachings—like those of the sacred society of the *Midewiwin* (Grand Medicine) Lodge.

Organized into independent migratory bands, the Ojibwe were ideally suited to the fur trade. They moved according to a seasonal subsistence economy—fishing in the summer, harvesting wild rice (above) in the fall, hunting, trapping, and ice-fishing in the winter, and tapping maple syrup (in "sugar

bush" camps) and spearfishing in the spring. Their main building material, *wiigwaas* (birch bark), could be transported anywhere to make a *wiigiwam* (lodge shelter). Social organization was somewhat egalitarian, and women played a strong economic role.

The decline of the fur trade transformed this traditional Ojibwe society. When the British ousted the French from the region, the Ojibwe allied with British traders and soldiers to drive away American settlers. After the U.S. took control of the region, the Ojibwe fell on hard economic times. The men took menial jobs in the timber industry, and the role of women weakened. Nevertheless, the bands' isolation enabled the Ojibwe to preserve much of their religion and cultural traditions through the 19th and into the 20th century.

Migration Scroll

A traditional migration chart (below) was etched on a birchbark scroll owned by *Midewiwin* leader James Red Sky. In 1960, he recounted the legend of the Ojibwe journey from the Atlantic Ocean to Minnesota. The modern map (below left) shows a historic migration route and the domain that the Ojibwe established. The chart tracing shows not only physical features the Ojibwe saw during the centuries-long migration, but also the deeper spiritual meaning of the journey and the landscape. According to the legend, *Gichi-Manidoo* (the Great Spirit) needed a creature to send a message about the Great Rules of Life to the people. The Bear carried the message, or "Pack of Life," across the ocean, until he encountered the sacred *megis* (cowrie shell). The sacred shell carried the Pack of Life up the St. Lawrence, Ottawa, Mattawa, and French rivers to Lake Nipissing and Lake Huron. Along the route, he met the Otter, who carried the message along the Lake Superior shore to Madeline Island, broke through a sand bar at Fond du Lac, and traveled up the St. Louis and Leech Lake rivers to Leech Lake, where he established the last in a series of *Midewiwin* centers. The Otter, overseen by the Crane bird-god, had to pass the malevolent underwater spirits of the Great Lynx and the Fish Monster and avoid wrong river paths (represented by snakes). The legend depicts some real dangers that the Ojibwe faced in their migration, and offers a spiritual explanation for their history and geography.

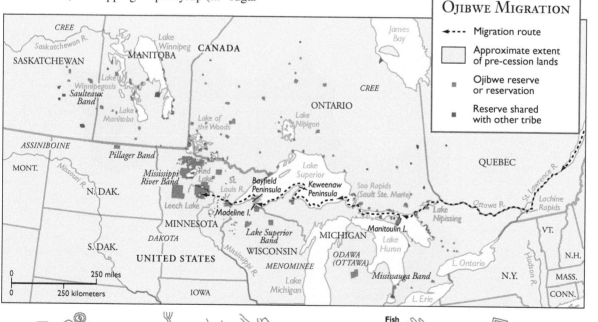

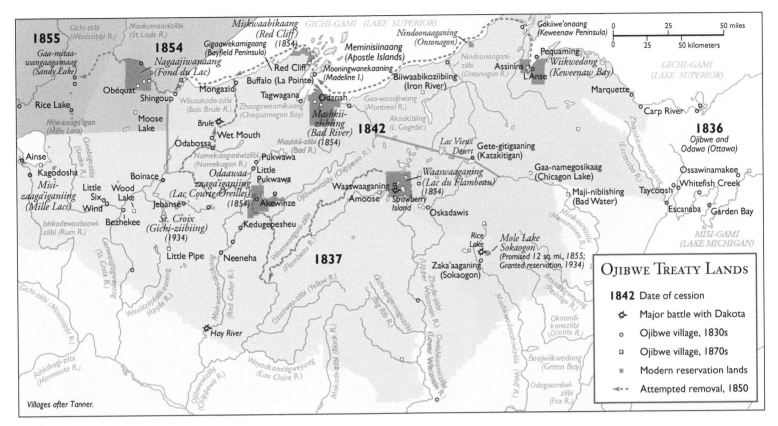

Villages after Tanner.

OJIBWE TREATY LANDS

1842	Date of cession
✦	Major battle with Dakota
○	Ojibwe village, 1830s
□	Ojibwe village, 1870s
■	Modern reservation lands
◄--	Attempted removal, 1850

OJIBWE TREATY CESSIONS

At first, American settlers avoided the northern Ojibwe country, preferring the farming areas to the south. The Canadian Shield underlies most of the region, which has mainly infertile soil, conifer forests, and granite bedrock. That combination, however, made it inviting for resource extraction.

The 1837 Treaty ceded vast tracts of forest in northwestern Wisconsin and east-central Minnesota, as did a Dakota treaty the same year. The "Pine Tree Treaty" allowed timber companies to cut the white pine stands (see *Timber*). Pine forests were not good for hunting, but the Ojibwe believed that they had reserved their hunting rights in other ceded forest lands. The treaty stated: "The privilege of hunting, fishing, and gathering the wild rice, upon the lands, the rivers and the lakes included in the territory ceded, is guaranteed to the Indians, during the pleasure of the President of the United States."

The 1842 Treaty ceded an area rich in copper and iron in northeastern Wisconsin and the western Upper Peninsula of Michigan. This "Copper Treaty" allowed mining companies to exploit the ore bodies (see *Mining*). Although Native peoples had carried out small-scale copper mining for centuries, the Ojibwe who signed the treaty were more interested in retaining their ways of life elsewhere. The completion of a canal around the Soo Rapids facilitated the copper rush into the region in the late 1840s.

An 1850 Removal Order by President Zachary Taylor attempted to move the Ojibwe west by transferring treaty payments from La Pointe to Sandy Lake, Minnesota. The Ojibwe were forced to travel in harsh winter conditions to accept the rations at Sandy Lake, where officials expected them to stay. Up to 400 Ojibwe died on the journey and during the walk home. Wisconsin residents, who saw the Ojibwe as good trading partners, raised an outcry, and President Millard Fillmore rescinded the order in 1852.

The 1854 Treaty permitted the Ojibwe to live on four reservations at Lac du Flambeau, Bad River, Red Cliff, and Lac Courte Oreilles. (The Mole Lake Sokaogon and St. Croix Ojibwe were overlooked and had to wait until 1934 for their tiny reservations.) Many Ojibwe felt that reservation life constricted their hunting and other subsistence activities, particularly after the state refused to honor their treaty rights (see column at right). In keeping with the decentralized Ojibwe political tradition, each of the six reservations has its own government. They are part of over 250 Ojibwe reserves in Michigan, Minnesota, North Dakota, Montana, Saskatchewan, Manitoba, and Ontario. Today, between 160,000 and 250,000 Ojibwe live in the U.S. (where they have the greatest range of any tribe) and in Canada.

Spearfishing

When the French first arrived in Wisconsin, they saw Native Americans spearing fish from canoes at night, using torches to illuminate the fishes' eyes. Because this fishing practice was particularly prevalent around the Ojibwe village of *Waaswaaganing* ("Place Where One Spears Fish"), the French named the village *Lac du Flambeau* ("Lake of the Torch"). The best time for spearfishing was early spring when the fish were spawning, and the male walleye and muskie were slow and in shallow water. The Ojibwe also speared fish through holes in the ice in winter, using small tents to cover the holes, and intricately carved wooden decoys to lure the fish. The state outlawed spearing from 1908 until 1983, when a federal court reaffirmed Ojibwe treaty rights, and the tradition legally resumed (above). The decision sparked a heated controversy (see *Land Conflicts*), with many anglers protesting what they saw as a potential threat to the fish resource. The Ojibwe replied that they took only a small percentage of the fish population. From 1986 to 1992 the conflict was most intense around Lac du Flambeau, where, in keeping with the local Ojibwe tradition, more fish were speared than elsewhere.

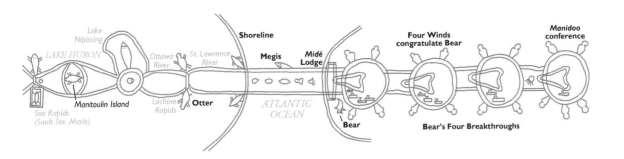

The Potawatomi Nation

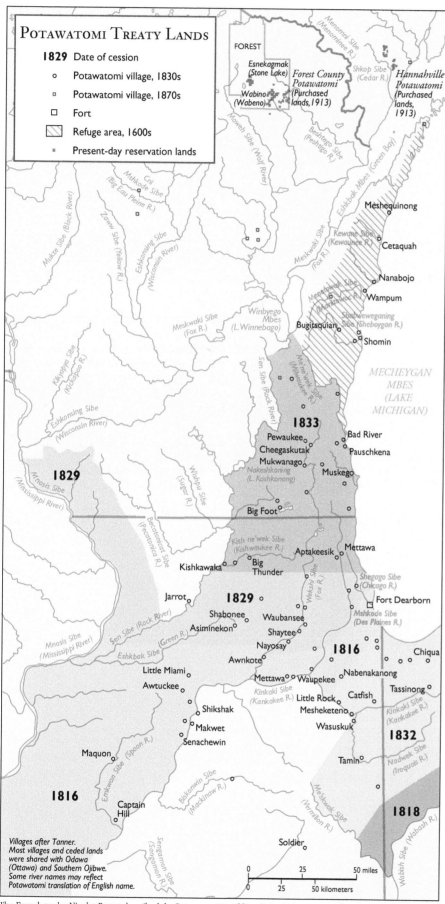

POTAWATOMI TREATY LANDS

1829 Date of cession

○ Potawatomi village, 1830s

▫ Potawatomi village, 1870s

☐ Fort

▨ Refuge area, 1600s

▪ Present-day reservation lands

FOREST

Esnekagmak (Stone Lake)

Forest County Potawatomi (Purchased lands, 1913)

Wabino (Wabeno)

Shkop Sibe (Cedar R.)

Hannahville Potawatomi (Purchased lands, 1913)

Menomini Sibe (Menominee R.)

Moweh Sibe (Wolf River)

Cni Mshkode Sibe (Big Eau Pleine R.)

Zaww Sibe (Yellow R.)

Eshkonsing Sibe (Wisconsin River)

Mukte Sibe (Black River)

Beshtego Sibe (Peshtigo R.)

Eshkbak Mbes (Green Bay)

Meshequinong

Kewane Sibe (Kewaunee R.)

Cetaquah

Meskwaki Sibe (Fox R.)

Nanabojo

Menekwak Sibe (Manitowoc R.)

Wampum

Winbyego Mbes (L. Winnebago)

Shabweweganing Sibe (Sheboygan R.)

Bugitsquian

Shomin

Meskwaki Sibe (Fox R.)

Kikyapya Sibe (Kickapoo R.)

Eshkonsing Sibe (Wisconsin River)

Sen Sibe (Rock River)

Mene Wek Sibe (Milwaukee R.)

MECHEYGAN MBES (LAKE MICHIGAN)

1833

Pewaukee

Cheegaskutak

Mukwanago

Nakeshkaning (L. Koshkonong)

Muskego

Bad River

Pauschkena

1829

Mnosis Sibe (Mississippi River)

Wishpu Sibe (Sugar R.)

Big Foot

Kish ne'wek Sibe (Kishwaukee R.)

Aptakeesik

Mettawa

Kishkawaka

Big Thunder

Shegago Sibe (Chicago R.)

Jarrot

1829

Wektshi Sibe (Fox R.)

Fort Dearborn

Shabonee

Waubansee

Mshkode Sibe (Des Plaines R.)

Asiminekon

Shaytee

Nayosay

1816

Chiqua

Awnkote

Little Miami

Mettawa

Waupekee

Nabenakanong

Awtuckee

Kinkaki Sibe (Kankakee R.)

Little Rock

Catfish

Tassinong

Shikshak

Mesheketeno

Kinkaki Sibe (Kankakee R.)

Makwet

Wasuskuk

Senachewin

1832

Maquon

Emkwan Sibe (Spoon R.)

Tamin

Nadwek Sibe (Iroquois R.)

1816

Captain Hill

Biskonwin Sibe (Mackinaw R.)

Meskwak Sibe (Vermillon R.)

1818

Soldier

Sengaman Sibe (Sangamon R.)

Wabish Sibe (Wabash R.)

Villages after Tanner. Most villages and ceded lands were shared with Odawa (Ottawa) and Southern Ojibwe. Some river names may reflect Potawatomi translation of English name.

Mnosis Sibe (Mississippi River)

Sen Sibe (Rock River)

Eshkbak Sibe

Becantonot Sibe (Pecatonica R.)

Mettawa

Little Rock

| 0 | 25 | 50 miles |
| 0 | 25 | 50 kilometers |

The Potawatomi are an Algonquian-speaking people who arrived in Wisconsin in the mid-17th century. According to legend, they migrated from Canada as part of the *Neshnabe*, or "Original People." As that group entered Michigan's Upper Peninsula, it split into three peoples—the Ojibwe, Odawa, and Potawatomi—each charged with a task by the Great Spirit. Most Ojibwe continued west, as the "Keepers of the Faith." Most Odawa (Ottawa) crossed into the Lower Peninsula, as the "Trader People." The Potawatomi—the "Keepers of the Sacred Fire People"—joined them there. Up to the present day, the "three brothers" have often lived in the same villages.

The Potawatomi settled in southwestern Michigan, along Lake Michigan's eastern shore. In the 16th and 17th centuries, intense political and trade conflicts in the East pushed other tribes (such as the Huron) westward. By 1641, during the Iroquois Wars, the Potawatomi fled to the western shore to seek safety. They found refuge in the Green Bay area, the Door Peninsula, and the islands at its tip. The area turned out to serve not only as a refuge, but also as an ideal location for the rebirth of the nation. It had rich soil, rice beds, and abundant fish and game.

The French traders with whom the Potawatomi came into constant contact frustrated their efforts to become middlemen in regional trade. Instead, the Potawatomi exploited a new role as arbiters, made brief alliances with powerful tribes in order to seize lands of smaller tribes, and, in little over a decade, became the dominant regional military power. The Potawatomi moved along river systems to the east and south, reaching Detroit by 1712 and St. Louis by 1769. They were aided by their close trade and marriage ties with the French, whom they joined in wars against the British and their allied tribes. They later supported the British during the Revolution and the War of 1812. By 1820, approximately 10,000 Potawatomi lived in 100 villages, and were being intensely pressured by the influx of American settlers, who took the best farming and hunting lands.

Potawatomi lands in Wisconsin were ceded to the U.S. in the 1829 Treaty of Prairie du Chien (covering the Lead District) and the 1833 Treaty of Chicago. Many Potawatomi who resisted removal fled northward, and wandered for decades in search of a secure land base; others returned from Kansas. Groups settled around Tripoli, Zoar, McCord, Star Lake, and Wisconsin Rapids. About 1894, some groups settled in Forest County. One of the earliest Native groups to buy back land, the Forest County Potawatomi used treaty payments in 1913 to purchase land that was placed into federal trust. The plots were in two clusters totalling 11,000 acres near Wabeno and Stone Lake (Lake Lucerne). Like most other Wisconsin tribes, the Potawatomi registered land claims with the U.S. Indian Claims Commission in the late 1940s. It was not until 1981 that they received payment for their treaty-ceded territories. For the lands that today include Milwaukee and Chicago, tribal members received only about $1,200 each.

The French trader Nicolas Perrot described the Potawatomi in 1668 as living in "utmost comfort," harvesting ample corn, fish, fowl, game, and wild rice. As their trade influence grew, the Potawatomi increasingly used canoes and horses for transportation. They settled into a seasonal migratory economy—northern fur hunting in the winter, springtime buffalo hunts in the south, farming in the summer, and trading in the fall. Canoe trading and buffalo hunting lessened by 1800 .

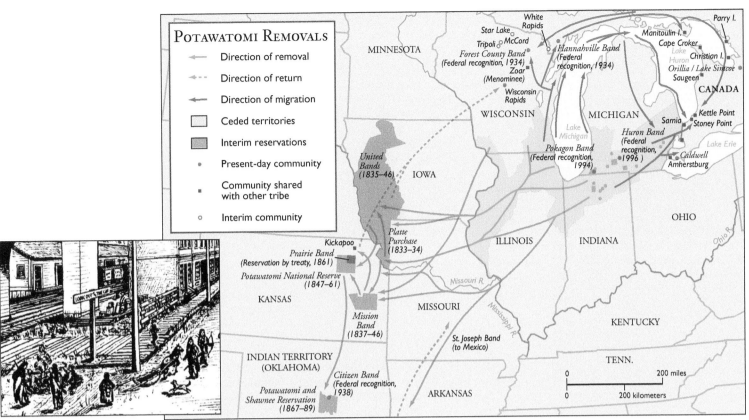

POTAWATOMI REMOVALS

- → Direction of removal
- ← - - Direction of return
- ← Direction of migration
- ☐ Ceded territories
- ▨ Interim reservations
- • Present-day community
- ▪ Community shared with other tribe
- ○ Interim community

Potawatomi in Milwaukee

In this 1860 street scene of Milwaukee, a group of Native Americans wait at a downtown railway depot at 3rd and Chestnut (West Juneau) streets. Since the 1830s, the Potawatomi had lost ownership of the Milwaukee area, and tribal members had been forced into economic dependence on the U.S. Once-powerful clans were being redefined according to their political relationships to the U.S. About 4,000 Potawatomi lived in the Milwaukee region, fencing their vast cornfields to protect them from their grazing pony herds. Even after their villages were uprooted following the 1833 treaty, some Potawatomi remained in the Milwaukee area for decades. The 1862 Dakota (Sioux) uprising in Minnesota made many whites in Wisconsin object to the presence of any Native Americans in the state. Fearing forced removal, most Potawatomi fled the Milwaukee area. It was not until almost a century later that many Potawatomi moved back to the city as part of a federal urban relocation program. In the 1990s, the Forest County Potawatomi put new plots of Milwaukee land in tribal trust status, in order to build a gaming establishment and an Indian community school. Through gaming, the tribe has reclaimed at least some of its past economic influence in the Milwaukee area.

POTAWATOMI REMOVALS

Of all Native American peoples, the Potawatomi were one of the most widely divided geographically by the federal removal policy. Today, tribal lands are scattered among five states and one Canadian province. Although relocation caused divisions within the tribe, the Potawatomi have retained their identity and kept in contact across vast distances.

The administration of Andrew Jackson (1829–37) enacted the 1830 Indian Removal Act to force all Native Americans onto reservations west of the Mississippi River. The Potawatomi lived in the way of the main route of American settlement to the west. The Potawatomi of northern Indiana and southern Michigan soon adapted to the heavy settlement in their area and attended mission churches and schools. This "Mission Band" owned its own private lands, and strongly resisted removal to the west. In

Members of the Skunk Hill (Wisconsin Rapids) Band of Potawatomi pose for a tourist postcard on a bluff near Arpin in Wood County, about 1920.

1841, most of its members were forced onto a reservation on the Osage River in eastern Kansas. Others remained on small reservations within their ceded lands, or migrated out of the area.

The Potawatomi of southern Wisconsin and northern Illinois came under less pressure from settlement, but clearly saw the coming deluge. They formed a "United Band" with some Odawa (Ottawa) and southern Ojibwe. Many Potawatomi fled to northern Wisconsin, and to northern Ojibwe and Odawa villages along the shores of Lake Superior and Lake

Huron. Some Potawatomi, however, agreed in 1833 to move to new reservations—first briefly in the Platte River country of northwestern Missouri. When Missouri settlers objected, they were then moved to the region around Council Bluffs in western Iowa. The "Prairie Band," as the group came to be called, fiercely guarded its traditional ways of life.

In 1846, the Mission Band and the Prairie Band were consolidated on the Potawatomi National Reserve around the Kaw River in northeastern Kansas. Some Potawatomi walked back to Wisconsin and settled in several northern villages. The federal government continued to forcibly remove these Potawatomi (and other Potawatomi who had resisted removal), from Wisconsin until 1851.

In Kansas, the cultural-political gap between the Mission and Prairie bands grew. In 1867, the Mission Band moved to Oklahoma, where it was renamed the "Citizen Band." The Prairie Band kept its language and religion alive, but lost over three-quarters of its reservation to private allotment. The isolation of the Potawatomi refugees who settled in Forest County in 1894 enabled them to preserve much of their culture, and treaty payments enabled them to purchase their own land. Although the Forest County Band established a federally recognized government in 1934, poverty forced it into dependence on unreliable timber jobs and government programs. Only in the 1990s did the band gain some economic self-sufficiency by building a casino and hotel complex, which also created new jobs for other area residents.

Conflicts over Native Land Resources

Before the 1830s, Native Americans controlled the lands that came to define Wisconsin. Their descendants today, about 40,000 people, make up less than 1 percent of the state's population. Wisconsin nevertheless has more reservations than any other state east of the Mississippi River.

Although they participated in many conflicts (see *Colonial Boundaries*), it was not warfare that defeated Wisconsin tribes. They fought in the Pontiac and Tecumseh rebellions, but mainly outside Wisconsin. Although the short-lived Black Hawk War ended in Wisconsin, it began in Illinois. White settlement, epidemics, trade dependency, tribal disputes, and refugee migrations all weakened the tribes.

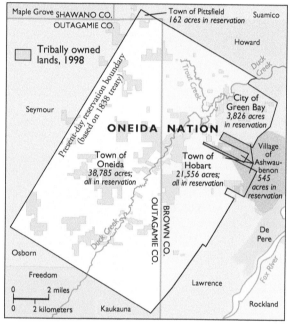

Native nations signed treaties to cede their lands to the U.S., and also to reserve land for reservations. Wisconsin tribes fixed intertribal boundaries in the 1825 Prairie du Chien Treaty (see map on facing page) to keep peace among themselves, but the U.S. used the boundaries as the basis for land cessions. Some tribes retained rights to continue using ceded lands for fishing, hunting, and gathering. As efforts at *removal* of tribes to lands west of the Mississippi River failed, the policy turned to *assimilation* of individuals into U.S. society. Some Native people adapted to U.S. culture, but others saw assimilation as a threat to their tribal identity and land base.

On the reservations. A major federal policy that affected reservations across the U.S. was *allotment.* The 1887 General Indian Allotment Act permitted the division of reservation lands into individual parcels. All members of a tribe received allotments (usually 160 acres); any left-over land was then open to public sale. About half of Wisconsin tribal lands were lost through surplus sales, tax default, division among multiple heirs, and fraudulent purchases from Native Americans who could not read or understand English. The result was a tribal/nontribal "checkerboard" of land ownership. Reservations with rich farmland (Oneida and Stockbridge-Munsee) lost

nearly all their tribal trust lands. Ojibwe reservations with timber and resort lakes lost half or more of their tribal lands (such as the Strawberry Island archeological site at Lac du Flambeau). A national survey of Native American affairs in 1928 criticized allotment, and the 1934 Indian Reorganization Act (IRA) halted allotments. Tribes got the chance to establish modern governments, and were able to recover some lands. The Oneida regained control over a small part of the land within their reservation (see map at left)—which also came under land pressure from adjacent cities—and the Stockbridge-Munsee had to wait until the 1970s to recover land. The Menominee, who were not affected by allotment or the IRA, were targeted for tribal status *termination* in the 1950s.

Off the reservations. In the 1950s–1960s, federal policy led to the *relocation* of Wisconsin tribal members to urban areas, where about half of them live today. Like termination, relocation was intended to eliminate tribal organization, but has had the unintended effect of enhancing intertribal unity in urban settings. Starting in the late 1940s, some tribes filed treaty settlement claims, but waited years for redress. A rise in activism in the 1960s led to greater efforts for sovereignty, and later to reclaiming treaty rights.

A central treaty dispute erupted over Ojibwe spearfishing, which the state Supreme Court outlawed in 1908 when tourism and sportfishing were becoming popular. Ojibwe who tried to spear fish off their reservations were cited or arrested, until a federal court upheld their treaties in 1983. Some sportsmen and others saw the decision as a threat to the fishery and to their own rights. During spring spearfishing seasons, protesters confronted the Ojibwe. Police in riot gear were deployed after reports of violence (particularly in Vilas and Oneida counties), including assaults on boats, sniper fire, and rock-throwing. A federal injunction against racial harassment, and greater awareness of Native cultures, decreased tensions by 1992. Some sportsmen began working with tribes to protect and enhance the fishery.

In the 1990s, some reservation economies began to improve as a result of gaming. Tribes became the largest employers in certain counties. New revenues financed more tribal programs and decreased local welfare rolls. As in previous efforts to enhance sovereignty, gaming has caused friction with some state officials and citizens. The increased prominence of Native Americans, however, has led to greater public understanding of the tribes' cultures and histories.

The Black Hawk War

Sauk chieftain Makataimeshekiakiak (Black Hawk) led the last major Native resistance in Wisconsin. The Sauk ceded their lands east of the Mississippi River in an 1804 treaty, but continued to live there. In 1827, the U.S. ordered them to move west of the river. A faction led by Keokuk agreed to move, but Black Hawk's "British Band" refused to give up its cornfields. When white squatters occupied its Saukenuk village, the British Band—with Meskwaki (Fox) allies—resolved to stay. In April 1832, the government mobilized state militia and federal troops, including Zachary Taylor, Abraham Lincoln, and Jefferson Davis. Black Hawk led his people on a retreat up the Rock River. Troops under Major Isaiah Stillman were routed when they attacked a Sauk truce party. Sauk fighters hid in Lake Koshkonong wetlands, raided army posts, and encouraged other tribes to join them. Troops chased them through Madison's isthmus in July and skirmished with them at the Wisconsin River. When the exhausted Sauk reached the Mississippi in August, at the confluence of the Bad Axe River, troops on a steamboat fired on Sauk who were carrying a truce flag. When the Sauk tried to cross the river two days later, at least 300 men, women, and children were killed by troops and Dakota warriors. After hiding out in a Ho-Chunk village, Black Hawk finally surrendered at Fort Crawford on August 21, 1832.

Intertribal unity increased around environmental issues in the 1980s–1990s. At right, representatives of the Ojibwe, Menominee, Potawatomi and Oneida led a 1995 walk to the proposed Crandon mine site near Mole Lake (see *Mining*).

Land conflicts between Native American nations and U.S. society in the 19th and 20th centuries, though different in form, share some common themes. Some conflicts involve *resource use*—the allocation of natural resources between Native and non-Native communities, including fish, game, and the land itself. Other conflicts involve *resource extraction*—the impacts on Native communities from the economic use of their lands for mining, timbering, or military operations. Although some *cultural conflicts* are specific to native peoples, such as the protection of burial sites and other sacred areas, some *racial conflicts* closely resemble the experiences of other "minority" ethnic groups in the U.S., including poverty and discrimination.

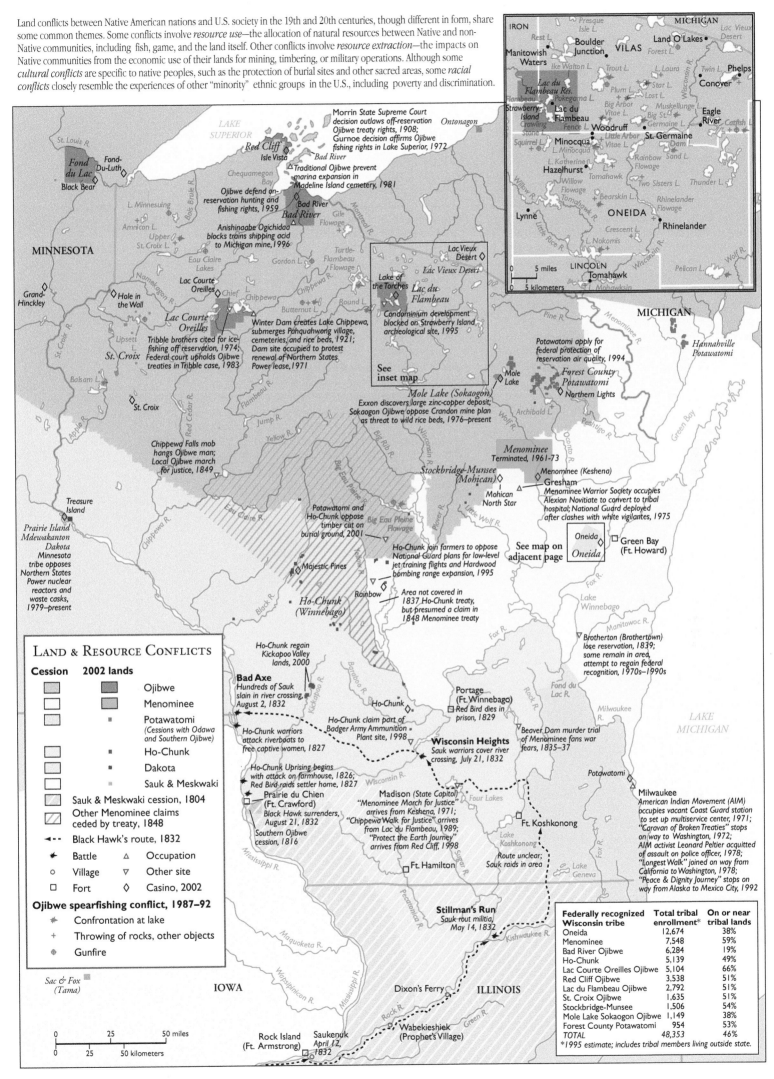

LAND & RESOURCE CONFLICTS

Cession   **2002 lands**

- Ojibwe
- Menominee
- Potawatomi (Cessions with Odawa and Southern Ojibwe)
- Ho-Chunk
- Dakota
- Sauk & Meskwaki

Sauk & Meskwaki cession, 1804
Other Menominee claims ceded by treaty, 1848

- - - Black Hawk's route, 1832

- ✸ Battle
- ○ Village
- □ Fort
- △ Occupation
- ▽ Other site
- ◇ Casino, 2002

Ojibwe spearfishing conflict, 1987–92

- ✸ Confrontation at lake
- + Throwing of rocks, other objects
- ⊕ Gunfire

Federally recognized Wisconsin tribe	Total tribal enrollment*	On or near tribal lands
Oneida	12,674	38%
Menominee	7,548	59%
Bad River Ojibwe	6,284	19%
Ho-Chunk	5,139	49%
Lac Courte Oreilles Ojibwe	5,104	66%
Red Cliff Ojibwe	3,538	51%
Lac du Flambeau Ojibwe	2,792	51%
St. Croix Ojibwe	1,635	51%
Stockbridge-Munsee	1,506	54%
Mole Lake Sokaogon Ojibwe	1,149	38%
Forest County Potawatomi	954	53%
TOTAL	48,353	46%

*1995 estimate; includes tribal members living outside state.

Anglo-Americans & British Isles Immigrants

In the 1820s, residents of the eastern and southern U.S. were looking toward the western territories for new land and economic opportunities. The American victory in the War of 1812 (see *Colonial Boundaries*), the completion of the Erie Canal and the National Road, the increasing availability of the steamboat, and the growth of eastern cities all contributed to the push westward. Southerners came by boat up the Mississippi River from Missouri, Tennessee, Kentucky, Virginia, and the Carolinas, mainly to mine lead in southwestern Wisconsin. Americans of British heritage from New York or New England, known as Yankees, took the Erie Canal to Buffalo, then traveled on by boat to Wisconsin (see map of routes below). Yankee settlers and land speculators were attracted to southeastern Wisconsin for its fertile soils and easy access to navigable waterways.

Yankee grit. English-speaking Anglo-Americans were unparalleled as pioneers. They combined an industriousness rising from their Protestant work ethic with a determination derived from a firm belief in their religious mission. They established themselves at the forefront of social, cultural, political, and commercial activities from the moment they arrived in Wisconsin. Many of Wisconsin's first politicians, physicians, lawyers, surveyors, and railroad promoters were Yankees. They also worked as merchants, printers, bankers, stockbrokers, teachers, and journalists. As the wealthiest Wisconsin settlers, Yankees owned the most property, and their homes tended to be the most prestigious, often with Irish or German servants. In the late 1840s, Kenosha, Elkhorn, and Janesville all had elaborate houses. The influence of Yankees shaped the state's culture and landscape in ways that far exceeded their numbers. The map below shows the county percentages of native-born citizens in 1850, at a time when the native-born tended to be Anglo-Americans. The largest concentrations were in the southeastern and southwestern counties.

Land speculation. Among the earliest Yankee settlers were *speculators,* or businessmen who invested in land. Speculators often moved ahead of settlement into Wisconsin's interior, buying prospective townsites and adjacent farmland, usually at sites accessible to water power and transportation. Land speculation was a lucrative business, as it had been in the eastern states and in other western territories. Speculators would survey and create a *plat* (land ownership map), similar to the map at bottom right, complete with streets and building lots. They would even name the "town" without any guarantee that it would actually grow on that spot. Many sites, however, became Wisconsin towns and cities. Milwaukee (see *Southeastern Industries*), Green Bay (see *Fox Valley*), and Madison (see *Statehood*) are examples of towns founded by Yankee land speculators.

Janesville

Henry Janes could be considered a pioneer on the "cutting edge" of the Wisconsin frontier. Born in Virginia, he settled on a bend in the Rock River in 1836. Like many other Anglo-American land speculators, Janes was drawn to the availability of water power. He platted the land on the east side of the Rock River and founded the town of Black Hawk, later renamed Janesville. Before Janes's arrival, settlers had been going to Milwaukee or Racine for their mail. Janes petitioned for a post office and was appointed the first postmaster. This post office became the distribution point for a large area, with settler families coming from 20 miles away for their mail. Janes also established the first ferry (near the present site of the Milwaukee Street bridge), enabling Janesville to become a focal point for movement to southwestern Wisconsin mining centers and the Mississippi River. Janes and his family joined the westward movement in 1839, but Janesville went on to become a major Wisconsin city, drawing many immigrant families. The map below, based on a 1873 plat map, shows the many English surnames (both from eastern states and from England), as well as Scottish and Irish surnames, of Janesville landowners.

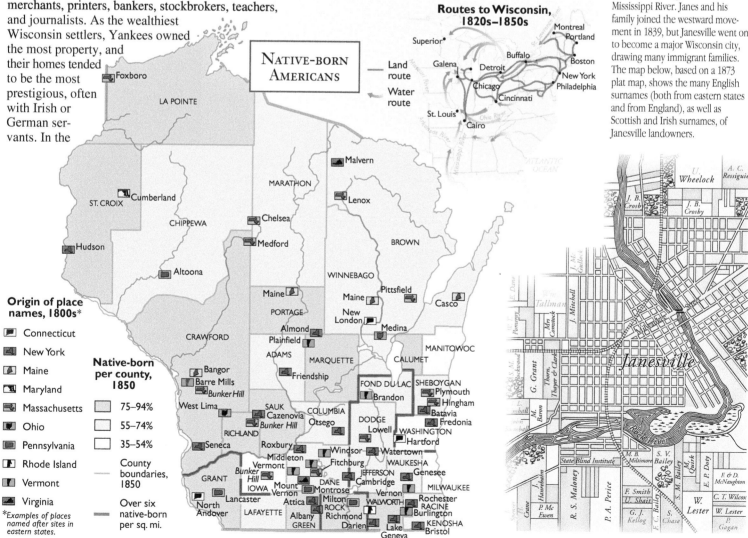

Origin of place names, 1800s*

- Connecticut
- New York
- Maine
- Maryland
- Massachusetts
- Ohio
- Pennsylvania
- Rhode Island
- Vermont
- Virginia

**Examples of places named after sites in eastern states.*

Native-born per county, 1850

- 75–94%
- 55–74%
- 35–54%
- County boundaries, 1850
- Over six native-born per sq. mi.

NATIVE-BORN AMERICANS

Routes to Wisconsin, 1820s–1850s

- Land route
- Water route

Dane County in the 1870s contained many examples of rural neighborhoods, or communities, of Anglo-Americans and British Isles immigrants (see map below). Names for these neighborhoods came initially from the natural surroundings, such as streams, hills, valleys, and prairies. Other place names were derived from family names or the names of the settlers' former homelands or hometowns. Communities of native-born Americans included Yankee Settlement and Vermont Settlement. English settlements were founded by the British Temperance Emigration Society (near Mazomanie in 1843) and the Potters Joint Stock Emigration Society, whose town leaders secured land in advance of immigration. Irish and Scottish immigrants also founded neighborhoods with names like Irish Lane and Scotch Grove. William McFarland, a Scottish immigrant, platted the village of McFarland around a railroad depot in 1856. He and his family are shown in the 1870s photo below, sitting with pride in front of their Exchange Street home.

English. In addition to American settlers of British descent, immigrants came to Wisconsin directly from the British Isles (Great Britain and Ireland), or as first-generation British immigrants who had lived elsewhere in the U.S. The first were miners from England's southwestern peninsula of Cornwall. Arriving in the late 1830s into the 1840s, the Cornish dominated Wisconsin's lead-mining industry until copper mining in the Upper Peninsula and the California gold rush drew many away from Wisconsin (see *Mining*). In the early 1840s, immigrants from other parts of Great Britain began to arrive in Wisconsin seeking better opportunities on farms and in factories. Most English immigrants settled among Yankees, though some arrived as members of communities whose leaders had selected a particular settlement site (see column at left). By the 1860s, British-born immigrants formed 6 percent of the workforce, and labored as farmers, machinists, masons, and miners. Many settlers of British heritage also came from Canada, which became independent of Britain in 1867, but under its dominion until 1931.

Irish. In the 1800s, all of Ireland was part of the United Kingdom, as were England, Scotland, and Wales (see map at right above). Some Irish immigrants came directly from Ireland, fleeing the potato famine of the 1840s. Most, however, arrived by more indirect routes. Some had worked in England and joined English emigrants in their voyages to America. Others went first to Canada or the eastern U.S., and spent years working their way to Wisconsin. Although most Irish were Catholics (and often victims of discrimination), a minority were Protestant Scots-Irish, mainly from northern Ireland. By the 1860s, the Irish constituted about 8 percent of the state's workforce. Most were farmers or farmworkers; others worked as day laborers, teamsters, canal or railroad builders, or workers on railroads. Before the Civil War (see *Military*), the Irish were widely scattered throughout the state. The formation of Irish militias and an Irish regiment during the war became a basis for growing ethnic pride. The Irish were gradually assimilated into society, particularly in Wisconsin's cities, where some emerged as political leaders. In 1990, they were the state's third-largest ethnic group.

Welsh and Scottish. Immigrants from Wales and Scotland were few in number compared to the streams of Irish and English arriving in Wisconsin. They largely practiced Protestant faiths and founded farming communities. Welsh immigrants began settling in clusters as early as 1840 in Waukesha County, and later in Columbia, Iowa, Racine, and Winnebago counties. Many Scottish immigrants came to Wisconsin via New York state, and tended to disperse among Yankee and English settlements. Although traces of Irish and Welsh culture persist today, English and Scottish influence have become virtually indistinguishable from the mainstream Anglo-American culture.

British Isles Settlement, 1940

Somerset · Erin · Elcho · Athelstane · Stratford · Albion · Amherst · Glenmore · Irish Valley · Irish Valley · Winchester · Ettrick · Melrose · Scots Junction · Ripon · Manchester · Dundee · Irish Ridge · English Valley · English Ridge · Woodstock · Cambria · Welsh Hollow · Leeds · Alderly · Erin · Irish Ridge · Irish Valley · Merton · Sussex · Boscobel · Avoca · London · Wales · Irish Hollow · Glen Haven · Albion · Caledonia · British Hollow · Exeter · Argyle · Benet Lake

After G.W. Hill

United Kingdom 1801–1922

SCOTLAND — Dundee, Glasgow, Edinburgh, Melrose, Ettrick
Scots-Irish
IRELAND — Dublin, Avoca
Ripon, Leeds, Manchester
WALES — ENGLAND — Woodstock
London, Merton, Winchester
Cornwall, Exeter

Foreign-born and children of foreign-born
Based on 1905 survey and 1940 census.

- English
- Scottish
- Welsh
- Irish
- Mixed ethnicity

Origin of place names, 1800s*

- England
- Scotland
- Wales
- Ireland
- Canada

*Examples of places named after sites in the British Isles by early settlers

Rural Neighborhoods of Dane County map

Prairie du Sac · Clifton · Sauk City · Roxbury · Steele or Dane Prairie · Scotch Grove · Morrisonville · Eagle Point · North Bristol · The Settlement or Hasemtosse · Eoli · Montrose · York · Roxbury · Brereton or Ohio Settlement · Dane · Vienna · De Forest · York Center · English Settlement or Superior City · Aldens Corners · Hyer's Corners · Fordville · Windsor · South Bristol · Bristol · Porter · Mazomanie · Waunakee · Token Creek · Sun Prairie · Deansville · British Temperance Emigration Society · Mazomanie · Poverty Hollow · Berry · Kingsley · Westport · Westport · Burke · Sun Prairie · Marshall · East Medina · Black Earth · Springfield · Fletcherville · Ashton · Norwegian Hill · Bailey · Pierceville · Medina · Mounds Creek · Black Earth · Cross Plains · Stros Karch · Middleton · Lake Mendota · Burke · Cottage Grove · Cottage Grove · Deerfield or Grace · Vermont · Cross Plains · Middleton Prairie · Middleton · Madison · Lake Monona · Blooming Grove · Cottage Grove · Deerfield · Kraghville · London North · Blue Mounds · Mount Horeb · Clontarf · Nine Mound Prairie · Fitchburg · Lake Waubesa · McFarland · Liberty Prairie · Koshkonong · Cambridge · Blue Mounds · Mound Prairie or Scotch Settlement · Verona · Syene Prairie · Yankee Settlement · Koshkonong · Clinton · Springdale · Mount Vernon · Scotch Lane · Verona · Irish Lane · Lakeview · Dunn · Lake Kegonsa · Pleasant Springs · Bovre · Utica · Rockdale · Christiana · Sharp's Corners · Irish Settlement · Paoli · Oak Hall · Fox Settlement · Hunt English · Starr or Stoughton · Wheeler Prairie · Albion Prairie · Perry · Primrose · Primrose · Montrose · Oregon · Hunt New England · Maine Settlement · Bass Lake · Dunkirk · Albion · Forward · Crokerville · Belleville · Vermont Settlement · Frog Pond or McCarthyville · Hardware · Edgerton · Brooklyn · Rutland

RURAL NEIGHBORHOODS OF DANE COUNTY

- Rural neighborhoods, 1870s
- Cities or villages, 1921
- - - Township lines

Becoming German American

In the 1840s, immigrants from German-speaking regions of Europe began coming to Wisconsin in large numbers. In the last half of the 19th century, more Germans arrived in the state than any other foreign immigrant group. These immigrants were extremely diverse in their regional, religious, and socio-economic backgrounds. Their numbers and wide distribution profoundly influenced Wisconsin.

A population boom and changing economic conditions encouraged emigration from German-speaking Europe. Wealthy landowners created a landless agricultural class by consolidating small farms into larger holdings, and a series of crop disasters convinced small farmers to look abroad. Industrialization displaced many skilled craftsmen, causing them to seek opportunities elsewhere. Political conditions stemming from the failed revolutions of

1848 motivated small groups of "Forty-eighters" to seek freedom in America. Other Germans sought to gain religious freedom or to avoid the military draft. Some German states subsidized emigration as a way to defuse social unrest. Whether the immigrants' motives were economic or political, their journey to America was eased by improvements in transportation. Railroads were extended, steamships were built, and transatlantic fares became more affordable.

German immigrants found Wisconsin to be the right destination, at the right time. In the 1840s and 1850s, they found a ready source of good farmland, either unsettled or being sold by earlier arrivals now moving west with the frontier. They were encouraged by a geography and climate similar to their homelands. After statehood, Wisconsin attracted immigrants by

German Cultural Societies

German cultural identity in the U.S. often centered around religious and community groups. In the late 19th and early 20th centuries Wisconsin had a robust and vibrant German culture. Some groups (usually rural) were made up of pious Catholics or Protestants, who focused on their own communities and religious institutions. More common were urban and rural community groups modeled on secular activities of the German working and middle classes in Europe. Their members came from many political, economic, and social backgrounds, and included political refugees, Forty-eighters, and atheists. Many organizations formed for practical reasons—volunteer fire companies, militias, and mutual aid societies. Some clubs were created as conversational and debating societies. Groups of "Free Thinkers" formed congregations seeking what they saw as "rational" alternatives to the authority and doctrines of organized religion. Other German Americans formed musical and singing societies, or developed competitions that displayed their culture to the nation. Dramatic societies grew into accomplished professional theater groups. The best-known German clubs were part of the *Turnverein* movement. "Turners" emphasized physical fitness and liberal nationalism. They established many Turner Halls and eventually emerged as a national organization that offered a framework for German American culture (see 1875 photo of Milwaukee Turners above). These clubs and other social institutions (such as the ever-present beer hall) facilitated the mixing of diverse German-speaking immigrants into new "German" communities. The weakening of German American identity in the 20th century, particularly during World War I, led to a decline in German cultural organizations. Groups and clubs can still be found in some rural communities around the state; legacies of German cultural society (such as Milwaukee's Pabst Theater and a few Turner Halls) are still present in some Wisconsin cities.

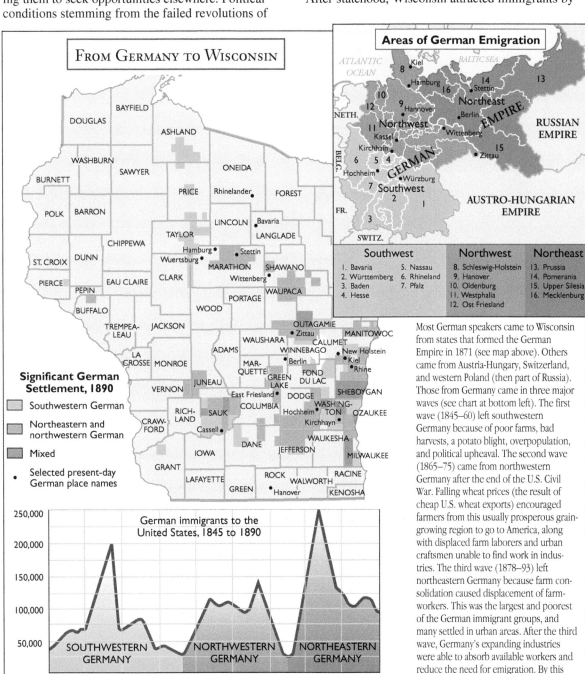

FROM GERMANY TO WISCONSIN

Areas of German Emigration

Southwest		Northwest		Northeast	
1. Bavaria	5. Nassau	8. Schleswig-Holstein		13. Prussia	
2. Württemberg	6. Rhineland	9. Hanover		14. Pomerania	
3. Baden	7. Pfalz	10. Oldenburg		15. Upper Silesia	
4. Hesse		11. Westphalia		16. Mecklenburg	
		12. Ost Friesland			

Significant German Settlement, 1890

☐ Southwestern German

☐ Northeastern and northwestern German

■ Mixed

• Selected present-day German place names

German immigrants to the United States, 1845 to 1890

SOUTHWESTERN GERMANY · NORTHWESTERN GERMANY · NORTHEASTERN GERMANY

Most German speakers came to Wisconsin from states that formed the German Empire in 1871 (see map above). Others came from Austria-Hungary, Switzerland, and western Poland (then part of Russia). Those from Germany came in three major waves (see chart at bottom left). The first wave (1845–60) left southwestern Germany because of poor farms, bad harvests, a potato blight, overpopulation, and political upheaval. The second wave (1865–75) came from northwestern Germany after the end of the U.S. Civil War. Falling wheat prices (the result of cheap U.S. wheat exports) encouraged farmers from this usually prosperous grain-growing region to go to America, along with displaced farm laborers and urban craftsmen unable to find work in industries. The third wave (1878–93) left northeastern Germany because farm consolidation caused displacement of farmworkers. This was the largest and poorest of the German immigrant groups, and many settled in urban areas. After the third wave, Germany's expanding industries were able to absorb available workers and reduce the need for emigration. By this time most of America's cheap public farmland had been settled.

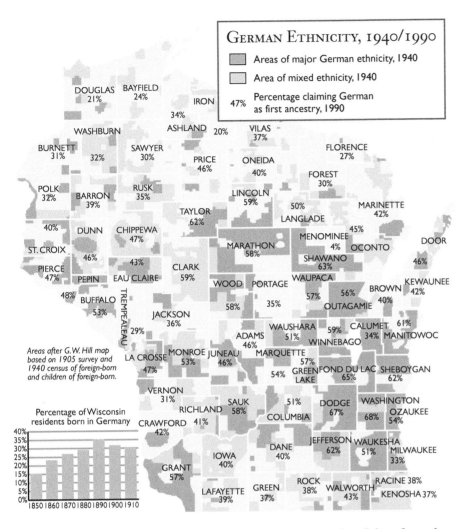

GERMAN ETHNICITY, 1940/1990

- ▪ Areas of major German ethnicity, 1940
- ▫ Area of mixed ethnicity, 1940
- 47% Percentage claiming German as first ancestry, 1990

DOUGLAS 21%
BAYFIELD 24%
IRON 34%
ASHLAND 20%
VILAS 37%
WASHBURN
BURNETT 31%
SAWYER 32%
SAWYER 30%
PRICE 46%
ONEIDA 40%
FLORENCE 27%
POLK 32%
BARRON 39%
RUSK 35%
LINCOLN 59%
FOREST 30%
40%
DUNN
CHIPPEWA 47%
TAYLOR 62%
50%
LANGLADE
MARINETTE 42%
ST. CROIX
46%
43%
MARATHON 58%
MENOMINEE 4%
OCONTO
DOOR 46%
PIERCE 47%
PEPIN
EAU CLAIRE
CLARK 59%
SHAWANO 63%
48%
BUFFALO 53%
TREMPEALEAU
JACKSON 36%
WOOD 58%
PORTAGE 35%
WAUPACA 57%
BROWN 40%
KEWAUNEE 42%
OUTAGAMIE
29%
ADAMS 46%
WAUSHARA 51%
59%
CALUMET 34%
MANITOWOC 61%
WINNEBAGO
LA CROSSE 47%
MONROE 53%
JUNEAU 46%
MARQUETTE 57%
GREEN LAKE 54%
FOND DU LAC 65%
SHEBOYGAN 62%
VERNON 31%
RICHLAND 41%
SAUK 58%
51%
COLUMBIA
DODGE 67%
WASHINGTON 68%
OZAUKEE 54%
CRAWFORD 42%
GRANT 57%
IOWA 40%
DANE 40%
JEFFERSON 62%
WAUKESHA 51%
MILWAUKEE 33%
LAFAYETTE 39%
GREEN 37%
ROCK 38%
WALWORTH 43%
RACINE 38%
KENOSHA 37%

Areas after G.W. Hill map based on 1905 survey and 1940 census of foreign-born and children of foreign-born.

Percentage of Wisconsin residents born in Germany

40% 35% 30% 25% 20% 15% 10% 5% 0%
1850 1860 1870 1880 1890 1900 1910

German American Bund

The German American Bund was one of the most notorious German American organizations in U.S. history. In 1924 the Free Society of Teutonia was founded in Chicago, with the aim of enlisting ethnic Germans around the world in the cause of German nationalism. After several name changes, it became known as the German American Bund in 1936. One of its largest chapters was in Milwaukee. Its philosophy reflected that of the Hitler regime. Members distributed Nazi propaganda and used Nazi salutes. Bund meetings displayed German swastika flags alongside the Stars and Stripes, and used uniformed Storm Troopers as security. The Bund established Camp Hindenberg, near Grafton, for youth group meetings and Storm Trooper drills. The group never made significant headway in recruiting Wisconsin German Americans, and mostly aroused public hostility against its cause. The Hitler regime dissociated itself from the Bund in 1937, fearing that the group's open Nazi advocacy would weaken American isolationism. The Bund dissolved after the U.S. entered World War II, but widespread suspicion of its former members continued. In the end, it further weakened German American culture in the U.S.

giving foreign-born settlers voting rights after only one year of residency. A prohibition on state borrowing for capital improvements kept taxes low, and progressive bankruptcy laws reduced the risk of homestead investments. The state established immigration commissions to advertise Wisconsin's attractions in Europe and to immigrants arriving on the East Coast. Perhaps of most importance, new immigrants sent home money and letters lauding Wisconsin's opportunities, convincing many others to follow in their footsteps.

BECOMING GERMAN

Although the original immigrants may have been "German," they were not from "Germany." They came from many states—such as Pomerania, Bavaria, and Prussia—in what was to become the German Empire in 1871 (see map on facing page). They identified primarily with their home regions but, for several reasons, began to think of themselves as "German" after their arrival in Wisconsin. First, the practical realities of life in an alien land led them to make cultural compromises. Second, community social clubs (see column on facing page) helped to develop a new "German" identity. Third, despite regional dialects, the use of a common written form of German encouraged a sense of community, and Americans generally identified immigrants by their language. Fourth, religious differences overpowered regional identities, and soon became the major dividing line within Wisconsin's German community (see *Religion*). It is interesting to note that these immigrants became "German" about the same time

as their homelands became a unified Germany. Becoming German in Wisconsin was a first step in the process of becoming "German American."

Many German immigrants came with money to establish homes, farms, and new businesses. Others were skilled tradesmen who easily found employment in port cities such as Milwaukee. Their presence both aided and encouraged others to come, and Milwaukee soon had one of the highest concentrations of German speakers in the U.S. German farmers first settled near Milwaukee, close to the established transportation network. As more Germans arrived, they moved farther west and north (see map on facing page). German farmers tended to develop their farms and buy additional land nearby, rather than engage—like their Yankee neighbors—in land speculation. Rural Germans thus tended to stay in the areas where they had originally settled, instead of moving west. They played a major role in the switch from wheat to dairy agriculture in the state (see *Crops*).

German American culture in Wisconsin was quite robust in the late 19th century. It encouraged numerous German-speaking churches, newspapers, and schools. German American political influence, however, never solidified into a single voting bloc. Divisions between Catholics and Protestants, between religious and secular perspectives, and between rich and poor inhibited strong unity. The community could unite, however, over particular issues. German American resistance to making English mandatory in schools, for example, swept the Republican governor and legislature out of power in 1890.

BECOMING AMERICAN

German immigration slowed dramatically in the late 19th and early 20th centuries, as Congress established immigration quotas and expanding urban industries in Germany attracted workers who otherwise might have emigrated. With fewer new immigrants renewing their culture, German Americans began to assimilate into mainstream culture. The outbreak of World War I in 1914, however, created widespread mistrust of their cultural expressions and political loyalties. Some German American institutions were actively suppressed after the U.S. joined the war against Germany in 1917. Anything closely identified with German culture was often deemed unpatriotic. (Sauerkraut, for example, was temporarily renamed "liberty cabbage.") When faced with the stark choice of becoming "American" or maintaining their German culture, many second- and third-generation Germans chose to dissociate themselves from their community institutions. German American culture never recovered.

World War II had a similar effect in "Americanizing" Wisconsin German Americans. German immigration continued in much smaller waves before and after the war and eventually reduced to a trickle. Except for some strong communities of German-speaking Amish (see *Religion*), Wisconsin's German American culture gradually fell victim to assimilation. Traces of German heritage, however, can still be found today in the cities, towns, and farms of Wisconsin.

Scandinavian Settlement

The term "Scandinavian" technically refers to people from Norway, Sweden, Denmark, and Iceland. But in Wisconsin, Finns, too, can be considered Scandinavian. Many came from Finnish groups that had lived for decades in Sweden, but for the most part had remained culturally and linguistically distinct.

Immigration from Scandinavia to North America in the 1800s began for several reasons. Throughout Scandinavia, the population increased rapidly from the 1750s through the 1800s. This growth, along with the transition of the traditional, semifeudal, subsistence agricultural system to one of production for profit, led to an increase in the number of landless laborers. Other causes of emigration included land subdivision, crop losses, and avoidance of the military draft. In Wisconsin and elsewhere in the Midwest, available land and opportunities for work in farming, lumbering, mining, and manufacturing attracted these immigrants.

Norwegians. The earliest and most numerous of the Scandinavian immigrants to Wisconsin were Norwegians, whose first settlements appeared in 1838. By the 1850s, large Norwegian communities had been established at Jefferson Prairie and Rock Prairie (Rock County), Muskego (Waukesha County), and Koshkonong (Jefferson County). These sites became important destinations for new immigrants, and staging areas for the development of other settlements in western and northern Wisconsin, western states, and Canada. Approximately 44,000 Norwegian settlers had arrived by 1860; almost half of the Norwegians in the U.S. then resided in Wisconsin. Many of them began to move to the "wheat frontier" in western Wisconsin (see *Crops*). By 1870, a quarter of the state's Norwegians lived in an area from Crawford County northward into Barron County. Other settlements developed away from this core area, notably in Winnebago and Manitowoc counties, and the "Indielandet" colony in Portage and Waupaca counties. In addition to farming, Norwegians were employed in shipbuilding and lumbering. An important characteristic of Norwegian settlements was their cohesiveness; immigrants sought out and settled among people from the same church parish, town, or valley from which they had come in the Old Country. These bonds enabled Norwegian settlements to retain their cultural distinctiveness longer than many other ethnic communities in Wisconsin.

Danes. Danish immigration began in the 1840s, when the first distinctly Danish settlements appeared in Hartland (Waukesha County) and New Denmark (Brown County). Racine became the primary destination of Danish immigrants who came to Wisconsin from the end of the Civil War through the early 1900s. Numerous Danes in Racine found work in the growing manufacturing sector; others found their way north and west to establish farms or work in lumbering. By 1900 Wisconsin had over 33,000 citizens of Danish lineage.

Swedes. Among the first Swedish settlements in Wisconsin was Pine Lake–New Uppsala (Waukesha County), founded by Gustav Unonius in 1841. A small number of Swedes arrived in the 1840s and 1850s, many settling among the Norwegians near Koshkonong. These early settlers differed from those who followed—they were not the landless poor, and they had left Sweden for philosophical or ideological reasons. The main period of Swedish immigration began in the 1860s (after devastating crop losses struck Sweden) and continued through the early 1900s. Because of their later arrival, Swedes found that much of Wisconsin's best agricultural land had already been settled. They turned to the task of farming and lumbering in the northern half of the state. Other Swedes found work in bridge, railroad, and road construction, and in the ports and mills of Ashland, Marinette, and Superior. The St. Croix Valley—particularly Burnett and Polk counties—attracted newly arriving Swedes (as did the adjoining area in Minnesota) and so developed as a distinct region of settlement in northwestern Wisconsin.

Finns. Significant numbers of Finnish immigrants did not arrive until the 1880s. Like the Swedes, Finns were later arrivals who settled what land remained in the northern region of the state. Some of the immigrants were ethnic Finns from Sweden, known as "Finland-Swedes." By 1910, Douglas, Bayfield, Ashland, Iron, and Price counties contained two-thirds of Wisconsin's Finns. Many Finnish immigrants found work in iron mines of the Gogebic Range and stone quarries of Marinette and Waushara counties (see *Mining*). Others established farms, worked in lumbering and commercial fishing, or labored in the factories and docks of Superior, Ashland, Kenosha, and Milwaukee (see *Great Lakes*). Spurred on by low-paying and often dangerous working conditions, Wisconsin's Finns became active in the growing American labor movement (see *Labor*). They mirrored developments in Finland,

The Davidson Windmill

Finnish immigrant and millwright Jaako Tapola (who later changed his name to Jacob Davidson) constructed this mill in Lakeside Township (Douglas County) in 1904. Eight wooden wings (a departure from the more common Dutch four-wing style) were covered with canvas sailcloth to catch winds off Lake Superior. The mill was built using local materials; the millstones came from the nearby Amnicon River bed. The mill was used for grinding flour and operated until 1926.

Tobacco Cultivation

Although Yankee farmers were the first to grow tobacco commercially in Wisconsin, tobacco cultivation later became synonymous with Norwegian settlements. The Baglien family's tobacco-stripping house (below) in Christiana Township (Vernon County) was constructed in 1869 as a store, and was later used as a milk-skimming station. Members of the Baglien, Engum, Larson, Lomen, Norbus, and Olson families pose holding cured tobacco leaves.

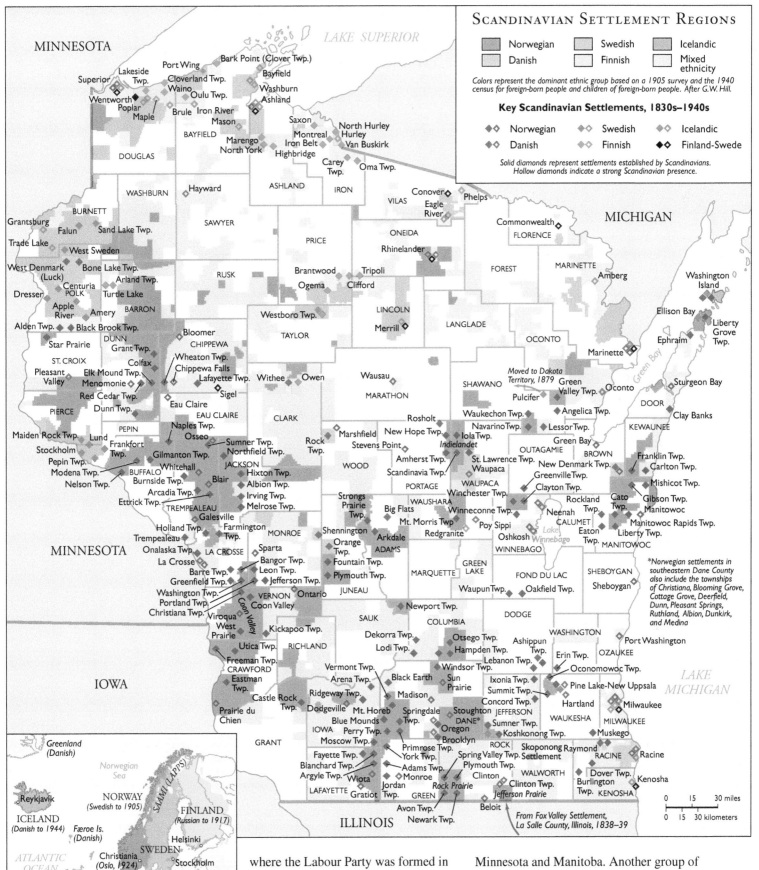

where the Labour Party was formed in 1899. Their communal spirit also led to the development of numerous cooperatives in Finnish rural settlements.

Icelanders. Icelandic immigrants arrived in the 1870s. Many found work on the docks and in the factories of Milwaukee. In 1870, Icelanders settled among the Danes on Washington Island, and worked in fishing, lumbering, and farming. The Washington Island settlement—recognized as the oldest Icelandic settlement in the U.S.—served as a staging point for the development of other Icelandic enclaves in Minnesota and Manitoba. Another group of Icelanders settled in 1875 near Pulcifer (Shawano County), but relocated four years later to Dakota Territory in search of better farmland. By 1924, over 1,000 Icelandic immigrants were located in northern Door County and Washington Island—one-tenth of the total number in the U.S.

The Scandinavian presence remains evident today in Wisconsin. Numerous annual folk festivals serve as a reminder of the songs, dances, food, ethnic costumes, folklore, and traditions of the original Scandinavian immigrants.

European Immigration

From the 1840s to the 1920s, European settlers arrived in large numbers in Wisconsin, searching for land, economic opportunity, or religious and political freedom. Many arrived soon after statehood from the German states (see *Germans*), Scandinavia (see *Scandinavians*), and the British Isles (see *Anglo-Americans*). Smaller numbers from other western European countries—the Netherlands, Belgium, and Switzerland—also came relatively early. Like other immigrants, they tended to settle near each other (see map on facing page). In the 1850s, Wisconsin enticed Europeans by giving male newcomers voting rights after only one year of residency, without requiring that they learn English. The main draw, however, was economic. Letters written by immigrants to family and friends back home promoted Wisconsin's virtues and encouraged others to come. In the 1870s, southern and eastern European immigrants began to arrive to work in the industrial cities such as Milwaukee and Racine (see column at right). Later immigrants to Wisconsin were rather evenly distributed between rural and urban areas (immigrants in most other states concentrated in the cities). By 1900, about 40 countries were represented among Wisconsin citizens.

Poles. Throughout the 19th century, Poland was divided among the German, Russian, and Austro-Hungarian empires. The vast majority of Poles arriving in Wisconsin came from the German-controlled region in the 1870s and 1880s. Their strong national and religious consciousness gave them a sense of cultural unity. They founded their own newspapers, social clubs, and (mostly Catholic) churches (see *Religion*). Poles settled mainly in Milwaukee County (see *Ethnic Milwaukee*), but also in rural communities, some with obvious names like Polonia, Krakow, Zachow, Pulaski, Sobieski, and Poniatowski. Today, Poles are the state's second-largest single ethnic group (see chart at right). Portage County has one of the country's oldest Polish farm districts, and Wisconsin leads the U.S. in Poles who work in agriculture.

French. The many French place names in Wisconsin come mainly from pre-1825 French Canadian explorers and settlers (see *Encounters*), not from later immigrants from France. The French made a lasting cultural impression, still evident in land subdivision patterns around Green Bay (see *Fox Valley*) and Prairie du Chien.

Italians. Immigrants from Italy began arriving in large numbers in the 1890s, mainly to work in the industries of southeastern Wisconsin, though many took northern mining or lumbering jobs. Most were farmers from Sicily or other poor regions of Italy, and some worked only a few years before returning to Italy. Many had lived in Chicago before moving to live in Milwaukee's Third Ward, Racine, Kenosha, Madison's Greenbush neighborhood, or rural farms.

Dutch. Wisconsin was a major destination for immigrants from the Netherlands from the 1850s to

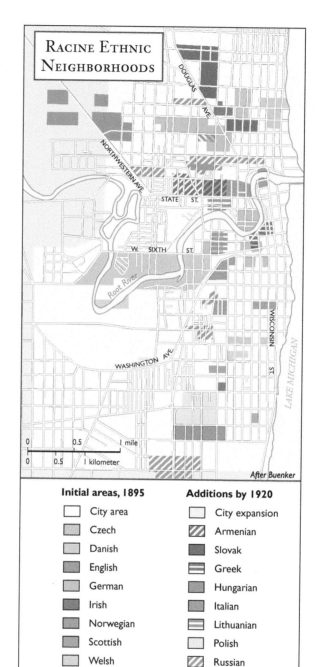

RACINE ETHNIC NEIGHBORHOODS

After Buenker

0   0.5   1 mile
0   0.5   1 kilometer

Initial areas, 1895

- City area
- Czech
- Danish
- English
- German
- Irish
- Norwegian
- Scottish
- Welsh

Additions by 1920

- City expansion
- Armenian
- Slovak
- Greek
- Hungarian
- Italian
- Lithuanian
- Polish
- Russian
- Yugoslav

Multicultural Racine

Racine has long been noted for its ethnic diversity. Named by French explorers, it was first settled by Yankees in the 1830s and 1840s, and its first European settler was a German known as "Dutch Pete." By 1910, Racine was called both "the most Danish city in America" and the "Czech Bethlehem." Racine County has such diverse place names as "English Settlement," "Scotch Lane," "Norway," "Little Armenia," "Polonia," and "The Barrio." At the turn of the century, 68 percent of Racine's population consisted of foreign-born immigrants or their children. The figure dropped to 60 percent in 1930, and as late as 1973 stood at 15 percent. Racine's immigrants came in three waves. The first wave, between 1840 and 1900, came mostly from the British Isles, Scandinavia, and German states, but included Czechs and other central European ethnic groups. The early 1900s saw a shift in immigration both from southern Europe—Italians and Greeks—and from eastern Europe—Poles, Slovaks, Hungarians, Lithuanians, and Yugoslavs (Serbs, Croatians, and Slovenes). Russians, Armenians, and Jews came from the Russian or Ottoman empires as well. The small African American community that had been in Racine since the Civil War grew during the two world wars (see *African Americans*). Mexican Americans also began to arrive in the 1950s (see *Newest Arrivals*). By the mid-1970s, African Americans and Hispanics together made up 11 percent of county residents. Because of its industrial base and its location between two major cities, Racine remains a prime example of ethnic diversity.

FIRST EUROPEAN ANCESTRY, 1990
Total population: 4,684,769

Ancestry	Population	Percent of state population	Ancestry	Population	Percent of state population
German*	2,209,701	47.2%	Yugoslav	12,940	0.3%
Polish	325,320	6.9%	Greek	10,382	0.2%
Irish**	281,309	6.0%	Lithuanian	10,295	0.2%
Norwegian†	257,345	5.5%	Ukrainian	4,479	0.1%
English**	211,729	4.5%	Austrian	4,059	0.1%
French	111,083	2.4%			
Italian	96,719	2.1%	**Other first ancestry reported, 1990**		
Swedish†	88,121	1.9%			
Dutch	86,556	1.8%	Racial or Hispanic groups††	341,293	7.3%
Czech	59,855	1.3%	United States or American	76,673	1.6%
Danish†	42,955	0.9%	French Canadian or Canadian	36,598	0.8%
Belgian	36,822	0.8%			
Swiss	36,281	0.8%	Arab	5,086	0.1%
Scottish**	29,922	0.6%	African	3,419	0.1%
Scots-Irish**	27,084	0.6%	Other groups	128,236	2.7%
Slovak	26,263	0.5%	Unclassified or not reported	55,713	1.2%
Finnish†	23,288	0.5%			
Russian	18,251	0.4%	*See Germans	††See African Americans and Newest Arrivals	
Hungarian	13,577	0.3%	**See Anglo-Americans		
Welsh**	13,415	0.3%	†See Scandinavians		

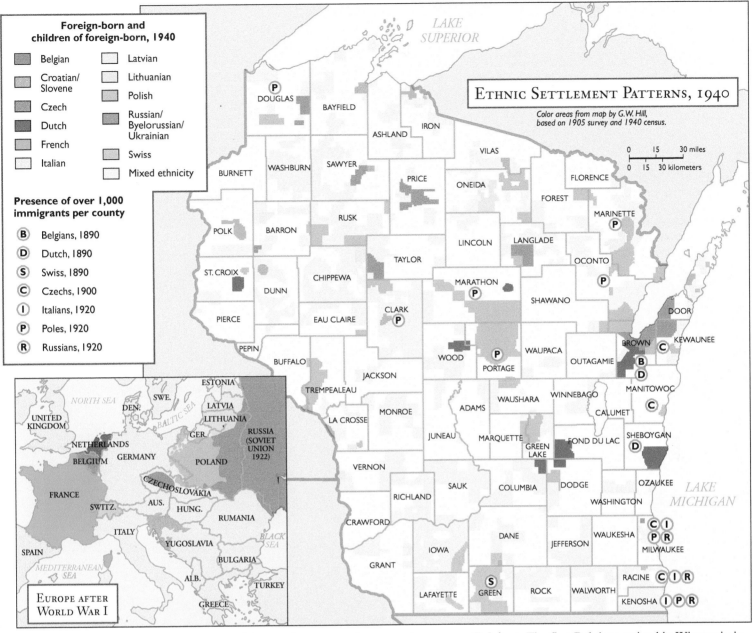

ETHNIC SETTLEMENT PATTERNS, 1940

Color areas from map by G.W. Hill,
based on 1905 survey and 1940 census.

Foreign-born and children of foreign-born, 1940

- Belgian
- Croatian/ Slovene
- Czech
- Dutch
- French
- Italian
- Latvian
- Lithuanian
- Polish
- Russian/ Byelorussian/ Ukrainian
- Swiss
- Mixed ethnicity

Presence of over 1,000 immigrants per county

- Ⓑ Belgians, 1890
- Ⓓ Dutch, 1890
- Ⓢ Swiss, 1890
- Ⓒ Czechs, 1900
- Ⓘ Italians, 1920
- Ⓟ Poles, 1920
- Ⓡ Russians, 1920

EUROPE AFTER WORLD WAR I

New Glarus Swiss

The New Glarus area was settled in 1845 by immigrants from Switzerland's Glarus Canton, who were searching for land for communal farming. Today, the Green County town continues to have a strong affinity for Swiss culture, and claims the title of "America's Little Switzerland." Annual events, begun in the 1930s, draw tourists, with Swiss foods, music, costumes, and folk dancing (see photo at right). They include the Heidi Festival (complete with yodeling and flag throwing), the Wilhelm Tell Pageant honoring a Swiss national hero, and the Swiss Volkfest marking Switzerland's independence day. New Glarus and the surrounding area are also the center of the state's Swiss cheese production (see *Dairyland*). In 1898 Green County boasted 200 cheese factories and creameries that manufactured 10 million pounds of cheese.

1880s. Dutch laborers, farmers, craftsmen, and tradesmen settled mainly in Brown, Sheboygan, Fond du Lac, and Outagamie counties. Like the Germans, some were Catholics and some Protestants.

Czechs. The earliest Slavic ethnic group to arrive in the state was the Czechs, who came from Bohemia, a region they shared with German-speaking groups. Primarily farmers and skilled tradesmen, Czechs settled along Lake Michigan from Racine to Kewaunee (founding towns such as Pilsen and Krok), and in southwestern Wisconsin. After World War I, Czechs and Slovaks unified as Czechoslovakia, and the two immigrant groups tended to settle together.

Swiss. Most Swiss in Wisconsin came for economic reasons, before 1870, from German-speaking parts of Switzerland. "Swissconsin" in Green County became the largest center of Swiss farming in the U.S. (see column at left).

Belgians. The first Belgians arrived in Wisconsin in the mid-1850s. At first, most were *Walloons* (French-speakers) who settled mainly in Door and Kewaunee counties, founding Brussels, Namur, and other towns. Later, some *Flemings* (Dutch-speakers) also arrived. Mostly Catholic, the Belgians quickly built churches, convents, and parochial schools.

Other European immigrants. Wisconsin later became the destination for other groups fleeing wars and economic upheavals in Europe. Russians and Ukrainians from the Russian Empire (the Soviet Union after World War I), Croatians, Slovenes, and Serbs (groups that formed Yugoslavia after World War I), Austrians, Hungarians, Lithuanians, and Latvians (groups that formed their own nations after World War I), Greeks, and others, made their homes in the state.

Americanization. European immigrants, by design and instinct, combined cultural elements from their homelands with the cultures of their new home. Their descendants "Americanized" at different paces, learning English and adapting to the predominant Anglo-American culture. Some ethnic groups kept much of their culture and language, while others were assimilated with few traces of either. The institutions and festivals that immigrants created still contribute to Wisconsin's diverse cultural heritage.

Ethnic Milwaukee

Historically, Milwaukee has been one of America's most "foreign" cities. Immigrants came in several waves, in response to the city's growth as a commercial and industrial center, and created neighborhoods shaped along ethnic and economic lines.

First wave. Germans and Czechs (Bohemians) fleeing repression, and Irish fleeing the potato famine, arrived in the 1840s. They quickly outnumbered native-born Americans, who nevertheless maintained a higher social status (see *Anglo-Americans*). Germans made up 35 percent of the population in 1880, concentrated in the Northwest Side's "German Town" (also known as the "Wooden Shoe District"). They were mainly skilled artisans and merchants, but there were some doctors and bankers. High culture flourished in the German-speaking parts of the city, which became known as a "German Athens." Cultural and political life centered on churches, taverns, theaters, and clubs (see *Germans*). Many Irish were grocers or railroad workers; they tended to intermingle with earlier British immigrants.

Second wave. Poles first arrived after the Civil War and had become the city's second-largest ethnic group by 1900 (see *European Immigration*). For a U.S. city to have two large predominant ethnic groups was unusual. Poles and Germans had much in common. Most Poles came from the German-con-

trolled section of Poland, and both Poles and Germans became homeowners. But Poles differed with Germans over European politics and over control of the local Catholic Church. The self-sufficient Polish South Side retained a strong sense of identity (see column on facing page). As the first-generation, foreign-born immigrants died out, some groups, such as the Irish, began to lose their distinct identities and their members scattered to other neighborhoods.

Third wave. Immigrants from southern and eastern Europe flocked to work in the city's growing industries from the 1880s to the 1910s. Italians (mainly from Sicily) moved into formerly Irish downtown areas, and developed other close-knit neighborhoods. Slovaks, Greeks, and Hungarians also settled downtown, as did Russian Jews fleeing persecution (including future Israeli Prime Minister Golda Meir). Slovenes, Croatians, and Serbs—from the area that became Yugoslavia after World War I—clustered around their Far South Side churches.

Fourth wave. The world wars weakened German American culture, at the same time that defense plants brought in many black southerners (see *African Americans*). The city developed a high level of racial segregation in housing and education (see *1960s*). Some members of other ethnic groups had moved to the suburbs as African Americans began

Occupational Patterns

Many immigrants arrived in Milwaukee with specific work skills, and others came to get jobs in the city's expanding industries. Ethnic and family ties were crucial both in getting jobs and in adjusting to economic changes and new job opportunities. The map below uses "grid cells," or representations of clusters of city blocks, to show the residential mosaic of Milwaukee in 1880 and 1900, including dominant ethnic groups and occupations. The city's native-born and English-born population had a large proportion of professionals and semiprofessionals. Germans were heavily represented in skilled craft trades, and tended to stay in those trades even as they declined. Many Norwegians worked in docks and shipyards. Most Irish were unskilled workers, but later moved into skilled trades. Czechs originally had a high proportion of laborers, but many moved into retail fields, particularly clothing. Poles were at first a large unskilled group, but many moved into manager positions. They were replaced as primary industrial workers by Italians, Greeks, and Eastern Europeans, and later by African Americans during World Wars I and II.

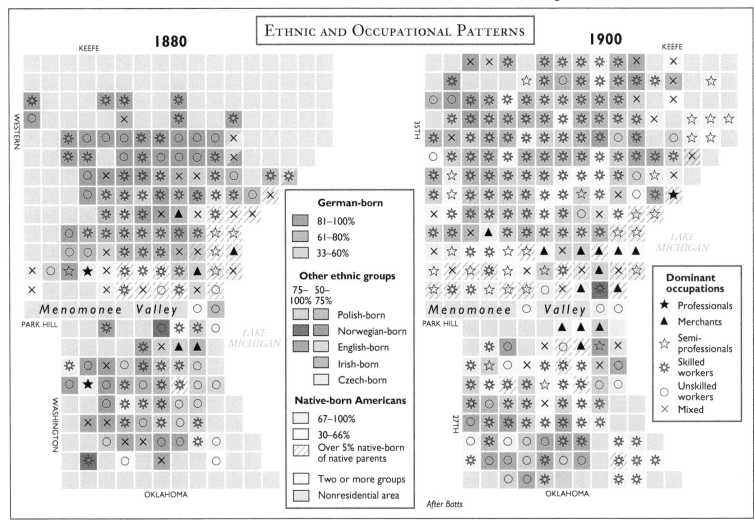

ETHNIC AND OCCUPATIONAL PATTERNS

1880   1900

German-born
- 81–100%
- 61–80%
- 33–60%

Other ethnic groups
75–100%   50–75%
- Polish-born
- Norwegian-born
- English-born
- Irish-born
- Czech-born

Native-born Americans
- 67–100%
- 30–66%
- Over 5% native-born of native parents
- Two or more groups
- Nonresidential area

Dominant occupations
- ★ Professionals
- ▲ Merchants
- ☆ Semi-professionals
- ❀ Skilled workers
- ○ Unskilled workers
- × Mixed

After Botts

ETHNIC AND RETAIL PATTERNS, 1850–1890

After M. P. and K. N. Conzen

GERMAN, CZECH, & DUTCH

POLISH

Milwaukee River

GERMAN & NATIVE BORN

Park

Laborers
POLISH

Wealthier classes

GERMAN CORE

RUSSIAN-JEWISH

NATIVE-BORN CORE

Wealthier classes

WATER ST.

GERMAN & NATIVE-BORN

MIXED ETHNICITY

Wealthier classes

AFRICAN AMERICAN

WISCONSIN AVE.

CBD

LAKE MICHIGAN

NATIVE-BORN CORE

IRISH CORE

Mechanics & laborers

IRISH CORE

Menomonee River

ITALIAN & RUSSIAN-JEWISH

Menomonee River course, 1860s

INDUSTRY

Artisans & laborers

GERMAN CORE

MIXED ETHNICITY

Park

Artisans & laborers

SCANDINAVIAN

Laborers

POLISH

INDUSTRY

Kinnickinnic River

Foreign-born population

	1850	1870	1890	
	20,061	71,440	204,468	Population
	12,839 (64%)	33,375 (47%)	79,742 (39%)	Foreign-born population

Predominant ethnic group

1850	1870	1890	
			German
			Native-born American
			Irish
			Czech and Dutch
			Scandinavian
			Polish
			Italian
			Russian-Jewish
			African American
			Mixed ethnicity

Retail districts

1850	1870	1890	
			Central business district (CBD)
			Industrial zone
			Regional district
			Neighborhood district
			Marginal district
			Horsecar routes
			Bridges

POLISH & GERMAN

ITALIAN

0   0.5 mi.
0   0.5 km

moving into their neighborhoods, in the process increasing the level of segregation. Many Mexicans and Puerto Ricans also moved to Milwaukee, which by 1980 had nearly half the state's Hispanic popula-tion (see *Newest Arrivals*). Although ethnicity remains a source of tension in Milwaukee, it has also become a source of identity and rediscovery, with cultural events and festivals drawing many visitors.

Retail Patterns

Milwaukee's main ethnic groups moved outward from "core" areas near the rivers as other ethnic groups moved into the city. The map at left shows the expansion of German and native-born (American) districts from 1850 to 1890. Native-born residents tended to control the city's early economy, and were identified with the wealthier "good classes." Germans grew in economic influence as their expanding neighborhoods became less ethnically concentrated. Unlike other groups, they opened many shops outside their ethnic areas to serve "regions" of the city. Czechs and later Poles also opened many businesses, but mainly in their own neighborhoods. Scandinavians (mainly Norwegians) were an example of a group that had few retail shops of their own. Retail centers outside the central business district formed along horsecar routes. Although these transporta-tion routes connected ethnic neigh-borhoods with Downtown, they did not connect the neighborhoods with each other. The replacement of horsecars with electric streetcars in 1890 allowed Milwaukee's ethnic districts finally to connect.

Milwaukee Poles

When Polish Catholics founded the St. Stanislaus Parish in 1866, they mortgaged their homes to build their first church. From the start, Milwaukee Polish identity was cen-tered on the church, parochial schools, and related social institu-tions. A strongly independent and self-reliant Polish community would grow in the city, and go on to erect the first Polish basilica in the U.S. (see *Religion*). The community also expanded economically—from 14 retail shops in 1880 to 142 in 1900. (Above, the Napieralski family stands in front of its South Side Bird Shop in about 1925.) Poles' growing politi-cal strength would be shown by their influence within the Democratic Party, the 1874 forma-tion of the Kosciuszko Guards state militia company, and the teaching of Polish in the public schools. By 1910 about 70,000 Poles lived in the city, only 58 percent of whom spoke English. They lived mainly on the crowded South Side, which expand-ed rapidly. About 118,000 Poles lived in the city in 1940—nearly half of all Poles in Wisconsin. Milwaukee is still one of the largest Polish centers in the country.

African American Settlement

The first African Americans came to Wisconsin in the fur-trade era. Later, during the 1820s lead rush, southern U.S. Army officers and lead miners brought in enslaved African Americans. After Wisconsin became a territory in 1836, Governor Henry Dodge freed his slaves and gave them each a piece of land.

By the 1850s, Wisconsin had become known for its support for the abolition of slavery and its opposition to the 1850 federal Fugitive Slave Law (see column at right). Some fugitives from the slave states passed through Wisconsin on the "Underground Railroad" to freedom in Canada or took refuge in the state. A network of sympathetic whites supported them. Wisconsin abolitionists helped found the Republican Party in 1854 to bring their fight into the political arena. An 1857 state Supreme Court ruling made Wisconsin the first state to defy the fugitive law.

The question of black *suffrage (*voting rights) was not easily settled in Wisconsin (see *Statehood*).

Referenda in 1849, 1857, and 1865 failed to enact suffrage. In 1866, however, the state Supreme Court enacted suffrage by reinterpreting the 1849 vote.

Although most African Americans settled in cities, some had established rural communities before the Civil War (1861–65). The best known were Pleasant Ridge in Grant County—home to the prosperous farmer Thomas Greene (below)—and Cheyenne Valley in Vernon County. Education was a priority for many of the settlers. Although youths began to look for jobs elsewhere in the 1880s, the communities lasted until after World War II. Other Wisconsin African Americans worked as farm laborers.

Despite the state's 1895 Civil Rights Act and the 1906 election of the first black assemblyman, economic conditions worsened in black communities throughout much of the 20th century. In 2000, African Americans made up 6 percent of the state's population; 80 percent of them lived in Milwaukee.

Joshua Glover escaped from slavery in Missouri and fled to Wisconsin. In March 1854, a deputy federal marshal in Racine bludgeoned Glover, arrested him under the U.S. Fugitive Slave Law, and transported him to a Milwaukee jail. Alerted to the arrest, abolitionist leader Sherman Booth and the Racine County sheriff led a crowd that demanded his release on a writ of habeas corpus. The crowd stormed the jail and freed Glover, spiriting him away to Waukesha, back to Racine, and then on a boat to freedom in Canada.

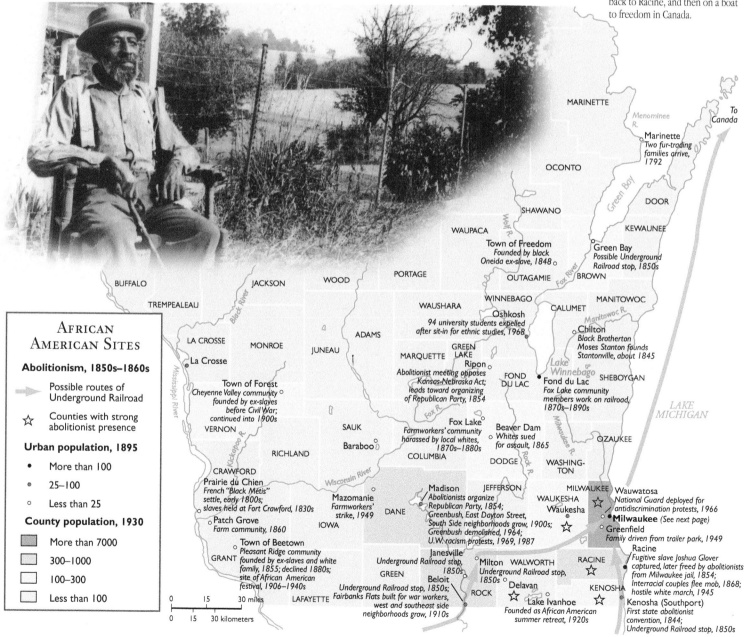

AFRICAN AMERICAN SITES

Abolitionism, 1850s–1860s

→ Possible routes of Underground Railroad

☆ Counties with strong abolitionist presence

Urban population, 1895

● More than 100

◦ 25–100

○ Less than 25

County population, 1930

▨ More than 7000

▢ 300–1000

▢ 100–300

▢ Less than 100

0   15   30 miles

0   15   30 kilometers

MARINETTE

To Canada

Menominee R.

Marinette
Two fur-trading families arrive, 1792

OCONTO

Green Bay

DOOR

SHAWANO

KEWAUNEE

WAUPACA

Town of Freedom
Founded by black Oneida ex-slave, 1848 ○

Green Bay
Possible Underground Railroad stop, 1850s

Wolf River

BUFFALO

JACKSON

WOOD

PORTAGE

OUTAGAMIE

Fox River

BROWN

TREMPEALEAU

Black River

WAUSHARA

WINNEBAGO

CALUMET

MANITOWOC

Manitowoc R.

LA CROSSE

MONROE

JUNEAU

ADAMS

Oshkosh
94 university students expelled after sit-in for ethnic studies, 1968 ●

Chilton
Black Brotherton Moses Stanton founds Stantonville, about 1845

La Crosse

Mississippi River

GREEN LAKE

MARQUETTE

Ripon ○

Lake Winnebago

SHEBOYGAN

Town of Forest
Cheyenne Valley community founded by ex-slaves before Civil War; continued into 1900s

VERNON

Kickapoo R.

Abolitionist meeting opposes
Kansas-Nebraska Act; leads toward organizing of Republican Party, 1854

FOND DU LAC

● Fond du Lac
Fox Lake community members work on railroad, 1870s–1890s

SAUK

Fox R.

Fox Lake ○
Farmworkers' community harassed by local whites, 1870s–1880s

Beaver Dam
○ *Whites sued for assault, 1865*

LAKE MICHIGAN

Baraboo ○

COLUMBIA

DODGE

Rock R.

OZAUKEE

RICHLAND

Wisconsin River

WASHING-TON

Milwaukee R.

CRAWFORD

Prairie du Chien
French "Black Métis" settle, early 1800s;
○ *slaves held at Fort Crawford, 1830s*

Mazomanie
Farmworkers' strike, 1949 ○

DANE

Madison
Abolitionists organize Republican Party, 1854; Greenbush, East Dayton Street, South Side neighborhoods grow, 1900s; Greenbush demolished, 1964; U.W. racism protests, 1969, 1987

JEFFERSON

WAUKESHA
Waukesha ☆

MILWAUKEE

Wauwatosa
☆ *National Guard deployed for antidiscrimination protests, 1966*

● Milwaukee *(See next page)*

○ Greenfield
Family driven from trailer park, 1949

○ Patch Grove
Farm community, 1860

IOWA

Town of Beetown
Pleasant Ridge community
GRANT *founded by ex-slaves and white family, 1855; declined 1880s; site of African American festival, 1906–1940s*

LAFAYETTE

Janesville
Underground Railroad stop, 1850s;

GREEN

Beloit
Underground Railroad stop, 1850s;

Milton
Underground Railroad stop, 1850s ○

WALWORTH

Delavan

ROCK

Lake Ivanhoe ☆
Founded as African American summer retreat, 1920s

RACINE ☆

Fairbanks Flats built for war workers, west and southeast side neighborhoods grow, 1910s

KENOSHA

Racine
/ *Fugitive slave Joshua Glover captured, later freed by abolitionists from Milwaukee jail, 1854; Interracial couples flee mob, 1868; hostile white march, 1945*

Kenosha (Southport)
First state abolitionist convention, 1844; Underground Railroad stop, 1850s

African Americans in Milwaukee

Legend:
- ○ Household, 1852
- • Household, 1860
- Household, 1870
- • Household, 1880
- Household, 1905
- ▨ "Bad Lands," 1905
- ⋯⋯ Inner Core, 1915
- – – Inner Core, 1932
- ▨ Inner Core, 1940

Map labels (streets): WRIGHT ST., MEINECKE ST., 14TH ST., 13TH ST., 12TH ST., 11TH ST., 10TH ST., 9TH ST., 8TH ST., 7TH ST., 6TH ST., 5TH ST., 4TH ST., 3RD ST., 2ND ST., 1ST ST., NORTH AVE., GARFIELD AVE., LLOYD ST., NORTH WATER ST., RESERVOIR ST., VINE ST., WALNUT ST., GALENA ST., CHERRY ST., VLIET ST., McKINLEY ST., (COLD SPRING BLVD.), JUNEAU ST., (CHESTNUT ST.), PRAIRIE ST., (HIGHLAND BLVD.), STATE ST., KILBOURN ST., (CEDAR ST.), WELLS ST., (GRAND AVE.), WISCONSIN AVE., SYCAMORE ST., CLYBOURN ST., ST. PAUL AVE., Menomonee River, GARDEN ST., OGDEN AVE., JOHNSON, MARTIN ST., JEFFERSON ST., MILWAUKEE ST., VAN BUREN ST., CASS ST., MARSHALL ST., ONEIDA ST., MASON ST., WISCONSIN ST. (AVE.), MICHIGAN ST., MARKET ST., Milwaukee River, HURON ST., DETROIT ST., BUFFALO ST., CHICAGO ST., MENOMONEE, WEST WATER ST., SOUTH ST., LAKE ST., OREGON ST., FLORIDA ST., LAKE MICHIGAN, VIRGINIA ST., GROVE ST., GREENBUSH ST., PARK ST., HANOVER ST., REED ST., CLINTON ST., BARCLAY ST., 6TH AVE., 5TH AVE., 4TH AVE., 3RD AVE., 2ND AVE., 1ST AVE., PIERCE ST., NATIONAL AVE., WALKER ST., MINERAL ST., SCOTT ST., MADISON ST., ORCHARD ST., Jones Island

0   0.5 mile
0   0.5 kilometer

Inset map: Expansion of the Core, 1940–80
0   1 mile
0   1 kilometer
Growth to 1980, Growth to 1960, Core in 1940
Labels: VILLARD AVE., HOPKINS ST., HAMPTON AVE., GREEN BAY AVE., 12TH ST., KEEFE AVE., CONCORDIA ST., BURLEIGH ST., CENTER ST., TEUTONIA AVE., CAPITOL DR., 27TH ST., HOPKINS ST., LOCUST ST., 20TH ST., WRIGHT ST., FOND DU LAC AVE., North Division High School, NORTH ST., SHERMAN BLVD., Lloyd St. School, LISBON AVE., WALNUT ST., 9th St. School, 35TH ST., HOLTON ST., 6TH ST., 3RD ST., Milwaukee R., JUNEAU AVE., STATE ST.

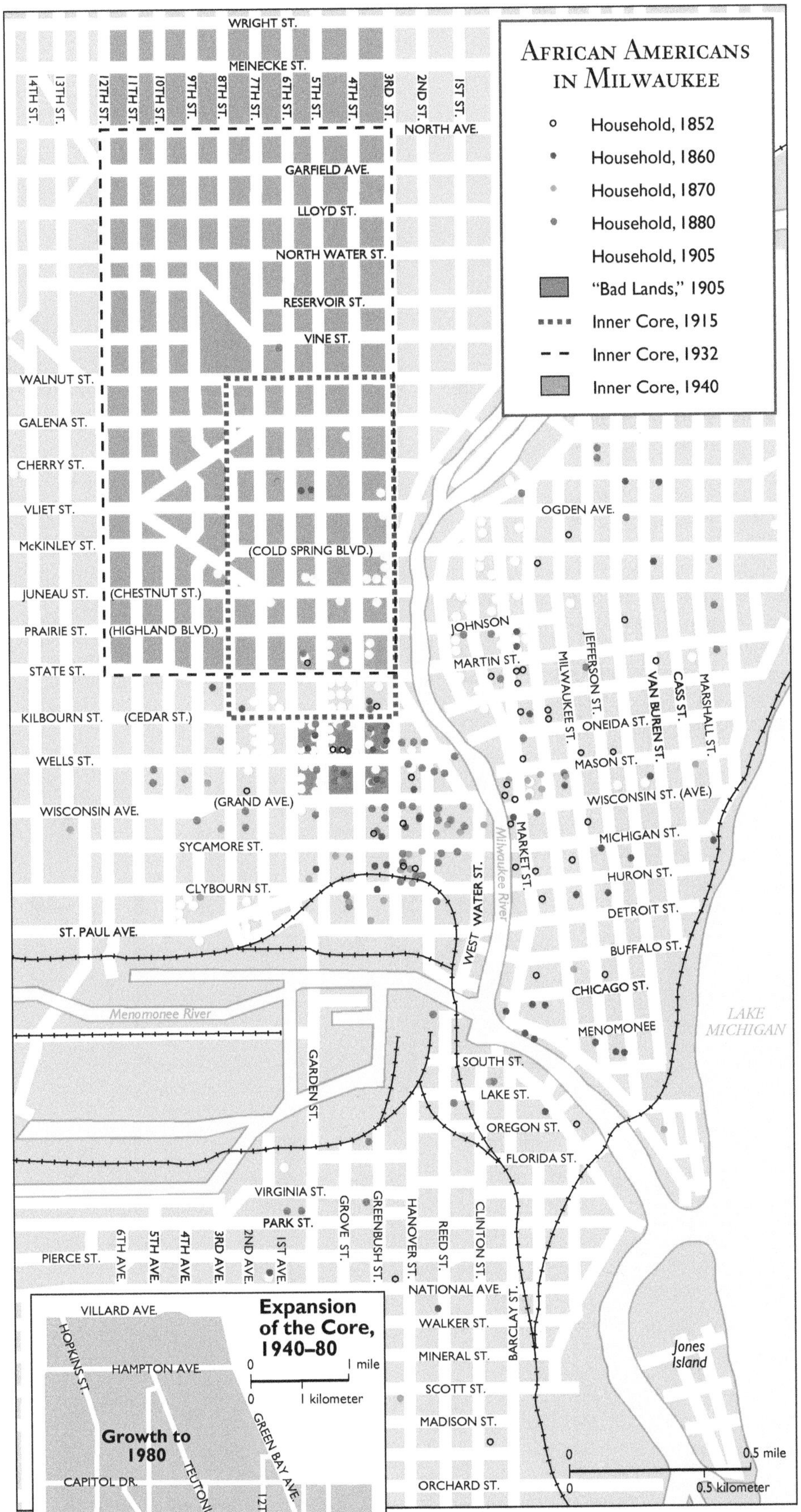

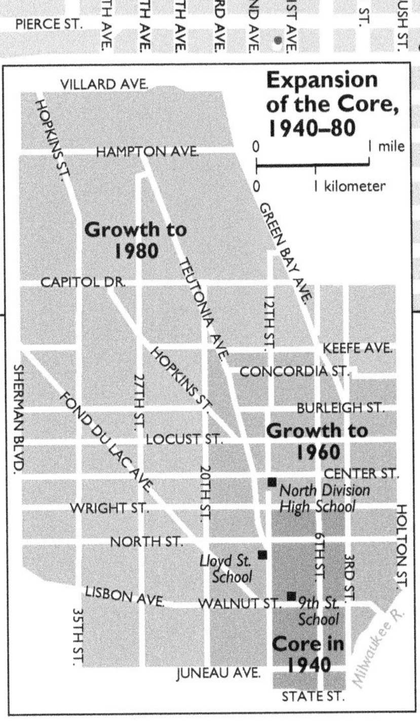

The first African American settlers in Milwaukee had no distinct neighborhoods of their own. The average size of African American households in the city grew steadily— from 2.2 persons in 1860 to 4.9 persons in 1905. Segregation increased after the turn of the century, and came to define an "Inner Core" district. As more African Americans arrived during both world wars, the Core, hemmed in by European immigrant neighborhoods on the south and east, expanded to the north and west. Of the 9,000 African Americans living in Milwaukee in 1940, 93 percent lived in the Core. Twenty years later, the population had grown to 62,000—96 percent in the Core. In 1980, 79 percent of the 147,000 African American residents lived in the Core.

AFRICAN AMERICANS IN MILWAUKEE

Milwaukee's first recorded African American citizens arrived in 1835. Before the Civil War, the city was a stop on the Underground Railroad, and newcomers could live wherever their circumstances allowed. The 1840s influx of European immigrants, however, turned the tide against African Americans (see *Ethnic Milwaukee*). Some immigrants saw freed slaves as a threat to their livelihood and feared they would take away jobs. Tensions boiled over during the Civil War when an Irish mob lynched an African American man.

Milwaukee began its long road to segregation after the Civil War. African Americans grouped together for security and formed their own churches and social institutions. As industrialization attracted more immigrants in the 1880s, black residency was restricted to a few neighborhoods, and black employment opportunities became limited to mostly service jobs. The resulting unemployment fed the growth of the "Bad Lands"—a downtown district known for its dens of vice, but also for its thriving, black-owned businesses. African Americans opposed discrimination by boycotting segregated theaters and establishing self-improvement groups.

Between 1890 and 1915 the African American population tripled to 1,500 as new industries attracted unskilled black laborers. Many were laid off in a 1908 recession, however, and replaced with machinery or immigrant labor. The city razed the "Bad Lands," eliminating many African American businesses and driving most African Americans into a new "Inner Core." The Core became notorious for its old, unsafe housing and high infant mortality rates.

The growth of Milwaukee industries in World War I drew many African American men from the South, including skilled and unskilled workers, educators, and church leaders. Their families joined them after the war, and the Inner Core expanded. The 1920s were also marked by Ku Klux Klan rallies, and the growth of African American rights groups. The Great Depression of the 1930s ravaged the community economically; it did not recover until new hiring laws affected war industries in World War II.

Postwar lawsuits forced open some white-collar jobs, which helped the growth of a black middle class. A large new influx of southern African Americans, however, was again met with discrimination in the skilled trades, housing discrimination turned much of the Core into exclusively black areas, and nearly all the whites transferred out of Core schools. In 1960, two-thirds of Milwaukee's African Americans had been born elsewhere, and three-fourths were blue-collar workers or unemployed.

Sit-ins and boycotts in the mid-1960s focused public attention on segregated schools. Marches for open housing in 1967 were confronted by angry white crowds and police (see *1960s*). The fight for school desegregation, often resulting in high school walk-outs, lasted into the early 1980s. Marches in the 1980s also opposed police brutality and substandard housing; Milwaukee's housing was the most segregated of any major U.S. city. In the 1990s African Americans worked toward "empowering" their community by establishing their own development plans, antigang programs, schools, and other institutions.

Newest Arrivals

Hispanics (Latinos) and Asians have lived in Wisconsin since statehood, but were few in number until the mid-20th century. Many of the new arrivals are members of families that came to Wisconsin from other parts of the country, as U.S. citizens. Most can trace their ancestry to two countries—Mexico and Laos—though many other ethnic groups today contribute to Wisconsin's cultural mosaic.

HISPANIC (LATINO) ARRIVALS

Mexicans have always been the largest Hispanic group in Wisconsin. Most have been Mexican Americans from the southwestern U.S. (part of Mexico before the 1840s), particularly the Rio Grande Valley in Texas. Immigrants who came directly from Mexico have lived in the state since 1850, but until the 1910s their population never exceeded 50.

In 1917, Congress passed a law requiring new immigrants from Europe to be able to read and write English to remain in the country. The resulting labor shortage led farm and factory owners to recruit Mexican Americans, who as U.S. citizens were exempt from the law. By 1930, 1,767 Mexican Americans lived in Milwaukee, with many working in the tanning and iron industries. In rural areas, seasonal farm and cannery workers became critical to the state's agricultural development. They harvested sugar beets, cucumbers (for pickles), peas, corn, and cabbage (for sauerkraut).

Many Mexican Americans left Wisconsin during the Great Depression of the 1930s. Labor shortages during World War II led to renewed recruitment of foreign farmworkers—mostly from Mexico, Jamaica, Barbados, and the Bahamas—and the use of some German prisoners of war. Mexican Americans returned to the factories during the war, and to the fields after the war. Some workers also came directly from Mexico as part of the federal "Bracero" program in 1951–64. The number of migrant workers

Farmworkers Organizing

Farmworkers in Wisconsin, as in the rest of the U.S., have long been vulnerable to exploitation. Mexican American migrant laborers have generally worked in the state only during the harvesting season, moving from one crop harvest to another (see U.S. map at left). Some were kept in debt to ensure their presence for the next year's harvest. They often lived in substandard housing and illegal camps. Their 1960 pay was only 37 percent of that for manufacturing workers. Child labor violations, hazardous conditions, pesticide exposure, and inadequate sanitary facilities were commonplace. Legal protections were rarely enforced for farmworkers, who were not covered by worker's compensation. As poor people not fluent in English, they were not able to get attention or help for their grievances. In 1966, a group of 24 farmworkers (above) held a protest walk from Wautoma to Coloma, and then south to the Capitol in Madison. Farm and cannery workers in Almond, Neshkoro, Cambria, Hartford, and other towns later joined the fight for the *Obreros Unidos* (United Workers) union. Union victories were usually short-lived, as farmworkers left the state, companies mechanized, and the farm lobby blocked wage reforms. Some farmworkers won better housing and health care, partly through federal legislation. Farm owners also began to recognize the value of a stable and healthy workforce.

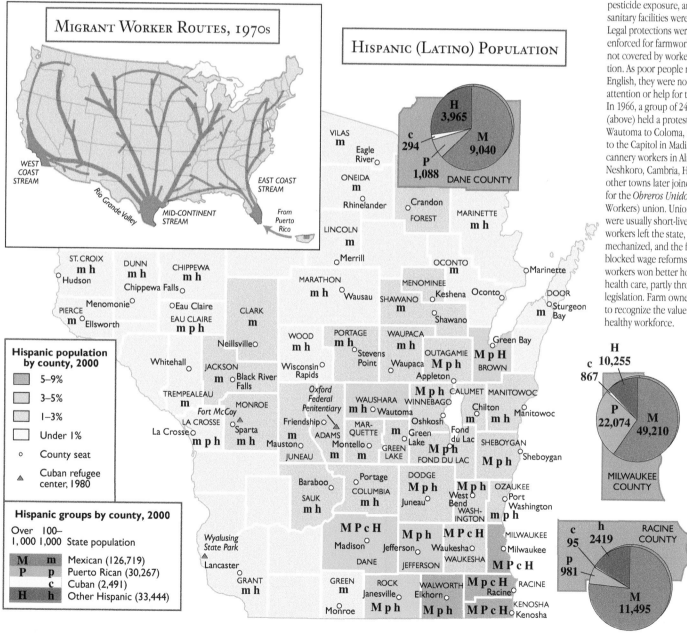

MIGRANT WORKER ROUTES, 1970s

WEST COAST STREAM

Rio Grande Valley

MID-CONTINENT STREAM

EAST COAST STREAM

From Puerto Rico

HISPANIC (LATINO) POPULATION

Hispanic population by county, 2000

- 5–9%
- 3–5%
- 1–3%
- Under 1%
- ○ County seat
- ▲ Cuban refugee center, 1980

Hispanic groups by county, 2000

Over 100– 1,000 / 1,000 State population

M	m	Mexican (126,719)
P	p	Puerto Rican (30,267)
	c	Cuban (2,491)
H	h	Other Hispanic (33,444)

DANE COUNTY — H 3,965 · c 294 · P 1,088 · M 9,040

MILWAUKEE COUNTY — H 10,255 · c 867 · P 22,074 · M 49,210

RACINE COUNTY — h 2419 · c 95 · p 981 · M 11,495

reached nearly 18,000 in 1961, including 5,000 under the age of 16.

Wisconsin farmworkers organized for their rights in the 1960s, as they did elsewhere in the country (see column at left). The mechanization of crop harvesting, however, reduced the number of migrant jobs to about 3,500 by 1978. Some migrant families gravitated to the cities; many moved to the neighborhood around Milwaukee's National Avenue and worked in area factories. Others settled year-round in rural areas, working for one farm or canning factory, and often raising Christmas trees. The state had about 5,570 migrant workers in 1990—only about one-tenth of the total Mexican American population.

Although Puerto Rico became a U.S. possession in 1898, few Puerto Ricans came to Wisconsin until after World War II. Milwaukee became the center of their community in the state. They worked in foundries, tanneries, and service jobs. From 1950 to 1980 the number of Puerto Ricans in Milwaukee jumped from 300 to 13,000; most lived on the city's northeast, west, and south sides. As U.S. citizens they moved freely between Wisconsin and Puerto Rico. Language barriers have put them and other Hispanics at a competitive disadvantage for jobs, and isolated them within schools. English training programs were instituted in the 1950s, and bilingual education in the 1970s, but many barriers persist.

Cuban refugees began arriving in the state in small numbers after Cuba's 1959 revolution. Fort McCoy became a major processing center for thousands of refugees from a 1980 boatlift at the Cuban port of Mariel, but only a few stayed in the state. South and Central American immigrants came in the 1980s and 1990s, often as refugees from wars in El Salvador, Nicaragua, and Colombia. As some immigrants are still undocumented, their numbers may be larger than census figures suggest.

ASIAN ARRIVALS

Asians have come to the U.S. for many of the same reasons as other immigrants. Asian immigration patterns, however, have been been profoundly shaped by U.S. foreign policy and by warfare. Small numbers of Asians arrived in Wisconsin in the 19th and early 20th centuries. Chinese became small-store owners and laborers. Filipinos began arriving after the Philippines became a U.S. colony in 1898. Some second-generation (*Nisei*) Japanese Americans were relocated from the West Coast to Wisconsin during World War II. They labored as farmworkers instead of being interned in camps like their family members. Some *Nisei* encountered hostility; others decided to stay in the state after the war and farm.

By far the largest groups of Asian Americans in Wisconsin have come from countries where the U.S. military fought in the Cold War against Communism. The first group arrived after the Korean War (1950–53). Four separate groups arrived as refugees after the U.S. war in Indochina (1960–75). Vietnamese and Cambodians arrived first, followed by Laotians from the lowlands of Laos, and Hmong from the highlands of Laos. Many Hmong tribal people had fought in a U.S.-backed guerrilla army, but most were left behind when the U.S. military effort collapsed (see column at right). The Hmong have proudly guarded their cultural identity under

difficult circumstances, using strong family ties to persevere in their new home. Many Hmong say they were drawn to Wisconsin partly by its school system. Although Hmong youth have faced cultural barriers in schools, they have scored well in reading tests. Hmong veterans had not been recognized for their military role in support of their newly adopted country until 1997, when Hmong and Laotian veterans were finally honored in a Capitol ceremony in Madison (above). The Hmong population more than doubled to over 39,791 by 2000, as new family members arrived in secondary migrations from other states. Wisconsin has become the third-largest Hmong center in the country—after California and Minnesota.

Other Asian immigrants have recently joined the mix, including Chinese students and Filipino and South Asian professionals and business owners. As Asian immigrants put down roots and their children grow up as Americans, they add to Wisconsin's economy and cultural diversity.

From Laos to Wisconsin

The Hmong (or "People") are from the highlands of Laos, one of the three countries that make up Indochina. Their historic isolation has enabled them to keep their distinct religion—based on reverence of ancestors and natural spirits. The ethnic Laotian majority in the lowlands is mainly Buddhist. During the Indochina War, the U.S. Central Intelligence Agency (CIA) used the historic division between the two ethnic groups to recruit Hmong into a guerrilla army. Hmong guerrillas fought against Communist Laotian rebels and North Vietnamese, in support of a U.S.-backed Laotian government. When Communist forces defeated that government in 1975, the CIA stopped supporting the Hmong. Some Hmong were killed, and many more fled to refugee camps in Thailand. Those who made it to the U.S. had to reconcile their culture, including strong clan and family ties, with life in a highly mobile, technological society.

Asian American Population

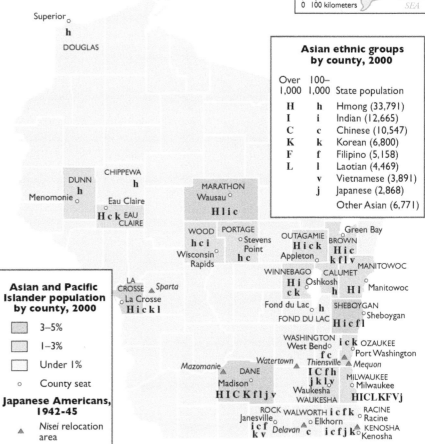

Asian ethnic groups by county, 2000

Over 1,000	100– 1,000	State population
H	h	Hmong (33,791)
I	i	Indian (12,665)
C	c	Chinese (10,547)
K	k	Korean (6,800)
F	f	Filipino (5,158)
L	l	Laotian (4,469)
	v	Vietnamese (3,891)
	j	Japanese (2,868)
		Other Asian (6,771)

Asian and Pacific Islander population by county, 2000

- 3–5%
- 1–3%
- Under 1%
- County seat

Japanese Americans, 1942-45

- ▲ Nisei relocation area

Immigrant Religious Patterns

As in the world over, religion and spirituality have been critical to Wisconsin's people ever since they have lived in the area (see *Early Cultures*). Roman Catholic Jesuit missionaries brought the first European religion to Wisconsin in the 1600s. They established short-lived missions to convert Native American peoples. French traders and settlers also practiced Catholicism (see *Encounters*).

Early settlement. Organized Christian church life began in the 1820s with the arrival of settlers in the southwestern Wisconsin "Lead District." Most were of British descent—English, Scottish, Welsh, Scots-Irish—of various Protestant denominations (see *Anglo-Americans*). Local Protestantism in 1820–50 mirrored developments in the eastern U.S., such as revivalism or the "Second Great Awakening," which brought new fervor to older church bodies and created new ones. Migrants from New England and New York sought to recreate religious communities or find solace in new religions. Protestant bodies formed "home" missionary associations to get churches started in new settlements. As the rest of Wisconsin was being settled in 1836, the Lead District already had as many as 53 Congregationalist and 32 Presbyterian churches. Episcopalians, Methodists, and Baptists also had toeholds in Wisconsin by the 1840s.

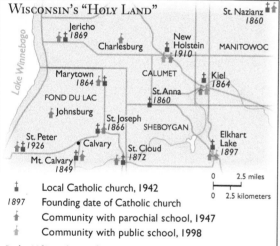

Wisconsin's "Holy Land"

Lake Winnebago

St. Nazianz 1860

Jericho 1869

Charlesburg

New Holstein 1910

MANITOWOC

Marytown 1864

CALUMET

Kiel 1864

St. Anna 1860

FOND DU LAC

Johnsburg

St. Joseph 1866

SHEBOYGAN

St. Peter 1926

Calvary

St. Cloud 1872

Elkhart Lake 1897

Mt. Calvary 1849

0   2.5 miles
0   2.5 kilometers

✝ Local Catholic church, 1942

1897 Founding date of Catholic church

✝ Community with parochial school, 1947

✝ Community with public school, 1998

In the 1860s, a cluster of communities northeast of Fond du Lac began using the ancient practice of naming their villages after their churches. This area was settled largely by southern German Catholic farmers. In contrast, nearby towns such as Kiel and New Holstein were settled mainly by northern German Lutherans. The rural communities retained their biblical names and a strong Catholic tradition, earning the area the name "Holy Land." Few public schools are found in this area, which has long relied on parochial education.

Immigration. In the 1830s and 1840s, many Catholic and Lutheran immigrants began to arrive in Wisconsin. By the late 1850s, they outnumbered earlier Protestant settlers. Scandinavians and northern Germans were predominantly Lutheran. Irish, Belgians, and southern Germans were predominantly Catholic, as were later arrivals such as Poles, Italians, and Croatians. Some immigrant groups, such as Czechs, Dutch, and Swiss, were divided between Catholic and Protestant affiliations. Many eastern Europeans were Eastern Orthodox Christian, or were

Jewish. Immigrants tended to create their own distinct villages or neighborhoods, often centered on a house of worship. Some of these "ethnic islands" recreated settlement patterns and religious divisions similar to those in their home communities. Throughout the late 1800s and early 1900s, much of the state's large foreign-born population viewed churches as central to politics and everyday life.

Influences on settlement life. Churches were often one of the first institutions established by rural or urban newcomers. Although only about half of Wisconsin's population regularly went to church, religious background strongly influenced personal and political behavior. Religion helped to maintain or create an identity for uprooted immigrant families. Churches brought a sense of morality and stability to otherwise lawless communities. A church often established the first parochial or public school in a community, with the priest or parson as the first schoolteacher. Churches sometimes even used public schools as a forum for promoting doctrine, and religious writings were used as textbooks. The presence of religious thinking influenced the development of government and social institutions in early communities. Ethnic and religious patterns coincided strongly with voting patterns, and at times played a greater role in elections than political party affiliations.

Catholics and Lutherans. Wisconsin's proportions of Catholics, Lutherans, and other Protestant denominations have stayed rather constant throughout most of its history. (Only Minnesota and North Dakota have a similar Catholic/Lutheran majority pattern.) About two dozen separate Lutheran *synods* (bodies), initially formed along ethnic lines, have operated in the state. Although the Catholic Church initially assigned priests to congregations speaking their languages, it later divided the state into *dioceses* based on geography rather than ethnicity. Wisconsin remained about half Catholic and a third Lutheran into the 1900s (see chart at right), forming a borderland between the heavily Catholic Great Lakes region and the heavily Lutheran Upper Midwest (see map on facing page). High Catholic and Lutheran churchgoing rates contribute to the state's above-average church attendance. The two groups have provided the state with some of its most distinctive architecture and its most popular social activities.

Conflicts and controversies. Along with their religious affiliations, immigrants brought religious differences and controversies. Differing interpretations of theology and scripture, friction with secular life, and competition for converts all stimulated a climate of controversy. Tensions existed not only among religions, but also within denominations. Churches in the 19th century were at the forefront of such issues as temperance, school and prison reform, and the abolition of slavery and child labor. Religious groups

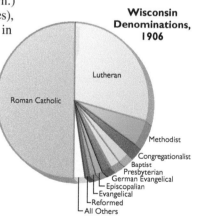

Amish Communities, 19

• Begun 1925
◆ Begun 1960–79
◆ Begun 1980–present
○ Former settlement

Exeland 1909-1927   Glen Flora 1920-1942

Clear Lake   Chetek   Curtiss   Medford   Athens
Greenwood   Owen   Bonduel
Durand   Augusta   Loyal   Granton   Marion   Amherst
1. Viroqua   Mondovi   Blair   Wautoma   New Holstein
2. Westby
3. Ontario   Dalton   Pardeeville
4. Norwalk   La Valle   Cambria
5. Cashton   Loganville
6. Wilton
7. Hillsboro   Bloomington
8. Cazenovia   New Glarus
9. Rising Sun   Monroe   Brodhead
10. Chaseburg
11. Readstown

Old Order Amish

The Old Order Amish stand as an example of a religious and ethnic community that has strongly maintained its identity in modern times. Although the German-speaking Amish remain concentrated in Pennsylvania, Ohio, and Indiana, Wisconsin has seen several waves of settlement. The state's first Amish community was established in 1909 in Sawyer County's impoverished "Cutover District" (see *Timber*). Many Amish worked on dairy farms in World War II, replacing hired hands serving in the military. A new wave of settlement began in the 1970s, as farm foreclosures made new agricultural lands available (see *Dairyland*). In 1972, Wisconsin Amish children became the center of a U.S. Supreme Court case. The Court's ruling—that the Amish have the right to establish their own schools and are not required to send their children to public high schools—strengthened religious freedom and helped preserve parental rights for all Americans.

Wisconsin Denominations, 1906

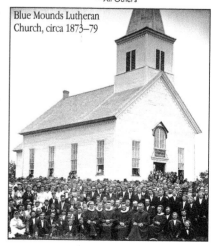

Lutheran

Roman Catholic

Methodist

Congregationalist
Baptist
Presbyterian
German Evangelical
Episcopalian
Evangelical
Reformed
All Others

Blue Mounds Lutheran Church, circa 1873–79

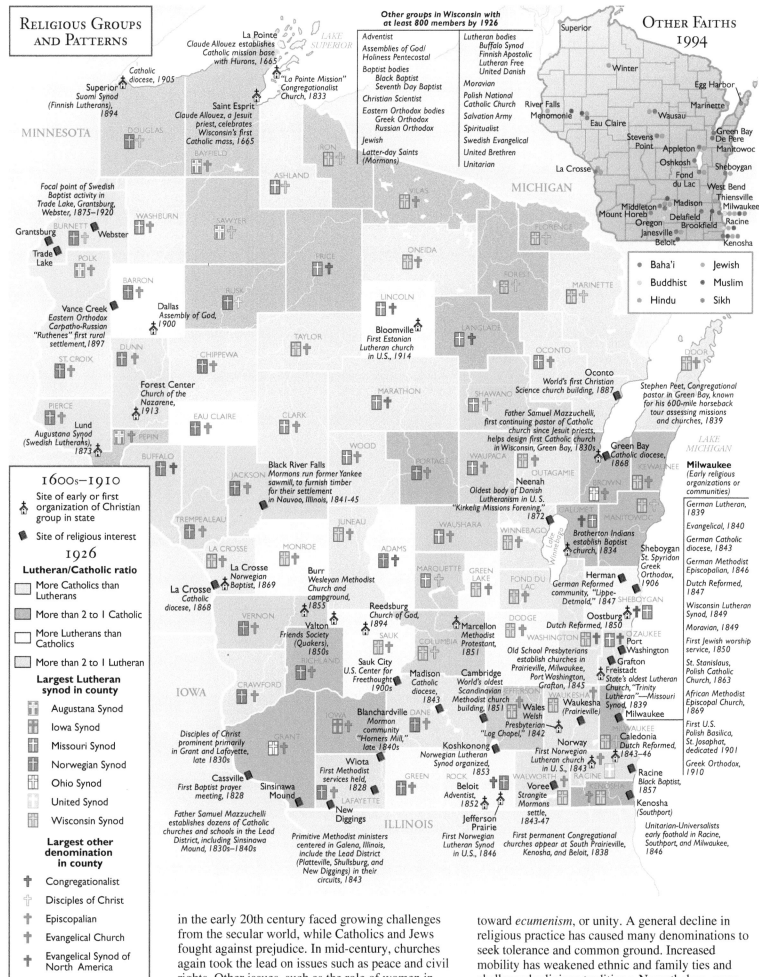

Religious Groups and Patterns

Other groups in Wisconsin with at least 800 members by 1926

Adventist
Assemblies of God/Holiness Pentecostal
Baptist bodies
  Black Baptist
  Seventh Day Baptist
Christian Scientist
Eastern Orthodox bodies
  Greek Orthodox
  Russian Orthodox
Jewish
Latter-day Saints (Mormons)

Lutheran bodies
  Buffalo Synod
  Finnish Apostolic
  Lutheran Free
  United Danish
Moravian
Polish National Catholic Church
Salvation Army
Spiritualist
Swedish Evangelical
United Brethren
Unitarian

Other Faiths 1994

- Baha'i
- Buddhist
- Hindu
- Jewish
- Muslim
- Sikh

La Pointe
Claude Allouez establishes Catholic mission base with Hurons, 1665

"La Pointe Mission" Congregationalist Church, 1833

Saint Esprit
Claude Allouez, a Jesuit priest, celebrates Wisconsin's first Catholic mass, 1665

Superior
Suomi Synod (Finnish Lutherans), 1894

Catholic diocese, 1905

Focal point of Swedish Baptist activity in Trade Lake, Grantsburg, Webster, 1875–1920

Grantsburg

Webster

Trade Lake

Vance Creek
Eastern Orthodox Carpatho-Russian "Ruthenes" first rural settlement, 1897

Dallas
Assembly of God, 1900

Forest Center
Church of the Nazarene, 1913

Lund
Augustana Synod (Swedish Lutherans), 1873

Bloomville
First Estonian Lutheran church in U.S., 1914

Oconto
World's first Christian Science church building, 1887

Father Samuel Mazzuchelli, first continuing pastor of Catholic church since Jesuit priests, helps design first Catholic church in Wisconsin, Green Bay, 1830s

Neenah
Oldest body of Danish Lutheranism in U.S. "Kirkelig Missions Forening," 1872

Green Bay
Catholic diocese, 1868

Stephen Peet, Congregational pastor in Green Bay, known for his 600-mile horseback tour assessing missions and churches, 1839

Black River Falls
Mormons run former Yankee sawmill, to furnish timber for their settlement in Nauvoo, Illinois, 1841–45

Brotherton Indians establish Baptist church, 1834

Sheboygan
St. Spyridon Greek Orthodox, 1906

Herman
German Reformed community, "Lippe-Detmold," 1847

Oostburg
Dutch Reformed, 1850

La Crosse
Norwegian Baptist, 1869

La Crosse
Catholic diocese, 1868

Burr
Wesleyan Methodist Church and campground, 1855

Reedsburg
Church of God, 1894

Valton
Friends Society (Quakers), 1850s

Sauk City
U.S. Center for Freethought, 1900s

Marcellon
Methodist Protestant, 1851

Madison
Catholic diocese, 1843

Cambridge
World's oldest Scandinavian Methodist church building, 1851

Old School Presbyterians establish churches in Prairieville, Milwaukee, Port Washington, Grafton, 1845

Port Washington

Grafton
Freistadt
State's oldest Lutheran Church, "Trinity Lutheran"—Missouri Synod, 1839

Wales
Welsh Presbyterian "Log Chapel," 1842

Waukesha (Prairieville)

Milwaukee

Disciples of Christ prominent primarily in Grant and Lafayette, late 1830s

Blanchardville
Mormon community "Horners Mill," late 1840s

Koshkonong
Norwegian Lutheran Synod organized, 1853

Norway
First Norwegian Lutheran church in U.S., 1843

Caledonia
Dutch Reformed, 1843–46

Cassville
First Baptist prayer meeting, 1828

Sinsinawa Mound

Wiota
First Methodist services held, 1828

Beloit
Adventist, 1852

Voree
Strangite Mormons settle, 1843–47

Racine
Black Baptist, 1857

Kenosha (Southport)

New Diggings

Father Samuel Mazzuchelli establishes dozens of Catholic churches and schools in the Lead District, including Sinsinawa Mound, 1830s–1840s

Primitive Methodist ministers centered in Galena, Illinois, include the Lead District (Platteville, Shullsburg, and New Diggings) in their circuits, 1843

Jefferson Prairie
First Norwegian Lutheran Synod in U.S., 1846

First permanent Congregational churches appear at South Prairieville, Kenosha, and Beloit, 1838

Unitarian-Universalists early foothold in Racine, Southport, and Milwaukee, 1846

Milwaukee (Early religious organizations or communities)

German Lutheran, 1839
Evangelical, 1840
German Catholic diocese, 1843
German Methodist Episcopalian, 1846
Dutch Reformed, 1847
Wisconsin Lutheran Synod, 1849
Moravian, 1849
First Jewish worship service, 1850
St. Stanislaus, Polish Catholic Church, 1863
African Methodist Episcopal Church, 1869
First U.S. Polish Basilica, St. Josaphat, dedicated 1901
Greek Orthodox, 1910

1600s–1910

- Site of early or first organization of Christian group in state
- Site of religious interest

1926

Lutheran/Catholic ratio

- More Catholics than Lutherans
- More than 2 to 1 Catholic
- More Lutherans than Catholics
- More than 2 to 1 Lutheran

Largest Lutheran synod in county

- Augustana Synod
- Iowa Synod
- Missouri Synod
- Norwegian Synod
- Ohio Synod
- United Synod
- Wisconsin Synod

Largest other denomination in county

- Congregationalist
- Disciples of Christ
- Episcopalian
- Evangelical Church
- Evangelical Synod of North America
- Methodist
- Northern Baptist
- Presbyterian
- Reformed Church in the United States

---

in the early 20th century faced growing challenges from the secular world, while Catholics and Jews fought against prejudice. In mid-century, churches again took the lead on issues such as peace and civil rights. Other issues, such as the role of women in society and sexual preference, continue as sources of religious controversy.

Ecumenism. After years of competition and conflict, Christianity today is often characterized by its trend toward *ecumenism*, or unity. A general decline in religious practice has caused many denominations to seek tolerance and common ground. Increased mobility has weakened ethnic and family ties and challenged religious traditions. Nevertheless, some religious bodies have managed to retain their identities and even flourish. Wisconsin's religious diversity and churchgoing devotion continue to affect public dialogue, and give Wisconsin's cultural landscape a unique flavor.

Cultural Figures

Wisconsin is not often considered a center for the arts, squeezed as it is between the cultural centers of Chicago and the Twin Cities. Even so, Wisconsin has been the home or birthplace of many talented and acclaimed individuals. Some were authors or artists who not only remained in Wisconsin but also chose the towns, cities, and countryside around them as settings for their writings and paintings. Drawn by the international reputation of the University of Wisconsin, some important educational figures have worked in the state, including inventors, scientists, and naturalists (see *Environment*). A number of entertainers with roots in Wisconsin also have gained national recognition.

Frank Lloyd Wright

(1867–1959) is recognized as perhaps the world's greatest architect of the 20th century. Born in Richland Center into a Welsh American family, he spent his formative years from 1879 to 1886 in Madison. Wright worked in Wisconsin for most of his life, building his Taliesin home near Spring Green in 1911. In a career spanning 70 years, he designed houses, public buildings, churches, and commercial structures throughout the U.S. and the world (see map). Wright's first distinctive buildings were designed in what became known as the "Prairie Style." His key Wisconsin works included the Taliesin complex, the Johnson Wax administration building in Racine, the Jacobs I Usonian house and the First Unitarian Society Meeting House in Madison. His innovative architecture emphasized the association of a building with its surroundings and used building materials appropriate to his "organic" approach. Wright's importance extended to design, urban planning, landscape architecture, and education. From 1903 until his death in 1959 Wright transformed the field of architecture, and became probably the best-known person ever to come from Wisconsin.

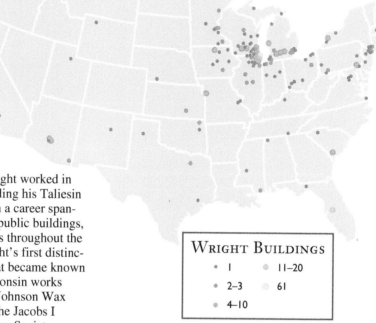

WRIGHT BUILDINGS

• 1	● 11–20
● 2–3	● 61
● 4–10	

Wright also designed buildings in Japan, Britain, and Canada.

The Green Bay Packers were founded in 1919 by George Calhoun and "Curly" Lambeau (who was backed by his employer, a meatpacking company). From the start, people from around the state embraced the Packers. They played not only in Green Bay, but also in Milwaukee, Madison, and (in their early years) Racine and Beloit. By 1921, the team had obtained a franchise in the new national professional football league. The Packers went on to win more championships than any other professional football team in history. Coach Vince Lombardi (below) led the team from 1959 to 1968, lifting the

Packers to world championships in 1961, 1962, 1965, 1966, and 1967. Noted for his drive and tenacity, Lombardi was inducted into the Pro Football Hall of Fame in 1971. The success of his team made Wisconsin a center of pro football, and other teams later began to train in the state (see map at left). Famous for his encouraging words, Lombardi once said, "Winning is not everything—but making an effort to win is."

Georgia T. O'Keeffe

(1887–1986) was born near Sun Prairie where her parents owned a considerable amount of land. As O'Keeffe grew up, she was inclined to be different from other children. Her parents were gentle and lenient with their children, and tried to nurture their talents. Her childhood in the country made her deeply sensitive to nature. She attended the one-room Town Hall schoolhouse, where she was a good student. When she was about 12, she began to take private art lessons from Sun Prairie resident Sarah Mann. She progressed quickly and was soon experimenting with colored pigment. Her mother encouraged her, and hoped she would eventually become an art teacher (at that time, it was unusual for a woman to pursue a career as an artist). O'Keeffe came to feel that, as an artist, she would have the freedom to do as she wished. When she was in high school, O'Keeffe's parents sold their farm and moved to Virginia. She stayed behind and lived with her aunt on Spaight Street in Madison, where she attended Madison High School (later the site of the downtown Madison Area Technical College). There, her art teacher showed students a jack-in-the-pulpit so that they could examine its unusual shapes and the shades of its interior. For the first time, it occurred to her to paint a living thing instead of simply copying a picture. More than two decades later she created a series of oil paintings based on that flower. In 1903, she left Wisconsin to join the rest of her family in Virginia. For the next 83 years, Georgia O'Keeffe would create highly renowned paintings, not only of flowers, but of such diverse subjects as New York skyscrapers, Texas plains, and New Mexico deserts. But it was her Wisconsin childhood that started her on the journey to becoming one of the most prominent American artists of the 20th century.

PROFESSIONAL FOOTBALL CHEESE LEAGUE

Green Bay, home of the Packers

Jacksonville Jaguars 1996 summer camp at Stevens Point

Kansas City Chiefs summer camp at River Falls

Milwaukee hosted Packer games from 1933 to 1994

Racine hosted Packer games in early days

New Orleans Saints 1988-1999 summer camp at La Crosse

Chicago Bears 1984-2001 summer camp at Platteville

Madison hosts preseason Packer games

Beloit hosted Packer games in early days

George C. Poage (1880–1962), a La Crosse native and University of Wisconsin student who represented the Milwaukee Athletic Club, was the first African American to compete in the Olympics, winning bronze medals in the 200- and 400-meter hurdles at the 1904 games in St. Louis.

Harry Houdini (1884–1926), considered the most famous magician and escape artist of all time, was born in Hungary as Ehrich Weiss. He grew up in Appleton and, in an attempt to Americanize himself, often claimed it as his birthplace. Also a pioneer aviator, he was the first on record to fly a plane in Australia.

August Derleth (1909–71), born in Sauk City, was one of Wisconsin's most prolific writers. His works included nature poetry, journals, and the fictional *Walden West*, as well as many novels. The author of more than 200 books, he was also well known as an editor and publisher.

Zona Gale (1874–1938), born in Portage, an activist for women's rights and a University of Wisconsin regent, was a nationally known author of novels, short stories, articles, and plays focusing on the lives of women. Her play *Miss Lulu Bett* won a Pulitzer Prize in 1921.

Edna Ferber (1885–1968), who won a Pulitzer Prize in 1925 for her novel *So Big,* used her life in Appleton as the source for much of her writing. Families, small towns, and working women were often the subjects of her work. Her 1926 book *Show Boat* was made into a popular musical comedy.

Orson Welles (1915–86), born in Kenosha and educated in Madison, was an actor and director who worked in theater, radio, television, and motion pictures. Among his accomplishments were the radio broadcast of *The War of the Worlds* (1938) and the film *Citizen Kane* (1941).

Frederick Jackson Turner (1861–1932), born in Portage, was a University of Wisconsin historian who won a Pulitzer Prize in 1932. He developed the "Frontier Thesis," which claimed that westward movement helped to develop American democracy—a theory that has been debated for over a century.

Thornton Wilder (1897–1975), the son of a Madison newspaper editor, was a playwright and novelist. He received a Pulitzer Prize in 1928 for his novel *The Bridge of San Luis Rey*, in 1938 for his play *Our Town*, and in 1942 for his play *The Skin of Our Teeth*.

Laura Ingalls Wilder (1867–1957), born in Pepin, used fictionalized tales of her childhood as the basis for writing her series of children's books, including *Little House on the Prairie* and *Little House in the Big Woods*.

Owen J. Gromme (1896–1991), born in Fond du Lac and known as a dean of wildlife painters, became the first artist honored by the American Museum of Wildlife Art. Ducks Unlimited chose him as its 1978 "Artist of the Year."

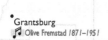

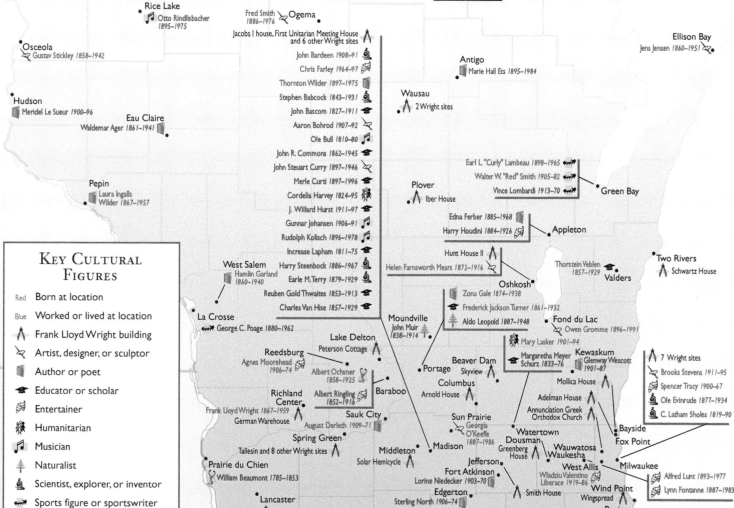

KEY CULTURAL FIGURES

Red — Born at location
Blue — Worked or lived at location
⋀ — Frank Lloyd Wright building
✎ — Artist, designer, or sculptor
📖 — Author or poet
❦ — Educator or scholar
🎭 — Entertainer
✿ — Humanitarian
🎵 — Musician
🌲 — Naturalist
⚗ — Scientist, explorer, or inventor
🏃 — Sports figure or sportswriter
⚕ — Surgeon or physician

Only deceased persons are included.

My friend tree
I sawed you down
but I must attend
an older friend
the sun

Along the river
            wild sunflowers
over my head
            the dead
who gave me life
            give me this
our relative the air
            floods
our rich friend
            silt

Black Hawk held: In reason
land cannot be sold,
only things to be carried away,
and I am old.

—Lorine Niedecker
        from
"My Friend Tree" (1961)

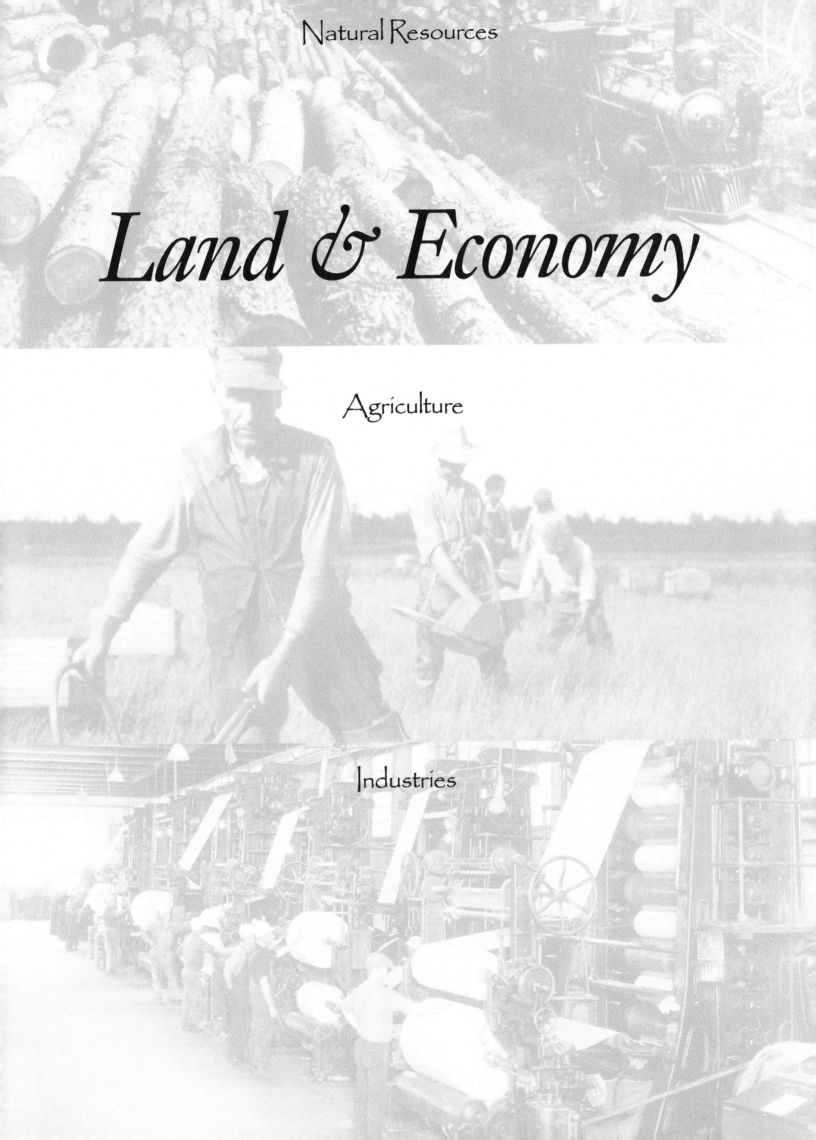

Land & Economy

Natural Resources

Agriculture

Industries

Glacial Landscapes

The Ice Age began about 2.4 million years ago, and continues to be characterized by alternating periods of cool and warm temperatures. Cooler periods produced a continuous buildup of snow near Hudson Bay. As the snow accumulated, it compressed and changed into ice. The weight of the ice caused it to flow outward, at rates from inches to miles per year. This process created *glaciers,* or huge sheets of ice. During warmer "interglacial" periods, the ice receded dramatically.

The advance and retreat of the massive sheets of ice scoured the land, pushing and carrying huge amounts of *drift,* or surface debris. This mixture of clay, silt, sand, pebbles, cobbles, and boulders was deposited beneath and in front of the glaciers, forming different types of glacial *topography* (landscapes).

The last series of glacial advances and retreats began about 25,000 years ago. Scientists call this the "Wisconsin Glaciation," because Wisconsin geologists were instrumental in first defining it. The farthest advance of this glaciation occurred about 15,000 years ago. Ice sheets flowed into the lowlands around what is now Lake Superior, Lake Michigan, and the Green Bay/Fox River Valley area. Their flow was shaped by the uplands of the Bayfield, Keweenaw, and Door peninsulas. The front of the advancing ice divided into six *lobes,* or "tongues," whose shape and speed were determined by the climate and the shape of the land. The ice sheets of the Wisconsin Glaciation and earlier glacial periods varied in how far they advanced (see maps on facing page).

Glaciers never covered the highlands of southwestern Wisconsin. This fact led scientists to call this region the *Driftless Area.* They later discovered that this plateau does contain some drift in the form of *outwash* (debris carried by meltwater) and glacial lake basins. This area has a much older topography influenced mainly by stream erosion, which left a rugged terrain of ridges and deep V-shaped valleys.

Elsewhere in Wisconsin, Ice Age landforms resulted from the actions of both glacial ice and meltwater flowing through and away from the ice.

Ice landforms. Ice action created such features as *moraines, drumlins,* and *collapsed till topography.*
• *Moraines* are ridges made up of *till* (rock debris,

Wisconsin's landforms were formed by the actions of both glaciers and glacial meltwater. The Parnell Esker (above), in Northern Kettle Moraine State Forest, was formed by a stream running through a glacier. Devil's Lake was formed by melting glaciers that stopped at the Baraboo Hills (below). Melting glaciers also formed the Wisconsin River, which subsequently drained a huge glacial lake. In modern times, the Wisconsin River was dammed near the Baraboo Hills, to form the smaller reservoir of Lake Wisconsin.

VIEW OF GLACIER'S EDGE OVER PRESENT-DAY BARABOO HILLS

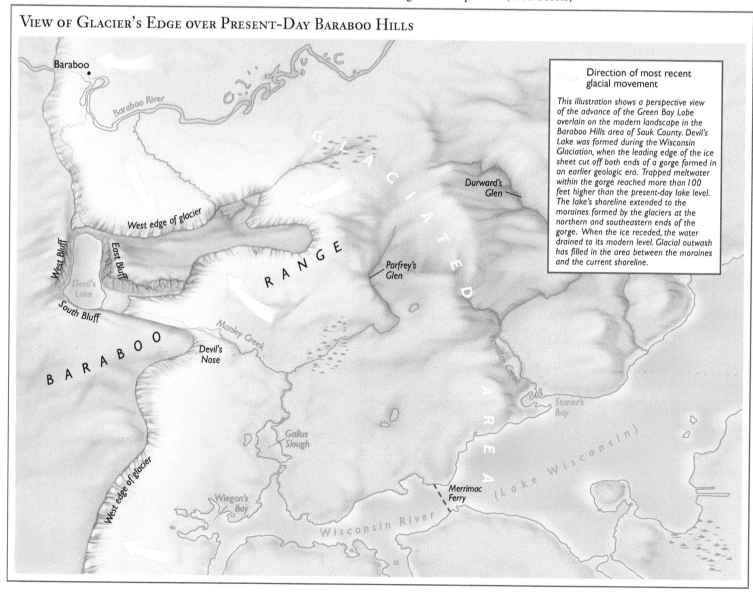

Direction of most recent glacial movement

This illustration shows a perspective view of the advance of the Green Bay Lobe overlain on the modern landscape in the Baraboo Hills area of Sauk County. Devil's Lake was formed during the Wisconsin Glaciation, when the leading edge of the ice sheet cut off both ends of a gorge formed in an earlier geologic era. Trapped meltwater within the gorge reached more than 100 feet higher than the present-day lake level. The lake's shoreline extended to the moraines formed by the glaciers at the northern and southeastern ends of the gorge. When the ice receded, the water drained to its modern level. Glacial outwash has filled in the area between the moraines and the current shoreline.

Ice Age in Wisconsin

The map at right shows glacial and nonglacial Ice Age landforms in present-day Wisconsin. Glacial lake basins and areas of glacial *outwash* (debris carried by water) were created by the actions of meltwater from the glaciers. Note that some outwash extends into the unglaciated Driftless Area. Moraines (brown), created by debris accumulated along the edge of a glacier, can be divided into two categories: *end moraines* show the farthest advance of a glacier; *recessional moraines* show where a retreating glacier stopped temporarily. *Till plains* (green) are areas where *till* (debris) atop the glacier settled unevenly on the land as the ice receded. This action often produced *collapsed till topography* (an uneven or rolling landscape). *Till plains* shown south and west of the terminal moraines are remnants of previous glacial advances. Parts of these areas are bare bedrock that show little evidence of glacial action.

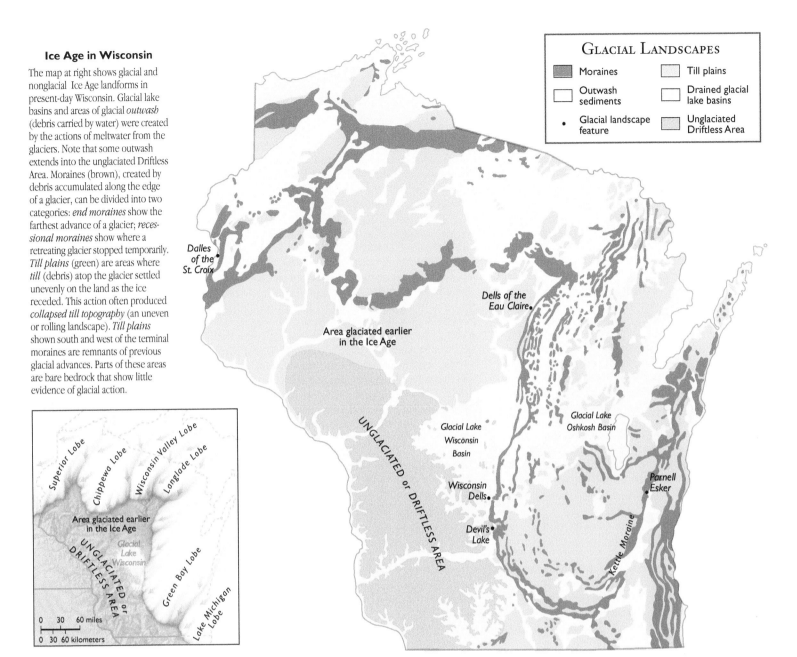

GLACIAL LANDSCAPES

- Moraines
- Outwash sediments
- Glacial landscape feature
- Till plains
- Drained glacial lake basins
- Unglaciated Driftless Area

Wisconsin Glaciation

The map above shows the farthest advance of the most recent glacier that affected Wisconsin. The unglaciated areas include land that was never glaciated (Driftless Area), and land that was covered by earlier Ice Age glaciations. The different glacial *lobes* (tongues) are shown with arrows pointing in the direction of their advance. Present-day state boundaries and shorelines for the Great Lakes are shown as gray lines. The Great Lakes were were created by glacial meltwaters as the ice sheet retreated north.

gravel, and sand dumped together without sorting by size or type of material) deposited along the edge of glaciers that have stopped moving for years or decades—long enough for accumulation to occur.
• *Drumlins* are long hills shaped like overturned canoes. They may represent "drag marks" of debris caught between the moving ice and the terrain. They are usually clustered in large groups, and "point" in the direction of the glacier's advance.
• *Collapsed till topography* describes areas where till scattered on top of receding glaciers settled to the ground as the ice melted unevenly beneath it. Some chunks of ice were better insulated and melted more slowly. The overlying till eventually collapsed, leaving depressions and rolling, uneven hills.

Meltwater landforms. Meltwater action created such features as *eskers, outwash plains, collapsed outwash topography,* and *kettles.*
• *Eskers* are long, winding, narrow hills formed by meltwater streams within glaciers. Sediments deposited by the streams built up over time within the channels or tunnels. When the ice melted, a long hill roughly parallel to the stream's direction remained (see photo).
• *Outwash plains* were formed when meltwater flowed away from the glacier and spread till in front of the glacier's edge.

• *Collapsed outwash topography* refers to uneven or rolling hills formed when outwash sediment buried large chunks of ice separated from a receding glacier. The ice later melted and the overlying sand collapsed, forming depressions. Both collapsed till and collapsed outwash topography formed most of today's natural lakes in Wisconsin.
• *Kettles* are a striking example of collapsed outwash topography. These kettle-shaped surface depressions resulted when buried blocks of glacial ice melted. They may be dry or filled with water.

Other landforms. Glaciers also created other important features on Wisconsin's landscape.
• *Erratics* are boulders carried great distances by glaciers from their areas of origin. (One such erratic can be seen on Observatory Hill at U.W.–Madison.)
• *Meltwater channels* were formed by meltwater rushing from rapidly melting glaciers or draining glacial lakes. They often cut sharp gorges known as *dells* or *dalles* (see map). One catastrophic meltwater breakthrough of the moraine damming Glacial Lake Wisconsin near Portage created the Wisconsin Dells.

Evidence of glaciers can be seen today in most of the state. Moving ice and water shaped two-thirds of Wisconsin's landforms.

Mining Districts & Discoveries

Wisconsin, though lacking coal, oil, and many other resources, has long had rich deposits of metallic ores and other minerals. People have mined copper and used lead in the area since ancient times (see *Early Cultures*). Metallic ores provided the "magnet" for the first wave of settlement in Wisconsin in the late 1820s and early 1830s. Settlers formed distinct "mining districts"—economic areas based on mineral extraction (see maps). Towns within the districts that had mines and processing facilities nearby became "mining centers." Miners first shipped ore or processed metal on nearby rivers, and later on roads to Great Lakes ports.

Early lead mining. Lead is found in the Unglaciated Area, or Driftless Area, of southwestern Wisconsin and in parts of Illinois and Iowa (see *Glacial*). Two French visitors—Nicolas Perrot (1680s) and Julien Dubuque (1780s)—mined lead in the area. Dubuque also *smelted* (heated) ore rock in furnaces to extract the lead. Native Americans who worked in the mines took over the operations after the French left the area, and used the lead as a trade item. The Sauk and Meskwaki (Fox) ceded much of the area to the U.S. in 1804, and miners began to arrive in the early 1820s.

Lead rush. The "Lead District" quickly became one of the world's leading mining centers for a brief time. Lead miners from Missouri and highly skilled Cornish miners from Great Britain and the southern U.S. (see *Anglo-Americans*) formed and initially governed their own distinct communities. The largest such settlement in Wisconsin was Mineral Point. Miners dug *galena* (lead sulfide) from tunnels and shafts, built small smelters, and later on began farming as well. Much of the "gray gold" was smelted for use as shot or ammunition (see column at right). By the 1840s, the lead boom had begun to decline. Miners had nearly exhausted the ore close to the surface, and could not sink shafts below the water table without pumps, which were expensive and unreliable. Nearly a third of Lead District residents left for Michigan's Upper Peninsula in the 1844 copper rush or for California in the 1849 gold rush.

Zinc mining. Using new technology in the 1850s, some miners began to extract zinc from deposits where it was found together with lead. For a short period in the late 19th century, Mineral Point had the world's largest zinc smelter. Plants also began to process the *sulfide* (sulfuric) ore for acid byproducts. The zinc industry expanded during the world wars but had ended by the late 1970s. Southwestern Wisconsin had been the longest-lived metallic mining district on the continent. Although lead and zinc mining left a legacy of contaminated wells and streams in some places, many area towns owe their creation to it.

Iron mining. Wisconsin iron mining began in 1849 in Dodge County, and increased after railroads reached the Gogebic Range near Lake Superior (see *Transportation*). In the 1880s, Ashland's port began to ship ore to feed steel mills around the region (see *Great Lakes*). As mining and steelmaking processes changed, cheaper Michigan and Minnesota ores eclipsed Wisconsin ores, but for decades the Gogebic Range was known for its rough-and-tumble mining towns. Author Edna Ferber (see *Cultural Figures*) described Hurley as a town of saloons, gambling, prostitution, and criminals in her 1910 book *Come and Get It.* The last Gogebic Range mines closed in the 1960s, but another iron mine operated in Jackson County from 1969 to 1983.

Copper mining. The U.S. acquired Wisconsin's Lake Superior shore in the 1842 Copper Treaty (see *Ojibwe*), but most copper deposits were discovered next door in Michigan. It was not until the 1970s that companies proposed to mine copper (and other metals) from sulfide ores near Ladysmith and Crandon. They also discovered other metallic deposits and proposed new mines in the north, where ancient bedrock of the Precambrian Shield (or Canadian Shield) lies close to the surface.

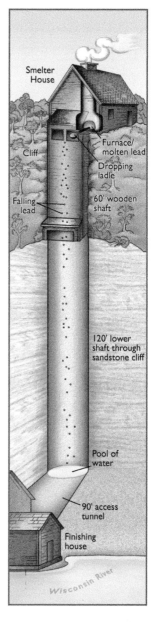

Helena Shot Tower

One important use of lead was to make ammunition. To turn the lead into *shot* (pellets), Yankee businessman Daniel Whitney founded the Helena processing center next to the Wisconsin River in 1830. Workers melted lead in a furnace, and poured the lead from a cauldron into a deep shaft dug into sandstone. As it fell, the molten lead formed round balls, which solidified after hitting a pool of water at the bottom. Up to 5,000 pounds of shot were produced and sorted each day. The shot was loaded onto barges for transport to Mississippi River cities or onto wagons for transport along "lead roads" to Lake Michigan ports (see map on facing page). On their return trips, the ox-drawn wagons brought new settlers and goods. The tower closed in 1861, since new rifles no longer required shot, and Helena later declined after a new railroad bypassed it. The shot tower and reconstructed smelter house can be seen today at Tower Hill State Park, on the old site of Helena.

Lead and Zinc District

- ☐ Lead District, 1820s–1850s
- ⚠ First continuous U. S. mining camps, 1824
- ✕ Concentrations of mines
- 🏛 Processing centers
- ═ Military Road, 1848
- (1848) Date of statehood
- ▨ Zinc District, 1850s–1970s
- — Present-day county boundaries

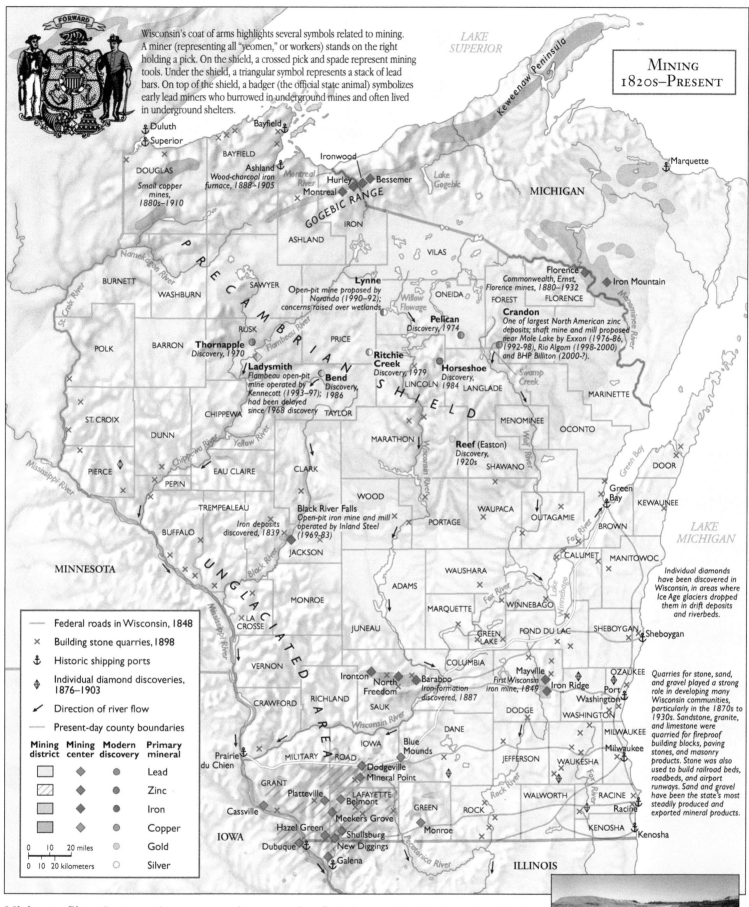

Wisconsin's coat of arms highlights several symbols related to mining. A miner (representing all "yeomen," or workers) stands on the right holding a pick. On the shield, a crossed pick and spade represent mining tools. Under the shield, a triangular symbol represents a stack of lead bars. On top of the shield, a badger (the official state animal) symbolizes early lead miners who burrowed in underground mines and often lived in underground shelters.

FORWARD

⚓ Duluth
⚓ Superior

LAKE
SUPERIOR

Keweenaw Peninsula

Bayfield ⚓

BAYFIELD

Ironwood

Marquette ⚓

DOUGLAS

Small copper mines, 1880s–1910

Ashland ⚓
Wood-charcoal iron furnace, 1888–1905

Montreal River

Hurley
Montreal
Bessemer

GOGEBIC RANGE

Lake Gogebic

MICHIGAN

IRON

ASHLAND

VILAS

Florence
Commonwealth, Ernst, Florence mines, 1880–1932

Iron Mountain

P R E C A M B R I A N

BURNETT

WASHBURN

SAWYER

Lynne
Open-pit mine proposed by Noranda (1990–92); concerns raised over wetlands

Willow Flowage

ONEIDA

FOREST

FLORENCE

Namekagon River

Pelican
Discovery, 1974

Crandon
One of largest North American zinc deposits; shaft mine and mill proposed near Mole Lake by Exxon (1976-86, 1992-98), Rio Algom (1998-2000) and BHP Billiton (2000-?).

Menominee River

St. Croix River

POLK

BARRON

RUSK

Thornapple
Discovery, 1970

PRICE

Flambeau River

Ritchie Creek
Discovery, 1979

Horseshoe
Discovery, 1984

Swamp Creek

MARINETTE

Ladysmith
Flambeau open-pit mine operated by Kennecott (1993–97); had been delayed since 1968 discovery

Bend
Discovery, 1986

LINCOLN
LANGLADE

S H I E L D

OCONTO

ST. CROIX

DUNN

CHIPPEWA

TAYLOR

Yellow River

Chippewa River

MARATHON

Reef (Easton)
Discovery, 1920s

MENOMINEE

Wolf River

SHAWANO

Mississippi River

PIERCE

PEPIN

EAU CLAIRE

CLARK

WOOD

Green Bay

DOOR

PORTAGE

Green Bay ⚓

KEWAUNEE

BUFFALO

TREMPEALEAU

Iron deposits discovered, 1839

Black River Falls
Open-pit iron mine and mill operated by Inland Steel (1969-83)

WAUPACA

OUTAGAMIE

BROWN

LAKE
MICHIGAN

MINNESOTA

U N G L A C I A T E D

Black River

JACKSON

WAUSHARA

Fox River

MANITOWOC

Individual diamonds have been discovered in Wisconsin, in areas where Ice Age glaciers dropped them in drift deposits and riverbeds.

MONROE

ADAMS

MARQUETTE

Lake Winnebago

WINNEBAGO

CALUMET

LA CROSSE

JUNEAU

GREEN LAKE

FOND DU LAC

SHEBOYGAN

Sheboygan ⚓

Federal roads in Wisconsin, 1848

× Building stone quarries, 1898

⚓ Historic shipping ports

◈ Individual diamond discoveries, 1876–1903

↙ Direction of river flow

Present-day county boundaries

Mining district	Mining center	Modern discovery	Primary mineral
▢	◆	●	Lead
▨	◆	●	Zinc
▤	◆	●	Iron
▦	◆	●	Copper
		●	Gold
		○	Silver

0 10 20 miles
0 10 20 kilometers

VERNON

A R E A

RICHLAND

CRAWFORD

SAUK

Ironton
North Freedom

Baraboo
Iron-formation discovered, 1887

COLUMBIA

Wisconsin River

Mayville

First Wisconsin iron mine, 1849

Iron Ridge

OZAUKEE

Port Washington ⚓

Quarries for stone, sand, and gravel played a strong role in developing many Wisconsin communities, particularly in the 1870s to 1930s. Sandstone, granite, and limestone were quarried for fireproof building blocks, paving stones, and masonry products. Stone was also used to build railroad beds, roadbeds, and airport runways. Sand and gravel have been the state's most steadily produced and exported mineral products.

DODGE

WASHINGTON

Prairie du Chien ⚓

MILITARY ROAD

IOWA

Blue Mounds

DANE

MILWAUKEE

Milwaukee ⚓

Dodgeville
Mineral Point

GRANT

Platteville
Belmont

Meekers Grove

LAFAYETTE

JEFFERSON

WAUKESHA

Rock River

WALWORTH

RACINE

Racine ⚓

Cassville

Hazel Green
Shullsburg
New Diggings

GREEN

ROCK

KENOSHA

Kenosha ⚓

Dubuque ⚓

IOWA

Monroe

Pecatonica River

⚓ Galena

ILLINOIS

Mining conflicts. Controversies over new mine proposals reflected the legacy of earlier mining eras. Some residents welcomed potential jobs, rural economic development, and contracts for the mining equipment industry (see *Southeastern Industries*). Others feared negative economic impacts on tourism, and burdens on local government services. Environmental concerns included potential acidic pollution from mine wastes, reduction of water tables by shaft pumping, and related effects on fish, wetlands, wild rice, and other resources. Mining firms maintained that new technologies would safeguard both the environment and the economy. Alliances of environmentalists, sportfishing groups, and tribes (see *Land*

Conflicts) contributed to the delay or cancellation of some projects. After 25 years of controversy and state permit procedures, the Ladysmith copper deposit was mined from 1993 to 1997 (see photo at right). In 1998, the state government required that a mining company must identify a metallic sulfide mine that has not polluted the environment before the company can open a similar mine in the state. Mining continues to play a role in Wisconsin history.

Timber, River & Mill

Significant commercial lumbering in Wisconsin began in the 1830s and 1840s with the appearance of sawmills in the southern and central regions. The industry grew rapidly from the 1850s through the 1890s, encouraging the settlement of the state's northern regions and the development of a wood products industry. Timber put the young state of Wisconsin in the national spotlight and made many timber "barons" fabulously wealthy.

Growth. Lumbering in Wisconsin grew dramatically for three reasons. First, the treaties of 1837 with the Dakota and Ojibwe made the timber lands available. Second, the agricultural frontier was advancing westward into the treeless prairie, as waves of settlers arrived in Illinois, Iowa, Kansas, and Nebraska. Finding rich soil but few building materials, the settlers looked to the northwoods timber for their lumber. Third, and most important, Wisconsin had an extensive network of waterways that flowed south from the woods to the prairies. The St. Croix, Chippewa, Black, Wisconsin, Wolf, and Menominee rivers (and their tributaries) provided transportation for the harvested logs to mills and markets, and provided power for the mills. Numerous sloughs, oxbows, lakes, and bays provided ideal holding areas for cut timber waiting to be milled and for building "log booms" for sorting and storage.

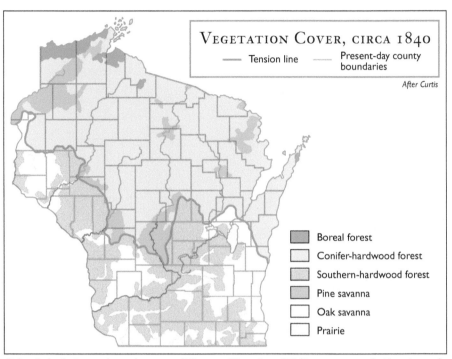

VEGETATION COVER, CIRCA 1840

— Tension line   — Present-day county boundaries

After Curtis

- Boreal forest
- Conifer-hardwood forest
- Southern-hardwood forest
- Pine savanna
- Oak savanna
- Prairie

Before the lumbering era, the northern parts of Minnesota, Wisconsin, and Michigan were covered with a mixture of softwood and hardwood forests, while the southern parts had predominantly hardwoods, mixed with pine and oak savanna. Where these two regions met was known as the *tension line* (or *tension zone*, where some species intermingle). The region north of this line was known as the "pinery," where softwood conifers (primarily white pine) were the desired species for harvest. Resinous and light, white pine resisted rot and was ideal for river transport. It was also soft and strong—making it easy to use in milling and carpentry. White pine was the wood of choice to make balloon-frame homes and farm buildings that were erected rapidly in the Midwest and Great Plains states.

Trains allowed deeper penetration into forests distant from navigable streams, and encouraged the harvest of nonbuoyant hardwoods.

Transport. Railroads were built into the northern forests beginning in the 1870s, and their presence had a profound effect on the timber industry (see *Transportation*). Trains led to a gradual decline in log driving and rafting on rivers, and enabled logging to continue year-round. Previously, logging had ceased in the summer months because of the difficulty of transporting logs overland to navigable streams. Railroads permitted deeper penetration into forested areas; spur lines made it possible to cut all marketable timber. Rail transport became essential as the availability of the prized softwoods declined; softwoods could float, but the less buoyant hardwoods were shipped by rail. Rail also linked Wisconsin lumbering areas to new markets west of the older markets in St. Louis and Chicago.

State lumber production grew steadily, peaking in 1892 at over four billion board feet. Between 1899

and 1905, Wisconsin led the nation in lumber production. Exhaustion of the resource, wasteful timber practices, and damaging fires (see *Weather Hazards*) led to a decline in production. The last stands of old-growth pine were harvested in the early 1930s.

Industry. The lumber industry helped to shape the state's industrial landscape. Wood product industries manufactured furniture, sashes, doors, blinds, barrels, wagons, carriages, housewares, caskets, and railroad ties. Small shops grew in the 1830s and 1840s to provide wood products for local markets. Wood industries grew rapidly in the 1860s and 1870s, with a large influx of skilled immigrant labor and access to new raw material. By 1900, Wisconsin had over 250 furniture factories. The lumber industry also enabled Wisconsin to become a leader in pulp and paper production. Changes in papermaking technology in the 1870s—away from cloth and straw and toward wood pulp—coincided with Wisconsin's lumbering boom. The cities of the Fox and Wisconsin river valleys became and remain major paper manufacturing centers (see *Fox Valley*).

As Wisconsin's timber was depleted, lumber interests turned their attention to the forests of the southern and northwestern U.S. This shift left many northern Wisconsin communities in the difficult position of encouraging settlers to move to the denuded "Cutover District." The state legislature and numerous northern counties established boards of immigration, receiving support from both lumber companies and land agencies. These boards published ads (above) touting northern Wisconsin as the ideal place to acquire cleared lands and establish farms. Thousands heeded the call and transformed much of the logged area into farmland. The lack of nearby markets, a short growing season, and acidic soils led to only marginal farming success. Many farmsteads were abandoned. Much of the land was declared tax-delinquent by the 1940s; a large part of it passed into public ownership and today accounts for many of Wisconsin's national, state, and county parks and forests.

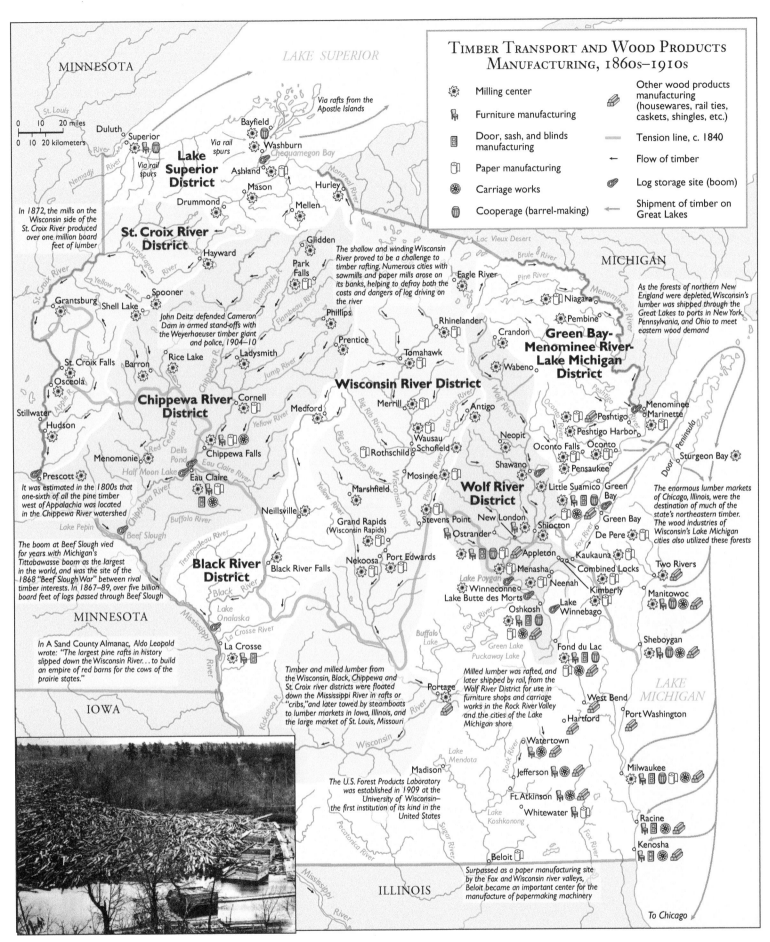

Milling center

Furniture manufacturing

Door, sash, and blinds manufacturing

Paper manufacturing

Carriage works

Cooperage (barrel-making)

Other wood products manufacturing (housewares, rail ties, caskets, shingles, etc.)

Tension line, c. 1840

Flow of timber

Log storage site (boom)

Shipment of timber on Great Lakes

MINNESOTA

LAKE SUPERIOR

Duluth
Superior

Via rail spurs

Via rafts from the Apostle Islands

Bayfield

Via rail spurs

Washburn

Chequamegon Bay

Lake Superior District

Ashland
Mason
Hurley
Drummond
Mellen

In 1872, the mills on the Wisconsin side of the St. Croix River produced over one million board feet of lumber

St. Croix River District

Glidden

The shallow and winding Wisconsin River proved to be a challenge to timber rafting. Numerous cities with sawmills and paper mills arose on its banks, helping to defray both the costs and dangers of log driving on the river

Park Falls

Hayward

Spooner

Phillips

MICHIGAN

Lac Vieux Desert

Brule River

Eagle River

Pine River

Niagara

As the forests of northern New England were depleted, Wisconsin's lumber was shipped through the Great Lakes to ports in New York, Pennsylvania, and Ohio to meet eastern wood demand

Grantsburg
Shell Lake

John Deitz defended Cameron Dam in armed stand-offs with the Weyerhaeuser timber giant and police, 1904–10

Rice Lake

Ladysmith

Rhinelander

Pembine

Crandon

Green Bay–Menominee River–Lake Michigan District

St. Croix Falls
Barron

Osceola

Stillwater

Hudson

Chippewa River District

Cornell

Medford

Merrill

Wisconsin River District

Antigo

Wabeno

Neopit

Menominee
Marinette

Menomonie

Dells Pond

Chippewa Falls

Half Moon Lake

Prescott

Eau Claire

It was estimated in the 1800s that one-sixth of all the pine timber west of Appalachia was located in the Chippewa River watershed

Buffalo River

Lake Pepin

Beef Slough

The boom at Beef Slough vied for years with Michigan's Tittabawasse boom as the largest in the world, and was the site of the 1868 "Beef Slough War" between rival timber interests. In 1867–89, over five billion board feet of logs passed through Beef Slough

MINNESOTA

In A Sand County Almanac, Aldo Leopold wrote: "The largest pine rafts in history slipped down the Wisconsin River... to build an empire of red barns for the cows of the prairie states."

IOWA

Wausau
Schofield
Rothschild

Mosinee

Marshfield

Neillsville

Black River District

Black River Falls

Grand Rapids (Wisconsin Rapids)

Nekoosa

Port Edwards

Lake Onalaska

La Crosse River

La Crosse

Timber and milled lumber from the Wisconsin, Black, Chippewa and St. Croix river districts were floated down the Mississippi River in rafts or "cribs," and later towed by steamboats to lumber markets in Iowa, Illinois, and the large market of St. Louis, Missouri.

Shawano

Wolf River District

Stevens Point

New London
Ostrander

Little Suamico

Oconto Falls
Oconto

Pensaukee

Peshtigo
Peshtigo Harbor

Sturgeon Bay

Door Peninsula

The enormous lumber markets of Chicago, Illinois, were the destination of much of the state's northeastern timber. The wood industries of Wisconsin's Lake Michigan cities also utilized these forests

Green Bay

De Pere

Kaukauna

Appleton
Menasha
Neenah
Kimberly

Combined Locks

Two Rivers

Winneconne
Lake Butte des Morts

Lake Poygan

Oshkosh

Lake Winnebago

Manitowoc

Buffalo Lake

Fond du Lac

Sheboygan

LAKE MICHIGAN

Green Lake
Puckaway Lake

Portage

Milled lumber was rafted, and later shipped by rail, from the Wolf River District for use in furniture shops and carriage works in the Rock River Valley and the cities of the Lake Michigan shore

West Bend

Hartford

Port Washington

Kickapoo R.

Wisconsin

Lake Mendota

Madison

The U.S. Forest Products Laboratory was established in 1909 at the University of Wisconsin— the first institution of its kind in the United States

Watertown

Jefferson

Rock River

Milwaukee

Pecatonica River

Ft. Atkinson

Whitewater

Lake Koshkonong

Racine

Sugar River

Beloit

Surpassed as a paper manufacturing site by the Fox and Wisconsin river valleys, Beloit became an important center for the manufacture of papermaking machinery

Kenosha

Fox River

ILLINOIS

Mississippi River

To Chicago

Driving logs downriver had its difficulties—most notorious among them being the logjam. An 1869 logjam on the Chippewa River contained approximately 150 million board feet of timber, backed up nearly 15 miles, and in places stood 30 feet above the level of the river.

Conservation. In less than 80 years the majestic forests of the state had been decimated. A permissive political climate that encouraged exploitation and discouraged conservation compounded the damage. It is estimated that nearly 40 percent of Wisconsin's forest resources never arrived at the sawmills because of fire and waste. As early as 1867, naturalist and cartographer Increase A. Lapham warned of the "disastrous effects" of forest destruction.

Awareness of the need for forest conservation grew slowly, but by the late 1890s the state legislature established a system of fire wardens and a forestry department, and developed regulations for cutting and experimental tree cultivation. Wisconsin is now home to a large county, state, and national forest system (see *Tourism*). It includes conservation and reforestation programs designed to balance recreational and commercial uses of the state's forests.

Harvesting the Crops

The cultivation of Wisconsin soil may have begun as early as 2,000 years ago, when Hopewell Culture settlements along the Rock and Wisconsin rivers harvested corn, squash, beans, and tobacco (see *Early Cultures*). Some later indigenous peoples also supplemented their hunting, fishing, and gathering with farming. It was not until the 1830s, however, that Wisconsin prairies and forests would begin to be transformed into an agricultural heartland.

Early crops. Corn, oats, and other crops were grown by settlers in the territorial era, but wheat was the primary cash crop. Wheat cultivation helped determine where people settled, and it established the state's identity as an agricultural "Eden." Wheat was an ideal crop for poor immigrants and settlers with limited resources, because it required little capital or labor once land had been cleared. After the initial plowing and planting, it could be left alone until harvest. The influx of settlers, available land, the use of mechanized harvesters and threshers, and the demand generated by the Civil War enabled Wisconsin to become a wheat-producing powerhouse throughout the 1860s and into the early 1870s (see map and charts below). This abundance led to a vigorous milling industry and established Milwaukee as an important grain port (see *Great Lakes*). Wheat production declined after the 1870s because of soil exhaustion (primarily nitrogen depletion), diseases like stem rust, and insect infestations. Better wheat lands in Minnesota and the Dakota Territory also drew wheat production westward out of Wisconsin. Despite decreased production, the state maintained a sizable milling industry into the 1900s (see *Southeastern Industries*), fed by rail connections to western wheat-producing areas (see *Transportation*). The reduction in wheat growing was quickly compensated for by diversified crops; the most important were feed crops for dairying (see *Dairyland*).

Period of transition. The shift to diversified crops brought numerous new crops into the state. Some earlier "boom and bust" crops (notably hops and flax) had peaked and declined rapidly in the 1860s. Other crops introduced in the period— including tobacco, sugar beets, sorghum, and cranberries— remain part of the state's agricultural output today (see column at right).

Feed-crop cultivation. The primary feed crops— corn, oats, and hay—had long been cultivated in Wisconsin, but did not play a dominant role until wheat farming began to decline in the 1870s. As dairy farming rose to prominence, the cultivation and storage of feed and forage crops (made possible by the newly introduced silo) became the cornerstone of the state's agriculture. Beginning in the 1890s, the U.W. College of Agriculture's aggressive studies of cows' dietary needs and of plant science led to the development of improved strains of hay seed and, later, hybrid corn. These scientific advances— combined with the growing use of labor-saving machines including reapers, plows, planters, and threshers—enabled crop cultivation to expand and push into the northern counties. Barley (historically important to the state's brewing industry), rye, soybeans and buckwheat appeared in the state's fields in the 1870s and 1880s, but were limited to a few counties by the 1940s and 1950s (see map on facing page). Corn, oats, and hay remain vital to the state's agricultural output; in 1999 Wisconsin ranked first in the U.S. in oat production and corn for silage, and among the top five in dry hay.

Fruit and vegetable cultivation. Gardens and orchards on family farms began producing vegetables and fruits as cash crops well before the 1900s,

Specialty Crops

"Specialty crops" were originally cultivated in Wisconsin as an income source to supplement dairying and feed-crop or cash-crop farming. The few specialty crop farms that grew to be large-scale operations were located in areas where the climate, landscape, and labor force made their success possible. Tobacco, mint, hemp, and honey production were introduced from other areas in the country; maple syrup production, berry-picking, and wild rice harvesting originated in Native American traditions. Farmers also flooded many central and northern Wisconsin bogs for cranberry cultivation, eventually making the state second only to Massachusetts in cranberry production. The photo above shows manual cranberry harvesting technique in use about 1950 in a cranberry bog near Warrens (Monroe County), where an annual cranberry festival is still held. In the early 1900s fur farms (primarily fox and mink) were established. Since the 1960s, the cultivation of ginseng (chiefly in Marathon County) has capitalized on expanding Asian and domestic markets.

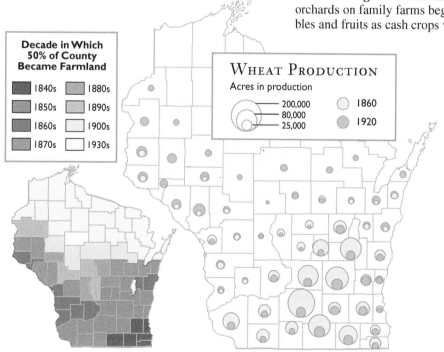

Decade in Which 50% of County Became Farmland

1840s	1880s
1850s	1890s
1860s	1900s
1870s	1930s

WHEAT PRODUCTION

Acres in production

- 200,000
- 80,000
- 25,000
- 1860
- 1920

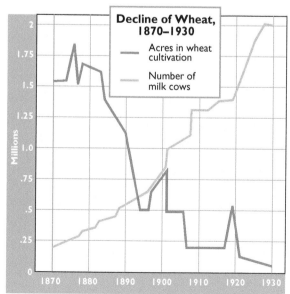

Decline of Wheat, 1870–1930

— Acres in wheat cultivation
— Number of milk cows

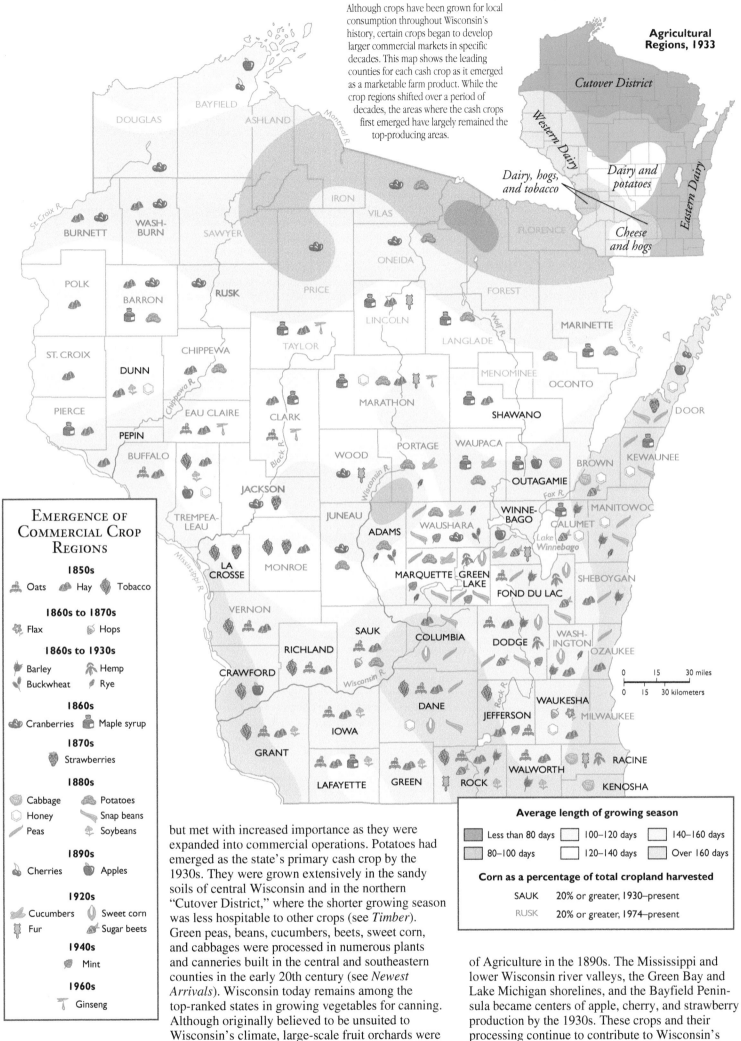

Although crops have been grown for local consumption throughout Wisconsin's history, certain crops began to develop larger commercial markets in specific decades. This map shows the leading counties for each cash crop as it emerged as a marketable farm product. While the crop regions shifted over a period of decades, the areas where the cash crops first emerged have largely remained the top-producing areas.

Agricultural Regions, 1933

Cutover District

Western Dairy

Dairy, hogs, and tobacco

Dairy and potatoes

Eastern Dairy

Cheese and hogs

EMERGENCE OF COMMERCIAL CROP REGIONS

1850s
Oats   Hay   Tobacco

1860s to 1870s
Flax   Hops

1860s to 1930s
Barley   Hemp
Buckwheat   Rye

1860s
Cranberries   Maple syrup

1870s
Strawberries

1880s
Cabbage   Potatoes
Honey   Snap beans
Peas   Soybeans

1890s
Cherries   Apples

1920s
Cucumbers   Sweet corn
Fur   Sugar beets

1940s
Mint

1960s
Ginseng

Average length of growing season

Less than 80 days	100–120 days	140–160 days
80–100 days	120–140 days	Over 160 days

Corn as a percentage of total cropland harvested

SAUK   20% or greater, 1930–present
RUSK   20% or greater, 1974–present

but met with increased importance as they were expanded into commercial operations. Potatoes had emerged as the state's primary cash crop by the 1930s. They were grown extensively in the sandy soils of central Wisconsin and in the northern "Cutover District," where the shorter growing season was less hospitable to other crops (see *Timber*). Green peas, beans, cucumbers, beets, sweet corn, and cabbages were processed in numerous plants and canneries built in the central and southeastern counties in the early 20th century (see *Newest Arrivals*). Wisconsin today remains among the top-ranked states in growing vegetables for canning. Although originally believed to be unsuited to Wisconsin's climate, large-scale fruit orchards were established on an experimental basis by the College

of Agriculture in the 1890s. The Mississippi and lower Wisconsin river valleys, the Green Bay and Lake Michigan shorelines, and the Bayfield Peninsula became centers of apple, cherry, and strawberry production by the 1930s. These crops and their processing continue to contribute to Wisconsin's agricultural economy, identity, and landscape.

America's Dairyland

The shift from wheat farming to dairy farming in Wisconsin began in the late 1800s, when yields of wheat declined, and the wheat frontier moved westward (see *Crops*). Before the specially bred dairy cow was introduced for its milk production, farmers had used "dual purpose" cattle for milk and meat, supplying households and local markets.

The "new butter region." Wisconsin's first marketable dairy product, butter, was made in the home. Butter, churned from the cream of milk, at first was usually consumed by the family that produced it. Butter sold at market often ended up as a lubricant for wagon wheels; it was known as "western grease" because of its poor quality. As dairying expanded, a "new butter region" grew up in western Wisconsin where cooperative creameries were formed. In 1895, Trempealeau County led the state in butter production, with over two million pounds. Cheese used whole milk and kept better than butter, but few farmers had the skill to produce it at home.

The industrialization of cheese. As wheat farming declined, farmers, especially those from New York, turned to dairying and to manufacturing cheese. Wisconsin's first neighborhood cheese factory was built in 1864 in Ladoga (Fond du Lac County) by

New York dairyman Chester Hazen. Getting milk made into cheese at the factory was beset with problems. The milk might spoil on the way, milk from different farms might be of uneven quality, or the cheese might be improperly aged. Many cheesemakers in the state were descendants of dairy farmers from England (cheddar cheese), Switzerland (limburger and Swiss cheeses), and Germany. Cheesemaking was concentrated in distinct regions of the state, depending on ethnic settlement, farmland quality (see map on facing page), and proximity to urban markets. Fluid milk production concentrated near cities; refrigerated railroad cars (introduced in 1871) helped to keep milk from spoiling and opened up more distant markets. In 1872, William D. Hoard helped found the Wisconsin Dairymen's Association to improve the quality, uniformity, and packaging of cheese and butter. Wisconsin cheese began to compete with New York and British cheese.

Emergence of the dairy farm. The seven-days-a-week job of running a dairy farm required discipline and a costly investment. Nevertheless, the number of Wisconsin milk cows more than doubled from 1869 to 1889 because farmland was expanding by about four million acres a decade. The difficult issue of milk quality was solved in 1890 with the invention

Dairy Breeds

Like the immigrants who brought them, the various breeds of dairy cattle in Wisconsin come from many nations. "Major," the first purebred dairy sire in Wisconsin (above), was an Alderney registered in 1860. Holsteins, brought from the Netherlands, make up around 93 percent of the state's dairy herds (see illustration on facing page). Recognized by its black and white coat, a Holstein produces about six gallons of milk per day. Jerseys, the smallest of the dairy breeds, place a distant second in number, but produce a higher-fat milk than Holsteins—rich in cream. Jerseys are found most often in southwestern Wisconsin. Brown Swiss, docile descendants of hardy animals raised in the mountains of Switzerland, are much larger than Jerseys. Guernseys, once found widely across the state, are now considered a minor breed. Their coats are similar to Holsteins in pattern, but are red and white in color. Guernseys, Jerseys, and Alderneys originated on British isles off the coast of France. Ayrshires, originating in Scotland, constitute the lowest percentage of the dairy cattle breeds in the state. They are hardy animals with coats of cherry-red and white.

Wisconsin was first called "America's Dairyland" in the 1930s. To promote dairying beyond the Upper Midwest, the federal government began a pricing system in 1937. It set prices for fluid milk based on the distance from Eau Claire, then deemed the center of dairy production. The minimum price was based on a "class-one differential"—the top subsidy paid to farmers. If a northern Wisconsin farmer was paid $1.04 for 100 pounds of milk in 1996, a southern Florida farmer received $4.18. A few states such as California have their own pricing systems. Wisconsin farmers strongly opposed the systems as "unfair" and "obsolete," and in 1997 a federal court ordered it equalized. Further reformation in 2000 divided the country into 11 orders.

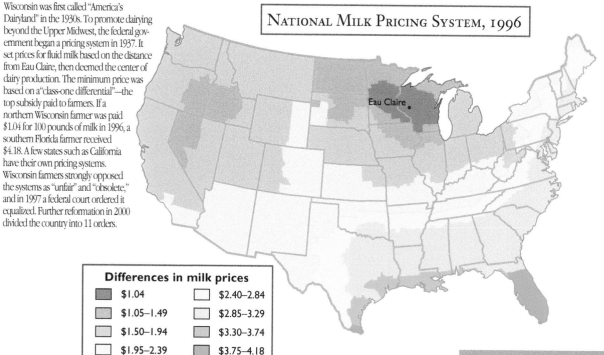

NATIONAL MILK PRICING SYSTEM, 1996

Eau Claire

Differences in milk prices

$1.04	$2.40–2.84
$1.05–1.49	$2.85–3.29
$1.50–1.94	$3.30–3.74
$1.95–2.39	$3.75–4.18

German forebay barn about 1900

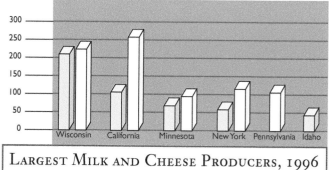

LARGEST MILK AND CHEESE PRODUCERS, 1996

| | 10 million pounds of cheese | | 100 million pounds of milk |

Loss of Family Farms

In the Great Depression of the 1930s, many family farmers went into debt. Some had their farm *foreclosed* (reclaimed by banks to redeem a mortgage), which often resulted in the sale of the farm. In 1932 in Chili (Clark County), farmers began to use the "penny sale"—bidding only pennies as a tactic to disrupt auctions at which farms were to be sold to pay off banks. In the late 1970s another farm crisis began as dairy prices stabilized but the cost of milk production began to quadruple. Family dairy farms were again foreclosed throughout the 1980s and 1990s. Many farms were sold at auction, such as the 1996 Eau Claire County auction shown above. Some farmers revived the penny sale, but large bidders bought the operations from the banks and turned them into "factory farms." In many cases, the new owners were absentee agribusiness companies. From 1970 to 2000, the number of Wisconsin's dairy farms declined from 64,000 to 21,000. Many families had to give up land that had been theirs for several generations, suffering emotional distress and losing a way of life. With fewer farms, the rural tax base was reduced, causing local businesses to fail and young people to seek jobs in cities. In the 1990s, surviving family farmers began to feel that new technologies favored the large-scale dairy operations that could afford them. Bovine Growth Hormone (BGH) increased a cow's milk production, but generated controversies over high costs and alleged side effects. In 1997, the American Breeders Service in Windsor (Dane County) carried out the world's first successful cloning of a calf for commercial purposes. Like the BGH controversy, cloning aroused debate over its biological implications and over the advantage that large-scale farms would gain from having numerous high-yield milk cows. These technological disputes are part of a larger debate over the future of Wisconsin's dairy industry. Some farmers express a need to save what is left of family farms, but some fear that there is too much to do in too little time.

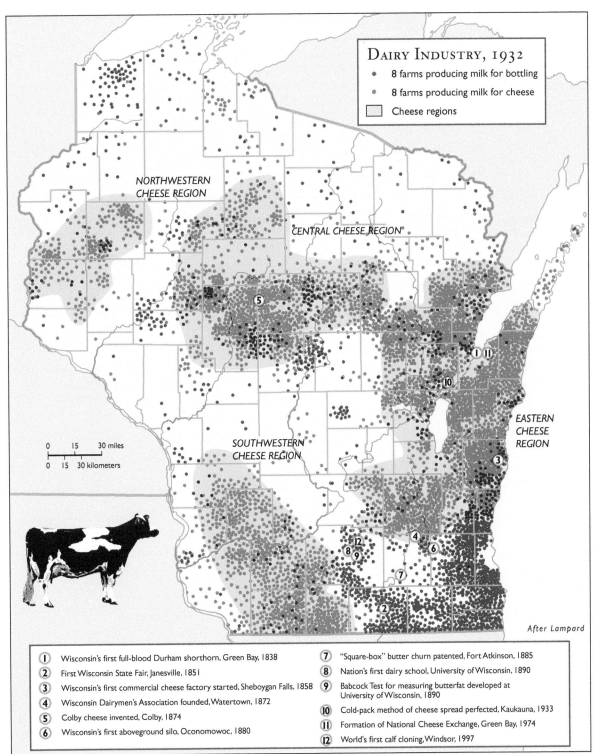

DAIRY INDUSTRY, 1932
- 8 farms producing milk for bottling
- 8 farms producing milk for cheese
- Cheese regions

NORTHWESTERN CHEESE REGION

CENTRAL CHEESE REGION

SOUTHWESTERN CHEESE REGION

EASTERN CHEESE REGION

0   15   30 miles
0   15   30 kilometers

After Lampard

① Wisconsin's first full-blood Durham shorthorn, Green Bay, 1838
② First Wisconsin State Fair, Janesville, 1851
③ Wisconsin's first commercial cheese factory started, Sheboygan Falls, 1858
④ Wisconsin Dairymen's Association founded, Watertown, 1872
⑤ Colby cheese invented, Colby, 1874
⑥ Wisconsin's first aboveground silo, Oconomowoc, 1880
⑦ "Square-box" butter churn patented, Fort Atkinson, 1885
⑧ Nation's first dairy school, University of Wisconsin, 1890
⑨ Babcock Test for measuring butterfat developed at University of Wisconsin, 1890
⑩ Cold-pack method of cheese spread perfected, Kaukauna, 1933
⑪ Formation of National Cheese Exchange, Green Bay, 1974
⑫ World's first calf cloning, Windsor, 1997

of the Babcock Test, a world standard for the simple measurement of butterfat content, by Stephen Babcock at the University of Wisconsin. The influence of the university's College of Agriculture grew through its dairy science research and outreach extension programs. By 1890, over 17 percent of Wisconsin farms were considered dairy farms, and over 90 percent reported having dairy cattle.

Another boon for dairying was the importation of the silo for the production of *silage* (green corn fermented in an enclosed space). This allowed for a longer feeding and milking season. Silo technology has changed in the 20th century, from wood, brick, or concrete bins to metal towers, and finally to shrink-wrap methods. Dairying was also given a boost by a state ban on colored oleomargarine from 1895 to 1967, an attempt to increase butter sales.

Dairy economy. Milk prices fluctuated in the first three decades of the century, with prices at their peak during World War I and in the late 1920s. During the Great Depression of the 1930s, prices spiraled downward. Large dairy companies forced smaller dairies out of business, sparking milk strikes among small dairy farmers (see *Progressives*). After World War II, large "agribusiness" firms began buying up or consolidating family dairy farms, particularly in eastern Wisconsin, where flatter terrain encouraged large farm operations. The process accelerated in the 1970s–1980s as many family farms throughout the state were foreclosed because of high debts (see column at left). Family dairy farms still thrive in some communities, particularly in the southwestern part of the state, while others struggle to survive. In 1996, Wisconsin produced more than two billion pounds of cheese, yet lost over 1,000 family dairy farms. That year, California's large agribusiness operations surpassed Wisconsin in milk production, though Wisconsin remained the leader in cheese production (see chart on facing page). "America's Dairyland" has a proud past and an uncertain future.

Weather Hazards

A wide range of weather conditions, some of them hazardous, have always affected Wisconsin. Compared to other states that suffer major disturbances, such as volcanoes, hurricanes, avalanches, tidal waves, or major earthquakes, Wisconsin is relatively safe. Yet large natural disasters such as floods, droughts, fires, and severe storms have plagued the state, causing agricultural losses, property damage, injuries, and loss of life. Through weather-related hazards, nature has left a lasting imprint on human history in Wisconsin. Human activity, however, has also created or worsened some so-called natural disasters.

Floods. Flooding, along with wind and ice, created most of Wisconsin's landscape. As the glaciers receded, meltwaters carved river valleys and dells, and transported fertile topsoils from the northern to southern regions (see *Glacial*). Certain rivers have flooded repeatedly in modern times, damaging homes or farms in the flat floodplains along their banks (see map below). Floods have taken place suddenly after snow melts in the spring, or after heavy summer or fall rains. They also have resulted from slow build-ups of rivers and streams. The construction of towns and the draining of many wetlands (see *Environment*) have removed a natural "sponge" that would normally absorb floodwaters. Dams and levees have been constructed or proposed to control flooding (see column at right).

Dams for Flood Control

Most dams in Wisconsin were built not to control floods, but to make it easier to transport logs, prevent erosion, generate electrical power, create recreational opportunities, or (especially in the case of the Mississippi River) improve commercial navigation through lock systems. The relocation of homes and businesses and the construction of *levees* (river embankments) are more common strategies for flood control and have been used in such vulnerable river cities as La Crosse and Prairie du Chien. In the 1950s and 1960s, numerous proposals were made to build large flood-control dams around the state. The Eau Galle River village of Spring Valley, which had been nearly destroyed in a 1942 flood, was protected by a new dam (above). Other dam proposals were blocked because of ecological concerns (see *Environment*). The most widely publicized was the proposed La Farge dam. In 1961, the U.S. Army Corps of Engineers, responding to public request, developed a proposal for a dam along the scenic but flood-prone Kickapoo River. The Corps purchased the land along the river in 1969—displacing many farmers and other landowners—and began construction in 1971. Citing environmental studies and growing costs, Senators William Proxmire and Gaylord A. Nelson withdrew support for new federal project funds in 1975. Officials devised new strategies to reduce flood damage, including levees, small dams, and community relocation (part of the village of Soldiers Grove, for example, was relocated to higher ground to avoid flood waters). Much of the 8,600 acres of land around the La Farge dam site grew wild; the area was transferred to state control in 1995. Two years later, the state signed an agreement to create a 7,400-acre, locally managed recreational reserve—and to also return 1,200 acres to the Ho-Chunk Nation. Today, a lone concrete tower still stands at the La Farge dam site.

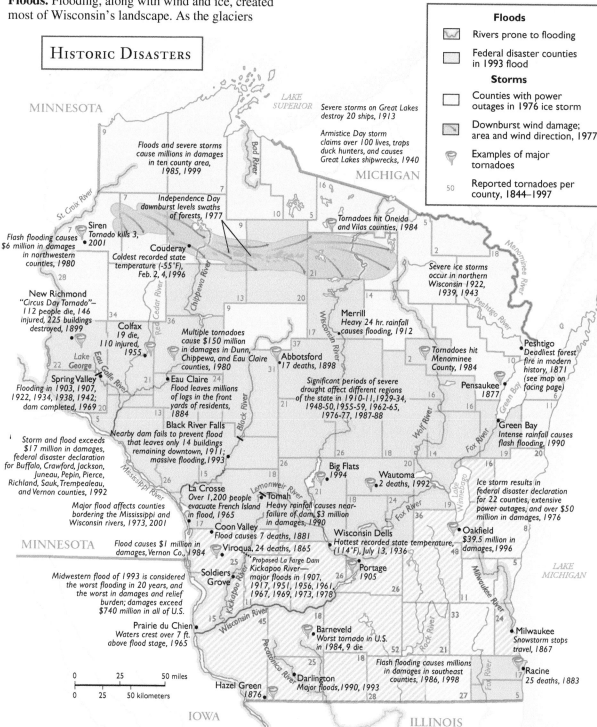

HISTORIC DISASTERS

MINNESOTA

LAKE SUPERIOR

MICHIGAN

Floods
- ⌇ Rivers prone to flooding
- ▢ Federal disaster counties in 1993 flood

Storms
- ▢ Counties with power outages in 1976 ice storm
- ◣ Downburst wind damage; area and wind direction, 1977
- ▽ Examples of major tornadoes
- 50 Reported tornadoes per county, 1844–1997

Severe storms on Great Lakes destroy 20 ships, 1913

Armistice Day storm claims over 100 lives, traps duck hunters, and causes Great Lakes shipwrecks, 1940

Floods and severe storms cause millions in damages in ten county area, 1985, 1999

Independence Day downburst levels swaths of forests, 1977

Tornadoes hit Oneida and Vilas counties, 1984

Siren Tornado kills 3, 2001

Flash flooding causes $6 million in damages in northwestern counties, 1980

Couderay Coldest recorded state temperature (-55°F), Feb. 2, 4, 1996

Severe ice storms occur in northern Wisconsin 1922, 1939, 1943

New Richmond "Circus Day Tornado"– 112 people die, 146 injured, 225 buildings destroyed, 1899

Merrill Heavy 24 hr. rainfall causes flooding, 1912

Colfax 19 die, 110 injured, 1955

Multiple tornadoes cause $150 million in damages in Dunn, Chippewa, and Eau Claire counties, 1980

Abbotsford 17 deaths, 1898

Tornadoes hit Menominee County, 1984

Peshtigo Deadliest forest fire in modern history, 1871 (see map on facing page)

Spring Valley Flooding in 1903, 1907, 1922, 1934, 1938, 1942; dam completed, 1969

Eau Claire Flood leaves millions of logs in the front yards of residents, 1884

Significant periods of severe drought affect different regions of the state in 1910-11, 1929-34, 1948-50, 1955-59, 1962-65, 1976-77, 1987-88

Pensaukee 1877

Lake George

Storm and flood exceeds $17 million in damages, federal disaster declaration for Buffalo, Crawford, Jackson, Juneau, Pepin, Pierce, Richland, Sauk, Trempealeau, and Vernon counties, 1992

Black River Falls Nearby dam fails to prevent flood that leaves only 14 buildings remaining downtown, 1911; massive flooding, 1993

Green Bay Intense rainfall causes flash flooding, 1990

Big Flats 1994

Wautoma 2 deaths, 1992

Ice storm results in federal disaster declaration for 22 counties, extensive power outages, and over $50 million in damages, 1976

La Crosse Over 1,200 people evacuate French Island in flood, 1965

Tomah

Heavy rainfall causes near-failure of dam, $3 million in damages, 1990

Major flood affects counties bordering the Mississippi and Wisconsin rivers, 1973, 2001

Coon Valley Flood causes 7 deaths, 1881

Wisconsin Dells Hottest recorded state temperature (114°F), July 13, 1936

Oakfield $39.5 million in damages, 1996

MINNESOTA

Flood causes $1 million in damages, Vernon Co., 1984

Viroqua, 24 deaths, 1865

Midwestern flood of 1993 is considered the worst flooding in 20 years, and the worst in damages and relief burden; damages exceed $740 million in all of U.S.

Soldiers Grove

Proposed La Farge Dam Kickapoo River— major floods in 1907, 1917, 1951, 1956, 1961, 1967, 1969, 1973, 1978

Portage 1905

LAKE MICHIGAN

Prairie du Chien Waters crest over 7 ft. above flood stage, 1965

Barneveld Worst tornado in U.S. in 1984, 9 die

Milwaukee Snowstorm stops travel, 1867

Hazel Green 1876

Darlington Major floods, 1990, 1993

Flash flooding causes millions in damages in southeast counties, 1986, 1998

Racine 25 deaths, 1883

0   25   50 miles
0   25   50 kilometers

IOWA

ILLINOIS

The Great Fires of October 8, 1871

Forest fires have posed a danger throughout Wisconsin history, particularly in times of drought. The wasteful practices of the early timber industry worsened the hazard by leaving behind huge amounts of dry wood and brush piles (see *Timber*). The inevitable disaster occurred in the drought year of 1871. On the night of October 8, hot winds from the south caused normally controllable small fires to shift suddenly and gather force. They swept through a 60-mile stretch north of Green Bay and a 50-mile stretch on the Door Peninsula, and collectively became known as the "Peshtigo Fire." The conflagration claimed an estimated 1,200–1,500 lives. Survivors later told of jumping into rivers to escape the flames, and witnessing firestorms, or "tornadoes of fire," that devastated enormous areas. The fire began on the same day as the Great Chicago Fire (which caused an estimated 250 deaths) and numerous fires on Michigan's Lower Peninsula. Because they started during the day, the Michigan fires claimed fewer lives, though they destroyed more land and timber. Newspapers of the time publicized the Chicago fire widely, making it the most infamous of the three disasters. The Peshtigo Fire stands today as the deadliest forest fire in modern world history.

1871 PESHTIGO FIRE

0 — 15 miles
0 — 15 kilometers

MICHIGAN

OCONTO

Birch Creek 22

Upper Sugar Bush
Middle Sugar Bush
Menominee
Marinette
255
Menekaune
Lower Sugar Bush
Peshtigo 600

At least 200 in outlying areas.

Oconto

Door Peninsula

LAKE MICHIGAN

Sturgeon Bay

Pensaukee

Williamsonville 59

Little Suamico

DOOR

Green Bay

KEWAUNEE

Origin and extent of fire

Direction of wind

Firestorm

Tobinsville 14

Estimated deaths
600

New Franken

Kewaunee

Green Bay

BROWN

Droughts. Extended and widespread droughts have been infrequent in Wisconsin's history; shorter droughts have been more common. Severe droughts are generated by a dry period lasting more than two or three months. They have resulted in heavy damage to agriculture, as in the early 1930s when the entire state was affected by the drought that created the "Dust Bowl" on the Great Plains. This drought extended throughout the state and is believed to be the worst in modern times. A 1948–50 drought struck northern and central Wisconsin, and a 1955–59 drought covered nearly the entire state (see map at left below). Droughts in 1976–77 and 1987–88 caused $624 million and $1.3 billion in damages, respectively (see map at right below). Although the 1987–88 drought was most severe in the north, every county in Wisconsin received federal disaster relief assistance. Hay and corn crop damage from drought increases feed prices, thus influencing the price of milk and the ability of dairy farmers to maintain their herds. Some scientists believe that droughts have grown in severity in recent years.

Fires. Fire has played a major role in shaping Wisconsin's vegetation patterns. Native Americans set fires to clear wooded areas and improve wildlife habitat for hunting. European settlers suppressed brush fires, causing forests to replace some large prairies (see photos). In northern Wisconsin, wasteful

timber-cutting practices led to disastrous forest fires, including the deadly 1871 Peshtigo fire (see map at left). In the early lumbering days, more timber was lost to fire than was actually harvested (see *Timber*). Today, wildfires still affect the logging, tourism, and recreational industries. Most fires strike between March and November; they occur particularly in drought years.

Prairies and savannas covered nine million acres in Wisconsin before European settlement began. These grassland ecosystems have since declined in area, partly because of the suppression of brush fires. The absence of fire enables trees to grow, shading out prairie grasses that thrive on sunlight and open spaces. The top photo shows Round Top Bluff, on the Wisconsin River opposite Prairie du Sac in 1870. Wollersheim Winery buildings are visible on the hillside. The bottom photo shows the same bluff in 1993, covered with trees. Only the tip of the winery (indicated by the blue arrow) is visible.

Storms. Because Wisconsin is located at the edge of seasonal weather systems, it is vulnerable to a variety of severe storms. The combination of cold winter air and Great Lakes moisture has often meant vast contrasts in snowfall—ranging from about 30 inches in south-central counties to over 100 inches in some north-central counties. In late fall and late winter, ice storms occur, particularly in southern Wisconsin, when rain or fog mixes with cold temperatures. The state also lies on the northern edge of the midwestern tornado belt (tornado season generally lasts from April to September). Tornadoes in Wisconsin occur most frequently in the southwestern and south-central regions of the state. No area in Wisconsin, however, is completely immune from tornado activity. Tornadoes are sometimes accompanied by downbursts—"collapsing" clouds that create intense straight-line winds. Like floods, droughts, and fires, severe storms are better understood today than in early Wisconsin history. Although weather hazards cause fewer casualties now, they still affect the state's economy and population distribution.

SEVERE 20TH-CENTURY DROUGHTS

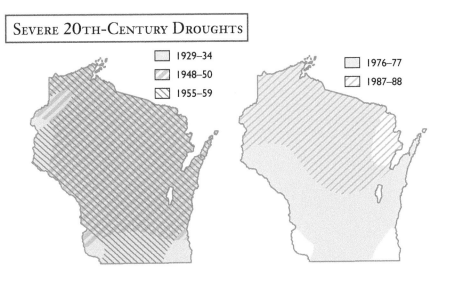

1929–34
1948–50
1955–59

1976–77
1987–88

Changes in Rural Society

Agriculture has been central to Wisconsin's economy and identity since territorial days. Changes in technology, communications, education, transportation, science, and public policy have profoundly shaped the rural landscape and transformed rural life.

Pioneer era, 1840s–1870s. The young state's best agricultural lands had been plotted and surveyed by the 1840s (see *Statehood*). Settlers quickly acquired them and began to transform the forests and prairies into farmsteads. At first pioneer farms were small— between 40 and 100 acres—and their operations very labor-intensive. Settlers cleared land, built homes, fences, and farm buildings, planted gardens for subsistence, and grew wheat as their first cash crop (see *Crops*). Roads were poor, so when railroads appeared in the 1850s they became the primary means of transporting harvested crops to urban markets (see *Transportation*). Farm communities were closely knit because of their isolation, family and church connections, and need for mutual aid.

Growth and consolidation, 1860s–1930s. Waves of immigrants poured into Wisconsin just as the "wheat frontier" pushed westward out of the state, replaced by dairying and diversified farming. Important changes during this time included the consolidation of small land holdings into larger farms and the introduction of modern farming technology, which included silos, large multipurpose barns, mechanical mowers and reapers, steam power for harvesting and threshing, and milk-testing devices. Labor shortages caused by the Civil War (1861–65) encouraged the adoption of mechanized farm implements. The 1880s also saw the creation of the university's College of

Agriculture in Madison, agricultural research stations, and extension programs for the dissemination of information to farmers. Farm communities remained closely knit and largely self-reliant, but began to embrace new ideas and farming technology.

Modernization, 1930s–1960s. Damage sustained in the Dust Bowl of the 1930s made farmers throughout the nation aware of the need for soil protection and erosion control (see *Weather Hazards*). Wisconsin led the nation with the first projects of the newly created Soil Conservation Service. The 1930s and the 1940s saw the expanded use of both the internal

The Selim farmstead near Chaseburg (Vernon County) was extensively damaged by erosion in 1937 (see top photo) but was repaired and replanted a year later (see bottom photo).

Soil Conservation

Throughout Wisconsin history, the immediate demands of housing, food, land productivity, and return on investment have taken precedence over long-term stewardship of the land. As agricultural settlement expanded, the use of marginal lands, wetlands, and slopes for crops and grazing increased. Erosion and its resulting decline in productivity— compounded by 1920s floods and a 1930s drought—led to a wave of conservation programs. One of the nation's first soil conservation experiment stations was established in La Crosse in 1929, four years before the organization of the U.S. Soil Conservation Service (SCS). These agencies worked closely with farmers in implementing crop rotation, contour farming, reforestation, streambank repair, and the removal of marginal lands from production. The Coon Valley area in Vernon County was the site of the SCS's Project Number One, in which Civilian Conservation Corps workers built erosion control projects (see photos at left). Farm product surpluses in the 1950s led to the federal Soil Bank program, which paid farmers to take parts of their farms out of production and reserve them for future use. This program backfired, however, as farmers overworked and subsequently degraded remaining lands. The 1970s saw a growing world market for U.S. farm products, which led to increased production and additional erosion damage. To contain this second wave of damage, the 1985 Farm Bill introduced subsidies for removing sensitive and erodable land from production. Today, erosion remains a problem in many areas of the state, and many farmers continue to implement measures to protect the soil.

RURAL ELECTRIFICATION, 1934

▫	House/farm without electricity	--- Existing electricity distribution-transmission line, 1934
▢	House/farm with electricity	▢ Area not yet served by electrical cooperative
◇	Using home lighting plant	
......	Telephone line, 1934	▢ Area already served with electricity, or not included in initial electrification survey
——	Road, 1934	

School
Church
⟨27⟩ State Highway, 1934
- - - Interstate 94, 1998

Northfield Township   *Garden Valley Township*

JACKSON COUNTY

0 ___ 1 mile
0 ___ 1 kilometer

Northfield
Northfield
York

Garden Valley

Stockwell Cr.
Hagden Cr.
Pigeon Cr.
Beaver Cr.
May Coulee
Judkins Cr.
Burnett Cr.
Schermerhorn Cr.

⟨27⟩
⟨95⟩

Rural Electrification

To improve the quality of life and reduce the farmer's burden of hand labor, President Franklin D. Roosevelt created the Rural Electrification Administration in 1935 to provide loans to local electric cooperatives so they could extend services to rural areas. Farmers used the electricity for lighting, pumping water, milking dairy cows, and refrigeration. At left are Northfield and Garden Valley townships in Jackson County in 1934, illustrating where the co-ops would extend service from existing electric service lines.

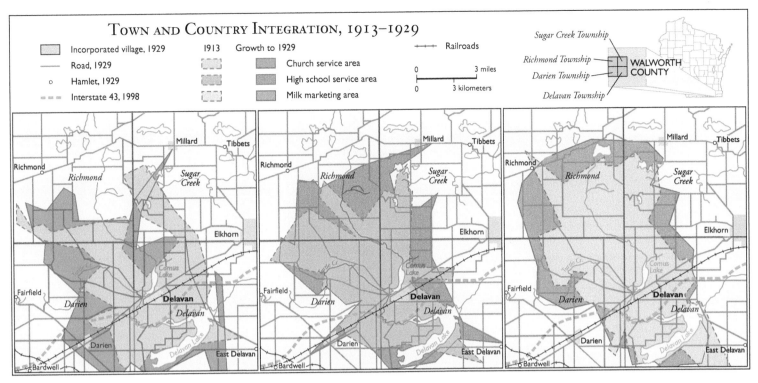

Legend:
- Incorporated village, 1929
- Road, 1929
- o Hamlet, 1929
- Interstate 43, 1998
- 1913 Growth to 1929
- Church service area
- High school service area
- Milk marketing area
- ┼┼┼┼ Railroads

0 3 miles
0 3 kilometers

Sugar Creek Township
Richmond Township
Darien Township
Delavan Township

WALWORTH COUNTY

combustion engine for plowing and transportation (which resulted in massive road construction) and increased access to electricity (see map on facing page).

Decline of the family farm, 1970s–2000s. The further consolidation of small farms into larger farms stemmed from the economic reasoning that farmers should increase their productivity so they could afford newly available technology, including chemical fertilizers, pesticides, supplemental animal feed, and hybrid crops. These changes transformed diversified, labor-intensive farm operations into capital-intensive and highly specialized operations, particularly in the open farmland of eastern Wisconsin. Many family farms were lost to foreclosures in the 1980s (see *Dairyland*) as farm ownership became more concentrated in fewer hands and urban sprawl intruded on other farmland near growing cities (see map at right). By the end of the 20th century, many Wisconsin farms had been transformed from family-owned enterprises into components of international "agribusiness" firms. Even so, a distinct rural culture still persists throughout the state, and successful, sustainable agricultural operations are increasing, particularly near urban markets.

Urban Sprawl

Eau Claire's development and expansion into its surrounding townships serves as an example of urban sprawl. Urban encroachment onto farmland presents problems for a growing number of Wisconsin farms. Many of the state's cities were initially founded as agricultural market and service centers, because of their proximity to the state's richest farmland. It is ironic that these same cities are now endangering the economy that helped create them. The increasing population and rising incomes of the 1940s–1960s led to a greater demand for housing, schools, and public and commercial facilites. Extensive road construction in the 1950s–1960s encouraged development on farmland around the cities. Shopping malls, office parks, and strip malls followed. Farms near cities were subject to new zoning, water, and sewage regulations as rural townships were annexed by the expanding cities. Taxes on farmland began to be based on the land's potential value for new construction, rather than its existing value for agriculture. Faced with these pressures, many farmers sold their land, which was then divided and developed, continuing the outward sprawl. Today, some communities are attempting to balance their growth and development with control of the environmental, cultural, and aesthetic damage of unchecked urban sprawl.

Before the 1910s, rural life was based on the local farming community. Many small churches, schools, creameries, and other important social institutions were located in "rural neighborhoods" outside populated villages (see *Anglo-Americans*). The rural economy was based on a system of mutual exchange (such as trading, bartering, and shared labor) offered through the extended family, church, or ethnic group. That system changed as economists and social scientists proposed a model of "progress" based on "efficiency" that would "uplift" rural life. They sought to integrate rural communities with nearby towns and villages (such as Delavan in the maps above) and tie the rural economy into the urban-based cash economy. Traditional rural institutions were "consolidated" and centralized in the towns and villages, which farmers had previously visited only on market day. In addition, beginning in the 1920s, the automobile also increased mobility between farms and population centers. The consolidation of rural churches increased the size of congregations, but sped up the assimilation of distinct ethnic groups within multi-ethnic village churches (see *Religion*). The consolidation of rural schools improved education, but was strongly resisted as being harmful to community life (see *Education*). The consolidation of milk-processing centers improved sanitation, but eliminated small creameries and cheese factories that provided a center for rural life (see *Dairyland*). These changes improved the material standard of living, but also eroded rural traditions and the sense of community.

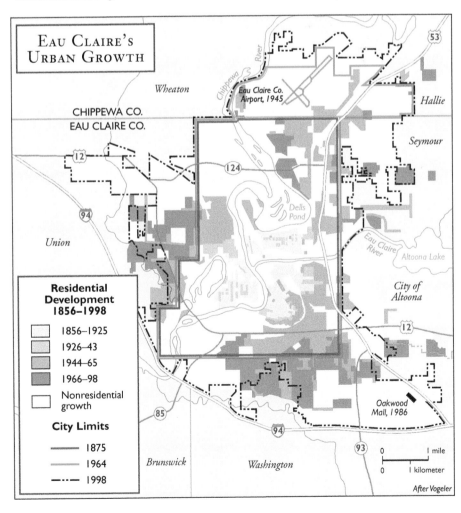

EAU CLAIRE'S URBAN GROWTH

Wheaton
Eau Claire Co. Airport, 1945
Chippewa River
CHIPPEWA CO.
EAU CLAIRE CO.
Hallie
Seymour
Dells Pond
Eau Claire River
Altoona Lake
Union
City of Altoona
Oakwood Mall, 1986

Residential Development 1856–1998
- 1856–1925
- 1926–43
- 1944–65
- 1966–98
- Nonresidential growth

City Limits
- ——— 1875
- ——— 1964
- –·–·– 1998

Brunswick
Washington

0 1 mile
0 1 kilometer

After Vogeler

Transportation Networks

How Wisconsin's transportation networks grew can provide insights into wider aspects of its history. They were used for fur trading, lead mining, troop movements, logging, immigration, farming, tourism, and more. Transportation networks are part of Wisconsin's past and present.

Waterways. Wisconsin's earliest transportation system was its natural network of rivers and lakes, which connected the two major natural transportation routes of the continent—the Great Lakes and the Mississippi River. These links made Wisconsin a focal point of colonial conflict and trade (see *Encounters*). The Fox-Wisconsin waterway was particularly integral to settlement and economic development (see *Fox Valley*). To facilitate steamboat traffic, companies built locks on the lower Fox and a canal between the Fox and Wisconsin rivers. Dreams of a canal connecting the Rock and Milwaukee rivers got only as far as one dam. Financial failures, competition from developing roads and railroads, and political intrigue over land grants prevented canals from fulfilling their potential in the state.

Road building. The first long roads in Wisconsin, connecting more than neighboring villages, were developed to ship ore and processed metals from the Lead District to Great Lakes ports (see *Mining*). State Highways 18 and 11 are examples of the routes these "lead roads" followed. The military built roads to connect forts and "secure the frontier" (see *Military*) and the federal government funded a few roads during the territorial era. The state constitution of 1848 prohibited the state government from funding internal improvements and made local governments responsible for road construction and maintenance. From 1849 to 1911, many local residents contributed their labor and tools to maintain roads, instead of paying taxes. This ineffective system kept taxes low, but created a crude and unreliable road system that inhibited economic growth.

Road improvement. Early campaigns for better roads resulted in a short period of plank-road construction in the early 1850s (see column at right). In the 1890s the "Good Roads Movement" brought together interest groups in support of public funding of state roads (see column on facing page). In response to the automobile, the State Aid Road Law of 1911 began direct state involvement in road construction. The Federal Aid Road Act of 1916 restarted federal aid for highways—initial funding was aimed at farm-to-market roads connected to rail lines. Wisconsin began to construct a State Trunk

Plank Roads

In Wisconsin's early years, plank roads were developed in the settled areas of the state. Boosters envisioned plank roads (see photo) connecting all the cities and towns in the state. Plank roads were privately owned toll roads. They were made of oak planks secured to wood beams set into the ground along the edge of the road. They improved travel considerably, with the most successful ones serving as feeder routes for railroads. Though they were initially considered cost-effective, competition from railroads and high maintenance costs made most plank roads marginal business enterprises. Few were constructed after 1853.

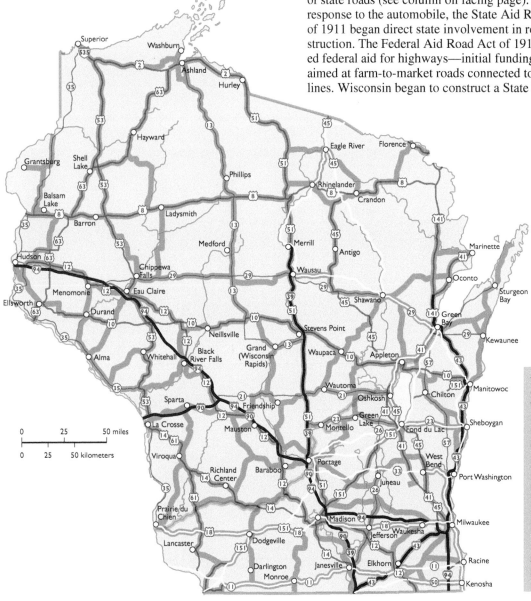

WISCONSIN ROADS AND WATERWAYS

- Fox-Wisconsin Waterway
- U.S. and military roads, 1848–70
- State Trunk Highway System, begun 1918
- ○ County seat, 1918
- Interstate, 2002
- U.S. Highways, 2002
- Principal stretches of selected state highways, 2002

Wisconsin's road system began before statehood with U.S. and military roads (white lines). In 1917 Wisconsin's legislature approved the construction of a State Trunk Highway System (grey lines), that would cover over 5,000 miles and connect all county seats and all cities with a population over 5,000. In 1919 another 2,500 miles were approved. The state was the first in the country to identify its highways with numbered route names. These efforts contributed to making Wisconsin a leader in highway development. This map also shows additional state highway segments classified as "principal through routes" (thin red lines) by the state Department of Transportation. These segments often followed earlier U.S. and state highways

Highway System in 1918, to connect every county seat (see map on facing page). Trucking along the system became a boon to most farmers, even though by then rail lines reached every corner of Wisconsin. Throughout the 1920s, the state and federal governments constructed new routes. In the Great Depression of the 1930s, road building continued under work relief programs. Road construction almost stopped during World War II, except for routes essential for defense. From the 1950s to the 1970s the federal government built the interstate highway system to meet anticipated defense needs during the Cold War. The interstate system deepened the nation's reliance on roads for economic needs and travel. It accelerated the population shift from rural to urban areas and the growth of suburbs, which had been stimulated by the automobile since the 1920s.

Impact of railroads. The push to build railroads in Wisconsin began in the territorial period, but rail lines did not cross the state until 1857. The presence of railroads (even primitive early versions) represented a fundamental change in everyday lives. Railroads connected the countryside to the city, and linked farms to markets. Rail lines brought in more immigrants from the East to farm the land and work in cities, and enabled farmers to switch from subsistence agriculture to wheat and dairy farming for a cash profit. Railroads brought more and cheaper goods into towns, which in turn drew more buyers. Markets for raw and finished goods such as lumber and furniture became more accessible (see *Timber*). Rail networks displaced older transportation systems such as plank roads and river systems. Major rivers and the Great Lakes were utilized to work in tandem with railroads; railroad companies commonly owned steamships and ferries.

Growth and decline of railroads. It took six years for rail lines to cross Wisconsin. In many cases, a lack of public financing and rivalries between communities for rail service turned each mile of laid track into a struggle. The acquisition of land and capital by railroads often led to a political drama fraught with corruption. When many of these railroads went bankrupt in the 1860s–1880s, hundreds of farmers were wiped out because they had mortgaged their farms to invest in them. Rail line construction declined during the Civil War, and then rebounded afterwards. State and federal land grants of over three million acres spurred the railroads to expand, and they soon extended into northern Wisconsin to haul timber and metal ores. Short lines were built to connect the major lines to local lumber yards, mines, and factories. From the 1860s to the 1880s, many small rail lines were consolidated into three major lines—the Chicago, Milwaukee and St. Paul (Milwaukee Road); the Chicago and North Western; and the Minneapolis, St. Paul and Sault Ste. Marie (Soo Line)—and also into smaller regional lines. Railroad construction peaked in Wisconsin in 1916; the miles of track have steadily declined since then. The depletion of timber and ore, competition from trucking, the switch to trucks and planes for carrying mail and packages, and growing reliance on the automobile and airplane for travel have caused railroads to become relics in many areas. Some cities have recently proposed new rail-based mass transit lines, much like the interurban lines that linked some Wisconsin cities in the early decades of the 20th century. Railroads may yet have a future in the transportation networks of Wisconsin.

The *Bob Ellis*

The "Bob Ellis" was the first train ever seen in Wisconsin, and the first locomotive of the Milwaukee and Mississippi Rail Road (one of the forerunners of the Milwaukee Road). Its first trip of five miles took place in November 1850. On February 25, 1851, it completed its first official run between Milwaukee and Waukesha.

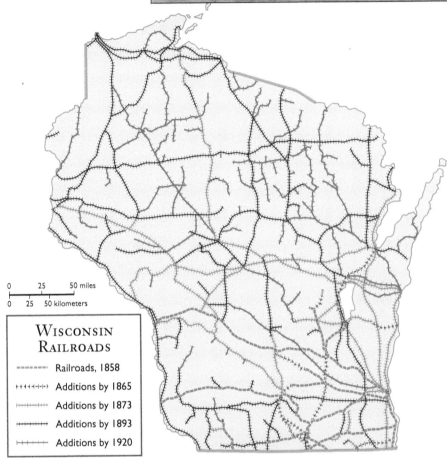

WISCONSIN RAILROADS

- ----------- Railroads, 1858
- ++++++++ Additions by 1865
- +++++++ Additions by 1873
- +++++++ Additions by 1893
- +++++++ Additions by 1920

State Highway 73 in Clark County in 1918 (above) and in 1938 (below).

Good Roads Movement

Early Wisconsin highways were often little more than cleared tracks in the countryside, maintained by local residents. In the 1890s a coalition of businessmen, progressive farm groups, university experts, engineers, and bicyclists formed the "Good Roads Movement." It campaigned for over a decade for a state-financed highway system. The primary obstacle was the resistance of rural residents who did not see the advantages of better roads and feared an increase in taxes. Much of the Good Road Movement's energy was devoted to convincing farmers that they would be better off with state-financed roads. It stressed positive aspects of public roads, such as reducing shipping costs, preventing milk spoilage, consolidating schools, and improving mail service and community life. A good economy and pressure from the Good Roads Movement and automobile owners enabled the constitutional amendment for state-funded roads to pass in 1908. State funding of highways began in 1911 when the State Aid Road Law was enacted—the first step in creating Wisconsin's highway network.

Southeastern Wisconsin Industries

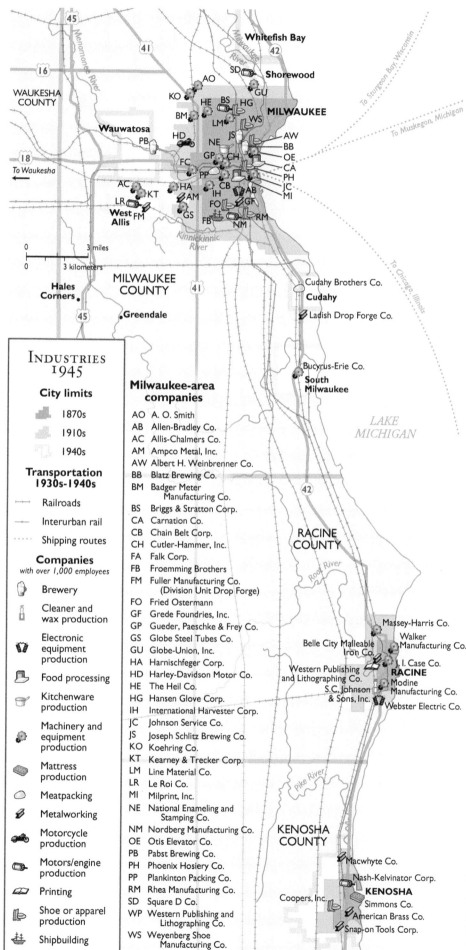

Milwaukee-area companies

AO A. O. Smith
AB Allen-Bradley Co.
AC Allis-Chalmers Co.
AM Ampco Metal, Inc.
AW Albert H. Weinbrenner Co.
BB Blatz Brewing Co.
BM Badger Meter Manufacturing Co.
BS Briggs & Stratton Corp.
CA Carnation Co.
CB Chain Belt Corp.
CH Cutler-Hammer, Inc.
FA Falk Corp.
FB Froemming Brothers
FM Fuller Manufacturing Co. (Division Unit Drop Forge)
FO Fried Ostermann
GF Grede Foundries, Inc.
GP Gueder, Paeschke & Frey Co.
GS Globe Steel Tubes Co.
GU Globe-Union, Inc.
HA Harnischfeger Corp.
HD Harley-Davidson Motor Co.
HE The Heil Co.
HG Hansen Glove Corp.
IH International Harvester Corp.
JC Johnson Service Co.
JS Joseph Schlitz Brewing Co.
KO Koehring Co.
KT Kearney & Trecker Corp.
LM Line Material Co.
LR Le Roi Co.
MI Milprint, Inc.
NE National Enameling and Stamping Co.
NM Nordberg Manufacturing Co.
OE Otis Elevator Co.
PB Pabst Brewing Co.
PH Phoenix Hosiery Co.
PP Plankinton Packing Co.
RM Rhea Manufacturing Co.
SD Square D Co.
WP Western Publishing and Lithographing Co.
WS Weyenberg Shoe Manufacturing Co.

The southeastern Wisconsin cities of Milwaukee, Racine, and Kenosha were founded in the 1830s as Americans advanced westward and European immigrants joined them. Settlers and townsite developers understood the trade and industrial possibilities offered by good harbors at the mouths of rivers giving access to inland farmland and timber (see map at left). The relatively flat topography of southern and central Wisconsin facilitated shipping to the ports, and the Great Lakes provided a corridor to urban markets. Industries expanded quickly because of the availability of raw materials around the Upper Great Lakes and the influx of both skilled and unskilled immigrant workers from the 1840s to the 1910s.

Early Milwaukee. With a protected harbor at the confluence of three waterways—the Menomonee River, the Milwaukee River, and Kinnickinnic River—the site of Milwaukee offered a natural economic advantage. In the 1830s developers established the town sites of Kilbourntown and Juneautown near the mouth of the Milwaukee River. The towns were united as Milwaukee in 1835, but retained their distinct identities and bitter rivalries as the East Ward and West Ward, respectively. The earliest industries were established along the waterways, with some light manufacturing concentrated on the lower east side. In the 1870s, the Menomonee River valley became a major center for lumber, brick, and coal yards. Milwaukee was 90 miles closer than Chicago to eastern U.S. markets via Great Lakes shipping routes (see *Great Lakes*), but the advent of cross-country rail service gave Chicago a primary economic position (see *Transportation*).

Agricultural links. Milwaukee became an early center for businesses and industries based on agricultural goods (see *Crops*). Milwaukee's flour mills flourished in the 1840s, and nearby barley fields fed a growing brewing industry (see column on facing page). In the 1860s, the city was for a short time the major flour-milling center in the Midwest. The many corn-fed hogs in southern Wisconsin gave rise to a meatpacking industry, which expanded during the Civil War. Tamarack trees around area marshes provided bark essential for tanning leather (from the hides of pigs, cattle, and deer), and tanning companies like Pfister and Vogel were founded. The city was the world's largest tanning center by 1872. In the 1860s New England investors and entrepreneurs developed an apparel industry specializing in men's clothing (often made from local wool) and leather boots and shoes. It grew during the Civil War by making uniforms, and by 1890 employed the city's largest labor force, including home-based workers.

Iron and steel. Milwaukee's metalworking industry began in the 1860s with the founding of the Milwaukee Iron Company in the Bay View neighborhood. Using iron and coal from mines around the Great Lakes region (see *Mining*), the company supplied the expanding railroad network with iron rails. By 1873 it was one of the city's largest employers and one of the country's most significant

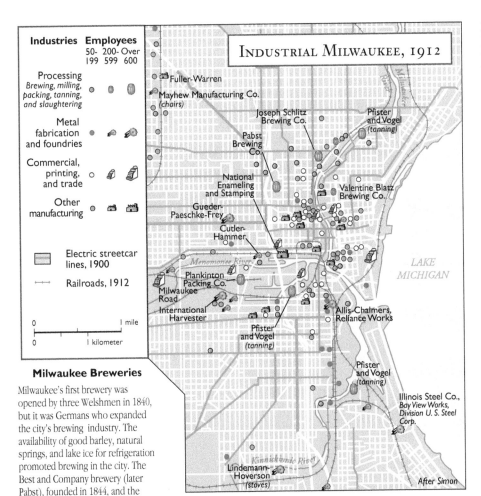

INDUSTRIAL MILWAUKEE, 1912

Industries	Employees		
	50-199	200-599	Over 600
Processing *Brewing, milling, packing, tanning, and slaughtering*	○	◑	◉
Metal fabrication and foundries	●	⬟	⬢
Commercial, printing, and trade	○	▨	▥
Other manufacturing	○	▦	▩

▭ Electric streetcar lines, 1900

†—† Railroads, 1912

0 — 1 mile
0 — 1 kilometer

Map labels:
- Fuller-Warren
- Mayhew Manufacturing Co. (*chairs*)
- Joseph Schlitz Brewing Co.
- Pabst Brewing Co.
- Pfister and Vogel (*tanning*)
- National Enameling and Stamping
- Valentine Blatz Brewing Co.
- Gueder-Paeschke-Frey
- Cutler-Hammer
- *Menomonee River*
- *LAKE MICHIGAN*
- Plankinton Packing Co.
- Milwaukee Road
- International Harvester
- Pfister and Vogel (*tanning*)
- Allis-Chalmers, Reliance Works
- Pfister and Vogel (*tanning*)
- Illinois Steel Co., Bay View Works, Division U. S. Steel Corp.
- *Kinnickinnic River*
- Lindemann-Hoverson (*stoves*)
- *After Simon*

Milwaukee Breweries

Milwaukee's first brewery was opened by three Welshmen in 1840, but it was Germans who expanded the city's brewing industry. The availability of good barley, natural springs, and lake ice for refrigeration promoted brewing in the city. The Best and Company brewery (later Pabst), founded in 1844, and the Joseph Schlitz Brewing Company, founded in 1849, emerged as industry leaders. The Miller Brewing Company began as a smaller operation, but expanded in the 1850s (see photo below). The 1871 Great Chicago Fire destroyed that city's breweries and gave Milwaukee the chance to gain a foothold in a wider market, fostering greater national distribution and advertising. By 1874, Best (Pabst) had become the nation's largest brewer; it kept that position for 25 years. Milwaukee brewers stayed on top of the industry by solving problems of uneven beer quality. Early brewers had dug caves in nearby bluffs to cool their product but later used refrigeration to regulate beer temperature. Milwaukeeans were the first to apply the pasteurization process to beer and to use the bottle cap, so they could ship their product to a larger market. Breweries declined temporarily during the Prohibition Era of 1919–33, producing cheese products and soft drinks instead. Since the 1960s, breweries, like other industries, have faced mergers and closings, and are being challenged by regional brands and "microbreweries."

ironworks. Foundries and metal fabricating plants that grew after the 1880s—such as the Cream City Iron Works, Milwaukee Harvester Company, and Harnischfeger Corporation—produced diversified machinery, milling machines, farming and mining equipment, tools, and implements. The Edward P. Allis Company built a large steam engine firm on Milwaukee's South Side in 1860, to provide equipment to sawmills and flour mills. A local businessman boasted in 1892 that Milwaukee had "the world's biggest iron foundry, the largest tannery, the largest brewery, and manufactures the biggest engines." By 1910, metal production and fabrication were employing the city's fourth-largest workforce.

Industrial growth and influence. In Milwaukee, dramatic growth in heavy manufacturing led to the development of industrial areas along the riverbanks and the Lake Michigan shoreline to the south. In the 1880s–1890s, industries began to move away from Milwaukee's central city core and establish industrial wards with distinct ethnic flavors. Firms such as the meatpacking company Patrick Cudahy and the industrial equipment manufacturer Bucyrus Company of Ohio (later Bucyrus-Erie) provided housing for their workers, and sold land for homesteads. Cudahy donated land to the Catholic Church to stimulate

Polish settlement (see *Ethnic Milwaukee*). The Edward P. Allis Company (later Allis-Chalmers) moved to the western outskirts and founded the community of West Allis. The Wisconsin Bridge and Iron Company provided a settlement site in north Milwaukee. The manufacturing industries of Milwaukee and the rest of southeastern Wisconsin adapted well to the production of equipment for mechanized warfare in the two world wars (see *Military*).

Racine and Kenosha. The major advantages of Racine and Kenosha as manufacturing centers were related to their location between Chicago and Milwaukee. Both were founded in the 1830s because of their potential as shipping ports, but the railroad proved to be a greater boon for industrial development after the 1850s. Even though Racine grew more rapidly from 1890 to 1920, both cities emerged as major manufacturing centers, drawing large numbers of immigrant workers (see *European Immigration*). In 1920, Racine and Kenosha ranked second and third behind Milwaukee in state manufacturing output and employment (and kept their ranking into the post–World War II years). The agricultural implement firm J. I. Case was Racine's largest employer from the 1860s to the 1970s. Like other Racine industries that extended into nearby towns, Case also opened a plant in Mount Pleasant Township. Racine's electrical machinery industry expanded rapidly from 1910 to 1950 and became a major employer. The city's early auto-related firms faced increased competition from Detroit and were largely gone by 1930. In contrast to Racine's extensive growth, Kenosha's growth was concentrated in its city center. Kenosha manufacturing was dominated by the bedding firm Simmons Company and by Nash Motors (later American Motors Corporation, or AMC). The two companies accounted for over half of Kenosha manufacturing employment from 1920 into the 1950s. The 1959 departure of Simmons was countered by the expansion of AMC. The 1988 closing of the former AMC auto assembly operations by its new owner, Chrysler Corporation, caused the loss of many jobs, but the city was able to develop a more diversified economic base less reliant on one or two large employers. In recent decades many northern Illinois residents have moved to Kenosha and commute by car or train to work in nearby Chicago and its suburbs.

1950s–present. Reliant on heavy manufacturing, southeastern Wisconsin industries did not adapt well to the Cold War defense industry of the 1950s–1980s, which was based largely on aerospace and high technology. The 1960s were characterized by the merging of companies (often family-owned) into large corporations. Although the mergers were usually amiable, some were the result of hostile "takeovers." Out-of-state corporations bought up some southeastern Wisconsin companies such as Allen-Bradley, Miller, Pabst, and Schlitz. But other southeastern Wisconsin firms such as Allis-Chalmers, Bucyrus-Erie, Johnson Controls, and A.O. Smith expanded by buying out other companies. Although from the 1970s to the 1990s some area firms closed certain operations and moved them to nonunion regions of the United States or lower-wage countries such as Mexico or China (see *Labor*), southeastern Wisconsin continues to be a national manufacturing center, and is moving toward high-technology and service industries.

Growth of the Fox Valley

The history of the Fox River Valley has been shaped largely by its location. The Fox River is a major waterway with excellent potential as a transportation route and power source. The river also lies at the intersection of agricultural and timber lands. It was once an "expressway" from the Great Lakes to the Wisconsin and Mississippi rivers. Its strong current began to provide power to a belt of industries in the 1800s. Today, Fox Valley cities are an important part of the U.S. paper industry.

Early settlement. The people who first lived in the area—including the Menominee, Ho-Chunk, Sauk, Meskwaki (Fox), Odawa (Ottawa), and Potawatomi—valued the Fox River highly as a trade route. After the French arrived in the 1630s, some Native American villages became sites for fur-trading posts and forts (see *Encounters*). Villagers gave some lands to French Canadian traders, who divided them into French-style "long lots"—narrow strips with one end at the river—so each settler would have shore frontage (see map on facing page). Yankee businessmen soon began to recognize the value of milling and woodworking in the area (see *Anglo-Americans*). They bought up land around the posts and forts for real estate speculation, displacing many French and Native American residents.

Water transportation. The Great Lakes were linked by the Erie Canal to the East Coast in 1825. Planners soon envisioned the Fox-Wisconsin waterway as a link to the Mississippi River and Gulf of Mexico. A few began to see Green Bay or Oshkosh as potential rivals to Chicago as the main Great Lakes port (Chicago won by linking Lake Michigan to the Illinois River in 1848). In the 1850s, the Fox and Wisconsin Improvement Company built locks and dams on the Fox, and completed a canal to the Wisconsin at Portage. The shallow upper Fox could be dredged satisfactorily only as far as Berlin, however, and sandbars made navigation undependable on the

Wisconsin. Although steamboats traveled the Fox-Wisconsin waterway for decades, they were not as reliable or cheap as railroads (see *Transportation*). New dams on the lower Fox laid the groundwork for more industrial development, by allowing the river's power to be harnessed (see lock diagram below).

Flour mills. The first industry to make use of this enormous water power was flour milling, centered in Neenah-Menasha. River transportation and new railroads brought grain to the mills, then took flour to distant markets. As wheat farming began to shift westward out of Wisconsin in the 1860s, the state's flour mills also declined (see *Crops*). The Fox River Valley remained a major regional player in agriculture, however, particularly in cheesemaking (see *Dairyland*). The valley's meatpacking industry expanded into the 1900s, and its "packers" gave their name to a Green Bay football team (see *Cultural Figures*).

Green Bay/Ashwaubenon

Procter & Gamble Paper Prods. 1892
Straubel Paper Co. 1907
Little Rapids Corp. 1926
Erving Paper Products 1928
Green Bay Packaging, Inc. 1933
Renard Machine Co. 1955
Fox Converting, Inc. 1962
Perini America, Inc. 1978
Wisconsin Converting, Inc. 1987
Fort James Corp. 1997
formerly Fort Howard Corp. 1919
and James River Corp. 1969

Appleton/Little Chute

Appleton Mills 1881
Fox River Paper Co. 1883
Valmet-Appleton, Inc. 1883
Asten Forming Fabrics, Inc. 1893
Pacon Corp. 1893
Riverside Paper Corporation 1893
Appleton Papers, Inc. 1906
B & J Supply, Inc. 1968
CBC Coating 1978
U. S. Paper Converters 1983
G & S Machine Co. 1986
Sulpaco West, Inc. 1990

De Pere

International Paper Co./
Nicolet Paper Co. 1892
Nekoosa Corp. 1918
U. S. Paper Mills Corp. 1971
Fox River Fiber Co. 1992

N

The Lower Fox River

The Fox is one of the few rivers in the U.S. that flow north. From its origin east of Portage to Lake Winnebago, the upper Fox flows slowly, often through wetlands. On its journey from Lake Winnebago to Green Bay, the lower Fox has a stronger and more dependable flow of water, ideal for water transportation and water power. The volume of water in the 215-square-mile lake increases the current of the lower Fox. Over a course of more than 40 miles, the river drops 170 feet—nearly the height of Niagara Falls (see diagram below). The power of its falls and rapids was harnessed by wheel mills in the 1830s, and by dams beginning in the 1850s. The dams were built with lock systems, to enable boats to travel the river. In 1882, the dams provided the power to operate the world's first hydroelectric central station in Appleton. The power of the river provided the fuel for the region's rapid industrial growth. Much as the Rhine River provided power for western Germany's larger-scale industrial boom in the same era, the Fox River helped industrialize east-central Wisconsin.

Kaukauna

International Paper Co./Thilmany 1883

Kimberly

Appleton Speciality Products, Inc. 1972
Inter Lake Papers, Inc. 1976

Neenah

Menasha Corp. 1849
P. H. Glatfelter Co. 1864
Kimberly, Clark & Co. 1872
J. J. Plank Corp. 1893
Gilbert & Nash Co., Inc. 1898
American National Can Co. 1901
Wisconsin Tissue Mills 1915
Atlas Tag & Label, Inc. 1931
Beloit Manhattan Division 1932
Bemiss-Jason Corp. 1934
Spencer-Johnston Co. 1960
James River Corp. 1969
Laminations Corp. 1972
Outlook Label Systems 1978
American Papers Converters 1979
Dunsirn Industries 1987

Menasha

Geo. A. Whiting Paper Co. 1882
Gilbert Paper Co. 1887
Appleton Wire, Inc. 1895
division of Albany International
Wisconsin Tissue Mills 1915
U.S. Paper Mills Corp. 1939
Great Northern Corporation 1962
Fort James Corp. 1997
formerly James River plant:
merged with Fort Howard
Corp. in 1997

Oshkosh

Georgia-Pacific Corp. 1927
Godshall Paper Box Co. 1930
Ponderosa Pulp Products, Inc. 1971
International Paper Co./Pluswood 1942

0   5 miles

0   5 kilometers

Kimberly-Clark paper mill,
Neenah, 1922

Neenah and Menasha

In the 1870 bird's-eye view below,
the twin cities of Neenah (background) and Menasha (foreground)
are divided by the lower Fox River
where it widens into Little Lake
Buttes des Mortes (not to be confused
with Lake Buttes des Morts on the
upper Fox River). The two communities were also divided by economic
standing—one reason they never
united as a single city. Neenah was
first known as the "flour city"
because of its flour mills along the
river. It later reflected the enormous
wealth generated by the paper industry. Besides Milwaukee, Neenah was
the only state city listed in the
Chicago Social Register. Its yacht
club (founded in 1874) was patronized
by mill owners and other wealthy
residents. By the 1880s, elegant
Victorian residences had been built
along "Park Row." Fewer mill owners
and more mill workers lived across
the river in Menasha. Because of
their economic differences, the two
cities developed a rivalry that continues today. The two communities,
however, have sometimes pulled
together to face the competition
from other Fox Valley cities.

Early paper mills. With the decline in flour production,
the flour industry turned to milling paper. At that
time, paper was made from rags. The Neenah Paper
Company set up one of the earliest Fox Valley paper
mills in 1866. Other new industries quickly fed the
growth in paper. A woolen mill in Appleton provided
felts for papermaking, and foundries and machine
shops made mill equipment. The increasing demand
for newspapers after the Civil War, and the 1869
invention of the first workable typewriter (by
Wisconsin legislator C. Latham Sholes), aided the
phenomenal expansion of the paper industry.

Pulp paper mills. New chemical processes began to
make wood pulp a major ingredient in paper in the
1870s. The Fox River was ideally situated downstream
from some of the country's largest timber stands (see
Timber). Lumberman John A. Kimberly founded a
company that led the development of the pulp paper
industry. Wisconsin forests supplied much of the
country's newsprint until the state's timber industry
declined in the early 1900s. Mills in Canada and the
southern U.S.—with access to cheaper timber—under-
cut the market in the 1910s and 1920s. The state's
paper firms survived by becoming experts in making
specialty and high-quality papers. By the early 1950s,
Wisconsin led the country in paper production. Today,
Fox River cities have a major place in the U.S. paper
industry, producing more than five million tons of
paper per year and employing over 50,000 people.

Paper mill pollution. The paper industry has always
needed clean water for processing, but ironically has
been known as a major water polluter. The public
began to address this dilemma in the 1920s, but little
changed. By the late 1950s, the industry accounted
for 80 percent of industrial waste in state waters. The
Fox was considered one of the country's 10 most
polluted rivers in the 1970s, and legislation was passed
to clean up the river (see *Environment*). The debate
continues today. Environmentalists say that contami-

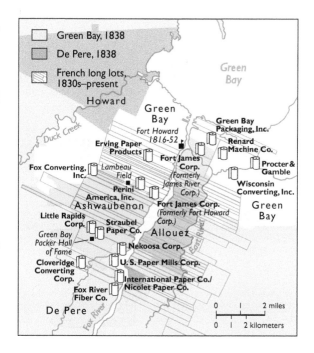

nants are still in the river, and have raised concerns
over waste sludge dumps and the chlorine used to
whiten paper. The paper industry says it is taking
voluntary initiatives to prevent water pollution and to
manage better the area forests that produce its wood.

Fox Valley today. The Fox Valley remains the
state's fastest-growing region and is still a hub of
transportation and power grids. Instead of moving on
riverboats, goods flow down U.S. Highway 41 or
Interstate 43. Instead of relying on hydro power,
industries use energy generated by coal and nuclear
plants. Instead of being only a means of water
transportation or power, the Fox River is a symbol of
modern industrial and environmental policy.
Wisconsin's agricultural, industrial, and natural
resource histories continue to converge in the Fox
River Valley.

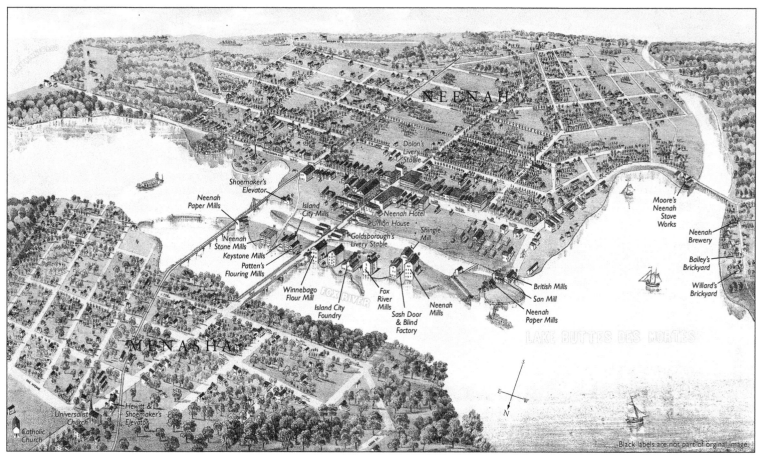

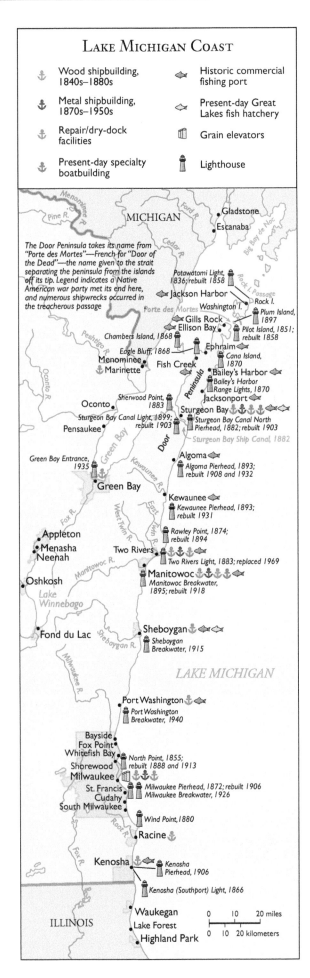

LAKE MICHIGAN COAST

⚓ Wood shipbuilding, 1840s–1880s

🐟 Historic commercial fishing port

⚓ Metal shipbuilding, 1870s–1950s

🐟 Present-day Great Lakes fish hatchery

⚓ Repair/dry-dock facilities

🏭 Grain elevators

⚓ Present-day specialty boatbuilding

🚨 Lighthouse

MICHIGAN

Menominee R.
Pine R.
Ford R.
Gladstone
Escanaba
Big Bay de Noc
Cedar R.

The Door Peninsula takes its name from "Porte des Mortes"—French for "Door of the Dead"—the name given to the strait separating the peninsula from the islands off its tip. Legend indicates a Native American war party met its end here, and numerous shipwrecks occurred in the treacherous passage

Potawatomi Light, 1836; rebuilt 1858
Jackson Harbor
Rock I. Passage
Rock I.
Porte des Mortes
Washington I.
Plum Island, 1897
Gills Rock
Ellison Bay
Pilot Island, 1851; rebuilt 1858
Chambers Island, 1868
Eagle Bluff, 1868
Ephraim
Cana Island, 1870
Menominee
Fish Creek
Peshtigo R.
Marinette
Bailey's Harbor
Bailey's Harbor Range Lights, 1870
Jacksonport
Oconto R.
Oconto
Sherwood Point, 1883
Sturgeon Bay
Pensaukee
Sturgeon Bay Canal Light, 1899; rebuilt 1903
Sturgeon Bay Canal North Pierhead, 1882; rebuilt 1903
Sturgeon Bay Ship Canal, 1882
Green Bay Entrance, 1935
Green Bay
Algoma
Algoma Pierhead, 1893; rebuilt 1908 and 1932
Kewaunee
Kewaunee Pierhead, 1893; rebuilt 1931
Fox R.
Appleton
Rawley Point, 1874; rebuilt 1894
Menasha
Neenah
West Twin R.
East Twin R.
Two Rivers
Two Rivers Light, 1883; replaced 1969
Oshkosh
Manitowoc R.
Manitowoc
Manitowoc Breakwater, 1895; rebuilt 1918
Lake Winnebago
Fond du Lac
Sheboygan R.
Sheboygan
Sheboygan Breakwater, 1915

LAKE MICHIGAN

Milwaukee R.
Port Washington
Port Washington Breakwater, 1940
Bayside
Fox Point
Whitefish Bay
North Point, 1855; rebuilt 1888 and 1913
Shorewood
Milwaukee
St. Francis
Cudahy
Milwaukee Pierhead, 1872; rebuilt 1906
Milwaukee Breakwater, 1926
South Milwaukee
Wind Point, 1880
Root R.
Racine
Kenosha
Kenosha Pierhead, 1906
Kenosha (Southport) Light, 1866
Fox R.
Waukegan
ILLINOIS
Lake Forest
Highland Park

0 10 20 miles
0 10 20 kilometers

From the past era of birchbark canoes to the modern era of enormous steel-hulled ships, the Great Lakes have afforded a unique advantage to Wisconsin. They have connected the people and resources of North America's interior to the rest of the continent and the world beyond. The Great Lakes have brought settlers and goods to the state and carried raw materials and manufactured goods to the world.

Lake Michigan. As settlers cultivated Wisconsin's prairies and forests, Milwaukee became a primary transshipment point for wheat and flour. The construction of grain elevators in the 1850s, rail links to wheat-producing areas, and the demand for grain in the Civil War enabled the city to vastly increase its trade. By 1862 Milwaukee was the leading wheat market in the world, but it was later eclipsed by Chicago. The port cities of Manitowoc, Racine, Sheboygan, and Green Bay also developed a minor role in the grain trade, which declined as the "wheat frontier" moved west out of the state (see *Crops*).

Primary ports. Competition with Chicago has been a recurring theme for Wisconsin's Lake Michigan ports. From the 1850s through the 1870s, the state and its port cities made harbor improvements and petitioned Congress to build lighthouses, range lights, and other navigation aids. Rail lines were not established north of Milwaukee along the Lake Michigan shore until the late 1860s. Chicago's earlier rail connections to the eastern seaboard, and its proximity to wheat, corn, and livestock production, enabled it to become Lake Michigan's primary port. Plans to develop the port of Green Bay as the "Chicago of the North" did not come to fruition (see *Fox Valley*). Green Bay did, however, become an important lumber port (see *Timber*), and today remains the primary manufacturing and distribution center in northeastern Wisconsin.

Shipping technology. The first true ship to navigate the Great Lakes was the *Griffon*, built in 1679 for French fur trader René-Robert Cavelier, Sieur de la Salle (see *Encounters*). In the 1830s and 1840s, wooden sailing schooners became the primary means of shipping. By the 1900s sailing vessels had completely given way to steam-powered vessels and metal ships, which were better suited to transport large volumes of cargo.

Shipbuilding. Wisconsin's ports were well suited for shipbuilding because of their protected lakeshore harbors and the availability of timber. As the demand for trade vessels increased, the shipyards of Milwaukee, Manitowoc, Two Rivers, and Sturgeon Bay built numerous fishing boats, scows, and schooners from the 1830s to the 1880s. In the 1870s and 1880s, shipbuilders began making steam-powered vessels, and steel-hulled and iron-hulled ships. The last "sailing ship" built on the Great Lakes was constructed in 1889 in Manitowoc, for commercial trade.

Shipyard expansion. Commercial growth and new technology encouraged Lake Michigan and Lake

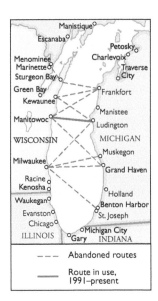

Manistique
Escanaba
Petosky
Menominee
Marinette
Charlevoix
Sturgeon Bay
Traverse City
Green Bay
Frankfort
Kewaunee
Manistee
Manitowoc
Ludington
WISCONSIN
MICHIGAN
Muskegon
Milwaukee
Grand Haven
Racine
Kenosha
Holland
Waukegan
Benton Harbor
Evanston
St. Joseph
Chicago
Michigan City
ILLINOIS
Gary
INDIANA

- - - Abandoned routes

—— Route in use, 1991–present

Lake Michigan Ferries

Even though Lake Michigan is an essential link for Great Lakes shipping, it is also a north-south barrier to the flow of land traffic between the east and west. Since the 1850s, Wisconsin and Michigan have used ferries to transport passengers and freight across this barrier. The first ferries—paddle vessels—carried grain and flour, primarily from Milwaukee to Muskegon and Grand Haven, Michigan. In the 1890s ferries began to transport loaded railcars across the lake, eliminating the need to transfer cargo at the ports. Numerous ferry lines operated from the 1910s to the 1970s. A decline in freight and passenger traffic, coupled with equipment failure and bankruptcy, had ended ferry service by the late 1980s. In 1991, however, the Lake Michigan Carferry began to serve summer tourists; it offers passenger and car ferry service between Manitowoc, Wisconsin, and Ludington, Michigan.

Lighthouses

Aids to navigation were important to Great Lakes trade and shipping. The Eagle Bluff Lighthouse (above) was constructed in 1868 to mark the east side of Strawberry Channel between the Door Peninsula and Chambers Island (see map at left). The lighthouse was automated in 1909, and is now a museum in Peninsula State Park.

Superior shipyards to expand their operations. By 1900 the shipyards of Superior constructed two-thirds of all new ships used on the upper Great Lakes. U.S. involvement in World War I (1917–18) and World War II (1941–45) led to construction of freighters, tugs, supply ships, minesweepers, tenders, and other vessels. The demand for ships dropped after 1945, and the costs of labor and materials rose. Many shipbuilders reduced their operations to dry-docking, repair work, and specialty boat construction.

Lake Superior exports. Modern shipping on Lake Superior really began in 1855 with the opening of the canal at Sault Ste. Marie that connected Lake Superior to the other Great Lakes. The Soo Locks were expanded five times over the next 110 years to accommodate increasingly larger ships. Duluth–Superior became the leading grain port in the 1870s, as the wheat frontier pushed westward out of Wisconsin into Minnesota and Dakota Territory. The primary cargo of Wisconsin's northern ports soon became iron ore. From the 1880s to the 1900s ore mining expanded in the Gogebic Range in Wisconsin and Michigan (see *Mining*), and the Mesabi, Vermilion, and Cuyuna Ranges in Minnesota. Enormous ore docks were constructed in Duluth, Superior, and Ashland for shipping the ore to steel mills and manufacturing plants (see map at right below). By the 1930s, the Lake Superior ranges were producing two-thirds of the world's iron ore, which along with coal and limestone was the critical ingredient in steelmaking. Ore shipping peaked in the 1950s, and then declined because of the exhaustion of local iron deposits and the growth of iron mining abroad. Grain again became the primary cargo at Duluth–Superior, particularly after wheat shipments to the Soviet Union increased in the 1970s.

Imports. Besides shipping out iron ore and grain, Wisconsin's ports brought in goods crucial to western expansion and settlement. These included manufactured iron products for railroad construction, coal for fueling train locomotives and generating electricity, and limestone used in cement, fertilizer, asphalt, and other industrial products.

Commercial fishing. The Great Lakes' rich fishing grounds initially enticed Native American and American settlers to the "inland sea." As the fur trade declined in the 1830s, a few fur-trade companies turned to fishing operations, and shipped their catch eastward. A modest commercial fishing industry grew throughout the 19th century, particularly in the Bayfield–Apostle Islands region, the Door Peninsula, and the Manitowoc–Two Rivers area. These areas had excellent natural harbors, little industrial development, and bountiful whitefish, herring, and lake trout. Wisconsin's fishing industry has steadily declined since the 1930s because of overfishing, the invasion of exotic species (such as the sea lamprey), and industrial development and pollution (see *Environment*). Since the 1950s, Wisconsin has worked with other Great Lakes states and Canada in exotic species control, environmental regulation, and fish restocking programs. Today, Wisconsin's Great Lakes ports retain their attraction for recreational fishing and boating.

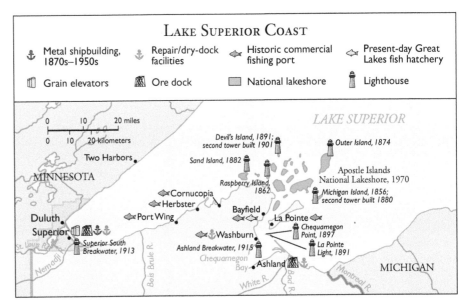

As the production of iron ore increased, existing schooners and steamers could not handle the volume of the trade. In 1889, ship designer Andrew McDougall developed the "whaleback" specifically for hauling iron ore. The shipyards of Superior constructed and launched more than 40 of these unique ships between 1889 and 1898.

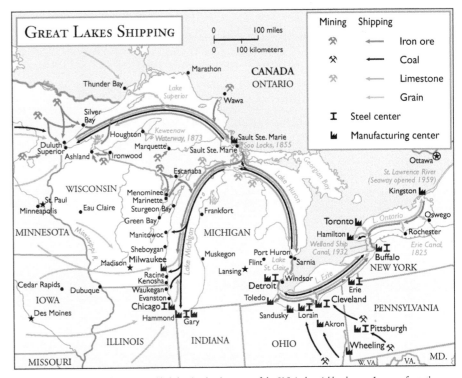

The Great Lakes provided an essential link for the development of the U.S. industrial landscape. Iron ore from the Lake Superior region and coal from Appalachia were essential in making steel. They fed enormous steel mills and manufacturing sites in New York, Pennsylvania, Ohio, Indiana, Michigan, Illinois, and Wisconsin. Limestone (mainly quarried in Michigan) was also needed for steel manufacturing and remains an important industrial material. Today, the pure magnetite and hematite iron ores have been exhausted but low-grade "taconite" is still processed and shipped. Grain from the Great Plains and low-sulfur coal from the western states are also important commodities in the Great Lakes global network.

Impacts on Wisconsin's Environment

Wisconsin has always been at the forefront of U.S. environmentalism—because of its diverse land use and industries and its progressive political traditions. As early as the 1850s, there was concern about such threats to public health as sewage, fish kills, and outbreaks of typhoid and black lung. Concerns over wasteful logging practices arose in the 1860s (see *Timber*). The Board of Health began investigating water pollution in 1911, and in 1915 the state formed a conservation commission to oversee fish, game, forests, and parks.

In the early 1900s, attempts began to reforest the Cutover District and control soil erosion (see *Rural Society*). The timber industry opposed power dams, which interfered with downriver shipment of cut logs. One of the first priorities of the 1960s environmental movement was to prevent the construction of dams (see *Weather Hazards*); it was able to secure protection for some wild and scenic rivers. Later on, Democratic Senator Gaylord A. Nelson (the founder of Earth Day in 1970) and Republican Governor

Warren Knowles led successful state efforts to curb paper mill and urban runoff pollution and to institute resource planning and environmental management. Among their strongest backers were sportsmen, who worked through their clubs and the Conservation Congress to enhance fish and game populations. In 1967, state departments of conservation and resource development combined to form the Department of Natural Resources (DNR).

In the 1970s, Wisconsin was the first state to focus on DDT's harm to bird reproduction—leading to a 1972 national ban on the pesticide. Other pesticides, such as Aldicarb (for potatoes) and Atrazine (for corn), continued to contaminate wells into the 1990s. Phosphate detergents killed many fish, and industry-generated toxic wastes such as polychlorinated biphenyls (PCBs), made some fish unsafe to eat (see purple waterways on facing page). The energy industry also became a primary concern of environmentalists. The burning of coal released sulfur dioxide that (along with other gasses) created acid rain. Northern

John Muir (1838–1914) is considered the founder of the "preservationist" wing of the environmental movement. He came from Scotland with his family at the age of 11, and lived on a farm on Fountain (Ennis) Lake in Marquette County. At age 22, he exhibited his wooden mechanical inventions at the state Agricultural Fair, and then enrolled in the university. Later, after five years of traveling, he settled in California's Sierra Nevada in 1868 and developed a reputation as a naturalist and writer. Muir's advocacy of a mystical vision of "wilderness" led to the establishment of Yosemite National Park and the Sierra Club. His efforts helped to expand the national park system and protect Yosemite from a proposed dam. Though often associated with the protection of western lands, Muir was strongly influenced by his Wisconsin boyhood. "When we try to pick out anything by itself," he wrote, "we find it hitched to everything in the universe."

Drainage and flooding have eliminated most wetlands in Wisconsin. A 1940 air photo (above left) shows Rowan Creek and Lake Wisconsin, in the Columbia County township of Dekorra, surrounded by wetlands (outlined in blue). By 1968 drainage ditches had converted most of the wetlands to farmland (above right). Once viewed as "swamps," wetlands are today recognized as important for wildlife habitat, flood control, and filtration of contaminants in the water.

Aldo Leopold (1887–1948), a wildlife ecologist and sportsman, was a key figure in modern conservationism. Born in Iowa and educated at Yale, Leopold joined the U.S. Forest Service in the Southwest, where he founded the first forest wilderness area. He moved to Madison to work at the Forest Products Laboratory. In the 1930s, he wrote a book on game management, and became the first chair of the U.W. Department of Game Management. He applied his ecological principles to an abandoned farm in Sauk County. A year after he died fighting a grass fire, his *A Sand County Almanac* was published. It was later recognized as a classic of ecological philosophy. In Leopold's words, "a land ethic changes the role of *Homo sapiens* from conqueror of the land-community to plain member and citizen of it."

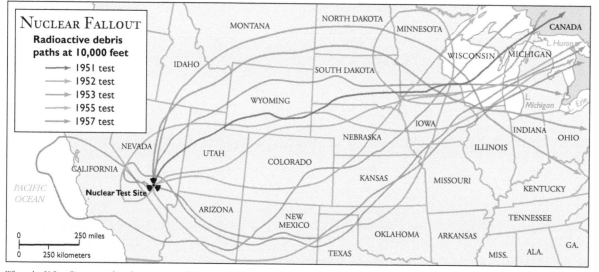

NUCLEAR FALLOUT

Radioactive debris paths at 10,000 feet

→ 1951 test
→ 1952 test
→ 1953 test
→ 1955 test
→ 1957 test

When the U.S. military tested nuclear weapons aboveground in Nevada early in the Cold War, some of the radioactive fallout drifted to Wisconsin. This map shows some of the paths along which atmospheric debris entered the state. Some of the earliest expressions of concern over fallout came from dairy farmers. The radioactive isotope strontium 90 resembles calcium in its chemical structure and so concentrates in milk. In 1956, the Atomic Energy Agency admitted that contaminated milk was the main source of strontium 90 contamination in food and could cause bone cancer. Fallout radiation that was concentrated in wetlands and mosses was passed to humans through venison. Wisconsinites helped lead public support for the 1963 Atmospheric Nuclear Test Ban Treaty, which moved U.S. and Soviet testing underground. Global testing, however, continued to spread fallout until it was curtailed in the 1990s.

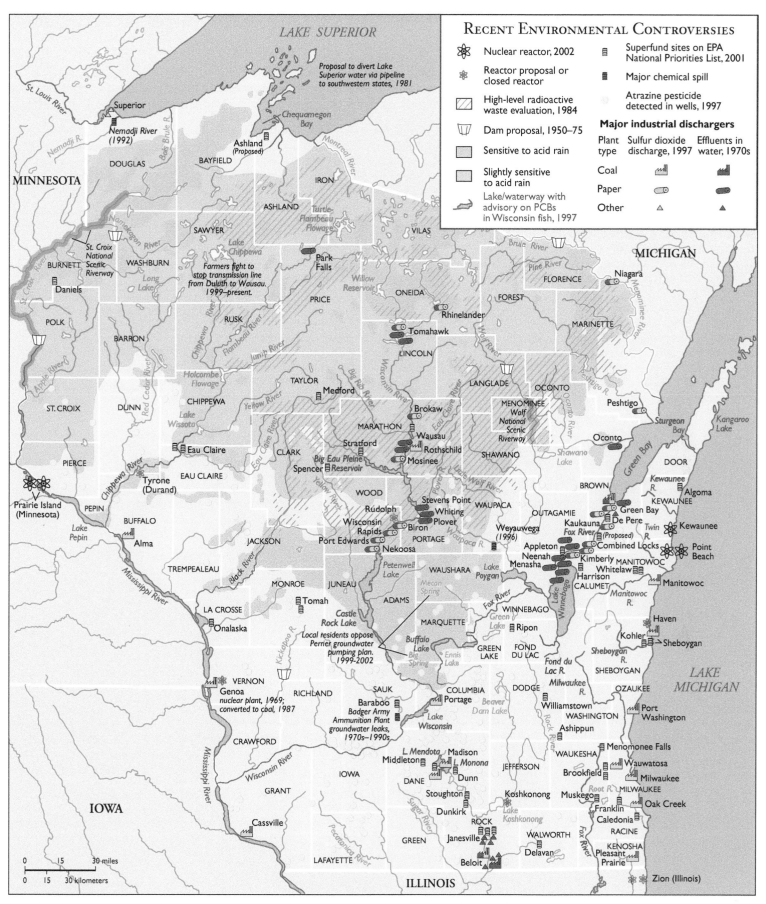

RECENT ENVIRONMENTAL CONTROVERSIES

- ⚛ Nuclear reactor, 2002
- ✳ Reactor proposal or closed reactor
- ▧ High-level radioactive waste evaluation, 1984
- ⛢ Dam proposal, 1950–75
- ▨ Sensitive to acid rain
- ▨ Slightly sensitive to acid rain
- ∿ Lake/waterway with advisory on PCBs in Wisconsin fish, 1997
- ▤ Superfund sites on EPA National Priorities List, 2001
- ▮ Major chemical spill
- ○ Atrazine pesticide detected in wells, 1997

Major industrial dischargers

Plant type	Sulfur dioxide discharge, 1997	Effluents in water, 1970s
Coal	⛰	⌂
Paper	⬭	⬬
Other	△	▲

LAKE SUPERIOR

Proposal to divert Lake Superior water via pipeline to southwestern states, 1981

St. Louis River

Superior

Nemadji River (1992)

Chequamegon Bay

Ashland (Proposed)

MINNESOTA

DOUGLAS — BAYFIELD — IRON

ASHLAND

SAWYER — Lake Chippewa

Turtle-Flambeau Flowage

VILAS

MICHIGAN

St. Croix National Scenic Riverway

BURNETT — WASHBURN

Daniels

Farmers fight to stop transmission line from Duluth to Wausau. 1999–present.

Park Falls

PRICE

Willow Reservoir

ONEIDA

Rhinelander

FOREST

FLORENCE

Niagara

MARINETTE

POLK — BARRON

Long Lake

RUSK

Flambeau River

Jump River

Tomahawk

LINCOLN

LANGLADE

OCONTO

Peshtigo

ST. CROIX — DUNN

TAYLOR

Medford

Brokaw

MENOMINEE Wolf National Scenic Riverway

SHAWANO

Sturgeon Bay

Kangaroo Lake

CHIPPEWA

Lake Wissota

MARATHON

Wausau

Stratford — Rothschild

Big Eau Pleine Reservoir

Mosinee

SHAWANO

Oconto

DOOR

PIERCE

Eau Claire

EAU CLAIRE

CLARK

Spencer

WOOD

Stevens Point

Whiting

Plover

WAUPACA

Weyauwega (1996)

OUTAGAMIE

Kaukauna

Fox River

Green Bay

De Pere

Kewaunee R.

Algoma

KEWAUNEE

Tyrone (Durand)

PEPIN

Prairie Island (Minnesota)

Lake Pepin

BUFFALO

Alma

Rudolph

Wisconsin Rapids

Biron

Port Edwards

Nekoosa

PORTAGE

Appleton

Neenah

Menasha

Kimberly

(Proposed)

Combined Locks

Point Beach

Kewaunee

JACKSON

TREMPEALEAU

Black River

MONROE

JUNEAU

Petenwell Lake

WAUSHARA

Mecan Spring

ADAMS

Lake Poygan

Fox River

Whitelaw

Harrison

CALUMET

MANITOWOC

Manitowoc R.

Manitowoc

Tomah

Castle Rock Lake

Local residents oppose Perrier groundwater pumping plan. 1999-2002

Buffalo Lake

Big Spring

Ennis Lake

MARQUETTE

WINNEBAGO

Lake Winnebago

Ripon

Green Lake

GREEN LAKE

FOND DU LAC

Fond du Lac R.

Haven

Kohler

Sheboygan

LA CROSSE

Onalaska

Kickapoo R.

VERNON

Genoa nuclear plant, 1969; converted to coal, 1987

RICHLAND

SAUK

Baraboo

Badger Army Ammunition Plant groundwater leaks, 1970s–1990s

COLUMBIA

Portage

Lake Wisconsin

DODGE

Beaver Dam Lake

Williamstown

Ashippun

SHEBOYGAN

Sheboygan R.

Port Washington

WASHINGTON

OZAUKEE

LAKE MICHIGAN

CRAWFORD

Mississippi River

Wisconsin River

IOWA

GRANT

L. Mendota — Madison

Middleton

L. Monona

Dunn

DANE

Stoughton

Dunkirk

Menomonee Falls

WAUKESHA

Brookfield

Wauwatosa

Milwaukee

MILWAUKEE

Muskego

Oak Creek

Cassville

GREEN

Janesville

ROCK

Koshkonong

Lake Koshkonong

WALWORTH

Delavan

Franklin

Caledonia

RACINE

Pleasant Prairie

KENOSHA

IOWA

Beloit

LAFAYETTE

ILLINOIS

Zion (Illinois)

0   15   30 miles
0   15   30 kilometers

Wisconsin soils could not neutralize acid rain, which contaminated many fishing lakes with mercury. Environmentalists also targeted nuclear plants and prevented the construction of new reactors. (At left, citizens protest the proposed Tyrone nuclear plant in 1973.) In the 1980s, they opposed the exploration of northern bedrock sites for a national high-level nuclear waste underground repository, and the construction of aboveground casks to store wastes from reactors. They joined farmers to stop high-voltage power lines (from coal and nuclear plants and dams), which they believed would harm human health and livestock.

Major concerns in the 1990s-2000s include urban sprawl, paper processing, mercury pollution, wetland and shoreland development, groundwater pumping, and mining (see *Mining*). Alliances of environmentalists, recreationists, wildlife groups, sports clubs, Native Americans, and farmers influence state environmental politics. Because of their efforts, Wisconsin remains a national environmental leader.

Tourism & Recreation

With its glacial lakes, scenic beauty, and location near large urban centers, Wisconsin is ideally situated to provide outdoor recreation and encourage tourism. One of the first resort centers in the Midwest developed in Wisconsin, and over the past 130 years the state's recreational industry has grown and changed dramatically. Tourism has shaped Wisconsin communities and landscapes, and has itself been shaped by technological, social, and environmental changes. These changes have created several different kinds of tourism that have overlapped in time, but yet all have enticed residents and visitors to spend their leisure time in Wisconsin.

Scenic tourism (1865–1915). After the Civil War, scenic spots that had been difficult to reach or explore were made more accessible by new railroads and passenger steamboats. Tourists from Chicago and Milwaukee could travel more easily to Wisconsin's "lake districts" to enjoy themselves on the water. Resorts and railroads marketed Wisconsin to wealthy urbanites as a healthy and scenic getaway from increasingly industrial cities. Some early tourist centers—such as Green Lake, Oconomowoc, Lake Geneva, and Door County—mainly drew elite tourists to exclusive resort hotels. Wisconsin's numerous circuses drew tourists and local people alike (see column at lower left). Other spots offered natural attractions, such as the mineral spring spas at Waukesha, or the rock

Circuses in Wisconsin

Wisconsin's first circus came in 1840 from New York state to Delavan, which remained the state circus capital through the 1870s. Other shows quickly followed, attracted partly by an ample supply of work horses, feed grain, and firewood. Circuses appealed to a largely European immigrant population. The Ringling Brothers made Baraboo a major circus center in the 1880s–1910s with their "World's Greatest Show." The era is remembered in the Circus World Museum (opened in 1959) and in an annual circus train excursion and Milwaukee parade.

The Chicago area (right) has long been the primary source of out-of-state tourists "escaping" to southern Wisconsin. In the 1910s Illinois tourists began to drive north, particularly to Door County and the "Lake Districts" of the Hayward area (Washburn and Sawyer counties) and the "Lakeland Area" (Vilas and Oneida counties). Today, attractions also include Milwaukee and the Madison area (including Wisconsin Dells and Spring Green).

Twin Cities-area tourists tend to visit the northwestern part of the state, including the Apple River and Bayfield Peninsula.

Legend

Over 1,000 Chicago tourists per average summer day, 1980s

Recreational housing units by county, 1990
- 0–2,000
- 2,000–4,000
- 4,000–6,000
- 6,000–8,000
- 8,000–12,000

70 County ranking for tourist spending, 1996

EARLY AND MODERN TOURISM

1840s–1920s
- Resort towns
- Historic circus towns

1920s–Present
- National Forest or wildlife refuge
- State Forest or reserve
- State park or recreation area
- State historic site
- 1927 Year established
- State or federal fish hatchery
- Trophy-potential fishing hot spots
- Scenic routes and trails
- Major highways
- Urban area and suburban extents

S.F. *State Forest*
N.W.R. *National Wildlife Refuge*
S.R.A. *State Recreation Area*

State parks in red type

0   15   30 miles
0   15   30 kilometers

Wisconsin Dells

The Dells of the Wisconsin River have been a major center for scenic tourism since 1873, when the first steamboats took sightseers to view the unusual rock formations. The map below, based on a map made by Charles Lapham around 1875, shows early tourist attractions. Promoters and railroad companies created an image of an "untouched" landscape, even though for years huge lumber rafts had floated down the Wisconsin River (see *Timber*). The stereographic photographs of H. H. Bennett helped transform the Dells into a natural "shrine," drawing visitors seeking inspiration. From the start, the area was a retreat for common people, with lower costs than elite resorts. By the early 1900s, 60,000 visitors a year visited Kilbourn City (renamed Wisconsin Dells in the 1930s). Promoters added Native American dances and folklore (see *Ho-Chunk*) to appeal to a growing interest in cultural tourism. After interstate highways improved access in the 1960s, entertainment tourism began appealing to children, with Disneyland-style amusement parks, and to adults, with shops, concerts, and golf courses. Today, the main attractions are based on water recreation and gambling, yet some tourists are still drawn by the natural and cultural appeal of the Dells.

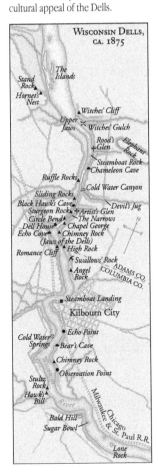

In 1933, Oneida County was the nation's first county to adopt a comprehensive rural zoning law, partly to keep the area forested and sparsely populated for tourism. At the time, the county mainly drew summer tourists and fishermen, and little land was used for private homes. However, while some private lands became part of state forests, more public lands were sold for private recreational use. *Small tracts*, or groups of vacation homes, grew in the 1950s (below). As snowmobiling and cross-country skiing grew in 1963–75, the number of winter lodging businesses increased from nine to 175. Small tracts expanded around area lakes into the 1990s. Tourism, which originally protected the county's rural character, now ironically alters the area by drawing new people and development.

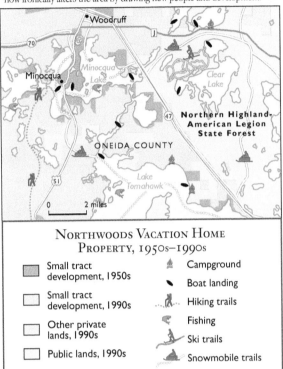

NORTHWOODS VACATION HOME PROPERTY, 1950s–1990s

- Small tract development, 1950s
- Small tract development, 1990s
- Other private lands, 1990s
- Public lands, 1990s
- Campground
- Boat landing
- Hiking trails
- Fishing
- Ski trails
- Snowmobile trails

formations at Wisconsin Dells (see column at left). Places like Devil's Lake and Wisconsin Dells drew both middle-class and working-class tourists for excursions and picnics.

Travel tourism (1915–45). The invention of the automobile and the construction of paved highways opened new areas to tourism (see *Transportation*). Tourists who drove could wander at their own pace (in what many called "gypsying") and spend the night in tents or roadside inns. Higher wages and a shorter work-week (see *Labor*) gave more people time and income for travel and recreation. Winter sports, always a favorite among the state's northern European population, also began to draw tourists, and were promoted by railroads that wanted to run their lines year-round. The new influx of tourist dollars came at just the right time for northern towns in the "Cutover District" as they tried to recover from the collapse of lumbering and their attempts at farming (see *Timber*). Northerners only gradually accepted the reforestation of former timber lands to create state and national forests. The forests attracted tourists and state residents who had begun to hunt and fish for sport, rather than just for food. Even during the Great Depression of the 1930s, the state promoted a string of new parks with the slogan "Relax in Wisconsin." The map on the facing page shows only state-owned tourist attractions; none of the hundreds of privately owned attractions is listed.

Cottage tourism (1945–75). The modern era of tourism was born out of the prosperous post–World War II era, the construction of multilane highways, and the transformation of Wisconsin's land and communities by recreation. Increased mobility meant that Chicagoans could drive to northern Wisconsin in

hours—a trip that had taken a day or more in the 1930s—and enjoy vacation homes or weekend cottages. Passenger train service ended, and new highways bypassed towns, which reinforced an impression of Wisconsin as primarily rural. Habitat preservation for hunting and fishing helped to transform the landscape into a patchwork of fields, woods, wetlands, and wildlife areas seldom matched elsewhere in the country. By the late 1950s tourism provided the primary source of income in much of Wisconsin, though mainly in the form of summer jobs. The state made more lands available for outdoor recreation in the 1960s, and the snowmobile (invented in Vilas County) vastly expanded winter tourism.

Weekend tourism (1975–present). Today, tourists take fewer long summer resort vacations, but have more weekend getaways. (With more women in the workforce, many families have to coordinate two vacation schedules.) Tourism and recreation continue to shape the landscape. Outdoor-exercise sports such as hiking, cross-country skiing, or bicycling—often on abandoned railroad beds—have increased support for public land preservation. Sentiment for preserving the "quaintness" of communities has also helped protect older architecture and "rustic roads," and promoted historical and cultural attractions like theaters and museums. Yet in other ways, such as the construction of lakefront homes, tourists' desire to enjoy nature may actually threaten it (see map at left). Wisconsin's unique blend of tourism and recreation continues to be a source of pride for its residents.

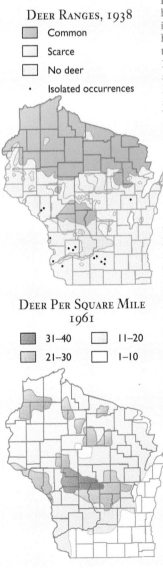

DEER RANGES, 1938

- Common
- Scarce
- No deer
- Isolated occurrences

DEER PER SQUARE MILE 1961

- 31–40
- 21–30
- 11–20
- 1–10

Deer hunting in Wisconsin has been affected by changes in the state's landscape, and has in turn helped to shape the landscape. In the mid-1800s, unrestricted hunting and the destruction of deer habitat reduced previously abundant herds in southern Wisconsin, until few deer were left in the area. But in northern Wisconsin, logging later created the type of "edge" habitat favorable for deer. By the 1930s, new conservation practices enabled deer herds in northern Wisconsin to expand to the point of overpopulation. In the 1940s, looser hunting regulations and the opening of more areas to hunting helped to decrease the northern deer population. Northern herds also began to dwindle because of the growth of thick forests that offered poor browsing. As farming declined in the central and southwestern counties in the 1960s, many residents permitted patches of forest to overtake former farmland. The resulting "edge" habitat, which permitted deer to feed on crops and find shelter in the woods, led to a rise in southern deer populations. The state's estimated 1962 autumn deer population of 500,000 tripled by 1995. Deer hunting, unlike fishing, which attracts many out-of-state visitors, is dominated by Wisconsin residents.

I had...absolute confidence in the people...it is a rare and exceptional people. The spirit of liberty stirring throughout Europe...gave us political refugees who were patriots and hardy peasants, seeking free government as well as homes...In every city and hamlet in the commonwealth are still living the last of these pioneers. And as a heritage to their children they are leaving the story of their oppression which forced them to abandon their native lands and intensified their devotion to self-government... To the character of the people of Wisconsin I attribute the progress which we were able to make...

—Robert M. La Follette
from
La Follette's Autobiography (1912)

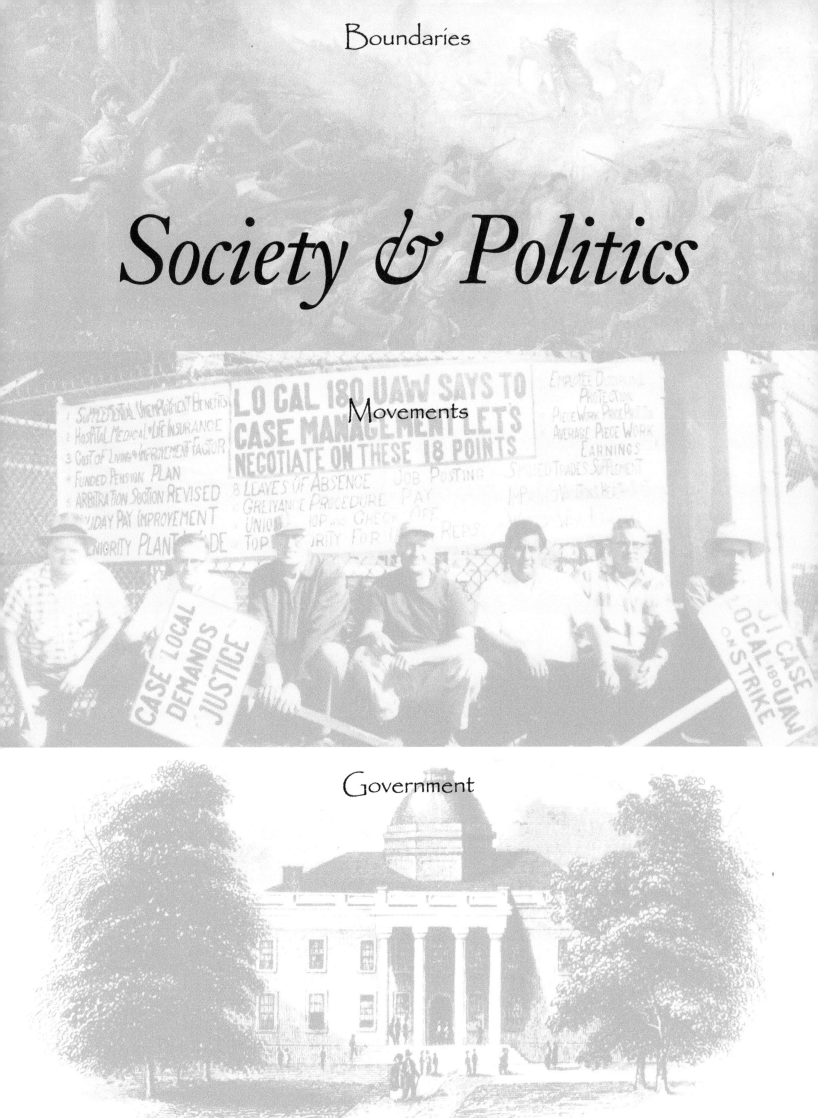

Boundaries

Society & Politics

Movements

Government

European Empires & Colonial Boundaries

Britain, France, and Spain had barely begun their struggle for control of North America when Jean Nicolet stepped ashore at what is commonly believed to be Red Banks, near Green Bay, in 1634. The area that was to become Wisconsin (outlined in gray on the three maps) would be in the French sphere of influence for over 100 years, until it was lost to Britain in 1763 (see *Encounters*). The struggle for empire in North America would lead to a series of wars (see timelines), with dramatic effects on Wisconsin. Shifts from French to British and finally to American control were carried out in a century of nearly continuous fighting among France, Britain, the U.S., and Native American nations.

New France. The French crown organized the royal colony of *Nouvelle-France* (New France) to exploit the fur trade and to counter British ambitions in the region. Unlike the British colonies, New France never became a destination for large-scale settlement. French settlers were too few in number to make a dramatic impact outside the Saint Lawrence River valley (see map at right). Dependent on resources from a king with frequently shifting priorities, and blocked from key western fur-trade routes by the Iroquois, the colony developed slowly.

Iroquois Wars. The British-allied Iroquois Confederacy was determined to gain control of the fur trade west of the Saint Lawrence. Starting in the 1640s, it attacked neighboring tribes, forcing them to flee westward. The massive disruptions had a domino effect stretching into the Great Lakes region. A mixed group of these refugees settled on Washington Island. In 1653, a large party of Iroquois

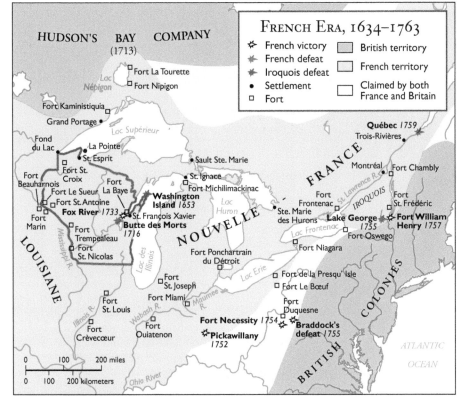

FRENCH ERA, 1634–1763
- ✳ French victory
- ✴ French defeat
- ✴ Iroquois defeat
- • Settlement
- ▫ Fort
- ▢ British territory
- ▢ French territory
- ▢ Claimed by both France and Britain

Flags of the Eras

In order on both timelines: The *Fleur-de-lis* was used by the French in North America. The British *Red Ensign* was in use until 1801. The *Grand Union* flag was used by American rebels in the Revolution. After the War of 1812, the U.S. flag had 15 stars and stripes.

BRITISH ERA, 1763–1775
- ▢ British territory
- ▢ Territory ceded to Britain in the Treaty of Paris, 1763
- ▢ French territory ceded to Spain, 1763
- ✳ British forts captured in Pontiac's Rebellion, 1763
- ✴ British victories in Pontiac's Rebellion, 1763

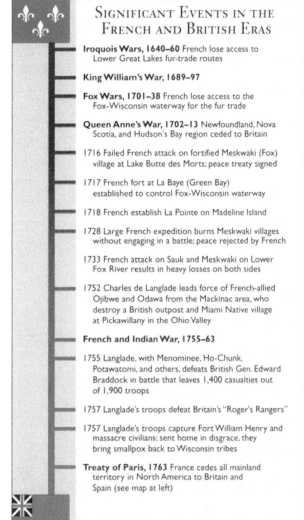

SIGNIFICANT EVENTS IN THE FRENCH AND BRITISH ERAS

Iroquois Wars, 1640–60 French lose access to Lower Great Lakes fur-trade routes

King William's War, 1689–97

Fox Wars, 1701–38 French lose access to the Fox-Wisconsin waterway for the fur trade

Queen Anne's War, 1702–13 Newfoundland, Nova Scotia, and Hudson's Bay region ceded to Britain

1716 Failed French attack on fortified Meskwaki (Fox) village at Lake Butte des Morts; peace treaty signed

1717 French fort at La Baye (Green Bay) established to control Fox-Wisconsin waterway

1718 French establish La Pointe on Madeline Island

1728 Large French expedition burns Meskwaki villages without engaging in a battle; peace rejected by French

1733 French attack on Sauk and Meskwaki on Lower Fox River results in heavy losses on both sides

1752 Charles de Langlade leads force of French-allied Ojibwe and Odawa from the Mackinac area, who destroy a British outpost and Miami Native village at Pickawillany in the Ohio Valley

French and Indian War, 1755–63

1755 Langlade, with Menominee, Ho-Chunk, Potawatomi, and others, defeats British Gen. Edward Braddock in battle that leaves 1,400 casualties out of 1,900 troops

1757 Langlade's troops defeat Britain's "Roger's Rangers"

1757 Langlade's troops capture Fort William Henry and massacre civilians; sent home in disgrace, they bring smallpox back to Wisconsin tribes

Treaty of Paris, 1763 France cedes all mainland territory in North America to Britain and Spain (see map at left)

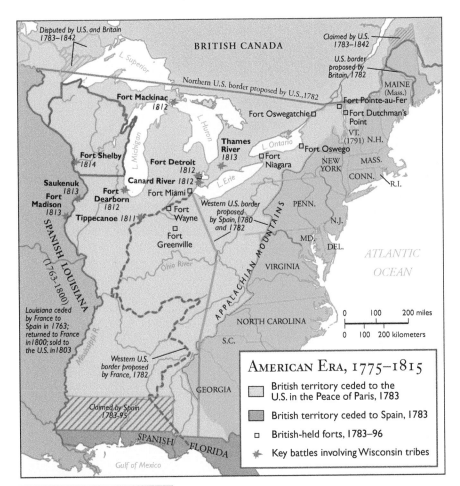

Map labels:

Disputed by U.S. and Britain 1783–1842

BRITISH CANADA

Claimed by U.S. 1783–1842

U.S. border proposed by Britain, 1782

Northern U.S. border proposed by U.S., 1782

L. Superior

Fort Mackinac 1812

MAINE (Mass.)

Fort Pointe-au-Fer

Fort Oswegatchie

Fort Dutchman's Point

L. Huron

L. Michigan

Thames River 1813

L. Ontario

Fort Oswego

VT. (1791) N.H.

Fort Shelby 1814

Fort Detroit 1812

Fort Niagara

Canard River 1812

L. Erie

NEW YORK

MASS.

CONN.

R.I.

Saukenuk 1813

Fort Madison 1813

Fort Dearborn 1812

Fort Miami

PENN.

Tippecanoe 1811

Fort Wayne

Western U.S. border proposed by Spain, 1780 and 1782

N.J.

SPANISH LOUISIANA (1763–1800)

Fort Greenville

APPALACHIAN MOUNTAINS

MD.

DEL.

Louisiana ceded by France to Spain in 1763; returned to France in 1800; sold to the U.S. in 1803

Ohio River

VIRGINIA

ATLANTIC OCEAN

Mississippi R.

Western U.S. border proposed by France, 1782

NORTH CAROLINA

0   100   200 miles

0   100   200 kilometers

S.C.

GEORGIA

Claimed by Spain 1783–95

SPANISH FLORIDA

Gulf of Mexico

AMERICAN ERA, 1775–1815

☐ British territory ceded to the U.S. in the Peace of Paris, 1783

■ British territory ceded to Spain, 1783

☐ British-held forts, 1783–96

✳ Key battles involving Wisconsin tribes

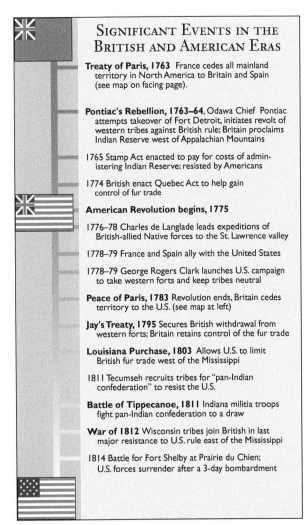

SIGNIFICANT EVENTS IN THE BRITISH AND AMERICAN ERAS

Treaty of Paris, 1763 France cedes all mainland territory in North America to Britain and Spain (see map on facing page).

Pontiac's Rebellion, 1763–64, Odawa Chief Pontiac attempts takeover of Fort Detroit, initiates revolt of western tribes against British rule; Britain proclaims Indian Reserve west of Appalachian Mountains

1765 Stamp Act enacted to pay for costs of administering Indian Reserve; resisted by Americans

1774 British enact Quebec Act to help gain control of fur trade

American Revolution begins, 1775

1776–78 Charles de Langlade leads expeditions of British-allied Native forces to the St. Lawrence valley

1778–79 France and Spain ally with the United States

1778–79 George Rogers Clark launches U.S. campaign to take western forts and keep tribes neutral

Peace of Paris, 1783 Revolution ends, Britain cedes territory to the U.S. (see map at left)

Jay's Treaty, 1795 Secures British withdrawal from western forts; Britain retains control of the fur trade

Louisiana Purchase, 1803 Allows U.S. to limit British fur trade west of the Mississippi

1811 Tecumseh recruits tribes for "pan-Indian confederation" to resist the U.S.

Battle of Tippecanoe, 1811 Indiana militia troops fight pan-Indian confederation to a draw

War of 1812 Wisconsin tribes join British in last major resistance to U.S. rule east of the Mississippi

1814 Battle for Fort Shelby at Prairie du Chien; U.S. forces surrender after a 3-day bombardment

Charles de Langlade

Thought to be Wisconsin's first permanent settler of partial European descent, Charles de Langlade (1729–1801) was raised in Michilimackinac (or Mackinac) by a French father and Odawa (Ottawa) mother. In 1752 he led a force of Odawa and Ojibwe that destroyed the British post and Miami Native village of Pickawillany. Commissioned in the French colonial army as an ensign in 1755, he led a group of Wisconsin Native troops (above) that defeated forces led by British General Braddock. Langlade helped take Fort William Henry (see map on facing page), where his troops massacred 200 captives. Sent home in disgrace, they inadvertently brought smallpox back to Wisconsin, which decimated area tribes. He later fought in other key battles of the French and Indian War. Langlade moved to Green Bay in 1764 and became an officer in the British Indian service. In 1776–78, he and Wisconsin Native troops fought in the East against American rebels. In 1778, he returned to Wisconsin to help the British prevent Native revolts. Charles de Langlade was a key player in colonial activity in Wisconsin. He personally participated in the change from French to British and then U.S. control of the region, but always on the losing side.

who came to attack them arrived starved and weakened. They begged for food from their intended victims, but were slaughtered instead. The Iroquois signed a treaty the following year and reopened routes important to trade in the Wisconsin area.

French in Wisconsin. The French built a fort at Green Bay in 1717 to tighten their hold on the western Great Lakes region. They became embroiled in a series of wars with the Meskwaki (Fox) Nation. The conflicts disrupted fur-trade routes along the critical Fox-Wisconsin waterway (see *Fox Valley*) to the Mississippi. The French developed a new route along the Maumee, Wabash, and Ohio rivers to bypass Wisconsin. This new trade route brought the French into sharper conflict with the British, whose colonists were seeking to claim the same areas. The British and French vied for control by courting local Native nations, but neither side was able to secure the region. The establishment of a series of French forts in the area prompted the colonists to take action. In 1754 Colonel George Washington led a Virginia militia force to demand removal of the forts, but had to retreat after a brief skirmish, the first in a series of encounters that led to war the following year.

French and Indian War. French colonies in North America, isolated from France by British domination of the seas, were left mostly to their own meager resources to carry out the war. Wisconsin Native tribes—including the Menominee, Ho-Chunk, Ojibwe, and Potawatomi—participated in military campaigns led by French army officer Charles de Langlade (see column at left). By 1760 the French had lost Quebec and Montreal to the British. In the 1763 Treaty of Paris that ended the war, France lost its mainland possessions in North America.

British control. Britain took on the tasks of controlling the French and Native fur trade. A rebellion led by the Odawa (Ottawa) leader Pontiac briefly united

many of the western tribes against Britain. Fearing further disruptions to the fur trade, Britain began appeasing the Native nations and restraining its colonists in the new territories. The British issued the Proclamation of 1763, which drew a line along the Appalachian Mountains to keep American colonists from encroaching on a new "Indian Reserve." In 1774, the British passed the Quebec Act to increase their control of the fur trade. Neither measure worked well, and by putting the cost of maintaining the reserve on the colonies, they stoked colonist resentment that would help lead to a revolution.

American Revolution. The colonial revolution in 1775 had little impact on Wisconsin. Charles de Langlade recruited tribal fighters for Britain and led them in battles near the St. Lawrence (see timeline). The tribes believed, as they had in 1763, that the American settlers' voracious appetite for land threatened their nations and ways of life. U.S.-British peace talks to end the war, joined by France and Spain, were marked by intrigue and conflicting boundary proposals (see map above). In the 1783 Peace of Paris, the U.S. unexpectedly gained control of most of the land east of the Mississippi.

War of 1812. Americans were slow to move into Wisconsin (see *Territorial Boundaries*). The British continued the fur trade on U.S. lands, encouraged Native nations to resist U.S. expansion, and repossessed some western forts. This contributed to the War of 1812, and the formation of a united Native army by the Shawnee leader Tecumseh. Wisconsin tribal forces again joined the British, fighting a brief battle at Prairie du Chien in 1814. Only with the end of the war in 1815 did the U.S. secure its claim to the area. It took another 20 years for the U.S. to take full military and economic control over Wisconsin.

Territorial Boundaries

U.S. TERRITORIES IN THE FUTURE WISCONSIN

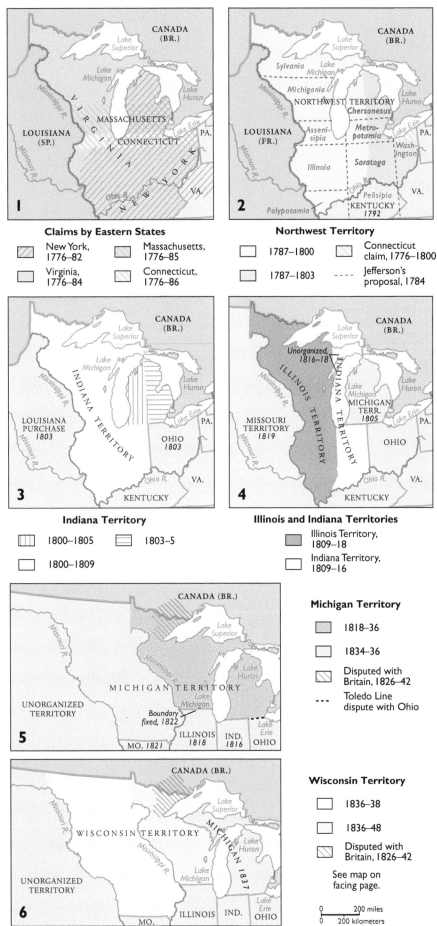

Claims by Eastern States

New York, 1776–82	Massachusetts, 1776–85
Virginia, 1776–84	Connecticut, 1776–86

Northwest Territory

1787–1800	Connecticut claim, 1776–1800
1787–1803	Jefferson's proposal, 1784

Indiana Territory

1800–1805	1803–5
1800–1809	

Illinois and Indiana Territories

Illinois Territory, 1809–18
Indiana Territory, 1809–16

Michigan Territory

1818–36
1834–36
Disputed with Britain, 1826–42
Toledo Line dispute with Ohio

Wisconsin Territory

1836–38
1836–48
Disputed with Britain, 1826–42

See map on facing page.

0   200 miles
0   200 kilometers

For more than seven decades after the American Revolution, what is now Wisconsin was part of various U.S. territories. Citizens living in territories did not have all the rights that citizens living in states did. Territories served an important function in setting the stage for eventual statehood.

Eastern claims and Northwest Territory. In the years after 1776, Wisconsin was part of the region known as the Northwest. The British maintained forts in the Northwest until the 1790s, and briefly retook much of the region in the War of 1812 (see *Colonial Boundaries*). During the same period, four eastern states—Virginia, New York, Massachusetts, and Connecticut—had overlapping claims in the region. These were gradually ceded to the federal government (see map 1 at left). In 1784, then-Congressman Thomas Jefferson proposed dividing the Northwest into 10 states (labeled in red on map 2). Congress issued a land ordinance in 1785 that directed how the area should be surveyed for land sales and settlement. In 1787, it issued the Northwest Ordinance, authored by Nathan Dane, establishing the Northwest Territory (see map 2). That ordinance banned slavery in the territory, established a bill of rights, and enabled any part of the territory with at least 60,000 citizens to ask for full statehood.

Indiana and Illinois territories. The first state to be carved out of the Northwest Territory was Ohio in 1803. Most of the rest of the area had already been reorganized as Indiana Territory (see map 3). For greater ease in administration, Congress later organized the Illinois and Michigan territories (see map 4). Most of present-day Wisconsin lay within Illinois Territory. The Door Peninsula (and part of the Upper Peninsula) lay within Indiana Territory, because the boundaries were drawn straight north-ward from the main part of Indiana. Territorial boundaries were drawn in Washington, with little consideration for the people living in the region. All of the future Wisconsin was still under the sover-eignty of Native American nations. These nations gave some lands near Green Bay and Prairie du Chien to French-Canadian settlers, who divided the lands into French-style "long lots" (see *Fox Valley*). Special commissioners later recorded these early land holdings for the U.S. government.

Michigan Territory. In 1818, after both Illinois and Indiana had become states, left-over parts of their territories were joined to Michigan Territory (see map 5). The territorial capital was in Detroit—too far away for people living on the western side of Lake Michigan. Their numbers swelled in the 1820s because of the lead rush (see *Mining*), and improved access from the East Coast to the Great Lakes via the Erie Canal. Michigan Territory settlers wanted the Illinois state border fixed at the southern tip of Lake Michigan, so they could control Chicago and all of the Lead District, and objected when the border was fixed 61 miles to the north. In 1824, Federal Judge James Doty proposed that this region join the rest of Michigan Territory (after the anticipated statehood

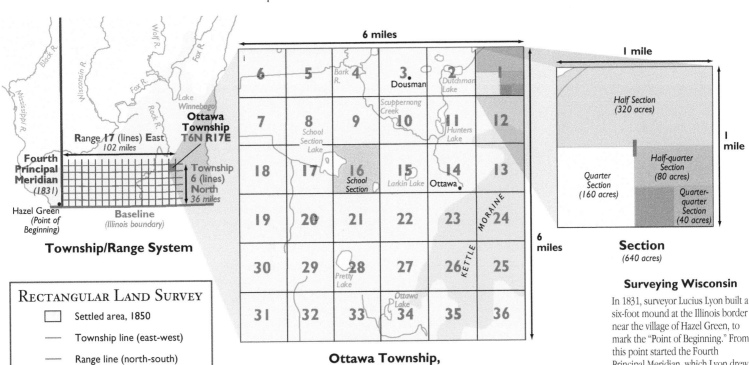

Township/Range System

RECTANGULAR LAND SURVEY

- Settled area, 1850
- Township line (east-west)
- Range line (north-south)
- **9** Section number

Ottawa Township, Waukesha County

Section
(640 acres)

Half Section (320 acres)

Quarter Section (160 acres)

Half-quarter Section (80 acres)

Quarter-quarter Section (40 acres)

Surveying Wisconsin

In 1831, surveyor Lucius Lyon built a six-foot mound at the Illinois border near the village of Hazel Green, to mark the "Point of Beginning." From this point started the Fourth Principal Meridian, which Lyon drew northward along the present-day eastern boundary of Grant County. Surveyors used the Illinois boundary as a *baseline* (or first mapped line) to draw east-west *township lines*. They used the Fourth Principal Meridian as the basis for drawing north-south *range lines*. Since the 1785 land ordinance had deemed townships to be six-by-six miles in area, each township line was six miles from the next one; the same was true for each range line. For example, Ottawa Township (in modern Waukesha County) was mapped at T6N R17E. At T6N—or Township Six North—it is six township lines, for a total of 36 miles, north of the Illinois border. At R17E—or Range Seventeen East—it is 17 range lines, for a total of 102 miles, east of the Fourth Principal Meridian. Every point in Wisconsin can be identified using this township/range system, and further defined by the 36 sections within each township. This rectangular land survey system explains the right angles seen on Wisconsin landscapes. Roads often run along section lines, and large trees often mark the intersection of the lines.

for the Lower Peninsula) to form a new "Chippewau Territory." But instead, in 1834, Michigan's territorial boundaries were extended west to the Missouri River—far beyond the original Northwest. When Michigan finally became a state in 1837, it consisted of both the Lower Peninsula and Upper Peninsula, and had given up its claim over Toledo. By this time, most of southern and eastern Wisconsin had been ceded by Native nations, and was being settled by European Americans.

Early Wisconsin Territory. In 1836, the remaining part of Michigan Territory was renamed Wisconsin Territory (see map 6); Henry Dodge served as its first governor. There were only 22,218 citizens living in the vast region—only 11,683 of them east of the Mississippi River. Two of the communities first proposed as territorial capital—Burlington and Dubuque—were in the western region. Belmont became the first capital, but many other towns and prospective towns were eager to become the permanent capital (see map at right). Doty promoted his own site of Madison, and later in 1836 won over lawmakers with promises of choice lots in the future city. Doty's victory intensified Dodge's longstanding rivalry with him. Though both men were Democrats and Anglo-Americans, Dodge's political base was in the Lead District, where many miners (including himself) from the southern U.S. lived. Doty was strongest along the Lake Michigan shore, which was becoming quickly populated by Yankees (see *Anglo-Americans*). Political struggles between their two camps involved battles over offices, privileges, federal funds, and land.

Land fever. The Michigan and Wisconsin territorial periods were marked by intensive land speculation and settlement. The 1785 land ordinance directed that new territories be mapped using an English grid system, and divided into square, six-mile by six-mile *townships* (see diagram above). Each township, in turn, would be divided into 36 *sections* of one square mile each, or 640 acres. The 16th section was set aside as a "School Section," which was withheld from sale until settlement had occurred, when

proceeds would be invested to support schools. The sections could be subdivided into halves or quarters for sale—the most common being a plot of 40 acres. In 1831, surveyor Lucius Lyon began mapping Wisconsin by marking a "Point of Beginning" on the Illinois border (see column at right). The rectangular survey could precisely locate lands for sale, which made possible the "Land Fever" of 1834–37, when more than one million acres were sold. Two-thirds were sold to land speculators, and one-third to settlers—many of whom had to await federal legislation to get clear title to their homesteads.

Late Wisconsin Territory. The western region of Wisconsin Territory was split off to form Iowa Territory in 1838. Doty was governor of Wisconsin Territory from 1841 to 1844. To make a profit and develop Wisconsin's economy, he and other speculators promoted incorporating new canals, railroads, toll roads, banks, and mining companies. By 1848, the Native American nations had ceded all the remaining regions of Wisconsin, and the long-disputed Canadian border had been set. The citizen population had increased tenfold since the establishment of Wisconsin Territory, which now awaited statehood.

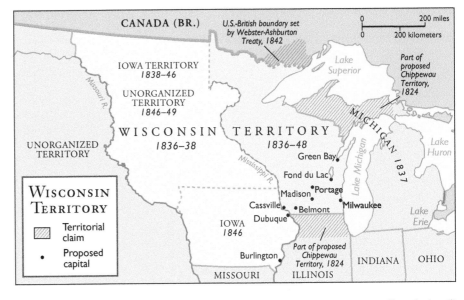

WISCONSIN TERRITORY

- ///// Territorial claim
- • Proposed capital

Statehood

Wisconsin's becoming a state in 1848 was the culmination of many internal struggles among political parties, politicians, and businessmen. The year 1848 also saw important events not only in Wisconsin, but around the world. That year, European armies crushed liberal revolutions, causing many people to flee to America. The U.S. signed a treaty ending the Mexican-American War, annexed the entire Southwest, and thereby completed its Manifest Destiny march to the Pacific. The discovery of gold in California increased the pace of western settlement and worsened tensions over the westward expansion of slavery into new territories and states.

Since 1841, Wisconsin territorial governors had been advocating statehood, but repeated referenda asking Congress for the right to go forward had failed. Residents at first preferred territorial status. The federal government generously provided financial support for roads, canals, harbors, and other internal improvements, and it levied low taxes.

In 1845, however, incentives to remain a territory waned. A new president, James Polk, reinstituted policies that limited federal involvement in the economy. Polk vetoed bills for internal improvements and Congress reduced funding for territorial expenses. Large numbers of newcomers brought new attitudes toward statehood. A threshold of 60,000 citizens was needed to apply for statehood (see *Territorial Boundaries*). Wisconsin's population in 1840 was 30,945, but by 1846 it had increased to 155,277—well above the requirement. The new settlers, mostly Yankees (see *Anglo-Americans*), were willing to reconsider statehood.

Congress had also made statehood more attractive. The federal government owned all the land in a territory. In 1841, it promised a donation of 500,000 acres of public land to each new state upon its admission to the Union—lands that a new state could sell. In addition, it promised a "school section" in every township, and a grant of 72 sections in each state for a public university (see *Education*). Finally, Congress returned 5 percent of federal land sale revenues within a new state to fund public roads.

Many congressmen were eager to see Wisconsin become a state. Texas and Florida had been admitted as slave states in 1845, changing the balance with free states that had been maintained since the 1820 Missouri Compromise. Northerners backed statehood for Iowa and Wisconsin to restore a balance.

Statehood would bring with it more freedom from federal control, and more electoral influence in local and national affairs. Federally appointed administrators and judges had made decisions that angered many Wisconsin residents, who wanted to begin electing their own representatives. Territorial status limited Wisconsin residents' participation in the tumultuous debates between the North and South. Many of these residents also wanted to cast votes in the critical 1848 election.

Another referendum on statehood was held in April 1846. Voters approved it overwhelmingly—12,334 for and 2,487 against. A new census determined representation for a constitutional convention, in which delegates would write a constitution for the new state. Congress passed an Enabling Act that allowed Wisconsin's residents to draw up a constitution and apply for statehood, with federal approval.

In October 1846, 124 elected delegates assembled for the constitutional convention in Madison—103 Democrats, 18 Whigs, and 3 independents. With such an overwhelming advantage, the Democrats should have been able to dictate the constitution, but their party was divided between Lead District interests and Lake Michigan commercial interests, and between reformers and conservatives. Whigs and independents were able to write some progressive provisions into the 1846 constitution, with support from some Democratic factions on certain issues. Divisions among Democrats, a lack of formal rules and limits, and a cumbersome size led to a long and rancorous convention.

Old State Capitol

The first territorial Capitol in Madison was completed in 1838 (above). It became the State Capitol in 1848 and was used until about 1865. The second Capitol in Madison was gradually built onto the first, eventually replacing it. Begun in 1857, it was first occupied in 1865 and was finished in 1869. Two wings were added between 1882 and 1884. A fire burned much of the Capitol in 1904, and construction of a new one was begun in 1906. The Capitol we have today was first occupied in 1909 and was finished in 1917.

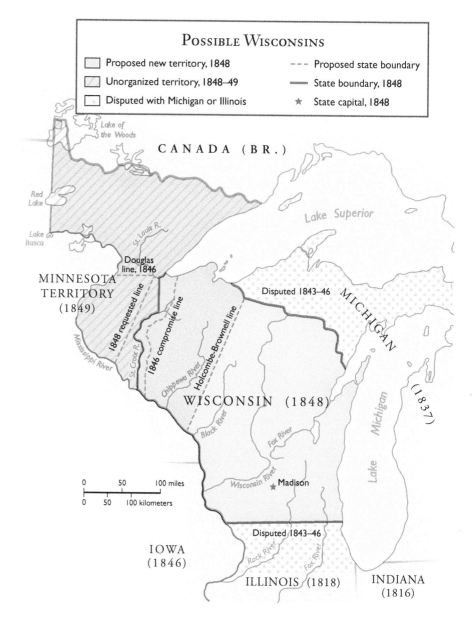

POSSIBLE WISCONSINS

- ☐ Proposed new territory, 1848
- ▨ Unorganized territory, 1848–49
- ☐ Disputed with Michigan or Illinois
- - - - Proposed state boundary
- —— State boundary, 1848
- ★ State capital, 1848

CANADA (BR.)

Lake of the Woods

Red Lake

Lake Superior

Lake Itasca

St. Louis R.

Douglas line, 1846

MINNESOTA TERRITORY (1849)

1848 requested line

1846 compromise line

Holcombe-Brownell line

Disputed 1843–46

MICHIGAN

(1837)

Mississippi River

St. Croix R.

Chippewa River

WISCONSIN (1848)

Black River

Fox River

Lake Michigan

0   50   100 miles

0   50   100 kilometers

Wisconsin River ★ Madison

Disputed 1843–46

IOWA (1846)

Rock River

Fox River

ILLINOIS (1818)

INDIANA (1816)

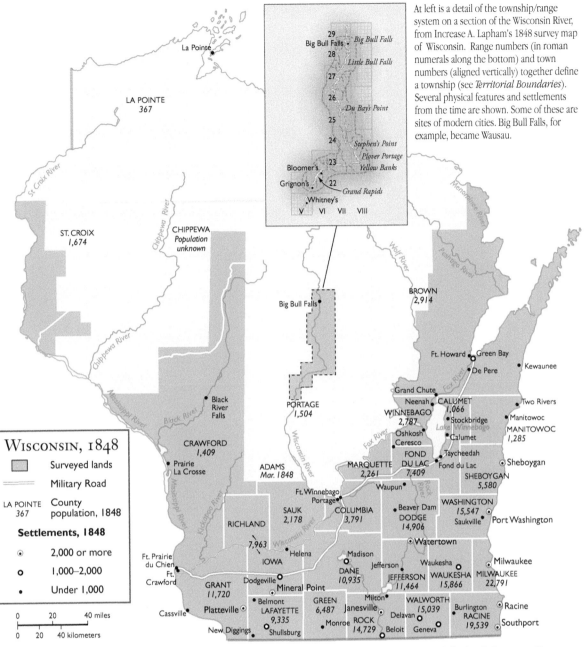

At left is a detail of the township/range system on a section of the Wisconsin River, from Increase A. Lapham's 1848 survey map of Wisconsin. Range numbers (in roman numerals along the bottom) and town numbers (aligned vertically) together define a township (see *Territorial Boundaries*). Several physical features and settlements from the time are shown. Some of these are sites of modern cities. Big Bull Falls, for example, became Wausau.

Possible Wisconsin Boundaries

The shape of the proposed state of Wisconsin was far from decided when delegates met for the first constitutional convention in 1846. Many delegates believed that northern Illinois and the Upper Peninsula of Michigan should become a part of the new state (see *Territorial Boundaries*), but the federal government did not support their claim. Wisconsin's northwestern boundary became the most contentious border issue. Most delegates assumed it would conform to the old Northwest Territory boundary—the Mississippi River. In the 1846 Enabling Act that approved Wisconsin's statehood vote, Illinois Congressman Stephen Douglas proposed a boundary going from the western tip of Lake Superior straight west to the Mississippi. The act was amended to draw the boundary along its present course straight *south* from the western tip of Lake Superior, and then along the St. Croix River, but it allowed the state constitutional convention to suggest new boundaries. New proposals included a secret plan by a group of developers to establish a new territory (and later a state), centered on the timber-rich St. Croix River valley. A delegate from the area, William Holcombe, proposed the separation of the northwestern part of Wisconsin Territory (shown in orange on the map at left), cutting off the rest of Wisconsin from Lake Superior. The delegates had previously been largely unconcerned about the boundary issue, but this proposal was too much to bear. They approved a compromise proposal that retained Wisconsin's access to Lake Superior, but not the St. Croix River. This border would have been official had voters approved the 1846 constitution. At the second constitutional convention in 1847, St. Croix County delegate George Brownell revived the Holcombe scheme. The delegates, newly aware of the area's value, instead asked Congress for a boundary farther west that would encompass all of the St. Croix River valley and present-day St. Paul. In 1848, Congress ignored the request, and also rebuffed a third attempt to implement the Holcombe-Brownell line. Instead it approved the border along the St. Croix River as first proposed in the amended 1846 Enabling Act. The left-over part of Wisconsin Territory became part of the new Minnesota Territory in 1849.

Wisconsin had many examples of constitutions from which to draw. State constitutions were being made and revised all around the country. Many influential convention delegates had originally come from New York, and turned to its newly revised constitution for ideas. Delegates easily decided upon executive and legislative branches with structures similar to those of other states. After lengthy debate, they decided that state judges should be elected.

The most heated debates revolved around economic and social issues, especially a proposed ban on banks and bank notes. Many delegates saw banks as untrustworthy tools of the rich. Despite broad-based opposition, the provision was retained. African American voting rights were to be considered in a separate—and ultimately unsuccessful—referendum (see *African Americans*).

Delegates did adopt some progressive provisions, including the right of a married women to retain property in their own names and the right of foreign-born residents to vote after living in the state one year (and declaring an intent to become citizens). Delegates prohibited debtors' prisons and exempted family homesteads (up to a value of $1,000) from seizure for debt. They also prohibited the state government from incurring debt for internal improvements and limited the overall state debt to $100,000.

After an intense campaign for and against the proposed constitution, it was submitted to a popular vote. Different issues alienated people in different parts of the territory, but the banking prohibition was the most strongly opposed—especially by Yankees who had strongly backed statehood. Voters rejected the constitution by a vote of 20,333 to 14,119.

Statehood supporters organized a second constitutional convention in December 1847. Smaller and more tightly controlled, the convention revised the 1846 constitution. Delegates dropped the issue of married women's property and deferred the chartering of banks to later state referenda. Other constitutional provisions stayed essentially the same.

In March of 1848 Wisconsin voters finally accepted the new constitution by a vote of 16,754 to 6,384. Before Congress could act on admission, eager voters elected two members to the U.S. House of Representatives, members of the state Senate and Assembly, and their first state governor, Nelson Dewey. President Polk signed the law on May 29, 1848, and Wisconsin became the 30th state in the Union.

County Boundaries

The county. Since becoming a territory, Wisconsin has always had strong governments at the local level. City, village, and township governments handle many community affairs. County government serves as an intermediary power between these communities and state government. In Wisconsin, counties administer some state functions, such as law enforcement, road maintenance, and health and social services. Around 1900, counties began to establish their own schools, parks, and other institutions. The county seat was often placed in the central area of the county, or on a key waterway. Wisconsin's extensive network of rivers and lakes made it possible to divide large counties into smaller ones that retained access to water transportation.

Creation of counties. Wisconsin's first counties were established in 1818, just after the area became part of Michigan Territory. Territorial Governor Lewis Cass partitioned what would become Wisconsin into the counties of Crawford, Brown, and (until 1836) Michilimackinac. Milwaukee and Iowa counties were also created during Michigan territorial rule. Wisconsin's territorial period (1836–48) saw the creation of an additional 25 counties. Upon statehood in 1848, Wisconsin had 29 counties, the best-defined of which were in the south and east, where settlement had begun.

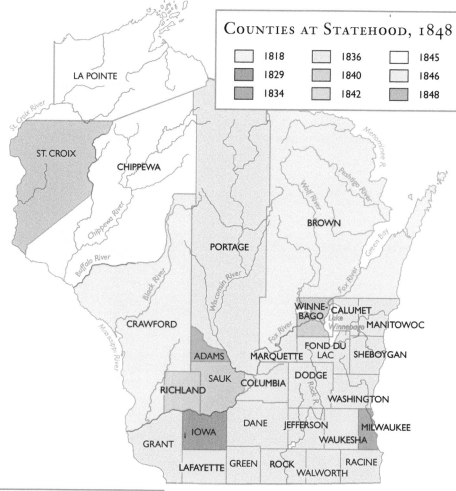

COUNTIES AT STATEHOOD, 1848

1818	1836	1845
1829	1840	1846
1834	1842	1848

COUNTIES IN 1861

1850	1853	1858
1851	1854	1859
1852	1856	1860

The expansion of counties. Article IV of the state constitution gives the legislature the power to establish and regulate counties. The number of counties doubled from 29 to 58 between 1848 and 1861. Lumbering, farming, and railroads encouraged the settlement of new regions of the state. As their populations grew, new counties were created to provide administrative structures and government services. The process of creating counties, however, involved more than just population growth. Land speculators and real estate interests lobbied the legislature to create new counties and establish county seats in locations that would increase the value of their land holdings. "Wars" occurred over the placement of county seats, as with the movement of the Iowa County seat from Mineral Point to Dodgeville in 1855 and the Bayfield County seat from Bayfield to Washburn in 1892 (see maps on facing page).

Counties today. Wisconsin's final 14 counties were created between 1861 and 1961, bringing the total number to 72. The years between 1874 and 1901 saw counties established in predominantly rural northern regions where, after lumbering ended, land became available for purchase and settlement (see *Timber*). Wisconsin's newest county, Menominee, was created in 1961.

Counties of the future. A 1997 proposal called for the creation of a 73rd county (tentatively named "Century") out of portions of Clark, Marathon, and

Wood counties. Many citizens in and around the growing city of Marshfield felt distanced from existing county services in Neillsville, Wausau, and Wisconsin Rapids (see map at right). Some feel a new county, centered on Marshfield, would serve them better. If approved, Century County would be established after 2000. The proposal suggests that Wisconsin's process of county formation may not be over.

Governor Gaylord A. Nelson (seated above), with Menominee tribal leaders, signs into law the creation of Menominee County. It was created from Menominee reservation lands in Oconto and Shawano counties. The law took effect in 1961 (see *Eastern Nations* and *Land Conflicts*).

County Boundary Changes

Counties often had their borders changed, and in some cases their county seats moved. Northwestern Wisconsin provides an excellent example of how counties were created and realigned. La Pointe County was partitioned off from St. Croix County in 1845, with the old Madeline Island fur-trade center of La Pointe as the county seat. The expectation that rail lines would reach Superior and Ashland (to create "inland seaports") led to the establishment of Douglas and Ashland counties. Lumbering, mining, and the promise of farming the Cutover District (see *Timber*) drew settlers northward and led to the creation of Iron, Sawyer, Washburn, Price, and Vilas counties.

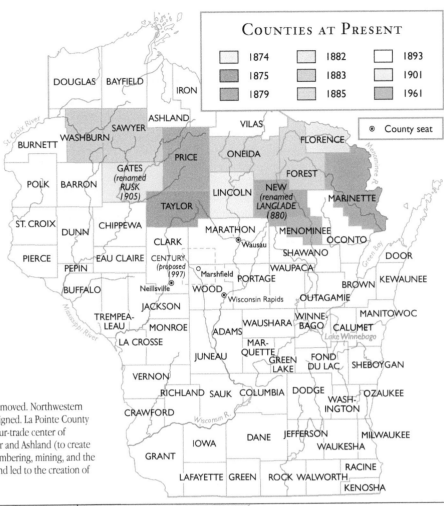

COUNTIES AT PRESENT

1874	1882	1893
1875	1883	1901
1879	1885	1961

⊙ County seat

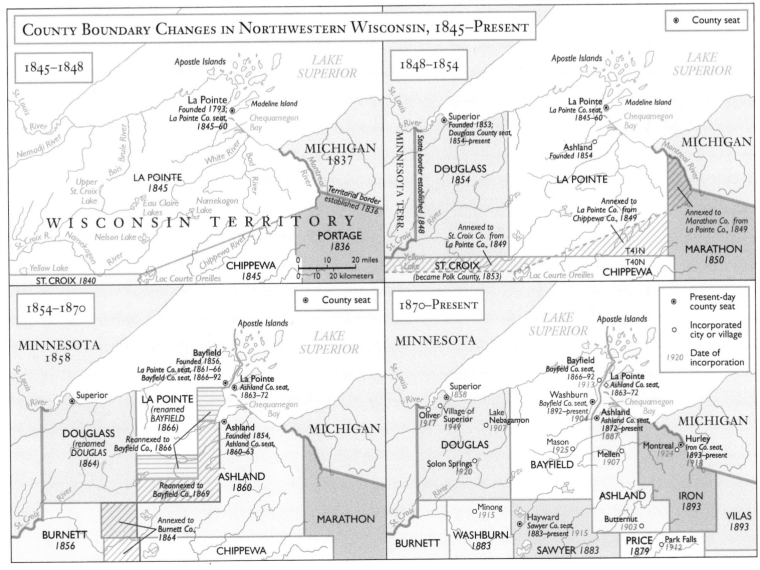

Progressive Era

Progressivism arose in the 1890s from a variety of campaigns for political and social reform, especially those in favor of economic protections for farmers and small business owners. From the Civil War to the 1890s, Wisconsin's political system had been dominated by political "bosses" and machines that played on ethnic and religious divisions. The Republican Party controlled nearly all of Wisconsin, except for some lakeshore counties where Catholic ethnic groups, who tended to vote Democratic, predominated (See *State Government*). Politicians offered voters little in the way of policy, but secured government jobs for their party members and supporters. Each political party had a behind-the-scenes boss who dispensed *patronage* (jobs and favors), perhaps his most important task. The boss controlled day-to-day activities and acted as a go-between for large financial interests. Under this political system, railroads, utilities, and other interests competed for economic advantage, at the expense of small farmers, business owners, and consumers.

Sources of reform. Wisconsin and several other midwestern states had large numbers of northern and western European immigrants who were experienced in political movements, familiar with oppression, and sympathetic to calls for reform. In the 1870s and 1880s, rural political protests arose in the form of the Grange farmers' league, the Greenback Party, and the People's Party (also known as the Populists). They had short-term success, but were not able to attract a large enough urban following to survive. The rise of industrialism and urban population growth in the 1870s and 1880s resulted in a stronger working class, which formed labor unions and socialist parties. Economic recessions, which widened the gaps between rich and poor, and between politicians and their constituents, gave momentum to these movements. An 1872–73 recession bolstered the Grangers, Greenbackers, and Populists, and led to the election of Grange-backed Democrat William R. Taylor as governor (see map on facing page). A severe 1893–98 depression motivated their political

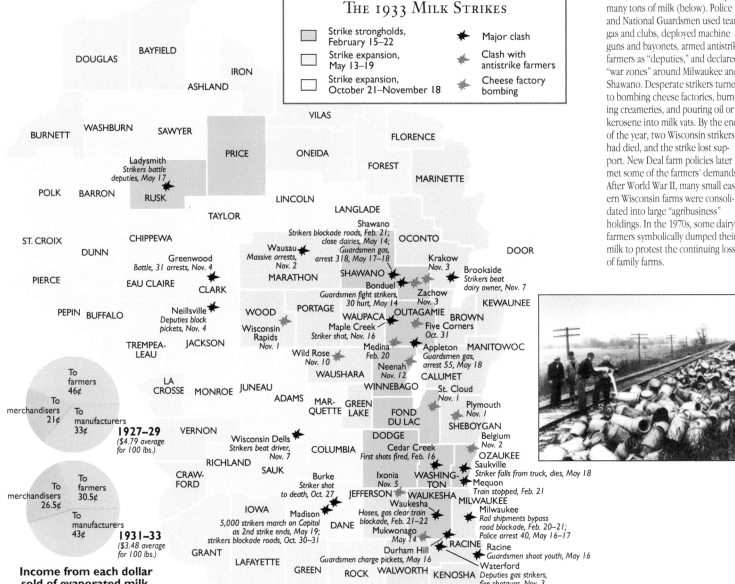

THE 1933 MILK STRIKES

- ▢ Strike strongholds, February 15–22
- ▢ Strike expansion, May 13–19
- ▢ Strike expansion, October 21–November 18
- ★ Major clash
- ★ Clash with antistrike farmers
- ★ Cheese factory bombing

DOUGLAS · BAYFIELD · IRON · ASHLAND

BURNETT · WASHBURN · SAWYER · PRICE · VILAS · ONEIDA · FLORENCE · FOREST · MARINETTE

Ladysmith
Strikers battle deputies, May 17

POLK · BARRON · RUSK · TAYLOR · LINCOLN · LANGLADE

ST. CROIX · CHIPPEWA · DUNN

Greenwood
Battle, 31 arrests, Nov. 4

Wausau
Massive arrests, Nov. 2

Shawano
Strikers blockade roads, Feb. 21; close dairies, May 14; Guardsmen gas, arrest 318, May 17–18

OCONTO · DOOR

Krakow
Nov. 3

PIERCE · EAU CLAIRE · CLARK · MARATHON · SHAWANO

Brookside
Strikers beat dairy owner, Nov. 7

Neillsville
Deputies block pickets, Nov. 4

Bonduel
Guardsmen fight strikers, 30 hurt, May 14

Zachow
Nov. 3

KEWAUNEE

PEPIN · BUFFALO · WOOD · PORTAGE · WAUPACA · OUTAGAMIE · BROWN

Wisconsin Rapids
Nov. 1

Maple Creek
Striker shot, Nov. 16

Five Corners
Oct. 31

TREMPEA-LEAU · JACKSON

Wild Rose
Nov. 10

Medina
Feb. 20

Appleton MANITOWOC
Guardsmen gas, arrest 55, May 18

To farmers 46¢
To merchandisers 21¢
To manufacturers 33¢
1927–29
($4.79 average for 100 lbs.)

Neenah
Nov. 12

LA CROSSE · MONROE · JUNEAU · ADAMS · WAUSHARA · WINNEBAGO · CALUMET

St. Cloud
Nov. 1

Plymouth
Nov. 1

MAR-QUETTE · GREEN LAKE · FOND DU LAC · SHEBOYGAN

VERNON

Wisconsin Dells
Strikers beat driver, Nov. 7

DODGE

Belgium
Nov. 2

COLUMBIA

Cedar Creek
First shots fired, Feb. 16

OZAUKEE

To merchandisers 26.5¢
To farmers 30.5¢
To manufacturers 43¢
1931–33
($3.48 average for 100 lbs.)

RICHLAND · CRAW-FORD · SAUK

Burke
Striker shot to death, Oct. 27

Ixonia
Nov. 5

WASHING-TON

Saukville
Striker falls from truck, dies, May 18

Mequon
Train stopped, Feb. 21

JEFFERSON · WAUKESHA · MILWAUKEE

Waukesha
Hoses, gas clear train blockade, Feb. 21–22

Milwaukee
Rail shipments bypass road blockade, Feb. 20–21; Police arrest 40, May 16–17

IOWA

Madison
5,000 strikers march on Capitol as 2nd strike ends, May 19; strikers blockade roads, Oct. 30–31

DANE

Mukwonago
May 14

Durham Hill
Guardsmen charge pickets, May 16

RACINE

Racine
Guardsmen shoot youth, May 16

GRANT · LAFAYETTE · GREEN · ROCK · WALWORTH · KENOSHA

Waterford
Deputies gas strikers, fire shotguns, Nov. 3

Income from each dollar sold of evaporated milk

Reform politics in Wisconsin sprang from different parties and regions at different times (see *State Government*). In 1873 Grange-backed William R. Taylor won 55 percent of the vote by opposing railroad corruption. In 1910, Republican Francis E. McGovern won 59 percent at the height of the strength of his progressive faction. In 1942, Progressive Orland S. Loomis won 50 percent against two opponents, just four years before the collapse of the Progressive Party. Though reform politics played a role in shaping these voting patterns, traditional party loyalties and ethnic/religious differences also strongly influenced the distribution of votes.

The Wisconsin Idea

The "Wisconsin Idea" is a concept developed in the Progressive Era, and defined in several ways. In the main, it involved the use of experts in drafting legislation and staffing regulatory commissions, together with providing outreach education. The University of Wisconsin was the primary resource for these experts. University President Charles Van Hise and his former classmate Governor Robert M. La Follette, Sr., did much to advance both cooperation and outreach. The most prolific of the experts used by progressive politicians was Professor John Commons. In 1905, he fashioned the state's Civil Service Law, and his later bills on workers' compensation and the Industrial Commission became models for other states (see *Labor*). A major player in the advancement of the Wisconsin Idea was Charles McCarthy, who was appointed as a documents clerk in 1901. From this position, he skillfully created the Legislative Reference Library. Sometimes called the "Bill Factory," it brought together documentary resources, academic and industry experts, and library staff to craft legislation and regulations. Wisconsin's educational system was recast during this period into a wide-ranging set of local, county, state, and vocational schools (see *Education*). By 1912 the Wisconsin Idea had been recognized around the nation. The Wisconsin Idea survived a backlash after the decline of progressivism. Its legacy can still be seen in the University extension system and the Wisconsin Legislative Reference Bureau.

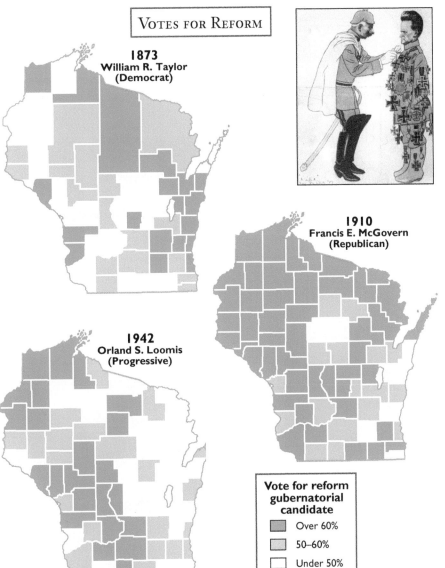

VOTES FOR REFORM

1873
William R. Taylor
(Democrat)

1910
Francis E. McGovern
(Republican)

1942
Orland S. Loomis
(Progressive)

Vote for reform gubernatorial candidate

Over 60%

50–60%

Under 50%

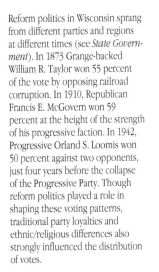

"Fighting Bob"

Separating the history from the legend of "Fighting Bob" La Follette is difficult. In the public's mind, he successfully merged the identity of a movement with his own. He did not start in politics as a reformer, but took up the cause after coming into conflict with corrupt party leadership. Ambitious and dedicated, he tried to create an organization loyal to him rather than to the party. He often saw his enemies, and sometimes his allies, as acting from the worst motives. La Follette's oratory made him a fearsome campaigner and national leader for the progressive movement. Never a liberal in the modern sense, he valued the liberties necessary for the "self-made man." His marriage to Belle Case La Follette—an ardent advocate of women's rights and social justice and an excellent politician—undoubtedly influenced him. He focused on the machinery of democracy—curbing industrial monopolies, unfair taxation, and irresponsible financial power. Adamant about maintaining U.S. neutrality in World War I, he was inaccurately vilified for being "pro-German." (The carton above depicts the German leader Kaiser Wilhelm II pinning a medal on La Follette). La Follette's actions sincerely reflected his ideals and those of his constituency, at political and personal cost to himself. He remains the most powerful icon in the history of Wisconsin.

successors, who developed a core following among farmers and small business owners, and cut across many ethnic, class, and party lines. This coalition later came to be called "progressive."

Rise of progressivism. Public disenchantment with "bossism" and unfettered corporate power simmered throughout the 1890s. Frustrated by Republican bossism, Madison attorney and former congressman Robert M. La Follette, Sr., joined the reformers and became their most articulate and popular spokesman. His skillful oratory won national attention. La Follette's failure to receive the 1896 Republican gubernatorial nomination caused his complete break with the party leadership. He and his group of ambitious politicians took up reform causes and formed what came to be known as the progressive wing of the Republican Party. Conservative party members, and moderates who did not care for La Follette's methods, became known as "stalwarts." La Follette's election as governor in 1900 marked the start of the "Progressive Era." His initial reforms included the direct primary, which allowed popular participation in the selection of each party's candidates—a move that struck at the heart of boss politics. Other reforms included railroad regulation, railroad tax reform, and anticorruption legislation—putting Wisconsin on the map as a leader in reform. After he moved to the U.S. Senate in 1906, successive progressive governors employed the "Wisconsin Idea" (see column at left) and enacted reforms including worker safety laws and civil service regulation.

Progressivism falters. Although progressivism grew into a national movement, it was weakened by differences between rival national leaders La Follette and Theodore Roosevelt, as well as by local factions. After stalwarts regained the governorship in 1914, progressivism began to lose momentum. La Follette was severely condemned for his stand on neutrality early in World War I but he rebounded and even ran for president as a Progressive Party candidate in 1924. After his death in 1925, his son Robert, Jr., became senator. In 1930, after the Great Depression began, his younger son Philip was elected governor. Philip's support for unemployment compensation, new labor laws, and government work relief programs received national attention (see *Labor*). Fed up with the stalwarts, Philip and Robert, Jr., left the Republican Party in 1934 and formed a state Progressive Party. While working with Democratic President Franklin D. Roosevelt, the Progressives had helped implement some key New Deal programs. The 1936 formation of the Farmer-Labor Progressive Federation brought the new party into a powerful alliance with farmers' groups, labor unions, and the Socialist Party. After two years of electoral success, the coalition collapsed (when farmers opposed union organizing in food processing plants), and Philip lost the governorship. When he broke with Roosevelt to seek the presidency himself, the Progressive Party began to come apart. After World War II the party dissolved, the La Follettes rejoined the Republican Party, and some younger progressives moved to the Democratic Party.

Industrial Labor Unions

From the 1840s to the 1910s, Wisconsin's industrial workers often labored six days a week for 10 to 12 hours a day, often in dangerous conditions, earning from less than a dollar up to two dollars a day. To care for coworkers and their families in case of illness, injury, or death, they formed mutual aid societies. They came together in unions to fight for better working conditions, shorter hours, and higher wages.

1840s–1870s. Wisconsin's first union was founded by Milwaukee construction workers in 1847; the first strike was held by the city's shipbuilders the following year. Early unions were started by skilled workers, such as tailors, cigar makers, railroad engineers, printers, iron workers, and coopers (barrel makers). To reduce union members' power, companies began to employ low-wage workers—particularly women, children, newly arrived immigrants, and later African Americans. Union members objected to these new employees, many of whom later joined unions themselves. During the Civil War unions made gains, but lost many of them in the economic slump that followed. In 1867, Wisconsin shoemakers formed the Knights of St. Crispin, which expanded into the nation's largest union for a brief time. In the 1860s and 1870s, the unions' main demand was for a shorter work day. The national Knights of Labor began organizing in the state in 1878 for an eight-hour day.

1880s–1910s. Lumber was the state's largest industry in 1881, the year that Eau Claire sawmill workers went on strike for a 10-hour day. For the first time, the state deployed militia against strikers. In 1886, Milwaukee workers joined a national strike for an eight-hour day, and at least seven of them were killed (see map at right). Blamed for the violence, the Knights of Labor lost members in Wisconsin. In 1893, the Wisconsin State Federation of Labor was chartered; it was affiliated with the American Federation of Labor (AFL) and later closely tied to the Socialist Party. Major strikes took place among northern timber and wood workers in the 1890s, among metalworkers and machinists in the early 1900s, and among paper workers in the 1900s–1920s (see map on facing page). Employers fought back by hiring spies and strikebreakers, "locking-out" union workers, hiring nonunion workers, and "blacklisting" fired union workers. They often required new hires to sign "yellow dog contracts" that forbade union membership, formed compliant "company unions," and secured injunctions against strike picketing and product boycotts. Under progressive Republican Governor Francis E. McGovern (1911–15), the long-term struggle for change resulted in new labor laws and an "Industrial Commission" to enforce them. The laws limited child labor, set a minimum wage for women, increased workplace safety, and created the nation's first workers' compensation system for injured employees, and the first state vocational education system (see *Education*).

1920s–1930s. World War I saw another increase in union strength, followed by counterattacks by employers. Many brewery workers lost their jobs because of Prohibition (see *Southeastern Industries*), and union membership dropped in the 1920s. The labor movement, however, made some important gains, such as the formation of the University of Wisconsin's "School for Workers," and the nation's first lasting ban on yellow dog contracts. The Great Depression of the 1930s brought high unemployment, which initially hurt unions. Partly to prevent social unrest, progressive Governor Philip F. La Follette (see *Progressives*) pushed through new labor laws that provided models for the federal "New Deal." In 1931, the legislature passed a labor code that limited employer injunctions and in 1932 passed the nation's first law for compensating unemployed workers. The American Federation of State, County and Municipal Employees (AFSCME), born in the state in 1936, eventually became one of the nation's largest unions. The Congress of Industrial Organizations (CIO), founded as a militant rival to the AFL, began organizing auto and metalworking plants—by 1937 the number of strikes in the state had nearly quadrupled, including *sit-down strikes* (plant occupations). That year the Wisconsin Labor Relations Act banned anti-union spies, blacklisting, company unions, and mass firings of union workers, and required employers to bargain with unions chosen by their employees. In 1939, however, conservative Republican Governor Julius Heil took office, and his Employment Peace Act banned sit-down strikes, *closed shops* (compulsory union workplaces), and some forms of picketing and boycotts.

BAY VIEW MASSACRE, 1886

Saturday, May 1
Milwaukee *Journal* estimates that 10,000 workers are on strike. Ten percent of the workforce walks out of the Allis Reliance Works. Brewery workers strike for more demands after winning concessions.

Sunday, May 2
Huge demonstrations and a grand parade at the Milwaukee Garden.

Monday, May 3
A crowd of about 1,000 invades the Milwaukee Road Car shops, forcing them to close. Strikers attempt to shut down the Allis Reliance Works, but are turned away by plant workers. Brewery workers march on the Falk Brewery, but fail to produce a strike. Some employees of the Bay View Rolling Mills go out on strike. Governor Rusk arrives and sets up his headquarters at the Plankinton House.

Schilling's meeting at the West Side Turner Hall fails to calm leaders on both sides.

Tuesday, May 4
Mass meeting at the Milwaukee Garden, followed by a march to Brand & Co. Stove Works, forcing it to close. A large crowd marches from St. Stanislaus Church to Bay View Rolling Mills. After a tense confrontation, National Guardsmen are deployed. They include the Kosciuszko Guards, whose involvement angers the mostly Polish strikers. Guardsmen fire warning shots.

Wednesday, May 5
A crowd of about 1,500 returns to the Bay View Rolling Mills from St. Stanislaus Church. After consulting the governor, the National Guard commander warns the crowd to stop at over 400 yards. Guardsmen open fire at about 200 yards, killing seven and wounding more than ten.

Bay View Massacre

In the 1880s, Milwaukee was the scene of industrial expansion and labor unrest. The city's many new immigrants competed with rural people for jobs that required working at least 10 hours a day. Workers and their unions were divided along ethnic lines and between skilled and unskilled jobs. When unskilled workers organized against harsh working conditions, they were usually replaced. Most strikes lacked support from the chiefly rural public and ended in violence or defeat. Labor unions nevertheless began to overcome these odds. The Eight Hour League, formed in 1886 by Robert Schilling of the Knights of Labor, became the rallying point for reform. Schilling avoided strikes as counterproductive, but militants quickly gained control of the League and planned a national strike for May 1. Thousands of workers took to Milwaukee streets in festive rallies and tense confrontations between May 1 and May 5. Strikers attempted to shut down several plants or force non-striking workers to walk out (see map and chart). In response on May 4, city officials asked Governor Jeremiah Rusk to deploy National Guard units at several plants. On May 5, the day after a strike-related bombing in Chicago's Haymarket Square, tensions escalated. National Guardsmen, nervous and unsure of their orders, opened fire on strikers marching toward the Bay View Rolling Mills—killing seven people and wounding at least ten. The casualties included a boy carrying schoolbooks and an elderly man feeding his chickens. Polish workers felt betrayed by the Polish "Kosciuszko Guards" who had opened fire, while many other citizens considered the guardsmen and the governor to be heroes. Employers voided most existing eight-hour day agreements, and any hope for new concessions was lost until socialists and progressives made gains in the late 1890s.

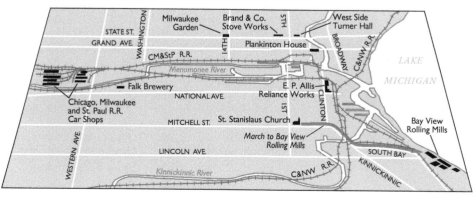

1940s–1960s. Unemployment dropped during World War II, and unions voluntarily limited most strikes. Prices rose after the war, but wages stayed the same, sparking a series of bitter strikes in machinery and metalworking plants, such as J. I. Case, Kohler, and Allis-Chalmers. Later, a telephone workers' strike made unions more visible in smaller towns where they were scarce. In 1946 the state Progressive Party collapsed, and CIO members expelled union leaders they believed were tied to the Communist Party. Unions increasingly supported the state's revitalized Democratic Party. The Wisconsin AFL and CIO merged in 1958, combining over 1,100 union locals. The AFL-CIO has played a strong political role in the state, contributing to political candidates and lobbying for new labor laws. A 1959 state law backed public employees' right to organize.

1970s-2000s. With a decline in industrial employment, public employee unions took a more central role in the labor movement. A 1974 teachers' strike in Hortonville led the legislature to pass a binding arbitration law in 1977 that required employers and unions to settle strikes. Union membership declined in the 1980s, because of a growth of nonunion service and high-tech industries and changes in federal labor policies. In what unionists opposed as "runaway shops," some Wisconsin companies began to shift production plants and subcontracts to nonunion Sunbelt states and low-wage Third World countries. Some Wisconsin unions carried out successful organizing drives and strikes in the 1990s, which often focused on job security or health and safety issues rather than wages. Wisconsin unions still remain among the strongest in the nation.

Strike at J. I. Case Company in Racine, 1960

NOTABLE STRIKES AND LOCKOUTS

Auto, transportation equipment workers
Eau Claire 1919 (Gillette Rubber)
Janesville 1937 (Fisher Body), 1945–46 (General Motors), 1961 (Fisher/GM), 1970 (GM)
Kenosha 1933–34 (Nash Motor)
Milwaukee 1934 (Seaman Body Corp.), 1974/1983 (Briggs & Stratton), 1974 (Harley-Davidson), 1992 (Teledyne Wisconsin Motors)
Racine 1934 (Nash Motor)
Stoughton 1988 (Stoughton Trailers)

Brewers
Milwaukee 1886, 1888, 1948, 1953, 1993

Cigar makers
Milwaukee 1881–82

Clothing, garment makers
Kenosha 1928–29 (Allen-A Hosiery)
Milwaukee 1853/1860 (tailors), 1855 (shoemakers), 1879 (tanners), 1911/1928 (clothing makers), 1937
Oshkosh 1915 (glove makers)
Racine 1991 (Rainfair)

Communications workers
Madison 1973 (Channel 3)
Milwaukee 1883 (telegraphers)
Statewide 1947 (telephone workers)

Construction workers
Madison 1904, 1948
Milwaukee 1847 (bricklayers), 1889

Coopers (barrel makers)
Milwaukee 1848, 1866, 1868, 1872

Dockworkers
Milwaukee 1880, 1881, 1971
Superior 1984 (Fraser Shipyards)

Electrical workers
Milwaukee 1969–70 (General Electric)
Waukesha 1969–70 (General Electric)
Wausau 1937, 1950 (Marathon Electric)

Food processing workers, meatpackers
Cambria 1969 (Fall River Canning)
Chippewa Falls 1973 (Packerland)
Cudahy 1978, 1987–88 (Patrick Cudahy)
Cudahy 1997–99 (Patrick Cudahy)
Franksville 1937 (canners)
Madison 1934 (Oscar Mayer), 1972–73 (General Beverage)
Milwaukee 1886 (bakers), 1878 (flour millers), 1968 (meatpackers), 1978 (Peck)
Wautoma 1967 (Libby)

Machinists
Beloit 1903 (Berlin Machine Works), 1972 (Beloit Corp.)
Cudahy 1901
Green Bay 1988 (Krueger), 1983 (G.B. Paper Converting), 1994 (Alwin)
Madison 1970 (Gisholt)
Milwaukee 1901, 1906, 1937 (Lindemann-Hoverson), 1937/1938 (Harnischfeger), 1941/1946–47 (Allis-Chalmers), 1974 (A.O. Smith)
Port Washington 1990 (Simplicity)
Racine 1899/1902/1905–7/1934–35/ 1936–37/1945–47/1960/1990 (J. I. Case Co.), 1992 (Acme Die Casting), 1993 (Dumore)
West Allis 1947 (Allis Chalmers), 1992 (Pressed Steel Tank), 1996 (Siemens)

Metalworkers
Beloit 1902 (Fairbanks-Morse), 1903
Green Bay 1971/1976 (FMC)
Madison 1919
Milwaukee 1876/1879 (coal heavers), 1873 (heaters), 1899, 1902, 1906–7 (molders), 1873, 1881, 1882, (ironworkers), 1983 (Briggs & Stratton), 1994 (Ampco Metals)

Papermakers
Appleton 1902, 1904
Biron 1902
Brokaw 1902
Clintonville 1998
Combined Locks 1904
De Pere 1987
Eau Claire 1902
Green Bay 1921
Kaukauna 1892, 1902, 1922
Marinette 1902
Neenah-Menasha 1902, 1904, 1922, 1992
Nekoosa-Port Edwards 1902, 1919–22
Plover 1902
Rhinelander 1921–22
Stevens Point 1902
Wausau 1992
Whiting 1902
Wisconsin Rapids 1902

Plumbers, plumbing equipment workers
Kohler 1897, 1934–41/1954–60 (Kohler Co.)
Madison 1903 (plumbers)
Milwaukee 1885 (plumbers)

Printers, publishing/ newspaper workers
Green Bay 1976
Madison 1977 (Madison Newspapers, Inc.), 1983 (Straus Printing)
Milwaukee 1852, 1863, 1872, 1881, 1882, 1884, 1907, 1936, 1961 (Journal), 1962 (Sentinel)
Neenah-Menasha 1976 (Banta)

Public employees
Milwaukee 1966 (Sewage District), 1967 (Milwaukee County)
Statewide 1977 (State of Wisconsin)

Railroad, streetcar workers
La Crosse 1909
Milwaukee 1853/1877/1880/ 1881/1885 (railroads), 1892 (Homestead), 1894 (Pullman), 1896, 1912, 1934
Stevens Point 1872

Retail, restaurant, hotel workers
Milwaukee 1934 (Boston Store), 1937

Sailors
Milwaukee 1851, 1862, 1864
Mississippi River 1866 (steamboats)

Shipbuilders
Milwaukee 1848, 1861

Teachers
Beloit 1973, 1976
Hortonville 1974
Kenosha 1972, 1973
Madison 1970/1976/1980 (U.W. teaching assistants), 1976
Milwaukee 1977
Racine 1973, 1977
Superior 1969, 1970, 1973, 1976
Wausau 1971
West Allis 1971
Wisconsin Rapids 1971, 1974

Timber, lumbering, wood workers
Ashland 1890
Chippewa Falls 1898
Eagle River 1881, 1892
Eau Claire 1892
La Crosse 1873, 1892
Manawa 1892
Marinette 1885–86, 1892, 1899, 1903, 1904, 1916
Merrill 1892
Neenah-Menasha 1885, 1896, 1897, 1899, 1904
Oshkosh 1864, 1898, 1920
Pineville 1885
Rhinelander 1892
Schofield 1892
Sheboygan 1899–1900
Stevens Point 1892
Two Rivers 1900
Washburn 1890
Wisconsin Rapids 1892
Woodboro 1892

Truckers, delivery workers
Statewide 1970 (U.S. Postal Service), 1974 (truckers), 1983 (Greyhound Bus), 1997 (United Parcel Service)

Superior
Washburn
Ashland
Eagle River
Woodboro Rhinelander
Pineville
Merrill
Brokaw Marinette
General strike, 1916
Chippewa Falls Wausau Schofield
Eau Claire
Clintonville
Stevens Point Green Bay
Whiting Manawa De Pere
Biron
Port Edwards Plover Hortonville
Nekoosa Wisconsin Appleton Kaukauna
Rapids Menasha Combined Two Rivers
Neenah Locks
Wautoma Oshkosh
Sheboygan
General strike, 1895
La Crosse Kohler
Cambria
Port Washington
Madison Milwaukee
General strike, 1886
Waukesha
Stoughton West Allis Cudahy
Franksville
Janesville Racine
Beloit Kenosha

St. Croix River
Montreal R.
Brule River
Menominee River
Wisconsin River
Wolf River
Chippewa River
Black River
Fox River
Mississippi River
Rock River

Certain strikes by workers, and lockouts of union members by management, have galvanized Wisconsin's labor movement. Although most strikes were directed by one union against one company, others involved multiple unions, multiple companies, or even (in the case of general strikes) multiple trades. Some unions repeated strikes numerous times until their demands were met or the unions were broken. Hundreds of strikes not listed on this chart also played a role in changing workplaces.

Women's Influence

Women's movements have been defined not by geography, but by the simple fact that women have always been everywhere. The movements have been centered on the everyday lives of women at home and at work, and the issues involved have affected all aspects of society. Before settlers arrived in Wisconsin, women in certain Native American nations took active leadership roles in social, economic, and sometimes political affairs. Native women often resented the lower status they were accorded in colonial society after Europeans arrived. Later, many female descendants of the settlers also came to question their own lower status.

Social activity. In Wisconsin's early years, work and social activity were largely segregated according to sex. This was particularly true in rural areas, where visits among relatives were important in building social, family, and work ties (see the photo at right). Women tended to associate with other women or with their own male relatives. At the center of women's culture were the relationship between mothers and daughters and the lifelong bonds between female relatives and friends. In Wisconsin towns and cities, all-women's clubs became a strong moral and social force in the late 19th century, when the focus of society was on the individual woman. Women took a lead on issues such as abolition (see *African Americans*), property rights of wives (see *Statehood*), temperance (see column on facing page), prison and school reform, and suffrage.

Woman suffrage. Public sentiment grew very slowly in Wisconsin for woman *suffrage* (the right to vote). Throughout the 19th century, Wisconsin did not permit women to vote in state elections. Although the Assembly backed suffrage in an 1867 resolution, it was not upheld by the next legislature. In 1869, suffragist leaders Susan B. Anthony and Elizabeth Cady Stanton visited the state to help organize the Wisconsin Woman's Suffrage Association. Milwaukee physician Laura Ross Wolcott led the group through years of legislative efforts. The cause was joined by reformers Belle Case La Follette (see *Progressives*), Zona Gale (see *Cultural Figures*), the Reverend Olympia Brown (the first ordained female minister in Wisconsin), Carrie Chapman Catt (later a founder of the League of Women Voters), Ada L. James, and many others around the state (see map on facing page). Finally, recognition of women's contributions to the war effort in World War I increased support for suffrage. Congress granted suffrage by passing the 19th Amendment to the U.S. Constitution, and sent it for ratification to the states, which raced to vote on it. On June 10, 1919, Wisconsin became the first state to ratify the amendment, notifying Congress only minutes before Illinois did. Considering Wisconsin's previous stance on suffrage, some were surprised that the state had taken the lead on the amendment.

Women in rural areas. In rural areas, suffrage changed women's everyday lives very little. On farms, women often worked in the fields and barns

Norwegian mother Siri Rustebakke posed with her daughters and daughter-in-law spinning at Black Earth in the late 1870s.

WISCONSIN WOMEN

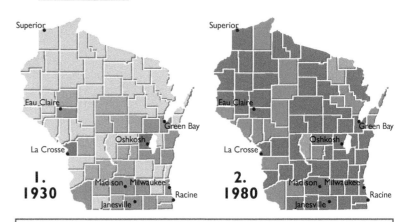

Women as Percentage of Total Population

Over 50% | 49.0–49.9% | 48.0–48.9% | Less than 48%

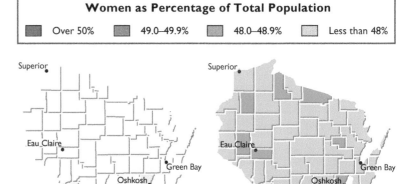

Women as Percentage of Total Employed

44–50% | 36–43% | 29–35% | Less than 29%

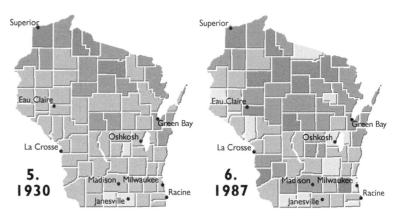

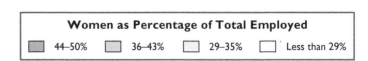

Woman-Operated Farms as Percentage of Total Farms

6.6–18% | 4.6–6.5% | 2.1–4.5% | Less than 2.1%

Temperance

Many Wisconsin women worked not only for their own rights, but for the moral improvement of society. Both temperance and prohibition of liquor became popular causes among women concerned about drunkenness and immorality. Some pioneer women went as far as knocking the heads off whiskey barrels to put saloons out of business. In the 1870s, women established local temperance clubs, and the Prohibition Party attracted a following that included many men. The Woman's Christian Temperance Union (WCTU), led by Janesville-raised educator Frances Willard, attracted evangelical women who believed in defending the Christian home (see 1913 photo of parade float, above). Through her Home Protection Party, Willard promoted the family-centered "politics of the mother heart." With her slogan "Do Everything," she led many WCTU members in supporting suffrage. Other women and men, particularly immigrants who worked in the brewing industry (see *Southeastern Industries*), feared the social and economic results of temperance and the equality of sexes. (Most came from countries such as Germany, where beer and wine were made and consumed routinely in the home.) When Congress enacted prohibition and suffrage in 1919, many women opposed them both. Wisconsin became a national center for both supporters and opponents of prohibition, which ended in 1933.

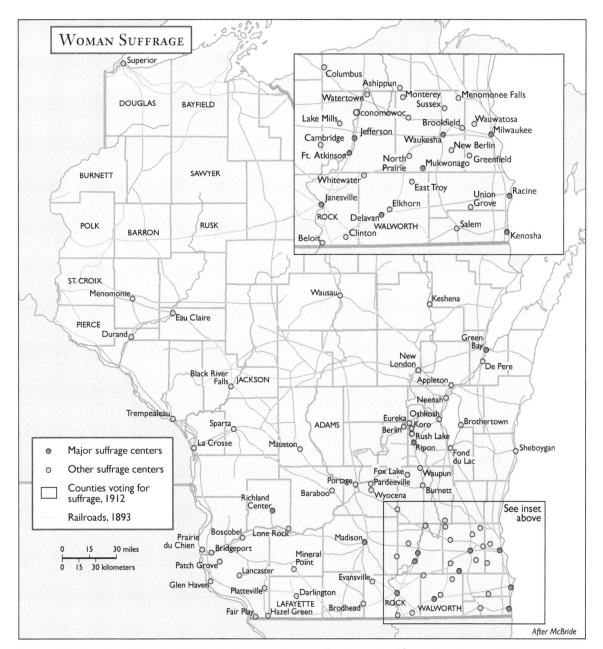

In a statewide referendum on November 4, 1912, male voters opposed woman suffrage by a margin of 63 percent to 37 percent. On the same day, four other states backed suffrage. Most of the 14 counties that backed suffrage were in the north, where relatively fewer women lived. Wisconsin granted women the full right to vote seven years later when the legislature ratified the 19th Amendment to the U.S. Constitution.

Women's Baseball

The All-American Girls Professional Baseball League was formed during World War II, when many male players served in the military. Teams in Wisconsin included the Racine Belles (see photo above from 1949), the Kenosha Comets, and the Milwaukee Chicks. A team manager asserted that one Belles game was the "greatest" game he had ever seen. In 1943, the Belles' Sophie Kurys stole 201 bases—a record that no professional player has since approached. Despite dawn-to-dusk training, the women players were required to attend "charm school" in the evening. Their league was discontinued in 1954.

with their spouses, while also managing the household, children, and family finances. Many did additional work, such as raising chickens, to earn "egg money" for household needs and children's education. Rural women's clubs formed work cooperatives, such as laundry services, for income and mutual support. Women were a smaller percentage of the population in the north (see maps 1 and 2); men were predominant there because of lumbering, though the industry was in decline after 1905. Some women operated their own farms (usually after the death of a husband); such farms were more frequently found in less fertile counties, particularly in the north (see maps 5 and 6).

Women in employment. World War II brought large numbers of women into the paid workforce to replace men who had entered military service (see photo of women workers in Fort Atkinson in 1946). After the war, many women were displaced by the returning men, but a significant number kept their jobs. By 1950 women made up about a quarter of the civilian labor force. During the 1960s, more women began to receive better education and training. By the end of the decade, women made up over a third of the labor force, and fewer than half were full-time homemakers. In comparison with men, however, more women worked part-time, and women had a smaller range of job opportunities.

Feminism. The feminist movement that gained momentum in the 1960s profoundly changed many aspects of society. As with earlier reform movements, it forged links to other social issues of its era (see *1960s*). Unlike earlier movements for specific reforms, it promoted the liberation of the entire community of women from all constraints—political, social, economic, and cultural. The social transformation that took place reached even small towns. By 1980 women made up over 40 percent of the work force in most counties (see maps 3 and 4). Despite the strides made by women, especially since the 1960s, women clearly have a long way to go to realize the goals of the movement.

The 1960s: Time of Turmoil & Change

The movement for black equality was not born in the 1960s (see *African Americans*). The 1960s civil rights movement, however, profoundly affected U.S. society. The first Milwaukee sit-in by the Congress On Racial Equality (CORE) coincided with the 1963 "March on Washington," where the Rev. Martin Luther King, Jr., gave his "I Have a Dream" speech. The local National Association for the Advancement of Colored People (NAACP) introduced his vision into schools, clubs, government, and neighborhoods.

Schools. In 1964–66, the Milwaukee United School Integration Committee (MUSIC) held a series of boycotts of segregated schools, one of which lasted 35 days. Some clergymen were arrested for symbolically blockading the schools. Clergy also set up temporary "Freedom Schools" in their churches. It was not until the 1980s that large-scale school integration took place in the Milwaukee metropolitan area.

Social discrimination. In 1966, the NAACP Youth League, joined by Father James Groppi, picketed the all-white Eagles Club and homes of public officials who were club members. The picketing of a Wauwatosa judge in August created a violent local reaction, and the National Guard was sent in for nine days. A few prominent club members resigned. The Ku Klux Klan then bombed NAACP headquarters, causing the Youth League to set up its own Freedom Houses.

Police brutality. African Americans had long objected to the unwarranted use of force by local police under the command of Chief Harold Breier. In July 1967, a few days after U.S. Army troops had quelled a large civil disturbance in Detroit, the resentment boiled over at a Milwaukee nightclub where police broke up a fight. Many youths marched north on 3rd Street, burning and looting some shops. Police used tear gas and battled snipers. Mayor Henry Maier began a 10-day curfew and called in 4,800 National Guard troops with armored vehicles. The disturbance resulted in 3 deaths, 70 injuries, nearly 200 arrests, and worsened interracial relations.

Housing. In 1967, after four attempts by Alderman Vel Phillips to pass a city open-housing law failed, the Youth League held a series of daily marches protesting housing discrimination. Many whites reacted violently to marches through the South Side (see column at right). Instead of calling in the National Guard to protect the marchers, Maier issued a three-day ban on all protests. Many of those who defied the ban were arrested or clubbed. The open-housing law passed in April 1968, only after Reverend King was killed and 15,000 Milwaukeeans marched in his honor.

Open-Housing Marches

The Milwaukee NAACP Youth League, also called the "Commandos," held a series of daily marches for open housing in 1967 (below). Their main target was what they saw as the bastion of housing discrimination—the South Side. It was populated mainly by Polish and Irish Catholics, who felt they were defending their neighborhood from unwanted change. People on both sides compared the South Side to the southern U.S. Presidential candidate George Wallace commented in 1964 that if he lived outside of Alabama, he would choose the South Side. African Americans referred to an Alabama civil rights struggle when they called Milwaukee "the Selma of the North." Father James Groppi (center) compared the Menomonee River Valley that divided the North and South sides to the "Mason-Dixon Line" that divided the North and South before the Civil War. On August 28, after receiving a permit for a rally in Kosciuszko Park in the heart of the South Side, about 260 open-housing marchers crossed the valley on the 16th Street viaduct. When they arrived they were met by a crowd of 8,000 whites—mainly youths— some of whom chanted, "White Power" and "We want slaves." The next day, 200 marchers, escorted by shotgun-wielding police, were stopped before reaching the park by a crowd of about 13,000, throwing rocks and carrying an effigy of Groppi. After six days of violence, a peaceful civil rights march of 1,000 people wound through the South Side on September 2. The marches continued daily for 200 straight days until December 12—when a judge ruled in favor of open housing.

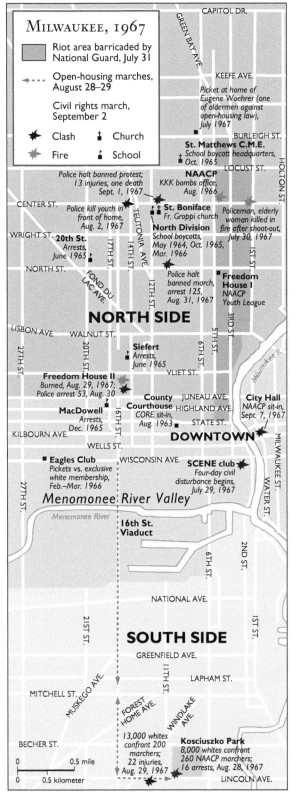

MILWAUKEE, 1967

Riot area barricaded by National Guard, July 31

Open-housing marches, August 28–29

Civil rights march, September 2

★ Clash   ╪ Church
✦ Fire   ╪ School

CAPITOL DR.
GREEN BAY AVE.
KEEFE AVE.

Picket at home of Eugene Woehrer (one of aldermen against open-housing law), July 1967

BURLEIGH ST.

St. Matthews C.M.E.
School boycott headquarters, Oct. 1965

LOCUST ST.
HOLTON ST.

Police halt banned protest; 13 injuries, one death Sept. 1, 1967

NAACP
KKK bombs office, Aug. 1966

CENTER ST.

Police kill youth in front of home, Aug. 2, 1967

St. Boniface
Fr. Groppi church
North Division
School boycotts, May 1964, Oct. 1965, Mar. 1966

Policeman, elderly woman killed in fire after shoot-out, July 30, 1967

WRIGHT ST. **20th St.**
Arrests, June 1965
NORTH ST.

TEUTONIA AVE.
17TH ST.
14TH ST.
12TH ST.
FOND DU LAC AVE.

Police halt banned march, arrest 125, Aug. 31, 1967

Freedom House I
NAACP Youth League

NORTH SIDE

1ST ST.
3RD ST.
5TH ST.
6TH ST.

LISBON AVE. WALNUT ST.

Siefert
Arrests, June 1965

27TH ST.
20TH ST.

VLIET ST.

Freedom House II
Burned, Aug. 29, 1967; Police arrest 53, Aug. 30

Milwaukee R.

County Courthouse
CORE sit-in, Aug. 1963

JUNEAU AVE.
HIGHLAND AVE.
STATE ST.

City Hall
NAACP sit-in, Sept. 7, 1967

MacDowell
Arrests, Dec. 1965

16TH ST.

KILBOURN AVE.

WELLS ST.

DOWNTOWN

MILWAUKEE ST.
WATER ST.

Eagles Club
Pickets vs. exclusive white membership, Feb.–Mar. 1966

WISCONSIN AVE.

SCENE club
Four-day civil disturbance begins, July 29, 1967

27TH ST.

Menomonee River Valley

Menomonee River

16th St. Viaduct

6TH ST.
2ND ST.
1ST ST.

NATIONAL AVE.

21ST ST.

SOUTH SIDE

GREENFIELD AVE.

11TH ST.

LAPHAM ST.

MITCHELL ST.
MUSKEGO AVE.
FOREST HOME AVE.
WINDLAKE AVE.

13,000 whites confront 200 marchers; 22 injuries, Aug. 29, 1967

Kosciuszko Park
8,000 whites confront 260 NAACP marchers; 16 arrests, Aug. 28, 1967

BECHER ST.

0   0.5 mile
0   0.5 kilometer

LINCOLN AVE.

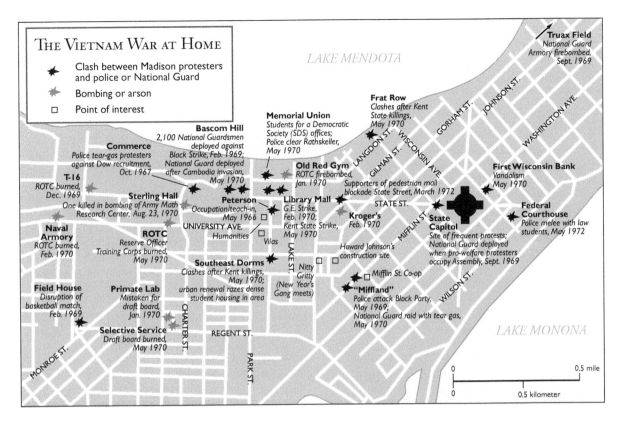

THE VIETNAM WAR AT HOME

★ Clash between Madison protesters and police or National Guard

✳ Bombing or arson

□ Point of interest

LAKE MENDOTA

Truax Field
National Guard
Armory firebombed,
Sept. 1969

Frat Row
Clashes after Kent
State killings,
May 1970

Memorial Union
Students for a Democratic
Society (SDS) offices;
Police clear Rathskeller,
May 1970

Bascom Hill
2,100 National Guardsmen
deployed against
Black Strike, Feb. 1969;
National Guard deployed
after Cambodia invasion,
May 1970

Commerce
Police tear-gas protesters
against Dow recruitment,
Oct. 1967

T-16
ROTC burned,
Dec. 1969

Sterling Hall
One killed in bombing of Army Math
Research Center, Aug. 23, 1970

Peterson
Occupation/teach-in,
May 1966

UNIVERSITY AVE.
Humanities

Old Red Gym
ROTC firebombed,
Jan. 1970

Library Mall
G.E. Strike,
Feb. 1970;
Kent State Strike,
May 1970

Supporters of pedestrian mall
blockade State Street, March 1972

STATE ST.

Kroger's
Feb. 1970

First Wisconsin Bank
Vandalism
May 1970

**Federal
Courthouse**
Police melee with law
students, May 1972

**Naval
Armory**
ROTC burned,
Feb. 1970

ROTC
Reserve Officer
Training Corps burned,
May 1970

Vilas

**State
Capitol**
Site of frequent protests;
National Guard deployed
when pro-welfare protesters
occupy Assembly, Sept. 1969

Howard Johnson's
construction site

Southeast Dorms
Clashes after Kent killings,
May 1970;
urban renewal razes dense
student housing in area

Nitty
Gritty
(New Year's
Gang meets)

□ Mifflin St. Co-op

Field House
Disruption of
basketball match,
Feb. 1969

Primate Lab
Mistaken for
draft board,
Jan. 1970

"Miffland"
Police attack Block Party,
May 1969;
National Guard raid with tear gas,
May 1970

LAKE MONONA

Selective Service
Draft board burned,
May 1970

REGENT ST.

0 ——— 0.5 mile
0 ——— 0.5 kilometer

The Bombing of
Sterling Hall

Foreign interventions commonly result in violence within the intervening country. The U.S. intervention in Indochina (Vietnam, Cambodia, and Laos) led to a small-scale "war at home," and nowhere was it more evident than in Wisconsin. On January 1, 1970, two young Madison men, angered by the U.S. "carpet-bombing" of Vietnam flew a light plane over the Badger Army Ammunition Plant near Baraboo. The "New Year's Gang" dropped a bomb that failed to detonate, but the group's action exploded on front pages around the country as the only aerial bombing in the U.S. during the war. The underground group also attacked U.W. ROTC offices and attempted to bomb a Sauk City electrical substation and Madison draft board offices. (Other clandestine groups firebombed military targets on the Milwaukee and Whitewater campuses, and elsewhere in the U.S.) The group saw university research and institutions as complicit in a war effort that killed many Indochinese civilians and also killed some student protesters. Some antiwar activists supported the group, but many others criticized it for using the same violent tactics as the military. On August 23, 1970, the New Year's Gang detonated a van packed with explosives next to Sterling Hall, intending to destroy the Army Math Research Center. The 3:42 AM blast destroyed part of the building (above), injuring some researchers and killing postdoctoral physics fellow Robert Fassnacht, one of the few casualties in the U.S. resulting from the Indochina War. Authorities apprehended three of the bombers (one remains at large to this day). Antiwar protests continued in Madison for two more years, but on a less militant level. More than 58,000 Americans and two million Indochinese lost their lives in the war.

THE "SIXTIES" ON CAMPUS

Turmoil and change had marked many periods in Wisconsin history before the late 1960s and early 1970s. The state had seen campus antiwar activism (opposition to intervention in Central America in the 1920s), left-wing militancy (see *Labor*), feminist rallies (see *Women*), and critical social thinking (see *Cultural Figures*).

What made the 1960s different was the *variety* of movements and the ways they reinforced each other. College students, in particular, challenged many of society's political and cultural assumptions. Campus activists came from both conservative families and families with longstanding reform politics.

These tendencies came together in Madison, which became known as the radical center of the Midwest. Students, professors, and community members joined in early 1965–66 actions against the Vietnam War. They included peaceful 40-mile walks to the Badger Army Ammunition Plant near Baraboo, and protests against examples of the "military-industrial complex": the draft board, the Reserve Officer Training Corps (ROTC), and military research contracts on campus.

Police and National Guard troops in tear gas masks detain a protester on Bascom Hill at the University of Wisconsin in February 1969.

As U.S. participation in the war escalated in Southeast Asia, militancy on campus increased. A youth "counterculture" grew out of the feeling that society had to be transformed. In 1967, National Guardsmen disrupted a summer youth festival at Lake Geneva, and police maced and clubbed

Madison students protesting recruitment by Dow— a firm that made the jellied gasoline *napalm* used in Vietnam. As similar clashes spread around the U.S., the local left-wing newspapers *Daily Cardinal* and *Kaleidoscope* predicted a "revolution," though many still backed the use of the military to fight communism in Southeast Asia.

Antiwar, feminist, and other movements drew much inspiration from civil rights activism. "Minority" college students brought that activism onto campus by demanding ethnic studies programs. In Oshkosh, 94 students who held a 1968 sit-in were expelled. A 1969 "Black Strike" in Madison was countered by National Guard troops.

Officials also took a "law-and-order" line against white student activists. Madison police cracked down on the countercultural Mifflin Street Block Party in 1969, and had running battles with antiwar protesters. Guardsmen were again deployed after the reaction to the 1970 Cambodia intervention, and the killing of a total of six students at Kent State in Ohio and Jackson State in Mississippi. Protesters attacked not only military offices, but also businesses seen as exploiting students. Militant tactics lessened after the fatal bombing of an Army research lab (see column at left).

Many Madisonians preferred to join peaceful marches and tried to forge broad-based community alliances. Madison voters elected student activist Paul Soglin as mayor in 1974. The U.S. military withdrew from Indochina in 1975, but Madison's reputation as a radical hotbed did not easily fade.

Federal Elections in Wisconsin

Wisconsin is known nationwide for its high voter turnout, voters splitting their tickets between parties, and the historic strength of several "minor" parties. The state's political patterns from the 1840s to 1940s were largely formed along ethnic and religious lines, and heavily favored the Republican Party (then a very different party in Wisconsin than in the rest of the U.S.). State voters have chosen the winning candidate 30 out of 39 times in presidential elections held every four years (see chart on facing page). Elections for the U.S. House of Representatives are held every two years (see *Population*), and, since popular voting for senators began in 1914, elections for the two U.S. Senate seats have alternated every six years. Federal election results show the strength of state parties throughout different political eras.

Former President Theodore Roosevelt (center) leaving Milwaukee after being injured in a 1912 assassination attempt. Roosevelt was campaigning to return to the White House as a "Bull Moose" Progressive. An eyeglass case, folded speech, and heavy overcoat stopped the assassin's bullet from killing Roosevelt. In the election later that year, he split the Republican vote with former ally President William Howard Taft, which led to a victory for Democrat Woodrow Wilson in Wisconsin and the U.S.

Democratic dominance (1843–55). Just before and after statehood, Democrats held a stronger position than Whigs in Wisconsin politics. In 1854, many Whigs joined antislavery abolitionists in founding the new Republican Party—which gained its first major successes in Wisconsin. Republican Abraham Lincoln was elected to the White House in 1860.

Republican dominance (1856–1900). The Republican Party was virtually unbeatable in Wisconsin for many decades. It lost federal elections in the state mainly in times of economic distress. Rural Scandinavians and Yankees typically voted Republican (although some voted for Prohibition candidates). German Catholics tended to vote Democratic until the 1890s, when they began to blame Democrats for an economic depression and for promoting the Protestant evangelical beliefs of presidential candidate William Jennings Bryan.

Progressive Era (1901–45). The most tumultuous era in global history—with two world wars and massive economic changes—also turned Wisconsin politics upside down (see *Progressives*). The era was marked by the reign of Robert M. La Follette, Sr., as governor (1901–6) and U.S. senator (1906–25). He came to represent the progressive faction of the

Republican Party, and was strongly opposed by members of the *stalwart* (conservative) faction (see *State Government*). Scandinavian and German Protestants tended to support La Follette's populist platform of equal opportunity, popular participation in government, and public education; Anglo-Americans tended to back his stalwart opponents. Yet together, the two Republican factions mobilized a sizable majority of voters. Democrat Woodrow Wilson won Wisconsin's 1912 presidential vote only because Republicans split between two candidates. His subsequent support of World War I convinced more ethnic Germans to support Senator La Follette, who had opposed the war (along with other figures such as Milwaukee Socialist Congressman Victor Berger). La Follette ran for president as a Progressive in 1924, winning a majority only in his home state, and over 16 percent nationally. When he died the following year, his son Robert, Jr., took over as senator. In 1934 he helped to form the state Progressive Party to oppose what he saw as "pro-war" Democrats and "probusiness" Republicans. This was the time of the Great Depression, however, and President Franklin D. Roosevelt's "New Deal" was identifying Democrats with many progressive economic issues. La Follette nevertheless accused Roosevelt of timidity on economic issues and of embroiling the U.S. in foreign conflicts.

Time of transition (1946–57). Robert La Follette, Jr., was defeated for reelection in 1946 by conservative Appleton Republican Joseph R. McCarthy. McCarthy presented himself as a World War II veteran and, like the La Follettes, as a "man of the people." He later chose to carry out his populist crusade against communism (see column at right). The Progressive Party disbanded, and at first Republicans picked up most of the pieces. Influenced by Roosevelt's legacy, however, some other (mostly younger) Progressives regrouped under a new Democratic liberal banner. Areas of the state—such as the northwestern counties—that had been heavily Republican or Progressive before World War II began to vote more Democratic (see maps on facing page). Conservative counties that had generally voted Democratic before the war (such as Milwaukee suburbs and many rural areas) began to vote more Republican. The parties shifted their messages at the same time as the state's population was shifting toward the cities and suburbs, and ethnic and religious loyalties were losing their hold.

Two-party system (1957–present). The senatorial victories of William Proxmire in 1957 and of then-Governor Gaylord A. Nelson in 1962, gave Democrats control of Wisconsin's U.S. Senate delegation for two decades. Both were helped by a strengthened Democratic base in Milwaukee, Dane. and other urban counties, a large bloc of independent voters, and crossover votes from Republicans. The state's unpredictable open primary system has allowed for crossover votes. As late as the 1980s, many backers of Republican President Ronald Reagan also voted for Proxmire. Wisconsin's

McCarthy's Crusade

In the 1946 Republican senatorial primary, former Appleton circuit judge Joseph R. McCarthy (above) won a stunning upset over Senator Robert M. La Follette, Jr., and went on to win the election. McCarthy was a conservative World War II veteran who opposed La Follette's progressive and isolationist politics. The two men represented different wings of Wisconsin's populist tradition—La Follette as a "left-wing" populist and McCarthy as a "right-wing" populist. McCarthy won national headlines in 1950 by charging that Communists had infiltrated the State Department, though he could not identify any individuals by name. In 1952 he became chairman of a subcommittee on investigations, where for two years he made allegations of Communist influence in the federal government. His crusade was eventually termed by some—such as Madison's *Capital Times* newspaper— as an unjustified "witch hunt." After he accused the Army of harboring Communists, the U.S. Senate condemned him in a rare censure vote. McCarthy died in 1957, but "McCarthyism" still stands for the fears of the Cold War and the undermining of civil liberties.

U.S. SENATORS

Isaac P. Walker	1848–1855
Henry Dodge	1848–1857
Charles Durkee (UR)	1855–1861
James R. Doolittle	1857–1869
Timothy Howe (UR)	1861–1879
Matthew Carpenter	1869–1875
Angus Cameron	1875–1885
Philetus Sawyer	1881–1893
John C. Spooner	1885–1891
William F. Vilas	1891–1897
John L. Mitchell	1893–1899
John C. Spooner	1897–1907
Joseph V. Quarles	1899–1905
Robert La Follette, Sr.	1906–1925
Isaac Stephenson	1907–1915
Paul O. Husting	1915–1917
Irvine L. Lenroot	1918–1927
Robert La Follette, Jr.	1925–1935
John J. Blaine	1927–1933
F. Ryan Duffy	1933–1939
Robert La Follette, Jr.	1935–1947
Alexander Wiley	1939–1963
Joseph R. McCarthy	1947–1957
William Proxmire	1957–1989
Gaylord A. Nelson	1963–1981
Robert W. Kasten, Jr.	1981–1993
Herbert H. Kohl	1989–
Russell D. Feingold	1993–

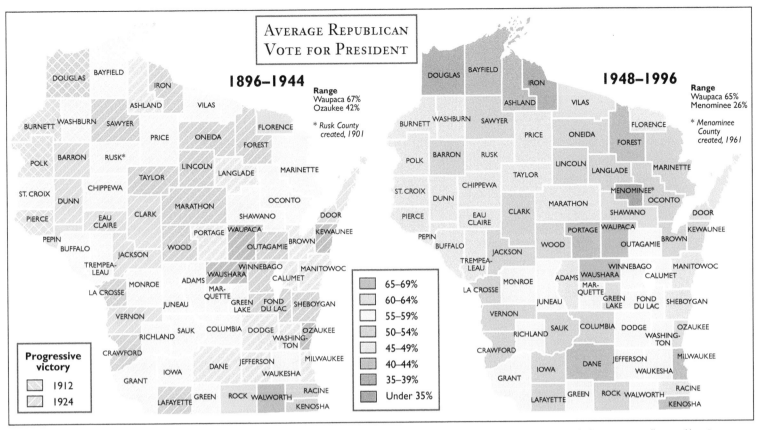

Average Republican Vote for President

1896–1944

Range
Waupaca 67%
Ozaukee 42%

* Rusk County created, 1901

Progressive victory
- 1912
- 1924

1948–1996

Range
Waupaca 65%
Menominee 26%

* Menominee County created, 1961

- 65–69%
- 60–64%
- 55–59%
- 50–54%
- 45–49%
- 40–44%
- 35–39%
- Under 35%

The two maps above show average voting patterns for Republican presidential candidates ifrom 1896 to 1996. Counties not won by a Republican (blue shades) were generally carried by a Democrat (red shades). The exceptions occurred when Progressive candidates Theodore Roosevelt (1912) or Robert M. La Follette, Sr. (1924) won counties in the state, as shown by the yellow patterns. The chart below shows the top three Wisconsin finishers in presidential elections, by candidate and party. Candidates listed in the first row won in Wisconsin, and those listed in italic letters won the election in the country as a whole. Wisconsin's share in the electoral college—the representative body that actually elects the president—has been dropping relative to other states since the 1930s.

position midway through the presidential primary season has enabled certain candidates to make a decisive showing, as John F. Kennedy did in 1960. Wisconsin's two-party era has been marked by weakened party allegiance, vote splitting, and an upsurge in personality politics. The focus on two parties has ironically narrowed political space in a state that once had harbored the most powerful "third parties" in the country. The state's maverick history could still be seen, however, in the 1980 independent vice-presidential bid by former Governor Patrick Lucey and in strong third-place showings by a few presidential candidates outside the two parties.

Politicians in the modern era have learned from Wisconsin's populist political history. They have found that they are most successful when they appeal to the interests of the "common people" and least successful when they are perceived as representing institutions. Whatever their place on the ideological spectrum, Wisconsin politicians often portray their programs as bringing "power to the people."

Political affiliations of presidential candidates and U.S. senators

- Democrat
- Republican
- Progressive
- Prohibition
- Socialist
- Whig
- Other party
- Independent (no party)

A	American	PP	People's Progressive
C	Constitution	RF	Reform
DL	Democrat and Liberal Republican	SD	Social Democrat
FS	Free Soil	SO	Southern Democrat
G	Greenback		
GR	Green	SW	Socialist Workers
IP	Independent Progressive	U	Union
		UR	Union Republican
L	Libertarian		

Presidential Elections in Wisconsin
National victor in italics

Election (electors)	Wisconsin victor Popular vote	Second-place finisher Popular vote	Third-place finisher Popular vote
1848 (4)	Lewis Cass 15,001	*Zachary Taylor* 13,747	Martin Van Buren (FS) 10,418
1852 (5)	*Franklin Pierce* 33,658	Winfield Scott 22,210	John P. Hale (FS) 8,814
1856 (5)	John C. Frémont 66,090	*James Buchanan* 52,843	Millard Fillmore (A) 579
1860 (5)	Abraham Lincoln 86,113	Stephen A. Douglas 65,021	John Breckinridge (SO) 888
1864 (8)	Abraham Lincoln 83,458	George B. McClellan 65,884	No candidate
1868 (8)	*Ulysses S. Grant* 108,857	Horatio Seymour 84,707	No candidate
1872 (10)	*Ulysses S. Grant* 104,994	Horace Greeley (DL) 86,477	Charles O'Connor 834
1876 (10)	*Rutherford B. Hayes* 130,668	Samuel J. Tilden 123,927	Peter Cooper (G) 1,509
1880 (10)	*James A. Garfield* 144,398	Winfield Hancock 114,644	James B. Weaver (G) 7.986
1884 (11)	James G. Blaine 161,157	*Grover Cleveland* 146,477	John P. St. John 7,656
1888 (11)	*Benjamin Harrison* 176,553	Grover Cleveland 155,232	Clinton B. Fisk 14,277
1892 (12)	*Grover Cleveland* 177,352	Benjamin Harrison 171,101	John Bidwell 13,136
1896 (12)	*William McKinley* 268,135	William J. Bryan 165,523	Joshua Levering 7,507
1900 (12)	*Willam McKinley* 265,760	William J. Bryan 159,163	John G. Wooley 10,027
1904 (13)	*Theodore Roosevelt* 280,164	Alton B. Parker 124,107	Eugene V. Debs (SD) 28,220
1908 (13)	*William H. Taft* 247,747	William J. Bryan 166,632	Eugene V. Debs (SD) 28,164
1912 (13)	*Woodrow Wilson* 164,230	William H. Taft 130,596	Theodore Roosevelt 62,448
1916 (13)	Charles E. Hughes 220,822	*Woodrow Wilson* 191,363	Allan Benson 27,631
1920 (13)	*Warren G. Harding* 498,576	James M. Cox 113,422	Eugene V. Debs 80,635
1924 (13)	Robert La Follette 453,678	*Calvin Coolidge* 311,614	John W. Davis 68,096
1928 (13)	*Herbert Hoover* 544,205	Alfred E. Smith 450,259	Norman Thomas 18,213
1932 (12)	*Franklin D. Roosevelt* 707,410	Herbert Hoover 347,741	Norman Thomas 53,379
1936 (12)	*Franklin D. Roosevelt* 802,984	Alfred M. Landon 380,828	William Lemke (U) 60,297
1940 (12)	*Franklin D. Roosevelt* 704,821	Wendell Willkie 679,206	Norman Thomas 15,071
1944 (12)	Thomas Dewey 674,532	*Franklin D. Roosevelt* 650,413	Norman Thomas 13,205
1948 (12)	*Harry S Truman* 647,310	Thomas Dewey 590,959	Henry Wallace (PP) 25,282
1952 (12)	*Dwight Eisenhower* 979,744	Adlai E. Stevenson 622,175	Vincent Hallinan (IP) 2,174
1956 (12)	*Dwight Eisenhower* 954,844	Adlai E. Stevenson 586,768	Coleman Andrews (C) 6,918
1960 (12)	Richard M. Nixon 895,175	*John F. Kennedy* 830,805	Farrell Dobbs (SW) 1,792
1964 (12)	*Lyndon B. Johnson* 1,050,424	Barry Goldwater 638,495	Clifton DeBerry (SW) 1,692
1968 (12)	*Richard M. Nixon* 809,997	Hubert Humphrey 748,804	George Wallace (A) 127,835
1972 (11)	*Richard M. Nixon* 989,430	George McGovern 810,174	John G. Schmitz (A) 47,525
1976 (11)	*Jimmy Carter* 1,040,232	Gerald R. Ford 1,004,987	Eugene J. McCarthy 34,943
1980 (11)	*Ronald Reagan* 1,088,845	Jimmy Carter 981,584	John Anderson 160,657
1984 (11)	*Ronald Reagan* 1,198,800	Walter Mondale 995,847	David Bergland (L) 4,884
1988 (11)	Michael Dukakis 1,126,794	*George Bush* 1,047,499	Ronald Paul (L) 5,157
1992 (11)	*Bill Clinton* 1,041,066	George Bush 930,855	Ross Perot 544,479
1996 (11)	*Bill Clinton* 1,071,971	Bob Dole 845,029	Ross Perot (RF) 227,339
2000 (11)	Al Gore 1,242,987	*George W. Bush* 1,237,279	Ralph Nader (GR) 94,070

Population & Representation

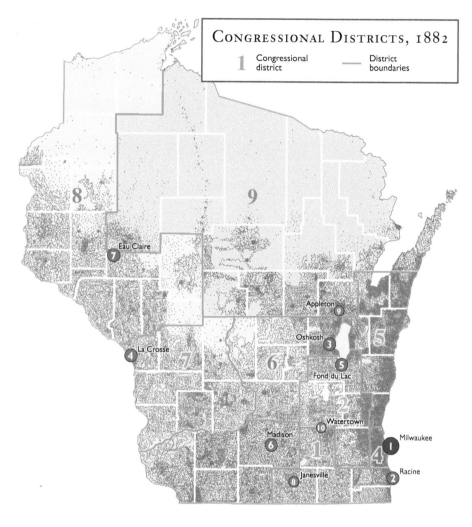

CONGRESSIONAL DISTRICTS, 1882

1 Congressional district — District boundaries

Wisconsin's population has increased since statehood, when about 300,000 citizens lived within its boundaries. Since 1848, the state's population has grown steadily at an average rate of about 25 percent in each decade. In 1870, Wisconsin, with a population of just over one million, ranked 15th out of 37 states. Wisconsin's 2000 population of 5,363,675 made it 18th out of the 50 states.

Population distribution. Wisconsin's population has always been distributed unevenly. Early European American settlement was concentrated in the southern and eastern parts of Wisconsin (see *Territorial Boundaries*). The population grew primarily along Lake Michigan, in the Fox and Rock river valleys, and in the southwestern Lead District (see *Mining*). Massive immigration, agricultural growth, and railroads moved settlement to the north and west from the 1860s to the 1910s. Although settlers founded cities and villages throughout the state, the south and east remained the most populous regions.

Population shifts. The shift in distribution occurred mainly for economic reasons. Arriving immigrants both enlarged existing ethnic communities and created new communities. Rural dwellers moved to the cities to seek employment, and urban dwellers later moved to suburbs (see *Rural Society*). In the mid-1920s, the state's urban population first surpassed the rural population, and the trend has continued (see graph below). Changes in resources and industries also caused cities to lose or gain population. From 1882 to 2001, Oshkosh dropped from the third-largest city to the eighth-largest, while Madison grew from the sixth-largest to the second-largest city.

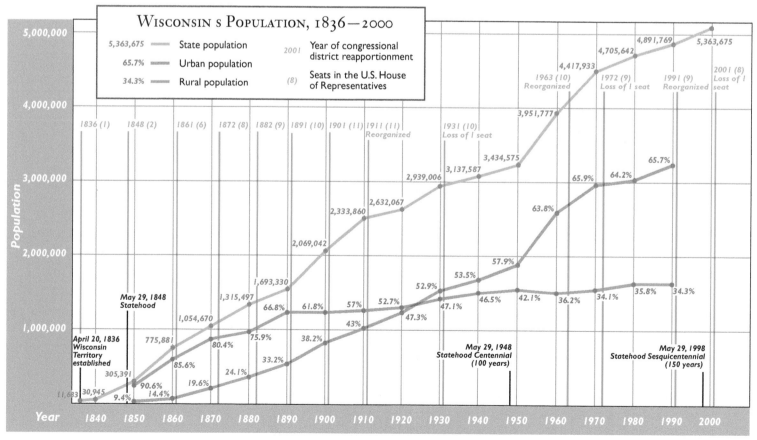

WISCONSIN'S POPULATION, 1836—2000

5,363,675 — State population
65.7% — Urban population
34.3% — Rural population

2001 Year of congressional district reapportionment

(8) Seats in the U.S. House of Representatives

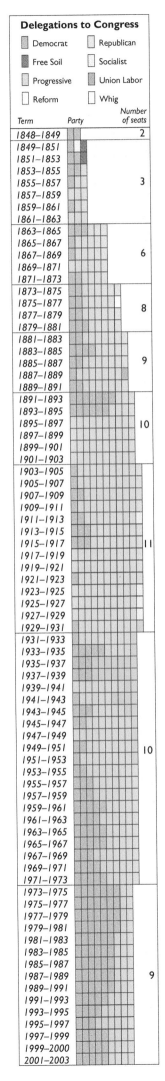

Delegations to Congress

▨ Democrat	▨ Republican
▨ Free Soil	☐ Socialist
▨ Progressive	☐ Union Labor
☐ Reform	☐ Whig

Term	Party	Number of seats
1848–1849		2
1849–1851		
1851–1853		3
1853–1855		
1855–1857		
1857–1859		
1859–1861		
1861–1863		
1863–1865		6
1865–1867		
1867–1869		
1869–1871		
1871–1873		
1873–1875		8
1875–1877		
1877–1879		
1879–1881		
1881–1883		9
1883–1885		
1885–1887		
1887–1889		
1889–1891		
1891–1893		10
1893–1895		
1895–1897		
1897–1899		
1899–1901		
1901–1903		
1903–1905		11
1905–1907		
1907–1909		
1909–1911		
1911–1913		
1913–1915		
1915–1917		
1917–1919		
1919–1921		
1921–1923		
1923–1925		
1925–1927		
1927–1929		
1929–1931		
1931–1933		10
1933–1935		
1935–1937		
1937–1939		
1939–1941		
1941–1943		
1943–1945		
1945–1947		
1947–1949		
1949–1951		10
1951–1953		
1953–1955		
1955–1957		
1957–1959		
1959–1961		
1961–1963		
1963–1965		
1965–1967		
1967–1969		
1969–1971		
1971–1973		
1973–1975		9
1975–1977		
1977–1979		
1979–1981		
1981–1983		
1983–1985		
1985–1987		9
1987–1989		
1989–1991		
1991–1993		
1993–1995		
1995–1997		
1997–1999		
1999–2000		
2001–2003		

Congressional representation. During its territorial era, Wisconsin had one nonvoting delegate in the House of Representatives. After statehood, Wisconsin began to be represented (like other states) by two U.S. senators serving six-year terms (see *Federal Elections*), and by varying numbers of House members serving two-year terms. Under the U.S. Constitution, congressional voting districts are based on population within a state. Members of the House represent the constituents of their districts. After every census a complex formula is used to determine the size of each state's congressional delegation. Depending on changes in state population and changes in the population of other states, a state may gain or lose representatives.

Reapportionment among states. Wisconsin representatives occupied two seats in the House of Representatives in 1848 (see *Statehood*). As the state's population grew, the number of Wisconsin seats increased steadily in each decade. In 1903 Wisconsin had 11 House members, but lost two seats in the reapportionments following the censuses of 1930 and 1970 (see chart at left). Wisconsin's population was still increasing, but not as fast as that of other states. Because Wisconsin's population as a percentage of the national population had declined, its share of representatives also dropped. The state lost one seat after the census of 2000, with Wisconsin voters choosing eight out of the 435 members of the House of Representatives, because the population of the *Sunbelt* (southeastern and southwestern states) is growing faster than Wisconsin's. The growth of suburbs and the Sunbelt is reshaping American politics.

Reapportionment within Wisconsin. During most of Wisconsin's history, congressional districts were drawn to include whole counties or groups of counties. In the 1960s

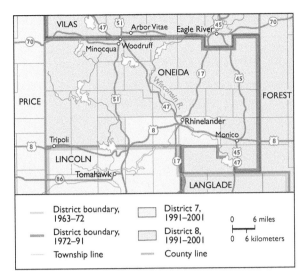

District boundary, 1963–72 · District boundary, 1972–91 · Township line · District 7, 1991–2001 · District 8, 1991–2001 · County line · 0 6 miles · 0 6 kilometers

it became necessary to break county lines in order to maintain an even population within each district. The goal of reapportionment is to create congressional districts with roughly the same populations. In 1991, for example, approximately 543,530 inhabitants were counted within each congressional district. In order to maintain this "equal representation," district boundaries are redrawn every ten years after each census. Districts that have lost more population than others will grow in area, while districts that gain population will shrink in area. In order to include the necessary number of people within its boundaries, District 7 (see map above) embraced the city of Rhinelander in the reapportionment of 1991. As Wisconsin's population continues to grow and its population becomes increasingly mobile, its map of political representation will change accordingly.

Delegations to Congress

Congressional elections, held every two years, serve as an important barometer of party strength (see chart at left). Congressional votes often mirrored choices for president (see *Federal Elections*) or governor (see *State Government*), but in other elections, voters chose candidates from different parties. Democrats did well in the first years after statehood. Republicans soon began to dominate congressional delegations, though they suffered a setback over an English-language school law in the 1890s (see *Germans*), and later split into progressive and conservative factions. Progressives formed their own party in 1934, and enjoyed success through World War II. Democrats rebounded after the war and peaked in the 1970s, following the Vietnam War and the Watergate scandal, however, Republicans gained more ground in the 1990s. The map at right shows proposed new congressional districts in February 2002. Controversy in the 2002 reapportionment centered on whether Milwaukee should be in one or two districts.

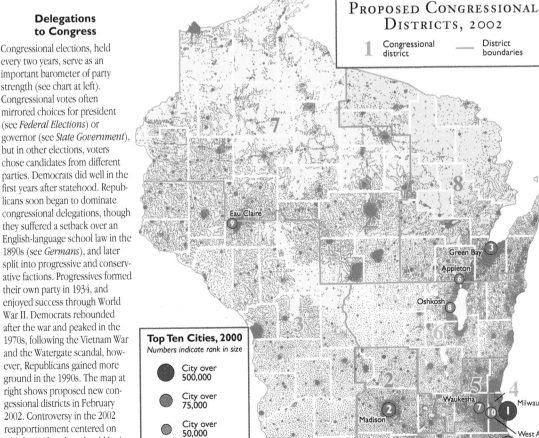

PROPOSED CONGRESSIONAL DISTRICTS, 2002

1 Congressional district — District boundaries

Top Ten Cities, 2000
Numbers indicate rank in size

● City over 500,000
● City over 75,000
● City over 50,000

One dot represents 25 inhabitants

State Government

Wisconsin's 1848 constitution was closely modeled on the U.S. Constitution: it created a legislative branch to make laws, an executive branch to carry out laws, and a judicial branch to interpret laws. All three branches—headed by a legislature, governor, and supreme court— help to develop public policy.

As population patterns have shifted around the state, legislative district boundaries of the *Senate* (upper house) and *Assembly* (lower house) have been *reapportioned* —or redrawn according to population— to distribute power in the legislature more fairly (see maps below). Although the numbers of state representatives and senators are roughly the same on the 1892 and 1998 maps, legislative districts are concentrated more in urban areas today. Assembly districts in 1892 were made up of either entire counties or divisions of counties. On the 2001 map, Assembly districts—apportioned by population—no longer exclusively follow county lines, and they show different population sizes in urban and rural areas.

The Wisconsin constitution in 1848 and many state law codes followed the constitution and law codes of New York. They incorporated traditions of political liberalism—including religious tolerance, election of judges, and separation of powers. They also reflected fiscal conservatism—supporting strong local government, opposing state-funded internal improvements, and limiting state debt.

Major issues in the 19th century included banking laws, the 1853 ban on capital punishment, African American voting rights, temperance, the use of foreign languages, women's property rights, railroad regulation, and currency reform. Agriculture took center stage under

Governor Jeremiah M. Rusk (later the first U.S. Secretary of Agriculture), whose administration was also marked by social reforms and labor unrest (see *Labor*).

The 1900 election of progressive Robert M. La Follette, Sr., the first Wisconsin-born governor, put Wisconsin on the national political map. A new progressive era made Wisconsin a leader in social welfare legislation (see *Progressives*). During this time, the Republicans were split into progressive and *stalwart* (conservative) factions, but their wide spectrum of opinion enabled them to dominate state politics. In most of the 1920s, the more conservative Democrats ran a distant third in the Assembly to the Republicans and Socialists (the latter mainly from Milwaukee, where they held the mayor's office for most of the

years between 1910 and 1960). La Follette died in 1925—after serving as both governor and U.S. senator —and his son Philip went on to become governor in 1931–33 and 1935–39. The progressive faction included governors McGovern, Blaine, and Zimmerman. Republican stalwarts were represented by governors Davidson, Philipp, and Kohler. Independent-minded voters, however, continued to split their tickets between the two parties. Progressives bolted to form their own party in 1934, and returned the younger La Follette to the governor's office. La Follette was defeated in 1938 by stalwart

Certain Wisconsin governors, such as the four pictured here, have taken state politics in new directions, either by initiating legislation or by representing a shift in party strength. Though decades apart, some statewide elections shared geographical similarities in party voting patterns.

2001 LEGISLATIVE DISTRICTS

36 Assembly district number
(Assembly districts indicated by color)

County boundaries

1892 LEGISLATIVE DISTRICTS

44 Assembly district number
(Assembly districts indicated by color)

County boundaries

□ Jeremiah Rusk
■ N. D. Fratt

1881 ELECTION
JEREMIAH M. RUSK

■ Philip La Follette
□ Albert Schmedeman

1934 ELECTION
PHILIP LA FOLLETTE

■ Gaylord Nelson
□ Vernon Thomson

1958 ELECTION
GAYLORD A. NELSON

■ Tommy Thompson
□ Anthony Earl

1986 ELECTION
TOMMY G. THOMPSON

Gubernatorial Elections

Vote percentages may total less than 100%.
Table shows only the figures for the first three places in each election and many of the percentages have been rounded.

Election	Victor / Birthplace / Term in office	% of votes	2nd place	3rd place
1848	Nelson Dewey / Connecticut / 1848–1852	56%	41%	3%
1849	Nelson Dewey	52%	36%	12%
1851	Leonard J. Farwell / New York / 1852–1854	50.5%	49.5%	
1853	William A. Barstow / Connecticut / 1854–1856	55%	39%	6%
1855	William A. Barstow / Court set aside election returns. / Coles Bashford served 1856–1858	50.1%	49.9%	
1857	Alexander W. Randall / New York / 1858–1862	50.2%	49.8%	
1859	Alexander W. Randall	53%	47%	
1861	Louis P. Harvey (died in office, 1862) / Connecticut / Edward Salomon served 1862–1864	54%	46%	
1863	James T. Lewis / New York / 1864–1866	60%	40%	
1865	Lucius Fairchild / Ohio / 1866–1872	55%	45%	
1867	Lucius Fairchild	52%	48%	
1869	Lucius Fairchild	53%	47%	
1871	Cadwallader C. Washburn / Maine / 1872–1874	53%	47%	
1873	William R. Taylor / Connecticut / 1874–1876	55%	45%	
1875	Harrison Ludington / New York / 1876–1878	50.1%	49.9%	
1877	William E. Smith / Scotland / 1878–1882	44%	40%	15% (G)
1879	William E. Smith	53%	40%	7% (G)
1881	Jeremiah M. Rusk / Ohio / 1882–1889	47%	41%	8%
1884	Jeremiah M. Rusk	51%	45%	3%
1886	Jeremiah M. Rusk	47%	40%	7%
1888	William D. Hoard / New York / 1889–1891	50%	44%	4%
1890	George W. Peck / New York / 1891–1895	52%	43%	4%
1892	George W. Peck	48%	46%	4%
1894	William H. Upham / Massachusetts / 1895–1897	52%	38%	7%
1896	Edward Scofield / Pennsylvania / 1897–1901	60%	38%	2%
1898	Edward Scofield	53%	41%	3%
1900	Robert M. La Follette, Sr. / Primrose, Dane County / 1901–1906	60%	39%	1%
1902	Robert M. La Follette, Sr.	53%	40%	4% (SD)
1904	Robert M. La Follette, Sr.	51%	39%	5% (SD)
1906	James O. Davidson / Norway / 1906–1911	57%	32%	8% (SD)
1908	James O. Davidson	54%	37%	6% (SD)
1910	Francis E. McGovern / Elkhart Lake, Sheboygan County / 1911–1915	51%	35%	12% (SD)
1912	Francis E. McGovern	45%	42%	9% (SD)
1914	Emanuel L. Philipp / Honey Creek, Sauk County / 1915–1921	43%	37%	10%
1916	Emanuel L. Philipp	53%	38%	7%
1918	Emanuel L. Philipp	47%	34%	17% (SD)
1920	John J. Blaine / Wingville, Grant County / 1921–1927	53%	36%	10%
1922	John J. Blaine	76%	11% (ID)	8%
1924	John J. Blaine	52%	40%	6%
1926	Fred R. Zimmerman / Milwaukee / 1927–1929	64%	14%	13%
1928	Walter J. Kohler, Sr. / Sheboygan / 1929–1931	55%	40%	4%
1930	Philip F. La Follette / Madison / 1931–1933	65%	28%	1%
1932	Albert G. Schmedeman / Madison / 1933–1935	52%	42%	5%
1934	Philip F. La Follette / Madison / 1935–1939	39%	38%	18%
1936	Philip F. La Follette	46%	29%	22%
1938	Julius P. Heil / Germany / 1939–1943	55%	36%	8%
1940	Julius P. Heil	41%	40%	19%
1942	Orland S. Loomis (died before inauguration) / Mauston, Juneau County / Walter Goodland served 1943–1945	50%	36%	12%
1944	Walter S. Goodland / Sharon, Walworth County / 1943–1947	53%	41%	6%
1946	Walter S. Goodland / (died in office) / Oscar Rennebohm served 1947	60%	39%	0.8%
1948	Oscar Rennebohm / Leeds, Columbia County / 1947–1951	54%	44%	1% (PP)
1950	Walter J. Kohler, Jr. / Sheboygan / 1951–1957	53%	46%	0.3% (PP)
1952	Walter J. Kohler, Jr.	62.5%	37.3%	0.2%
1954	Walter J. Kohler, Jr.	51.5%	48.4%	0.1%
1956	Vernon W. Thomson / Richland Center / 1957–1959	52%	48%	
1958	Gaylord A. Nelson / Clear Lake, Polk County / 1959–1963	53.6%	46.3%	0.1%
1960	Gaylord A. Nelson	52%	48%	
1962	John W. Reynolds / Green Bay / 1963–1965	50.4%	49.4%	0.2%
1964	Warren P. Knowles / River Falls, Pierce County / 1965–1971	51%	49%	
1966	Warren P. Knowles	53.5%	46.1%	0.4%
1968	Warren P. Knowles	52.9%	46.8%	0.2%
1970	Patrick J. Lucey / La Crosse / 1971–1977	54%	45%	0.6% (A)
1974	Patrick J. Lucey / Resigned to serve as ambassador to Mexico, 1977 / Martin Schreiber served 1977–1979	53%	42%	3% (A)
1978	Lee S. Dreyfus / Milwaukee / 1979–1983	54%	45%	0.4% (CO)
1982	Anthony S. Earl / Michigan / 1983–1987	57%	42%	0.6% (L)
1986	Tommy G. Thompson / Elroy, Juneau County / 1987–2001	53%	46%	0.6% (LF)
1990	Tommy G. Thompson	58%	42%	
1994	Tommy G. Thompson	67%	31%	0.7% (L)
1998	Tommy G. Thompson / Resigned to join White House Cabinet, 2001. / Scott McCallum serving 2001–	60%	39%	0.6% (L)

Legend:

Democrat	Socialist	A	American
Republican	Whig	CO	Conservative
People's (Populist)	Other party	G	Greenback
		ID	Independent Democrat
Progressive	Independent (no party)	LF	Labor-Farm
		L	Libertarian
Prohibition	No candidate*	PP	People's Progressive
		SD	Social Democrat

*Either no third-party candidate or no candidate with over 0.1% of the vote.

German immigrant Julius P. Heil, who began dismantling some of his reform programs.

"New Deal" Democrats adopted some progressive ideas during the Great Depression. The Progressive Party also lost ground because of political missteps by the La Follette family before and during World War II, and disbanded in 1946. La Follette rejoined the Republicans, but some younger Progressive leaders (including future governors Gaylord A. Nelson and John W. Reynolds) instead joined the Democratic Party.

Nelson's 1958 gubernatorial victory ushered in a more conventional two-party system, although many voters largely ignored party affiliations. From the 1960s to the 1980s, the legislature passed ethics codes, antidiscrimination laws, and tougher environmental regulations. Gubernatorial terms were changed from two to four years in 1970. Democrats alternated with Republicans in the governor's office, but dominated both legislative houses from 1975 to 1993. Republican fortunes rebounded with the 1986 election of Tommy G. Thompson, who has used the line-item veto more than any other governor and has introduced welfare reform legislation. Thompson served an unprecedented 14 years, before accepting an appointment to be the U.S. Secretary of Health & Human Services in 2001. It remains to be seen whether a new Republican era has begun, or whether state voters will continue to be unpredictable in their political behavior.

Wisconsin Firsts in Legislation, 1900s

Year		Year	
1901	Legislative Reference Library (Legislative Reference Bureau)	1925	Elderly pension plan
1903	Direct primary election enacted by legislation	1932	Unemployment compensation
1905	State civil service system	1933	Ban on racial or national origin discrimination against teachers
1907	Utilities regulation commission	1945	Aid to disabled persons
1909	City planning commissions	1951	Natural area management
1911	State income tax; state life insurance; workers' compensation; vocational education; labor commission	1957	Fiscal estimates of legislation
		1959	Public sector bargaining
1913	Prisoner work release	1963	Homestead tax credit
1914	Building codes	1965	Handicapped discrimination ban
1919	Food quality grading	1970	DDT pesticide ban
1921	Consumer protection laws; ban on sex discrimination in laws	1982	Ban on discrimination based on sexual orientation
		1990	Recycling business tax
		1997	"Wisconsin Works" welfare reform

The Military in Wisconsin

The U.S. military has helped to shape Wisconsin history in several ways. It has established installations in Wisconsin and has deployed troops in some local conflicts. It has recruited or drafted state residents to fight in wars around the world (see chart below) and has funded state defense industries.

Early presence (1816–60). The U.S. first acquired forts to control fur-trade routes along the strategic Fox-Wisconsin waterway (see *Colonial Boundaries*). In 1816 it established Fort Crawford north of the mouth of the Wisconsin River, Fort Winnebago at the portage between the Wisconsin and the Fox rivers, and Fort Howard at the mouth of the Fox. Settlements and farms grew around these forts, and roads connecting them to ports and mines were built (see *Transportation*). Militias built blockhouses and stockades in the Lead District during conflicts with the Ho-Chunk in 1827 and the Sauk in 1832 (see *Land Conflicts*). Troops removed Native Americans from the region and stopped using the forts by 1856.

The Civil War (1861–65). During the Civil War, Wisconsin raised 56 infantry, cavalry, and artillery regiments—far beyond initial expectations. Volunteer militias provided the recruits for many of these regiments, which were trained in 11 camps in the state (see column at right). They served in many key battles, among them Bull Run, Antietam, Chancellorsville, Vicksburg, Chattanooga, and the Wilderness. The Iron Brigade, named for its discipline under fire at the battle of South Mountain, was largely made up of Wisconsin regiments. It became one of the most famous and respected brigades of the war; it suffered heavy losses in the battle of Gettys-burg and was subsequently merged with units from the East. Militia units also suppressed riots against the military draft in Milwaukee and Ozaukee counties in 1862.

Militia and overseas expansion (1866–1917). After the Civil War the state militia took over some training camps. In the early 1880s the militia was reorganized into a professional National Guard. Twice in that decade it was used to suppress strikes—in Eau Claire in 1881 and Milwaukee in 1886 (see *Labor*). Wisconsin Guardsmen saw action in Puerto Rico during the 1898 Spanish-American War. Wisconsin troops also fought against rebels in

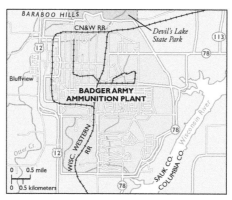

the Philippines (1899–1910) and Mexico (1917). In 1909, the Army purchased nearly 60,000 acres to build Camp McCoy (later renamed Fort McCoy) as a training, storage, and supply base.

The world wars (1917–45). Many Wisconsin citizens served in World War I in 1917–18, including federalized National Guardsmen who fought in the trenches of France. Nearly three times as many Wisconsin service members served in World War II from 1941 to 1945 (see chart bottom left). The military established several temporary bases around the state for weaponry, personnel, training, and housing prisoners of war. University classrooms were used to train technical personnel. The Air Force expanded Truax Field for its own use, and in the process helped to build Madison's economy. The Army built the Badger Ordnance Works near Baraboo to manufacture ammunition and explosives (see column at right). Existing manufacturing industries also expanded dramatically to serve defense needs (see *Southeastern Industries*), transforming the economy and lifestyle in some Wisconsin cities.

The Cold War (1946–90). After World War II, tensions began with the Soviet Union and other Communist countries. Wisconsin soldiers were sent to wars in Korea in 1950–53 and Indochina (Vietnam, Laos, and Cambodia) in 1960–75. When the Cold War intensified, Nike missiles were deployed near some Wisconsin cities (they were later withdrawn under treaty agreements). The Air National Guard expanded Mitchell Field in Milwaukee, built Volk Field at Camp Williams, and developed a tactical fighter wing. Army National Guardsmen were deployed to counter unrest over civil rights and the Indochina War (see *1960s*). The Air Force built communications stations in the state, and the Navy built Project ELF to communicate with its submerged submarines (see illustration on facing page). During this era, industries in Wisconsin received few military contracts compared to those in other states.

Post–Cold War era (1991–present). Conflicts involving the U.S. military continued in the 1990s, even as the superpowers reduced tensions. Fort McCoy was a major transshipment point for troops deployed for the 1991 Gulf War, and became a major

Wisconsin in Military Conflicts

Conflicts	Years	Number Served	Number Died
Civil War	1861–65	91,379	12,216
Spanish-American War	1898	5,469	134
Mexico	1917	4,168	NA
World War I	1917–18	122,215	3,932
World War II	1941–45	332,200	8,390
Korea	1950–53	132,000	729
Indochina	1960–75	165,400	1,239
Lebanon/Grenada	1983	400	1
Panama	1989	520	1
Gulf War	1990–91	10,400	11
Somalia	1992–94	426	2

Badger Army Ammunition Plant

After it entered World War II in 1941, the Army needed explosive fuel powder to propel ammunition shells. Plants needed to be located away from possible attack on the coasts and on large flat areas close to supplies of water and labor. The Army chose the Sauk Prairie, between the Wisconsin River and the Baraboo Hills. It acquired the fertile land from farmers and built the Badger Ordnance Works (see map at left). Thousands of workers came from around the state and elsewhere to work at the complex in 1943–45 and 1954–58. The renamed Badger Army Ammunition Plant produced fuel and explosives during the Indochina War in 1966–75, when it became a target of protests (see *1960s*). The plant, with over 1,400 buildings, was then put on standby. In the 1980s local residents were alarmed by pollution found in underground water supplies (see *Environment*) and by a "Star Wars" antimissile system proposed on the site. Ironically, the unfarmed 7,354-acre complex has become a haven for prairie grasses and animals. The site (closed in 1998) is due to be jointly managed by federal, tribal, state and local governments, primarily for prairie restoration, recreation, groundwater clean-up, and cultural-historical preservation.

Camp Randall

Camp Randall (above) was established after the start of the Civil War in 1861, at the Agricultural Society Fairgrounds on the western edge of Madison. It was named for Governor Alexander Randall, a staunch Republican and Union supporter. The camp trained most of the Wisconsin regiments that served in the war—a total of 70,000 men. Trainees were housed in poor conditions in tents and converted stables and cowsheds. Like other trainees around the state, they often received inadequate training from lower-level officers and lacked supplies and discipline. In the spring of 1862, the camp housed 1,260 Confederate prisoners of war taken in the capture of Island Number 10 in the Mississippi River. Many died from disease, and some are buried in Forest Hill Cemetery. The camp was closed in 1866; the land was later bought by the University of Wisconsin.

regional training center. The breakup of the Soviet Union later that year led to a reassessment of military priorities. Many National Guard and reserve units were either disbanded or consolidated. Some facilities were closed and operations scaled back. The Air National Guard dropped plans to expand low-level jet-training flights in 1996, after south-western Wisconsin farmers objected, but kept related plans to expand the Hardwood bombing range. Despite significant military cutbacks, Wisconsin National Guard units and active-duty personnel continue to be involved in military operations and deployments. The relatively low level of military resources invested in Wisconsin has helped insulate the state economically from the boom-and-bust nature of the modern defense industry.

Electrical current pulsed through the ground completes a circuit producing an Extremely Low Frequency (ELF) radio wave, with a wave length of about 2,500 miles. This wave is bounced between the earth's mantle and the ionosphere but penetrates seawater, allowing communication with submerged U.S. submarines.

Project ELF

In 1969 the Navy built an ELF (Extremely Low Frequency) test facility at Clam Lake, with a 28-mile antenna strung on aboveground utility poles. The facility was designed to carry messages to submarines at the bottom of the ocean (above). The system functioned best using the granite bedrock of northern Wisconsin and Michigan. The Navy first proposed to build "Project Sanguine"–a 6,000-mile network of underground antenna cables covering northern Wisconsin. Opposition by environmental and peace groups led to a scaled-down 1975 proposal for a 2,400-mile "Project Seafarer" in Michigan and finally in 1979 for "Project ELF." The final version, completed in 1989, twinned the original Clam Lake antenna and a connected 56-mile antenna in Michigan.

POW Camps
During World War II over 20,000 prisoners of war were housed in 39 camps throughout Wisconsin. Camp McCoy had more than 3,500 Japanese POW's, the most of any camp in the U.S. Prisoners were used to fill labor shortages, on farms, canneries and in logging. Temporary seasonal camps were often set up at county fairgrounds and former Civilian Conservation Corps camps. German prisoners would sometimes escape for a few hours or days in search of recreation. A few of these prisoners returned to settle in Wisconsin after the war.

Project ELF
(Clam Lake)
Naval submarine communications antenna, 28-mile cable on aboveground utility lines, 1969–present

Project ELF
(Republic, Mich.)
Naval submarine communications antenna, 56-mile cable on aboveground utility lines, coordinated with Clam Lake transmitter through phone lines, 1989–present

MICHIGAN

LAKE SUPERIOR

Osceola
Air Force Station
1942–45

Antigo Air
Force Station
Communications facility 1956–1970s

MINNESOTA

Fort McCoy
(Sparta)
1974–present
Camp McCoy, 1909–74
POW camp, 1942–45

Hardwood
Air-to-Ground
Weapons Range
Air National Guard base 1955–present

Fort Howard
(Green Bay)
1816–52

Camp Bragg
(Oshkosh)
Old fairgrounds; 1861–65

Volk Field and
Camp Williams
Air National Guard, Army National Guard base, 1961–present

Camp Fremont
(Ripon) *1861–65*

Camp Hamilton
(Fond du Lac)
1861–65

LAKE MICHIGAN

Lake Winnebago

MILITARY INSTALLATIONS

═══	Military roads, 1835–70
⊓	Federal fort, 1816–56
⊏	Military post or blockhouse, 1820–56
⊿	Civil War camp, 1861–65
◉	Major federal military installation, 1900s
✦	Nike missile site, 1960s
⚐	Army National Guard or Army Reserve facility, 2002
⚓	Navy/Marine Corps Reserve facility, 2002

Camp Salomon
(La Crosse)
1861–65

Fort Crawford
(Prairie du Chien)
1816–52;
Ft. Shelby 1813–14,
Ft. McKay (Br.), 1814–15,
moved to higher ground, 1828

Badger Army
Ammunition Plant
(Baraboo) *1963–75*
Badger Ordnance Works, 1942–63

Fort Winnebago
(Portage) *1828–45*

Truax Field
(Madison)
Air National Guard base, 1942–present

Camp Scott (Houlton)
1861–65

Camp Sigel (Reno)
1861–65

Camp Washburn
1861–66

General Mitchell Field
Air National Guard, Air Force Reserve base, 1951–present

Camp Utley
(Racine) *1861–65*
Artillery training;
1862 draftees' arson

Camp Harvey
(Kenosha)
1861–65

Fort Bluemounds

Camp Randall
(Madison) *1861–66;*
POW camp 1862;
soldiers mutiny, 1862

Fort Koshkonong

Fort Union
Fort Napoleon
Fort Defiance
Fort Jackson
Fort Hamilton

Camp Barstow
(Janesville)
1861–65

Williams Bay
Air Force Station
1942–45

Hazel Green

IOWA

ILLINOIS

0   15   30 miles
0   15   30 kilometers

Educational System

Schools have always helped to draw communities together, much like the churches that often appeared simultaneously with them in Wisconsin's early years (see *Religion*). Many early schoolhouses were simple log buildings built by volunteers and maintained without formal taxation, thus demonstrating the importance that communities placed on education. In 1848, the state constitution established free public schools, with funding for them and the university to come from interest earned on proceeds from sales of federal land grants. Between 1848 and 1900, the number of state school districts grew from 1,430 to 6,529. The vast majority were one-room schools; only 209 districts had high schools by 1900.

Consolidation. After 1900, improved transportation made it practical to consider the consolidation of districts into larger entities (see *Transportation*). The struggle of poorer rural districts to support schools created a disparity between them and schools in larger towns or cities. Consolidation supporters believed that by combining resources, smaller schools would be able to offer the quality and diversity of courses available in larger school districts. The state's urban population was far ahead of the rural population in the number of elementary school years students completed and in the percentage of students who went on to secondary and college levels. In 1940, Wisconsin's urban population ranked first in the nation in the proportion of 16- and 17-year-olds enrolled in school, while the state's farm population of the same age ranked 37th (girls) and 42nd (boys). Forced consolidation, however, aroused opposition from many people living on farms and in villages, who saw it as a threat to rural community values and democratic ideals and who considered

their schools integral to local pride and identity (see *Rural Society*). In 1947, the state backed consolidation, but communities were allowed to make decisions affecting their local schools (see map below). Consolidation worked gradually; the state had 2,731 districts in 1960 and only 426 by 1998.

University system. The University of Wisconsin System illustrates the value placed on education in the state. Three months after statehood, the legislature established the university on federally granted land in Madison. The first class—consisting of two men—graduated in 1854. By the 1890s, the university had a reputation around the state and the nation for its practical value in developing new ideas and disseminating knowledge to the general public. Progressive reformers of the early 1900s created the "Wisconsin Idea," and a partnership began between the university and state government in formulating public policy (see *Progressives*). Charles Van Hise, who led the university from 1903 to 1918, carried out many of these progressive programs. Under his leadership, the university grew in enrollment and served the public through an even wider range of programs, research, and extension work, becoming known as the one of the best public universities in the country. Elsewhere in the state, the first State Normal School for teacher training was founded at Platteville in 1866. It and similar institutions gradually expanded into two-year and four-year colleges, and in 1971 were consolidated as U.W. System campuses (see map on facing page).

Vocational and extension education. Between 1900 and about 1960, many counties operated normal schools and high schools for agricultural and home

Rural School Districts

Port Wing, on Lake Superior, was probably the first Wisconsin school district to provide its students with free, tax-supported transportation. A boom in the logging industry in the early 1900s increased the number of students, creating the need for more classroom space. To solve the problem, local residents T. N. Okerstom and James C. Daly proposed consolidating the rural districts into a larger school district with free transportation. Although some residents resisted the idea, the district began transporting children to a new school in horse-drawn, canvas-covered wagons known as "school rigs." It also provided sleighs in the winter months to take children to their new school building, which was completed in 1903. The consolidation of small schools into larger districts occurred in Marquette County from the 1940s to the 1960s (see map below). The process took place gradually, and individual schoolhouses were closed when the larger districts were formed. The high school grades in some schools (such as Oxford and Neshkoro) were subsequently further consolidated into high schools in larger towns.

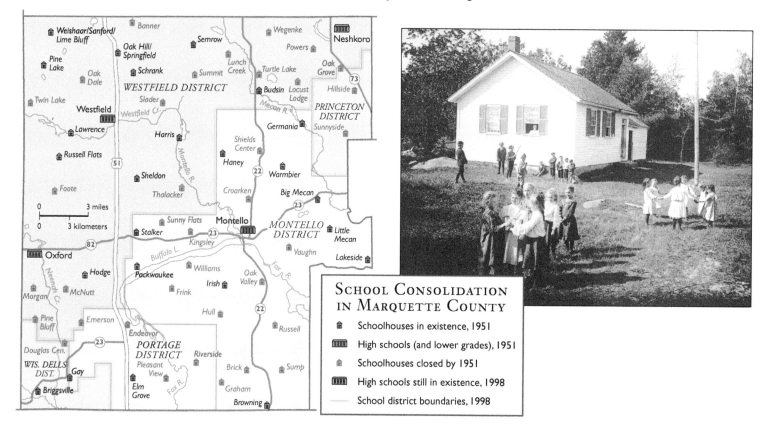

SCHOOL CONSOLIDATION IN MARQUETTE COUNTY

- Schoolhouses in existence, 1951
- High schools (and lower grades), 1951
- Schoolhouses closed by 1951
- High schools still in existence, 1998
- School district boundaries, 1998

PUBLIC AND PRIVATE COLLEGES AND UNIVERSITIES, 2002

PUBLIC AND PRIVATE COLLEGES AND UNIVERSITIES, 2002

- University of Wisconsin System four-year campus
- University of Wisconsin System two-year campus
- 1848   Founding date
- ◇   Wisconsin Technical College System campus (colors and area names indicate System districts)
- Private university, college, or theological seminary
- Private technical/professional college

U.W.–Superior 1893
Superior
Ashland
Northland College 1892
Hayward
Lac Courte Oreilles Ojibwe Community College 1982
WISCONSIN INDIANHEAD
Phillips
Minocqua
NICOLET AREA
Rhinelander
U.W.–Barron County 1966
Rice Lake
Ladysmith
Mount Senario College 1962
NORTHEAST WISCONSIN
New Richmond
CHIPPEWA VALLEY
Medford
NORTH CENTRAL
Antigo
Marinette
U.W.–Marinette 1966
U.W.–Stout 1891
Chippewa Falls
U.W.–Marathon County 1933
Wausau
College of the Menominee Nation 1993
Keshena
Sturgeon Bay
River Falls
Menomonie
Eau Claire
U.W.–Eau Claire 1916
Spencer
Wittenberg
U.W.–Green Bay 1968
U.W.–River Falls 1874
U.W.–Marshfield/ Wood County 1964
Bellin College of Nursing 1909
Immanuel Lutheran College 1959
Neillsville
Marshfield
U.W.–Stevens Point 1884
Stevens Point
Lawrence University 1847
Green Bay
De Pere
St. Norbert College 1898
Independence
MID-STATE
Wisconsin Rapids
Waupaca
U.W.–Fox Valley 1933
Black River Falls
Appleton
Silver Lake College 1869
U.W.–Manitowoc 1935
Neenah
U.W.–Oshkosh 1871
Chilton
Manitowoc
WESTERN WISCONSIN
Tomah
Wautoma
Oshkosh
Cleveland

Theological Seminaries
1. Immanuel Lutheran Seminary 1959
2. Nashotah House 1847
3. Sacred Heart School of Theology 1932
4. St. Francis Seminary 1845
5. Wisconsin Lutheran Seminary 1929

Sparta
U.W.–La Crosse 1909
La Crosse
Viterbo College 1890
Viroqua
Adams
Mauston
Ripon College 1851
Ripon
Marian College 1936
U.W.–Fond du Lac 1968
Fond du Lac
Sheboygan
Lakeland College 1862
U.W.–Sheboygan 1933
Reedsburg
Portage
MORAINE PARK
U.W.–Washington County 1968
Alverno College 1887
U.W.–Baraboo/ Sauk County 1968
Baraboo
Beaver Dam
West Bend
Cardinal Stritch College 1937
Richland Center
U.W.–Richland 1967
MADISON AREA
Concordia Univ. 1881
Mequon
Columbia College of Nursing 1901
Watertown
Nashotah
Carroll College 1846
MILW.
Marquette Univ. 1881
U.W.–Madison 1848
Pewaukee
Milwaukee
Medical College of Wisconsin 1913
Edgewood College 1927
Madison
Waukesha
U.W.–Waukesha 1966
W. Allis
Hales Cnrs.
Milwaukee Institute of Art and Design 1974
Fennimore
SOUTHWEST WISCONSIN
Fort Atkinson
WAUKESHA CO.
Milwaukee School of Engineering 1903
U.W.–Platteville 1866
Platteville
U.W.–Rock County 1966
Whitewater
U.W.–Whitewater 1868
Oak Cr.
Racine
Mt. Mary College 1913
BLACKHAWK
Janesville
Elkhorn
Burlington
U.W.–Milwaukee 1885
Monroe
GATEWAY
Kenosha
Beloit College 1846
Beloit
Carthage College 1847
Wisconsin Lutheran College 1973
U.W.–Parkside 1968

University of Wisconsin System

The University of Wisconsin was founded in Madison in 1848. In the photo above, the Class of 1876 poses on Bascom Hill. The university was a single institution in Madison until 1971, when former normal schools and state colleges were brought together under the U.W. System umbrella and a single board of regents. The U.W.–Madison remains an internationally important teaching and research institution.

economics education—a system virtually unique in the U.S. In the U.W. System, extension, agricultural, and vocational education have long played an important part. In 1911, Wisconsin became the first state to establish a state-supported system for vocational-technical and adult education, which grew to have a total enrollment of over 431,000 in 1995–96. The U.W. opened a Madison center for extension work and home economics in 1912, and later opened centers throughout the state. Today, the Extension offers a broad range of cooperative and continuing education programs, including electronic remote learning. In 1996, Extension enrollment exceeded 1.5 million; U.W. campus enrollment was about 150,000.

Private education. Since the mid-1800s, religious and secular groups have established many private schools in Wisconsin. Before the widespread opening of high schools, private academies offered the equivalent of a secondary-level education. Today, the state's private postsecondary learning institutions include 3 universities, 16 colleges, 4 technical/professional schools, 5 theological seminaries, and 2 tribal colleges. In 1990, Wisconsin created the nation's first private school voucher program, under which certain low-income Milwaukee students can attend private schools at public expense. This issue continues to be a topic of legal, political, and academic debate.

Bibliography
and Sources

Photograph and
Illustration Credits

Index

Bibliography & Sources

GENERAL SOURCES

Certain sources were used extensively in research for this atlas, as the most prominent references on Wisconsin history. They include *The History of Wisconsin* series, edited by William F. Thompson and published by the State Historical Society of Wisconsin (six volumes below), as well as other sources. In the Bibliography, these sources are indicated in **bold type**.

The *History of Wisconsin* series:

Smith, Alice. *The History of Wisconsin. Volume I: From Exploration to Statehood.* Madison: State Historical Society of Wisconsin, 1973.

Current, Richard Nelson. *The History of Wisconsin. Volume II: The Civil War Era, 1848–1873.* Madison: State Historical Society of Wisconsin, 1976.

Nesbit, Robert C. *The History of Wisconsin. Volume III: Urbanization and Industrialization, 1873–1893.* Madison: State Historical Society of Wisconsin, 1985.

Buenker, John D. *The History of Wisconsin. Volume IV: The Progressive Era, 1893–1940.* Madison: State Historical Society of Wisconsin, 1998.

Glad, Paul. *The History of Wisconsin. Volume V: War, a New Era, and Depression, 1914–1940.* Madison: State Historical Society of Wisconsin, 1990.

Thompson, William Fletcher. *The History of Wisconsin. Volume VI: Continuity and Change, 1940–1965.* Madison: State Historical Society of Wisconsin, 1988.

Other general sources:

Blue Book: Wisconsin Legislative Reference Bureau. *State of Wisconsin Blue Book.* Madison: Wisconsin Legislature. Years vary.

Nesbit and Thompson: Nesbit, Robert. *Wisconsin: A History.* Revised and updated by William F. Thompson. Madison: University of Wisconsin Press, 1989.

Risjord, Norman. *The Story of the Badger State.* Madison: Wisconsin Trails, 1995.

Wyatt, Barbara, project director. *Cultural Resource Management in Wisconsin: A Manual for Historic Properties.* Volumes 1–4. Madison: State Historical Society of Wisconsin, 1986.

TWO-PAGE SPREADS

Each two-page atlas presentation was coordinated by one or two Guild members, whose names are indicated beside the page numbers.

EARLY CULTURES pages 2–3 *Amelia Janes*

Beaver, Jan. "Wisconsin's Gigantic Eagle Mound." *The Ancient American* (September/October 1993): 32.

Birmingham, Robert, and Leslie E. Eisenberg. *Indian Mounds of Wisconsin.* Madison: State Historical Society of Wisconsin, 2000.

Birmingham, Robert, and Katherine Rankin. *Native American Mounds in Madison and Dane County*, 2d ed., 1–6, 8. Madison: State Historical Society of Wisconsin and City of Madison, 1996.

Coe, Michael, Dean Snow, and Elizabeth Benson. *Atlas of Ancient America.* Ed. Graham Speake, 50–57. New York: Facts on File, 1986.

Current, p. 180.

Gartner, William. "Four Worlds Without An Eden." In *Wisconsin Land and Life*, ed. Robert Ostergren and Thomas Vale, 331–50. Madison: University of Wisconsin Press, 1997.

Griffin, James. "Lake Superior Copper and the Indians: Miscellaneous Studies of Great Lakes Prehistory." *Anthropological Papers.* Ann Arbor: Museum of Anthropology, University of Michigan, no. 17 (1961): 34, 90.

Holliday, Diane, and Bobbie Malone. *Digging and Discovery: Wisconsin Archaeology*, 19–45. Madison: State Historical Society of Wisconsin, 1997.

Knauf, Mary. *Sheboygan Indian Mound Park: History and Nature Trail*, 5–11. Sheboygan, Wis.: Town and Country Garden Club, 1981.

Nesbit and Thompson, pp. 9–13.

Peterson, Robert. *The Wisconsin Effigy Mounds Project I*, 96. Decorah, Iowa: Luther College Archaeological Research Center, 1979.

Risjord, p. 6.

Salzer, Robert. "The Gottschall Site." *The Upper Midwest Rock Art Research Association*, ed. Charles Bailey. 1997. <www.pclink.com/cbailey/Gottsiteoverview.html> (1 October 1997).

Scherz, James, et al. *Mound Survey Report no. SR2* (unpublished map). University of Wisconsin–Madison, 1988.

Smith, pp. 124–25.

Stoltman, James, and Alice Kehoe. "Introduction to Wisconsin Archeology." *The Wisconsin Archeologist* 67, no. 3–4, ed., William Green. Madison: State Historical Society of Wisconsin and Wisconsin Archeological Survey (Sept.–Dec. 1986): 208, 223, 264, 285, 315.

Wisconsin Department of Natural Resources. *Aztalan State Park* (booklet). 1995.

Woodward, David, Robert Ostergren, Onno Brouwer, Steven Hoelscher, and Joshua Hane. *The Cultural Map of Wisconsin: A Cartographic Portrait of the State.* Madison: University of Wisconsin Press, 1996.

THANKS to William Gartner (University of Wisconsin–Madison Geography Department), Robert Birmingham, John Broihahn, and Diane Holliday (State Historical Society of Wisconsin), Janet Speth (Copper Culture State Park), Geraldine Flick (University of Wisconsin– Milwaukee Archeological Research Laboratory), Roxanne Owens (Ho-Chunk Historic Preservation Office), Larry Johns.

Native & European Encounters pages 4–5 *Jeffry Maas*

Adams, Arthur T., ed. *The Explorations of Pierre Esprit Raddison,* 40–41. Minneapolis: Ross and Haines, 1961.

Bieder, Robert E. *Native American Communities in Wisconsin 1600–1960.* Madison: University of Wisconsin Press, 1995.

Gilman, Rhoda R. "The Fur Trade." *Wisconsin Magazine of History* 58 (Autumn 1974): 3–18.

Kellogg, Louise Phelps. *The British Régime in Wisconsin and the Northwest,* 2–3, 7–11, 17, 25–27, 30, 33–48, 93–104, 115, 138–39, 146–47, 159, 176, 189–99, 232, 248–50, 267–70, 313–20. Madison: State Historical Society of Wisconsin, 1935.

Kellogg, Louise Phelps. *The French Régime in Wisconsin and the Northwest,* 108–9, 116–17, 146, 150, 152–55. Madison: State Historical Society of Wisconsin, 1925.

Holzhueter, John O. *Madeline Island and the Chequamegon Region,* 11, 15–20, 24. Madison: State Historical Society of Wisconsin, 1986.

Homberger, Eric. *The Penguin Historical Atlas of North America,* 40–41. London: Viking/Penguin Books, 1995.

Marshall, Albert M. *Brule Country.* St. Paul: North Central Publishing, 1954.

Mason, Carol I. *Introduction to Wisconsin Indians: Prehistory to Statehood,* 63–97. Salem, Wis.: Sheffield Publishing Co., 1988.

McKee, Russell. *Great Lakes Country,* 64–73, 75–95, 113–29. New York: Thomas Y. Crowell Co., 1966.

Oerichbauer, Edgar S. *A Final Report of Fur Trade Sites.* Madison: State Historical Society of Wisconsin, 1981.

Roberts, Robert B. *Encyclopedia of Historic Forts,* 849–53. New York: Macmillan, 1988.

Ross, Hamilton Nelson. *La Pointe: Village Outpost,* 17–72. St. Paul: Edwards Brothers, 1960.

Schmirler, A. A. A. "Wisconsin's Lost Missionary: The Mystery of Father Rene Menard." *Wisconsin Magazine of History* 45, no. 2 (Winter 1961–62): 99–114.

Smith, pp. 2–22, 28–31, 33–64, 67–68, 72–75, 85–97, 99–100, 104–5, 120–21.

Tanner, Helen Hornbeck, ed. *Atlas of Great Lakes Indian History,* 39–53, 57–66. Norman: University of Oklahoma Press, 1987.

Tanner, Helen Hornbeck, ed. *The Settling of North America,* 48–49, 58–63, 72–73. New York: Macmillan, 1995.

White, Richard. *The Middle Ground: Indians, Empires, and Republics in the Great Lakes Region, 1650–1815,* 2–19, 23, 30, 34–35, 78–79, 94–141, 191–201, 210–11, 476–85. New York: Cambridge University Press, 1991.

Wyatt, Volume 1, secs. 2, 3, 4.

THANKS to Jim Hansen (State Historical Society of Wisconsin), Aaron Maas (researcher, Superior), James Bokern (Marshfield).

Native Nations of Eastern Wisconsin pages 6–7 *Zoltán Grossman*

Brasser, T. J. "Mahican." In *Handbook of North American Indians,* ed. William C. Sturtevant. Vol. ed. Bruce G. Trigger, 198. Washington, D.C.: Smithsonian Institution, 1978.

Brotherton Indian Nation. *A Brief History of the Brotherton Indians of Wisconsin.* Beaver Dam, Wis.: Brotherton History Committee, 1982.

Oneida Nation in Wisconsin. *Oneida Nation,* 1995.

Oxley, Shelley. *The History of the Brotherton Indians.* Madison: Wisconsin Department of Public Instruction, 1982.

Oxley, Shelley. *The History of the Menominee Indians.* Madison: Wisconsin Department of Public Instruction, 1981.

Oxley, Shelley. *The History of the Oneida Indians.* Madison: Wisconsin Department of Public Instruction, 1981.

Oxley, Shelley. *The Stockbridge-Munsee Tribe: A History of the Mahican and Munsee Indians.* Madison: Wisconsin Department of Public Instruction, 1981.

Stockbridge-Munsee Historical Committee. *Brief History of the Mahikan/Stockbridge-Munsee Indian People* (booklet). December 1991.

Tanner, Helen Hornbeck, ed. *Atlas of Great Lakes Indian History,* 99–101, 126–27, 143–46, 165–66, 178–79. Norman: University of Oklahoma Press, 1987.

Wrone, David, and James Frechette, eds. *Traditional Menominee Clans Project,* maps 1–3. University of Wisconsin–Stevens Point, 1993.

THANKS to Dr. Carol Cornelius (Oneida Cultural Heritage Department), David Grignon (Menominee Historic Preservation Office), Nancy O. Lurie (Milwaukee Public Museum Head Curator Emerita), Arvid E. Miller Memorial Library Museum (Bowler), Lee Halbrook (Menominee Tribal Enterprises Forestry Center, Keshena), Professor David Wrone (University of Wisconsin–Stevens Point History Department), and Kenneth Fish (Menominee Treaty Rights and Mining Impacts Office, Keshena).

The Ho-Chunk & Dakota Nations pages 8–9 *Zoltán Grossman*

Great Lakes Indian Fish and Wildlife Commission (GLIFWC). Reservation GIS data.

Hocak Wazijaci Language and Culture Program, Mauston, Wis. (for Ho-Chunk original names of rivers).

Ho-Chunk Historic Preservation Department. "Ho-Chunk (Wisconsin Winnebago) Chronology," 1995.

Ho-Chunk Historic Preservation Department. "Ho-Chunk Village Sites," 1996.

Ho-Chunk Historic Preservation Department. "Road of the Ho-Chunk Warrior," n. d.

Lurie, Nancy Oestreich. "Winnebago." In *Handbook of North American Indians.* ed. William C. Sturtevant. Vol. ed. Bruce G. Trigger, 690–707. Washington, D.C.: Smithsonian Institution, 1978.

Reedsburg Remembers 150 Years: 1848–1998 (booklet), 32–33.

Royce, Charles C. *Indian Land Cessions in the United States.* 56th Cong., 1st sess. Pt. 2, H. Doc. no. 736. Serial 4015. Plate 64.

Shames, Deborah, ed. *Freedom with Reservation: the Menominee Struggle to Save Their Land and People.* Washington, D.C.: National Committee to Save the Menominee People and Forests, 1972.

Smith, pp. 13, 25, 100, 122, 129, 144–46, 155–56.

Tanner, Helen Hornbeck, ed. *Atlas of Great Lakes Indian History,* 140–44, 164. Norman: University of Oklahoma Press, 1987.

Waldman, Carl. *Atlas of the North American Indian,* 177. New York: Facts on File, 1985.

THANKS to Roxanne Owens and Nettie Kingsley (Ho-Chunk Historic Preservation Department, Black River Falls), Nancy O. Lurie (Milwaukee Public Museum Head Curator Emerita), Janice Rice (Madison), Kenneth Funmaker (Hocak Wazijaci Language and Culture Program, Mauston), Sherry Wilson (*Hocak Worak,* Black River Falls), Myron and Bertha Lowe (Waunakee), Dr. Helen Miner Miller (Madison), Brent Dershowitz (Minneapolis).

THE OJIBWE NATION pages 10–11 *Zoltán Grossman*

Dewdney, Selwyn H. *The Sacred Scrolls of the Southern Ojibway*, 1–5, 31–34, 57–80. Toronto: University of Toronto Press, 1975.

Great Lakes Indian Fish and Wildlife Commission (GLIFWC). Reservation and ceded territory GIS data.

National Geographic Society. *Close-Up Canada* (map series), 1978–80.

Nesbit, pp. 430–31.

Ritzenthaler, Robert. "Southwestern Chippewa." In *Handbook of North American Indians*. ed. William C. Sturtevant. Vol. ed Bruce G. Trigger, 743–59. Washington, D.C.: Smithsonian Institution, 1978.

Satz, Ronald N. *Chippewa Treaty Rights: The Reserved Rights of Wisconsin's Chippewa Indians in Historical Perspective*. Madison: Wisconsin Academy of Sciences, Arts, and Letters. *Transactions* 79 (1991): 1–85.

Tanner, Helen Hornbeck, ed. *Atlas of Great Lakes Indian History*, 123, 131, 144, 148, 176. Norman: University of Oklahoma Press, 1987.

U.S. Bureau of Indian Affairs. *Indian Land Areas* (map). Washington, D.C.: U.S. Government Printing Office, 1987.

Vogel, Virgil J. *Indian Names on Wisconsin's Map*. Madison: University of Wisconsin Press, 1991.

Waldman, Carl. *Atlas of the North American Indian*, 187, 193, 239–44. New York: Facts on File, 1985.

THANKS to Eugene Begay (Lac Courte Oreilles), Nancy O. Lurie (Milwaukee Public Museum Head Curator Emerita), Earl R. Nyholm (Professor of Ojibwe, Bemidji State University, Minnesota), Dana Jackson (Bad River Chippewa Education Department), Rand Valentine (University of Wisconsin–Madison), John Nichols (University of Manitoba), Museum of Ojibwa Culture (St. Ignace, Mich.), David Woodward and Judith Leimer (History of Cartography Project, University of Wisconsin–Madison), Richard Ackley.

THE POTAWATOMI NATION pages 12–13 *Zoltán Grossman*

Clifton, James A. "Potawatomi." In *Handbook of North American Indians*. ed. William C. Sturtevant. Vol. ed Bruce G. Trigger, 725–42. Washington, D.C.: Smithsonian Institution, 1978.

Clifton, James A. *The Prairie People: Continuity and Change in Potawatomi Indian Culture*, 54, 281, 286, 406. Lawrence: Regents Press of Kansas, 1977.

Edmunds, R. David. *The Potawatomis: Keepers of the Fire*, 240–75. Norman: University of Oklahoma Press, 1978.

Great Lakes Indian Fish and Wildlife Commission (GLIFWC). Reservation and ceded territory GIS data

Mitchell, Gary E. "A Chronology of Events for the Prairie Band of the Potawatomi Indian Tribe." <www.ukans.edu/~kansite/pbp/people/p_chronology.html> (24 October 1997).

Oxley, Shelley. *Keepers of the Fire: The History of the Potawatomie Indians*. Madison: Department of Public Instruction, 1981.

Prucha, Francis Paul. *Atlas of American Indian Affairs*, 33, 72. Lincoln: University of Nebraska Press, 1990.

Socolofsky, Homer E. *Historical Atlas of Kansas*, plates 12, 15. Norman: University of Oklahoma Press, 1972.

Tanner, Helen Hornbeck, ed. *Atlas of Great Lakes Indian History*, 134, 140, 144, 165, 176. Norman: University of Oklahoma Press, 1987.

Tanner, Helen Hornbeck, ed. *The Settling of North America*, 91. New York: Macmillan, 1995.

Vogel, Virgil J. *Indian Names on Wisconsin's Map*. Madison: University of Wisconsin Press, 1991.

THANKS to Clarice Werle (Potawatomi Historic Preservation Department), Nancy O. Lurie (Milwaukee Public Museum Head Curator Emerita), Donald A. Perrot (Hannahville Indian School), Jim Thunder (Stoughton), Mark Theil (Marquette University Archives), James McKinney (Iowa State University), Billy Daniels (Forest County Potawatomi Community).

CONFLICTS OVER NATIVE LAND RESOURCES pages 14–15 *Zoltán Grossman*

Current, p. 154.

Great Lakes Indian Fish and Wildlife Commission (GLIFWC). Reservation GIS data.

Indian Country Communications. "National Bingo and Casino Directory." *Explore Indian Country* (newspaper insert). Hayward, Wis., 1996.

Josephy, Alvin, ed. *American Heritage History of the Great West*, 155. New York: American Heritage Publishing, 1965.

Loew, Patty. *Indian Nations of Wisconsin: Histories of Endurance and Renewal*. Madison: Wisconsin Historical Society Press, 2001.

Lurie, Nancy Oestreich. *Wisconsin Indians*. Madison: State Historical Society of Wisconsin, 1987.

Midwest Treaty Network. *Witness for Nonviolence Reports*. Madison, 1989–90.

Midwest Treaty Network. <www.treatyland.com> (January 2002).

Oneida Geographic Land Information Systems Department. *Oneida Nation in Wisconsin* (map). Released 11 September, 1996.

Prucha, Francis Paul. *Atlas of American Indian Affairs*, 33. Lincoln: University of Nebraska Press, 1990.

Royce, Charles C. *Indian Land Cessions in the United States*. 56th Cong., 1st sess. Pt. 2., H. Doc. 736. Serial 4015. Plate 64.

Sandefur, Gary, and Miguel Ceballos. "Historical Factors Affecting Population Growth, Their Impact on the Future Population Change and Their Implications for American Indian Land Tenure in Wisconsin." University of Wisconsin–Madison, 4 June 1998.

Satz, Ronald N. *Chippewa Treaty Rights: The Reserved Rights of Wisconsin's Chippewa Indians in Historical Perspective*. Madison: Wisconsin Academy of Sciences, Arts, and Letters. *Transactions* 79 (1991): 101–28.

Smith, pp. 261–62.

Tanner, Helen Hornbeck, ed. *Atlas of Great Lakes Indian History*, 151–54. Norman: University of Oklahoma Press, 1987.

U.S. Department of the Interior. Bureau of Indian Affairs. *Indian Service Population and Labor Force Estimates*. 1995.

Waldman, Carl. *Atlas of the North American Indian*, 118–20. New York: Facts on File, 1985.

Whaley, Rick, and Walter Bresette. *Walleye Warriors*, 134–35. Philadelphia: New Society Publishers, 1994.

Woodward, David, Robert Ostergren, Onno Brouwer, Steven Hoelscher, and Joshua Hane. *Cultural Map of Wisconsin: A Cartographic Portrait of the State*. Madison: University of Wisconsin Press, 1996.

Wrone, David, and James Frechette, eds. *Traditional Menominee Clans Project*, maps 2–3. University of Wisconsin–Stevens Point, 1993.

THANKS to Nancy O. Lurie (Milwaukee Public Museum Head Curator Emerita), Stacy Sommers (GLIS Department), Oneida Land Committee, Oneida Business Committee, *News From Indian Country* (Hayward), Cathy Debevec (Madison).

Anglo-Americans & British Isles Immigrants pages 16–17 *Amelia Janes*

Barraclough, Geoffrey, ed. *The Times Concise Atlas of World History.* Maplewood, N.J.: Hammond, 1989.

Cassidy, Frederic G. *Dane County Place Names.* Madison: University of Wisconsin Press, 1968.

Combination Atlas Map of Rock County, Wisconsin: Compiled, Drawn and Published from Personal Examinations and Surveys by Everts, Baskin, and Stewart, 45, 48. Chicago: Everts, Baskin and Stewart, 1873.

Gara, Larry. *Westernized Yankee: The True Story of Cyrus Woodman,* 43–59. Madison: State Historical Society of Wisconsin, 1956.

Gard, Robert, and L. G. Sorden. *The Romance of Wisconsin Place Names.* Minocqua, Wis.: Heartland Press, 1988.

Hill, George W. *The People of Wisconsin According to Ethnic Stocks, 1940* (map). Madison: State Historical Society of Wisconsin, 1940.

Hudson, John C. "The Creation of Towns in Wisconsin." In *Wisconsin Land and Life,* ed. Robert Ostergren and Thomas Vale, 197–220. Madison: University of Wisconsin Press, 1997.

Kanetzke, Howard W. *Irish in Wisconsin.* Madison: State Historical Society of Wisconsin, 1978.

Kolb, J. H. *Rural Primary Groups: A Study of Agricultural Neighborhoods.* Madison: Agricultural Experiment Station of the University of Wisconsin, 1921.

Knowles, Anne Kelly. *Welsh Settlement in Waukesha County, Wisconsin, 1840–1873.* Madison: State Historical Society of Wisconsin, 1989.

Nelson, pp. 45–46, 59–60, 63, 66, 72, 78–79, 97, 117–21, 124–26, 128, 130, 137, 161, 205, 233, 423, 428, 498, 529, 551–54, 584.

Nesbit, pp. 272, 283–84, 299, 306–9, 312, 324–25, 337, 378, 550, 575.

Nesbit and Thompson, pp. 106–17.

Smith, pp. 45, 171–72, 182–88, 246–47, 348–49, 417–18, 432–35, 489–99, 506–7, 530.

Wicklein, Edward C. *The Scots of Vernon and Adjacent Townships, Waukesha County, Wisconsin.* Big Bend, Wis., 1974.

THANKS to Martin Perkins (Old World Wisconsin), Maurice Montgomery (Rock County Historical Society).

Becoming German American pages 18–19 *Michael Gallagher*

Bureau of the Census. *1990 U.S. Census Database.* C90STF3A, Summary level: State-County, "Persons with German Ancestry." <venus.census.gov/cdrom/lookup> (17 November 1997).

Conzen, Kathleen Neils. "Germans" In *Harvard Encyclopedia of American Ethnic Groups,* 406–25. Cambridge: Belknap Press of Harvard University, 1980.

Current, pp. 127–32, 489–92, 496, 572, 607–9

Eichhoff, Jürgen. "German in Wisconsin." In *The German Language in America: A Symposium,* 46–49. Austin: University of Texas Press, 1971.

Hill, George W., ed. *The People of Wisconsin According to Ethnic Stocks, 1940* (map). Madison: State Historical Society of Wisconsin, 1940.

Kanetzke, Howard W., ed. "Germans in Wisconsin." *Badger History* 27, no. 4 (1974): 4–11.

Lake, David L. "A Salute that Failed: The German-American Bund in Milwaukee." *Wisconsin Academy Review* (Spring 1993): 14–18.

Levi, Kate Everest. "Geographical Origin of German Immigration in Wisconsin." In *Collections of the State Historical Society of Wisconsin.* Vol. 14. Ed. Reuben Thwaites, 341–92. Madison: State Historical Society of Wisconsin, 1898.

Lewis, Herbert S. "European Ethnicity in Wisconsin: An Exploratory Formulation." *Ethnicity* 5 (1978): 174–88.

Nesbit and Thompson, p. 149.

Risjord, p. 6.

Smith, pp. 43–45, 60–63.

U.S. Senate. "Statistical Review of Immigration, 1820–1910." 61st Congress, 3rd sess. S. Doc. no. 756. In *Reports of the Immigration Commission.* Vol. 3, 1910. U.S. Serial 5878.

Wyatt, Volume 1, secs. 2.1– 2.18.

Zietlin, Richard H. *Germans in Wisconsin,* 1–29. Madison: State Historical Society of Wisconsin, 1977.

THANKS to Director Joseph C. Salmons and Outreach Specialist Mary Devitt (Max Kade Institute, Madison).

Scandinavian Settlement pages 20–21 *Jeffry Maas*

Fapso, Richard J. *Norwegians in Wisconsin,* 3–4, 10, 12–15, 27–28, 30, 37–39. Madison: State Historical Society of Wisconsin, 1977.

Hale, Frederick. *Danes in Wisconsin,* 3–7,10, 20–25, 28, 31. Madison: State Historical Society of Wisconsin, 1981.

Hale, Frederick. *Swedes in Wisconsin,* 3, 12, 14, 20–24, 26, 28, 30. Madison: State Historical Society of Wisconsin, 1983.

Hill, George W. *The People of Wisconsin According to Ethnic Stocks, 1940* (map). Madison: State Historical Society of Wisconsin, 1940.

Knipping, Mark. *Finns in Wisconsin,* 3, 5–9, 11, 13–16, 20–22, 24, 26, 32–33, 38. Madison: State Historical Society of Wisconsin, 1977.

Lake, David, George W. Hill, and John I. Kolemainen. *Haven in the Woods: The Story of the Finns in Wisconsin,* 27–33, 46–69, 152–60. New York: Arno Press, 1979.

Qualey, Carlton C. *Norwegian Settlement in the United States,* 5, 7–11, 13–15, 40–41, 44, 46–47, 49–60, 63–70, 72–75. Northfield, Minn.: Norwegian-American Historical Association, 1938.

Rippley, La Vern J. *The Immigrant Experience in Wisconsin,* 64, 67, 69, 72–79. Boston: Twayne Publishers, 1985.

Wyatt, Volume 2, secs. 5, 6.

THANKS to Mark Knipping (Wade House, Greenbush), Brian Olson (Norskedalen, Coon Valley), Sherry Huhn (Art Institute of Chicago).

European Immigration pages 22–23 *Marily Crews-Nelson*

Buenker, John D. "The Immigrant Heritage." In *Racine: Growth and Change in a Wisconsin County,* ed., Nicholas C. Burckel, 69–74. Racine, Wis.: Racine County Board of Supervisors, 1977.

Current, pp. 45, 61, 66, 79, 124.

Hill, George W. *The People of Wisconsin According to Ethnic Stocks, 1940* (map). Madison: State Historical Society of Wisconsin, 1940.

Lewis, Herbert S. "European Ethnicity in Wisconsin: An Exploratory Formulation." *Ethnicity* 5 (1978): 174–88.

Nesbit, pp. 306–7.

Nesbit and Thompson, pp. 150, 163–89.

Rippley, La Vern J. *The Immigrant Experience in Wisconsin*, 22. Boston: Twayne Publishers, 1985.

Vogeler, Ingolf. *Wisconsin: A Geography*, 70–72. Boulder, Colo.: Westview Press, 1986.

Woodward, David, Robert Ostergren, Onno Brouwer, Steven Hoelscher, and Joshua Hane. *The Cultural Map of Wisconsin: A Cartographic Portrait of the State*. Madison: University of Wisconsin Press, 1996.

Wyatt, Volume 1, secs. 1, 3, 4, 7, 8, 9.

Zaniewski, Kazimierz J., and Carol J. Rosen. *The Atlas of Ethnic Diversity in Wisconsin*. Madison: University of Wisconsin Press, 1998.

THANKS to Jack Holzhueter (State Historical Society of Wisconsin), Michael Gallagher, Doug Crews-Nelson.

ETHNIC MILWAUKEE pages 24–25 Zoltán Grossman and Jeffry Maas

Anderson, Harry, and Frederick Olson. *Milwaukee: At the Gathering of the Waters*, 57–60, 92–93, 97–98. Tulsa: Continental Heritage, 1981.

Borun, Thaddeus, ed. *We, the Milwaukee Poles: The History of Milwaukeeans of Polish Descent and a Record of Their Contributions to the Greatness of Milwaukee*. Milwaukee: Nowiny Publishing, 1946.

Botts, Howard Alan. "Commercial Structure and Ethnic Residential Patterns in the Shaping of Milwaukee: 1880–1900," 225–304. Ph.d. diss., University of Wisconsin–Madison, 1985.

Conzen, Kathleen Neils. "The German Athens": Milwaukee and the Accommodation of Its Immigrants 1839–1860." Ph.d. diss., University of Wisconsin–Madison, 1972.

Conzen, Kathleen Neils. *Immigrant Milwaukee 1836–1860: Accommodation and Community in a Frontier City*, 1–228. Cambridge: Harvard University Press, 1976.

Conzen, Kathleen Neils. "Mapping Manuscript Census Data for Nineteenth Century Cities." *Historical Geography Newsletter* 4, no. 1 (Spring 1974): 1–7.

Conzen, Michael P., and Kathleen Neils Conzen. "Geographical Structure in Nineteenth-Century Urban Retailing: Milwaukee 1836–90." *Journal of Historical Geography* (London) 5, no. 1 (1979): 45–66.

Cooper, Fiona. "Ethnic and Sexual Divisions of Labor: Milwaukee, 1880–1905." Master's thesis, University of Wisconsin–Madison, 1986.

Gurda, John. *The Making of Milwaukee*. Milwaukee County Historical Society, 1999.

La Piana, G. *The Italians in Milwaukee Wisconsin: A Survey*, 5–10. Associated Charities, 1915.

Rippley, La Vern J. *The Immigrant Experience in Wisconsin*, 9–27, 71–72. Boston: Twayne Publishers, 1985.

Thompson, pp. 42–43, 51–55.

THANKS to Michael P. Conzen (University of Chicago Geography Program), Kathleen Neils-Conzen (University of Chicago History Department), Howard Botts (University of Wisconsin–Whitewater Geography Department), Dr. Dirk Hoerder (Universität Bremen History Department, Germany).

AFRICAN AMERICAN SETTLEMENT pages 26–27 Zoltán Grossman

Buchanan, Thomas R. "Black Milwaukee 1890–1915," 1–14, maps A–F. Master's thesis, University of Wisconsin–Milwaukee, January 1973.

Cooper, Zachary. *Black Settlers in Rural Wisconsin*. Madison: State Historical Society of Wisconsin, 1994.

Current, pp. 26–67, 87, 146–47, 370, 389–91, 560–61, 567–74.

H. M. Gousha Company. *Street Map of Milwaukee*. 1995.

Nesbit, pp. 435–46.

Pfederhirt, Julia. "North to Freedom." *Wisconsin Trails* (March–April 1997): 98–105.

State Historical Society of Wisconsin. *To Answer Your Questions About Wisconsin: The Underground Railroad in Wisconsin* (booklet). Pub. no. 1000-1-DB20043.

Thompson, pp. 305–400; map, p. 312.

Trotter, Joe William, Jr. *Black Milwaukee: The Making of an Industrial Proletariat, 1915–45*, 22, 68, 177. Chicago: University of Illinois Press, 1985.

U.S. Department of the Interior. "Underground Railroad: Special Resource Study." September 1995.

Wyatt, Volume 4, secs. 12.1–12.10.

THANKS to Clayborn Benson (Wisconsin Black Historical Museum, Milwaukee), Milton Historical Society, Clarence Kailin (Madison), *Wisconsin Commonwealth* newspaper.

NEWEST ARRIVALS pages 28–29 Michael Gallagher and Zoltán Grossman

Berry-Cabán, Cristobal. *Hispanics in Wisconsin: A Bibliography of Resource Materials*. Madison: State Historical Society of Wisconsin 1981.

Blue Book, 2001–2002, p. 790.

Bureau of the Census. *2000 U.S. Census Database*. C90STF3A, Summary level: State-County, "Persons of Hispanic Origin" and "Race: Asian and Pacific Islander." <venus.census.gov/cdrom/lookup> (5 October 1997).

Encyclopædia Britannica. Vol. 22, p. 702. Chicago: Encyclopædia Britannica, 1997.

Office of Refugee Services. *Indochinese Refugee Population in Wisconsin* (map). 30 June 1997.

Oyarbide, Pancho, Maria Anita Sánchez, and Richard Kreusal. *Strangers: A Series of Dialogues on Mexican-American Alienation*, 50–58, 120. Appleton, Wis.: La Raza, 1973.

Salas, Jesús, and David Giffey. *Struggle for Justice* (brochure). Milwaukee: Wisconsin Labor History Society, 1997.

Slesinger, Doris. *Health Needs of Migrant Workers in Wisconsin, 22*. Madison: Department of Rural Sociology, University of Wisconsin–Extension. July 1979.

State Historical Society of Wisconsin. "Hispanics in Wisconsin." *Badger History* 33, no. 3 (1980): 15–17, 28–38.

Thompson, pp. 325–27.

U.S. Central Intelligence Agency. *Laos: Ethnic Groups* (map). 1970.

Vang, Shwaw. "About the Hmong." *Wisconsin Hmong Life* 1, no. 5 (August–September 1997): 1.

Vogeler, Ingolf. "Source Area and Travel Patterns of Wisconsin's Migratory Agricultural Workers." In *The Myth of the Family Farm: Agribusiness Dominance of US Agriculture*, 230. Boulder, Colo.: Westview Press, 1981.

Wisconsin. Governor's Commission on Human Rights. *Migratory Agricultural Workers in Wisconsin: A Problem in Human Rights*, 1–72. State Capitol, Madison, June 1950.

THANKS to David Giffey and Jesús Salas (Struggle for Justice project), Doua Vang (*Wisconsin Hmong Life*), Daniel Gaytan (Movimiento Estudiantil Chicano de Aztlán), Pancho Oyarbide.

IMMIGRANT RELIGIOUS PATTERNS pages 30–31 *Amelia Janes*

Bureau of the Census. *Religious Bodies: 1926*. Vol. 1, 270–73, 701–4. Washington, D.C.: U.S. Government Printing Office, 1930.

Official Catholic Directory, 138–49, 481–88. New York. P. J. Kennedy & Sons, 1947.

Smith, pp. 75–77, 559–617, 626–47.

Smith, Susan Lampert. "Wisconsin's Holy Land Retains Traditional Values." *Wisconsin State Journal*, 16 April 1995, p. 2A.

Thompson, pp. 59–61.

Tordella, Stephen J. *Religion in Wisconsin: Preferences, Practices and Ethnic Composition*, 19–45. Madison: Applied Population Laboratory, Department of Rural Sociology, 1979.

Works Progress Administration. Wisconsin Historical Records Survey Records, 1936–1942. Church Records Forms. Boxes 226, 228, 234.

Wyatt, Volume 3, secs. 1.1–19.31.

THANKS to Jack Holzhueter (State Historical Society of Wisconsin), Bill and Bette Janes (Asheville, N.C.), Barb Ballweg and Carla Rennolds (Educational Statisticians for Wisconsin Department of Public Instruction), Timothy Bawden (University of Wisconsin–Madison Geography Department).

CULTURAL FIGURES pages 32–33 *Marily Crews-Nelson*

Blue Book, 1995–1996, pp. 686–88; *1997–1998*, pp. 669–71.

Blum, Martha. *The Pro Arte Quartet: 50 Years* (booklet). University of Wisconsin–Madison School of Music, 1991.

Bowman, John C., ed. *Cambridge Dictionary of American Biography*, 74, 76, 357, 418, 419, 424, 507, 784. Cambridge: Cambridge University Press, 1995.

"Complete Listing of Extant Frank Lloyd Wright Buildings." <www.swc.com/flwlist.html> (10 November 1997).

Coopey, Judith Redline, and Michael Mentzer. *The World of Owen Gromme*. Madison: Stanton & Lee Publishers, 1983.

Davis, Tom. "Trailblazers." *Wisconsin Trails* 39, no. 1 (January 1998): 50–59.

"Frank Lloyd Wright Heritage Tour Site Index." <flw.badgernet.com/2080/htour.htm> (10 November 1997).

Gillispie, Charles Coulston, ed. *Dictionary of Scientific Biography*. Vol. 18, supp. 2, 849–51. New York: Charles Scribner's Sons, 1981.

"Green Bay Packers." <www.packers.com> (12 December 1997).

Grolier Multimedia Encyclopedia, Version 8.0.3. Danbury, Conn.: Grolier Electronic Publishing, 1996.

Hopkins, Joseph G. E., ed. *Concise Dictionary of American Biography*. 2d ed., 533. Charles Scribner's Sons, 1977.

Johnson, Allen, and Dumas Malone, eds. *Dictionary of American Biography*, Vol. 2, 32, 151; Vol 6, 483–84; Vol. 7, 616–77; Vol. 8, 235; Vol. 9, 122; Vol. 10, 194, 233, 495. American Council of Learned Societies, 1958.

Lisle, Laurie. *Portrait of an Artist: A Biography of Georgia O'Keeffe*, 3–24. New York: Seaview Books, 1980.

"Milwaukee Public Museum–Gromme." <www.mpm.edu/exhibit/gromme.html> (18 January 1998).

Moritz, Charles, ed. *Current Biography Yearbook 1975*, 471. New York: H. W. Wilson Company, 1975.

Our Times Multimedia Encyclopedia of the 20th Century. Licensed by Turner New Media. New York: Columbia University Press, 1995.

Peck, George W., ed. *Cyclopedia of Wisconsin*, 138, 190, 196. Western Historical Association, 1906.

"Vince Lombardi." <pilot.msu.edu/user/haradam/lombardi.htm> (25 October 1997).

Wisconsin State Journal. "Obituaries." 20 December 1997.

Woodward, David, Robert Ostergren, Onno Brouwer, Steven Hoelscher, and Joshua Hane. *The Cultural Map of Wisconsin: A Cartographic Portrait of the State*. Madison: University of Wisconsin Press, 1996.

World Book Encyclopedia. Vol. 7, p. 319; Vol. 12, p. 383; Vol. 21, pp. 159, 419. Chicago: World Book, 1986.

THANKS to Jack Holzhueter (State Historical Society of Wisconsin), Doug Crews-Nelson, Gretchen Farwell (University of Wisconsin–Madison Steenbock Library), Judy Buenzli (University of Wisconsin–Madison), Vince Lombardi, Jr.

GLACIAL LANDSCAPES pages 36–37 *Michael Gallagher and Amelia Janes*

Attig, John W., and Lee Clayton. *The Ice Age Geology of Devils Lake State Park*, 4–15. Wisconsin Geological and Natural History Survey Educational Series. no. 35, 1990.

Clayton, Lee, John W. Attig, David M. Mickelson, and Mark D. Johnson. *Glaciation of Wisconsin*, 1. Madison: Wisconsin Geological and Natural History Survey, 1984.

Hadley, D. W., and J. H. Pelham. *Glacial Deposits of Wisconsin*. Wisconsin Geological and Natural History Survey Educational Map Series. No. 10, 1976.

Risjord, pp. 1–8.

U.S. Department of the Interior. *Ice Age Trail: National Scenic Trail Wisconsin* (brochure with maps and diagrams). Washington, D.C.: National Park Service, 1993

University of Wisconsin–Extension. Wisconsin Geological and Natural History Survey. *A Short History of the Ice Age in Wisconsin* (handout). 1984.

Wisconsin Department of Natural Resources, State of Wisconsin and National Park Service, U.S. Department of the Interior. *Ice Age National Scientific Reserve Wisconsin* (brochure with maps and diagrams). 1976.

Wisconsin Geological and Natural History Survey. *Glacial Deposits of Wisconsin* (map). 1985.

THANKS to Dr. Lee Clayton (Wisconsin Geological and Natural History Survey) and Professor David Mickelson (Geology Department, University of Wisconsin–Madison).

MINING DISTRICTS & DISCOVERIES pages 38–39 *Amelia Janes*

Broughton, W. A. *Geology of the Upper Mississippi Valley Base-Metal District.* Information Circular no. 16, 1–5. Madison: Wisconsin Geological and Natural History Survey, 1978.

Cannon, W. F., and M. G. Mudrey, Jr. *The Potential for Diamond-Bearing Kimberlite in Northern Michigan and Wisconsin.* Geological Survey Circular 842. Washington, D.C.: Department of the Interior, 1981.

Crandon Mining Company. "Time Line of Mining in Wisconsin" and "Wisconsin's Mining History and Heritage." <www.crandonmine.com/mineh.html> (27 December 1997).

Current, pp. 9, 72, 102–3, 380, 482–83.

Gedicks, Al. *The New Resource Wars,* 57–135. Boston: South End Press, 1993.

Gedicks, Al. *Resource Rebels: Native Challenges to Mining and Oil Corporations,* 127–178. Boston: South End Press, 2001.

Hole, Francis D. Chap. 11 in *Geography of Wisconsin.* Madison: Department of Geography, University of Wisconsin–Madison, 1980.

Larsen, James A., ed. "Wisconsin's Geological History." *UIR/Research Newsletter* 11, no. 3. Madison: University of Wisconsin, University-Industry Research Program, 1977.

McCombs, Alice. "Earthwins Network." <www.earthwins.com> (8 October 1997).

Mudrey, M. G., Jr., T. J. Evans, R. C. Babcock, M. L. Cummings, E. H. Eisenbrey, and G. L. La Berge. *Case History of Metallic Mineral Exploration in Wisconsin, 1955 to 1991.* Madison: Wisconsin Geological and Natural History Survey, 1991.

Nesbit, pp. 129, 151, 162–65, 194.

Nesbit and Thompson, pp. 106–17.

Smith, pp. 45, 171–72, 182–88, 246–47, 348–49, 417–18, 432–33, 489–99, 506–7, 530.

Thompson, p. 14.

U.S. Geological Survey and Wisconsin Geological and Natural History Survey. *Mineral and Water Resources of Wisconsin.* Washington, D.C.: U.S. Government Printing Office, 1976.

Wisconsin Department of Natural Resources. *Tower Hill State Park* (map). Pub. no. PR137-96RRev. Spring Green, Wis.: Wisconsin Department of Natural Resources, 1996.

Wyatt, Volume 3, secs. 2.17, 3.16, 4.8.

THANKS to Wisconsin Geological and Natural History Survey (University of Wisconsin–Extension), Wisconsin Resources Protection Council (Rhinelander/La Crosse), Flambeau Mining Company (Ladysmith).

TIMBER, RIVER & MILL pages 40–41 *Jeffry Maas*

Cronon, William. *Nature's Metropolis: Chicago and the Great West,* 151–61, 171–72, 179–83. New York: W. W. Norton & Co. 1991.

Current, Richard N. *Wisconsin: A Bicentennial History,* 109–17. New York: W. W. Norton & Co., 1977.

Curtis, John T. *The Vegetation of Wisconsin: An Ordination of Plant Communities* (map adapted from book endpapers). Madison: University of Wisconsin Press, 1959.

Fries, Robert F. *Empire in Pine: The Story of Lumbering in Wisconsin 1830–1900,* 3–13, 16–21, 60–99, 239–54. Sturgeon Bay: William Caxton, 1981.

Hass, Paul H. "The Suppression of John F. Deitz." *Wisconsin Magazine of History* 57 (Summer 1974): 255–309.

Merk, Frederick. *Economic History of Wisconsin During the Civil War Decade,* 59–110. Madison: State Historical Society of Wisconsin, 1916.

Nesbit, pp. 46–86.

Rohe, Randall. "Lumbering: Wisconsin's Northern Urban Frontier." In *Wisconsin Land and Life,* ed. Robert C. Ostergren and Thomas Vale, 224–30. Madison: University of Wisconsin Press, 1997.

Twining, Charles. "The Apostle Islands and the Lumbering Frontier." *Wisconsin Magazine of History* 66, no. 3 (1983): 205–20.

Wyatt, Volume 2, secs. 5, 6.

THANKS to Randall Rohe (University of Wisconsin–Waukesha Center).

HARVESTING THE CROPS pages 42–43 *Jeffry Maas*

Clark, James I. *Wisconsin Agriculture.* Madison: State Historical Society of Wisconsin, 1956.

Collins, Charles. *An Atlas of Wisconsin,* 88–112. Madison: College Print and Typing Co., 1968.

Current, Robert N. *Wisconsin: A Bicentennial History,* 67–73. New York: W. W. Norton & Co., 1977.

Glad, pp. 165–94.

Kirkpatrick, E. L., et al. "Family Farm Living in Wisconsin." *University of Wisconsin Agricultural Experimental Station Bulletin* 114 (1933): 38–39.

Lampard, Eric E. *The Rise of the Dairy Industry in Wisconsin: A Study in Agricultural Change, 1820–1920,* 2, 4, 11, 15–16, 23–26, 30, 40–45, 47–50. Madison: State Historical Society of Wisconsin, 1963.

Merk, Frederick. *Economic History of Wisconsin During the Civil War Era,* 15, 19–22, 30–39, 42–44, 52, 54. Madison: State Historical Society of Wisconsin, 1916.

Nesbit, pp. 2–34, 36–45.

Shafer, Joseph. *A History of Wisconsin Agriculture.* Madison: State Historical Society of Wisconsin, 1922.

Thompson, John Griffin. "The Rise and Decline of the Wheat Growing Industry in Wisconsin." *Bulletin of the University of Wisconsin, Economics and Political Science Series* 5(3) no. 292 (1909): 221–29.

Wyatt, Volume 2, secs. 1–8, 11.

THANKS to Ingolf Vogeler (University of Wisconsin–Eau Claire Department of Geography), Nancy Sills (University of Wisconsin–Madison Department of Comparative Biosciences), Lee Clayton (Wisconsin Geological and Natural History Survey).

AMERICA'S DAIRYLAND pages 44–45 *Marily Crews-Nelson*

Apps, Jerry. *The Wisconsin Traveler's Companion,* 52, 94–97, 103–5. Madison: Wisconsin Trails, 1997.

Current, pp. 462–63.

Glad, pp. 409–10.

Lampard, Eric E. *The Rise of the Dairy Industry in Wisconsin: A Study in Agricultural Change 1820–1920.* Madison: State Historical Society of Wisconsin, 1963.

Nesbit, pp. 15–22, 41.

Nesbit and Thompson, pp. 274, 283–93, 489.

Pederson, Jane Marie. *Between Memory and Reality: Family and Community in Rural Wisconsin, 1870–1970,* 78–86. Madison: University of Wisconsin Press, 1992.

Uber, Harvey A. *Environmental Factors in the Development of Wisconsin,* 114–15. Milwaukee: Marquette University Press, 1937.

Vogeler, Ingolf. "The Cultural Landscape of Wisconsin's Dairy Farming." In *Wisconsin Land and Life*, ed. Robert C. Ostergren and Thomas R. Vale, 410–21. Madison: University of Wisconsin Press, 1997.

Vogeler, Ingolf. *The Myth of the Family Farm.* Boulder, Colo.: Westview Press, 1981.

Vogeler, Ingolf. *Wisconsin: A Geography*, 126–36. Boulder, Colo.: Westview Press, 1986.

THANKS to Ingolf Vogeler (University of Wisconsin–Eau Claire), Doug Crews-Nelson, Gina Keller (Wisconsin Milk Marketing Board, Madison), Nancy Riggio (U.S. Department of Agriculture, Lisle, Illinois), John Kinsman (Family Farm Defenders), Bruce Marion (University of Wisconsin–Madison), Mary Lippert (American Raw Milk Pricing Association, Madison).

WEATHER HAZARDS pages 46–47 *Amelia Janes*

Brinkmann, Waltraud. "Challenges of Wisconsin's Weather and Climate." In *Wisconsin Land and Life*, ed. Robert Ostergren and Thomas Vale, 49–61. Madison: University of Wisconsin Press, 1997.

Bureau of Water Regulation and Zoning. *The Floods of 1993: The Wisconsin Experience.* Ed. Gary Heinrichs. Madison: Wisconsin Department of Natural Resources, 1993.

Current, p. 180.

Fujita, Theodore. *Manual of Downburst Identification for Project Nimrod.* Chicago: Satellite and Mesometerology Research Project, Department of the Geophysical Sciences, University of Chicago, May 1978.

Glad, pp. 358, 396–97, 474–75.

Hennig, Laura, ed. *Natural Hazards Data Resources Directory.* Natural Hazards Research and Applications Center, and National Geophysical Data Center (Colorado). <www.ngdc.gov/seg/hazard/resource/hazdir.html> (16 November 1997).

Merritt, Raymond H. *Creativity, Control and Controversy: A History of the St. Paul District U.S. Army Corps of Engineers*, 331–50. Washington, D.C.: U.S. Government Printing Office, 1979.

Risjord, p. 115.

Portz, John. "The Rains Came." In *Badger History: Disasters in Wisconsin*, 349–50, 365–68, 414–17. Madison: State Historical Society of Wisconsin, 1979.

Wells, Robert. *Fire and Ice: Two Deadly Wisconsin Disasters.* Madison: Northword, 1983.

Wisconsin Division of Emergency Management. *Hazard Analysis for the State of Wisconsin.* Madison: Wisconsin Department of Military Affairs, 1996.

Wisconsin State Climatology Office. *Wisconsin: Floods and Droughts*, 567–74. Madison: University of Wisconsin–Extension Geological and Natural History Survey, 1997.

THANKS to Matt Mene (Wisconsin State Climatology Office), John Anfinson, (U.S. Army Corps of Engineers, St. Paul District historian), Jeb Barzen (International Crane Foundation), Mark Martin (Department of Natural Resources Bureau of Endangered Resources), Diane Kleiboer (Wisconsin Department of Military Affairs).

CHANGES IN RURAL SOCIETY pages 48–49 *Jeffry Maas*

Galpin, C. J. "The Social Anatomy of an Agricultural Community." *University of Wisconsin Agricultural Experimental Station Bulletin* 34 (1915): 2–34.

Glad, pp. 165–69, 187.

Goc, Michael J. *Where the Waters Flow: A Half Century of Regional Development, 1941–1991*, 10–17, 90–94. Friendship, Wis.: New Past Press, 1991.

Kolb, J. H., and R. A. Polson. "Trends in Town-Country Relations." *University of Wisconsin Agricultural Experimental Station Bulletin* 117 (1933): 3–37.

Olmstead, Clarence W. "Changing Technology, Values and Rural Landscapes." In *Wisconsin Land and Life*, ed. Robert Ostergren and Thomas Vale, 355–75. Madison: University of Wisconsin Press, 1997.

Risjord, pp. 127–29.

Thompson, pp. 103–10.

Wisconsin Emergency Relief Administration. *Rural Electrification Survey by Work Division, Northfield Township and Garden Valley Township Jackson County* (map in the collection of State Historical Society of Wisconsin). 1934.

THANKS to Ingolf Vogeler (Geography Department, University of Wisconsin–Eau Claire), Allen Ruff (historian, Madison), Renae Anderson and Kathleen Kelly (U.S. Soil Conservation Service, Madison).

TRANSPORTATION NETWORKS pages 50–51 *Michael Gallagher*

Campbell, Ballard. *Wisconsin Stories: The Good Roads Movement in Wisconsin, 1890–1911.* Madison: State Historical Society of Wisconsin, 1980.

Current, pp. 24–45, 110–12, 243–50, 437–51.

Nesbit, pp. 87–147; maps pp. 116–17.

Nesbit and Thompson, pp. 115, 190–206, 313–36; maps pp. 321–27.

Smith, pp. 179, 434–61; map p. 435.

State Highway Commission of Wisconsin. *A History of Wisconsin Highway Development 1835–1945,*1–45, 58–65, 77–79. Madison, 1947.

Wisconsin Department of Transportation. *1997/98 Official State Highway Map.* Madison, 1997.

THANKS to Michael Harrington (Middleton), Barbara Jenkin (Wisconsin Department of Transportation).

SOUTHEASTERN WISCONSIN INDUSTRIES pages 52–53 *Amelia Janes*

Anderson, Harry H., and Frederick I. Olson. *Milwaukee: At the Gathering of the Waters.* Tulsa: Continental Heritage Press, 1981.

Canfield, Joseph M. *TM, the Milwaukee Electric Railway & Light Company.* Chicago: Central Electric Railfans Association, 1972.

Illustrated Description of Milwaukee (newspaper insert). Milwaukee: Milwaukee Sentinel, 1890.

Keehn, Richard H. "Industry and Business." In *Racine: Growth and Change in a Wisconsin County,* ed. Nicholas C. Burckel, 279–343. Racine: Racine County Board of Supervisors, 1977.

Lankevich, George J. *Milwaukee: A Chronological and Documentary History, 1673–1977.* Ed. Howard B. Furer. Dobbs Ferry, N.Y.: Oceana Publications, 1977.

Lathrop, J., Jr. *Kenosha County, Wisconsin, 1861.* New York: H. F. Walling, 1861.

Nesbit and Thompson. pp. 143–45, 163–64, 277–78, 320–35, 510–11.

Rand McNally & Co. *Map of Racine and Kenosha, 1896.* Chicago: Rand McNally & Co., 1896.

Risjord, pp. 62–67.

Simon, Roger David. *The City-Building Process: Housing and Services in New Milwaukee Neighborhoods 1880–1910,* 10–15. Philadelphia: American Philosophical Society, 1978.

Simon, Roger David. *The Expansion of an Industrial City: Milwaukee, 1880–1910,* 20–90. Madison: University of Wisconsin Department of History, 1971.

State Highway Commission of Wisconsin, Public Roads Administration Federal Works Agency, Statewide Highway Planning Survey. *Traffic Map of the State of Wisconsin.* State of Wisconsin, 1942.

Wisconsin Manufacturers Association. *Classified Directory of Wisconsin Manufacturers, 1945.* Madison: Wisconsin Manufacturers Association, 1945.

Wisconsin Manufacturers Association. *Classified Directory of Wisconsin Manufacturers, 1948.* Madison: Wisconsin Manufacturers Association, 1948.

Wisconsin Manufacturers and Commerce. *Classified Directory of Wisconsin Manufacturers, 1991.* Madison: Wisconsin Manufacturers and Commerce, 1991.

THANKS to Richard H. Keehn (University of Wisconsin–Parkside Economics Department), Roger David Simon (Lehigh University History Department), Jeffrey Zimmerman (University of Wisconsin–Madison Geography Department).

GROWTH OF THE FOX VALLEY pages 54–55 *Amelia Janes*

American Directory Publishing Co. *Wisconsin Business Directory.* Nebraska: American Directory Publishing Co., 1997.

Current, pp. 21, 22, 381, 427, 468, 476, 479, 582, 583.

Fox Cities Chamber of Commerce. *Appleton Community Profile* (booklet). Appleton, Wis.: Fox Cities Chamber of Commerce, 1996.

Fox Cities Chamber of Commerce. *Guide to Fox Cities Manufacturers and Principal Employers.* Appleton, Wis.: Fox Cities Chamber of Commerce, 1994.

Glaab, Charles, and Lawrence H. Larsen. *Factories in the Valley: Neenah-Menasha, 1870–1915,* 23–39. Madison: State Historical Society of Wisconsin, 1989.

Glad, pp. 211, 236.

Kort, Ellen. *The Fox Heritage,* 172. California: Windsor Publications, 1984.

Nesbit, pp. 152, 163, 186, 187–90, 365–67.

Nesbit and Thompson, pp. 202, 203, 334, 365–67.

Olcott, Perry G. *Water Resources of Wisconsin Fox-Wolf River Basin.* Washington, D.C.: U.S. Geological Survey, 1968.

Smith, pp. 14, 27–31, 98, 155, 283, 291, 419, 439, 486, 499, 507–13, 528–29, 535.

Smith, Alice. *Millstone and Saw: The Origins of Neenah-Menasha,* 45–49, 50–58, 2–66, 74–79. Madison: State Historical Society of Wisconsin, 1966.

Thompson, pp. 162–64, 167, 171, 172, 178, 180, 206, 207, 221, 625, 626.

Wisconsin Paper Council. "A Brief History of Papermaking in Wisconsin." Neenah, Wis.: Wisconsin Paper Council. 1997.

Wisconsin Paper Council. "Fact Sheet." Neenah, Wis.: Wisconsin Paper Council, 1997.

THANKS to Greg Summers (University of Wisconsin–Madison Geography Department), Scott Rice (Wisconsin Paper Council, Neenah).

THE INLAND SEA: SHIPPING ON THE GREAT LAKES pages 56–57 *Jeffry Maas*

Ashworth, William. *The Late Great Lakes: An Environmental History,* 113–21. Detroit: Wayne State University Press, 1987.

Current, pp. 13–19, 240–43, 383–84, 446–48, 467, 590.

Downs, Warren. *Fish of Lake Superior,* 1–8, 20–21. Madison: University of Wisconsin Sea Grant Institute, 1984.

Eaton, Conan B. *Death's Door: The Pursuit of a Legend,* 24–31. Sturgeon Bay, Wis.: Bay Print, 1988.

Eaton, Conan B. *Rock Island,* 10–11, 13–14, 53–56. Sturgeon Bay, Wis.: Bay Print, 1988.

Holand, Hjalmar R. *Old Peninsula Days,* 105, 192–93. Madison: Wisconsin House, 1972.

Holzhueter, John O. *Madeline Island and the Chequamegon Region,* 31, 43–44. Madison: State Historical Society of Wisconsin, 1986.

Hyde, Charles K. *The Northern Lights: Lighthouses of the Upper Great Lakes,* 135–53, 184–89, 200–202. Detroit: Wayne State University Press, 1995.

McKee, Russell. *Great Lakes Country,* 198, 219–32. New York: Thomas Y. Crowell Co., 1966.

Merk, Frederick. *Economic History of Wisconsin During the Civil War Era,* 363–83, 386–91. Madison: State Historical Society of Wisconsin, 1916.

Merritt, Raymond H. *Creativity, Conflict and Controversy: A History of the St. Paul District U.S. Army Corps of Engineers,* 297–342. Washington, D.C.: U.S. Government Printing Office, 1979.

Nesbit, pp. 128–39.

Quaife, Milo M. *Lake Michigan,* 31–33, 320, 324. Indianapolis: Bobbs-Merrill Co., 1944.

Wisconsin Department of Transportation. Multimodal Planning Unit. *Passenger Ferry Service: An Overview and Study Proposal for Passenger Ferry Service in Wisconsin,* 1–4. Report prepared by Dawn Krahn and Daniel Yeh. Madison, 1994.

Wyatt, Volume 2, secs. 8, 14.

THANKS to Eric C. Reinelt (Port of Milwaukee), Patricia Maus (Northeast Minnesota Historical Center), Lisa Marciniak (Port Authority of Duluth).

IMPACTS ON WISCONSIN'S ENVIRONMENT pages 58–59 *Zoltán Grossman*

Huffman, Thomas R. *Protectors of the Land and Water: Environmentalism in Wisconsin, 1961–1968,* 1–8, 70–86. Chapel Hill: University of North Carolina Press, 1994.

Huver, Charles W., Gertrude A. Dixon, Naomi Jacobson, and George I. J. Dixon. *Methodologies for the Study of Low-Level Radiation in the Midwest.* Millville, Minn: Anvil Press, 1979.

Madison, F. W., A. B. Dickens, and T. May. "Wisconsin's Sensitivity to Acid Rain: The Role of Geologic Materials and Soils." Cooperative Extension Service, College of Natural Resources, University of Wisconsin–Stevens Point, 1987.

Miller, Richard L. *Under the Cloud: The Decades of Nuclear Testing,* 442–66. New York: Free Press, 1986.

Rogers, Deb, ed. *Threats to Wisconsin Communities.* Madison: People United in Respect for the Earth and Wisconsin Action Group for Environmental Responsibility, 1981.

U.S. Department of Energy. *Areas and Rock Bodies Identified by the U.S. Department of Energy for High-level Radioactive Waste Evaluation* (map). June 1984.

U.S. Environmental Protection Agency. "Superfund National Priorities List 2001." <www.epa.gov/superfund> (6 January 2002).

Wisconsin Department of Agriculture, Trade, and Consumer Protection. *Atrazine ES Exceedences* (map). Agricultural Resource Management Division, April 1997.

Wisconsin Division of Health and Wisconsin Department of Natural Resources. *Important Health Information for People Eating Fish from Wisconsin Waters,* 12–29. Pub. no. FH824-97, 1997.

Wisconsin Department of Natural Resources. *Standard SO2* (table). Air Quality Division, 20 March, 1997.

Wisconsin Department of Natural Resources. Water Quality Management Section maps: "Fox River WLA Modeling Report," "Area Modeled with RMA4," "Northern Mainstem Sub-Basin with Segment A Dischargers," "Central Mainstem Sub-Basin with Segment BC Dischargers," "Southern Mainstem Sub-Basin with D Dischargers," "Park Falls," "Oconto Falls" "Rock River Mainstem: Lake Koshkonong to State Line."

THANKS to Professor William Cronon (University of Wisconsin–Madison), Dale Patterson (Wisconsin Department of Natural Resources), Dwayne Gebkin (Wisconsin Department of Natural Resources), Lisa Morrison (Wisconsin Department of Agriculture), Will Fantle (Northern Thunder, Eau Claire), Becky Katers (Clean Water Action Council, Green Bay), Mark Martin (Wisconsin Department of Natural Resources), Dave Teske, Meg Turtleheiz (Madison).

TOURISM & RECREATION pages 60–61 *Amelia Janes*

Bawden, Timothy. "The Northwoods." In *Wisconsin Land and Life,* ed. Robert Ostergren and Thomas Vale, 450–69. Madison: University of Wisconsin Press, 1996.

Bersing, Otis S. *A Century of Deer in Wisconsin,* 1–15, 58, 78. Wisconsin Conservation Department: Game Management Division, 1966.

Cronon, William. *Nature's Metropolis: Chicago and the Great West,* 379–83. New York: W. W. Norton & Co., 1991.

Current, pp. 538–40.

Dells Country Historical Society. *Others Before You: A History of the Wisconsin Dells Country,* 1, 18, 24. Friendship, Wis.: New Past Press, 1995.

"Department of Tourism." Wisconsin Department of Tourism. <badger.state.wi.us/agencies/tourism/guide> (31 January 1998).

Glad, pp. 211–20, 248–60.

Hoelscher, Steven. "A Pretty Strange Place." In *Wisconsin Land and Life*, ed. Robert Ostergren and Thomas Vale, 424–49. Madison: University of Wisconsin Press, 1996.

Hole, Francis D. *Geography of Wisconsin*, 28.1–28.19, 33.1–33.9. Madison: University of Wisconsin: Department of Geography, 1980.

Imrie, Robert. "Mild Winter Means Lots of Happy Deer." *Wisconsin State Journal* 2 March, 1998, p. 1B.

Marcouiller, David W., Gary P. Green, Steven C. Deller, N. R. Sumathi, and Daniel L. Erkkila. *Recreational Homes and Regional Development*, 2. Madison: Cooperative Extension Publications, University of Wisconsin Extension, 1996.

Nesbit, pp. 528–32.

Nesbit and Thompson, pp. 515–17.

Ness, Erik. "The Deer Hunter." *Isthmus*. Madison, 21 November 1997.

"98 American Birkebeiner." *Winona*. <winona.com/birkie> (6 February 1998).

Rockford Map Publishers. *Land Atlas & Plat Book: Oneida County, Wisconsin*, 42–43. Rockford: Rockford Map Publishers, 1996.

Rockford Map Publishers. *Plat Book: Oneida County, Wisconsin*, 4–5. Rockford: Rockford Map Publishers, 1957.

Thompson, pp. 272–304.

U.S. Department of the Interior. *Ice Age Trail: National Scenic Trail Wisconsin*. Washington, D.C.: National Park Service, 1993.

U.S. Department of the Interior. *North Country Trail: National Scenic Trail Wisconsin*. Washington, D.C.: National Park Service, 1990.

Wisconsin Department of Natural Resources. *Wisconsin State Forests* (map). Pub. no. PUB-FR-034. Madison: Wisconsin Department of Natural Resources, revised 1997.

Wisconsin Department of Tourism. *Snowmobile Trail Map*. Madison: Wisconsin Department of Tourism, 1993.

Wisner, Frank O. *The Dells of the Wisconsin: An Illustrated Handbook*. Kilbourne City, Wis.: F. O. Wisner, 1875.

THANKS to Steven Hoelscher (Tulane University), Professor William Cronon (University of Wisconsin–Madison), Drew Hanson (GIS coordinator, Ice Age Park and Trail Foundation), Al Holfacker, Robert Granflaten (State Historical Society of Wisconsin), David Sceller (Wisconsin Department of Tourism), Suzanne J. Young (Rockford Map Publishers).

COLONIAL BOUNDARIES & EUROPEAN EMPIRES pages 64–65 *Michael Gallagher*

Nesbit and Thompson, pp. 1–17.

Pictorial Atlas of United States History, 54–115. Washington, D.C.: American Heritage Publishing Co., 1964.

Smith, pp. 36–121.

Tanner, Helen Hornbeck, ed. *Atlas of Great Lakes Indian History,* 49, 105–21. Norman: University of Oklahoma Press, 1987.

THANKS to Jim Hansen (State Historical Society of Wisconsin).

TERRITORIAL BOUNDARIES pages 66–67 *Zoltán Grossman*

Historical Atlas of the United States, 96–98. Washington, D.C.: National Geographic Society, 1988.

Nesbit and Thompson, pp. 118–31, 133, 151–54.

Pictorial Atlas of United States History, 118–21, 126–29, 133, 136, 145–46, 152–53, 158, 167. Washington, D.C.: American Heritage Publishing Co., 1964.

Smith, pp. 199–272, 662.

"Wisconsin Territorial Days." *Badger History* 27, no. 1 (September 1973).

THANKS to Jack Holzhueter (State Historical Society of Wisconsin).

STATEHOOD pages 68–69 *Michael Gallagher*

Lapham, Increase A. *A Sectional Map with Most Recent Surveys by I. A. Lapham* (map). Milwaukee: Hale & Chapman, 1848.

Nesbit and Thompson, pp. 211–25.

Quaife, Milo M., ed. *The Attainment of Statehood*, 112–30, 923. State Historical Society of Wisconsin Collections, vol. 29. Constitutional Series, vol. 4. Madison: State Historical Society of Wisconsin, 1928.

Risjord, pp. 72–75.

Smith, pp. 648–84; map, p. 435; map, p. 538; map, p. 662.

Wyatt, Volume 1, 2.1– 2.18.

THANKS to Peter Cannon and Richard Roe (Research Analysts, Wisconsin Legislative Reference Bureau).

COUNTY BOUNDARIES pages 70–71 *Jeffry Maas*

Blue Book, 1997–1998, pp. 714–23.

Clark, Anita. "New County for a New Century?" *Wisconsin State Journal*. 28 September 1997, p. 1.

Current, pp. 156–59.

Holzhueter, John O. *Madeline Island and the Chequamegon Region,* 50. Madison: State Historical Society of Wisconsin, 1986.

Lurie, Nancy Oestereich. *Wisconsin Indians*, 52–55. Madison: State Historical Society of Wisconsin, 1980.

Nesbit, pp. 111–12, 317, 332–33.

Ross, Hamilton Nelson. *La Pointe: Village Outpost,* 122–28. St. Paul: Edwards Brothers, 1960.

Thompson, pp. 678–79.

"The Urge to Merge: Let's Make a Century County Deal." *Wisconsin Trails* 39, no. 1 (January–February 1998): 14.

Wisconsin Historical Records Survey. *Origin and Legislative History of County Boundaries in Wisconsin,* 2–5, 8, 14–221. The Survey, 1942.

Wyatt, Volume 1, sec. 10.

THANKS to Bob Mackreth (Apostle Islands National Lakeshore), Kathryn and Robert Maas (Solon Springs).

PROGRESSIVE ERA pages 72–73 *Michael Gallagher and Zoltán Grossman*

Buenker, John D. *The History of Wisconsin. Volume IV: The Progressive Era, 1893–1940.* Madison: State Historical Society of Wisconsin, 1998.

Donoghue, James R. *How Wisconsin Voted, 1848–1972,* 97, 106, 114. Madison: Institute of Governmental Affairs, University of Wisconsin Extension, 1974.

Glad, pp. 296–347, 410–19, 435–47.

Hoglund, William A. "Wisconsin Dairy Farmers on Strike." *Agricultural History* 35, no. 1 (January 1961): 24–34.

Jacobs, Herbert. "The Wisconsin Milk Strikes." *Wisconsin Magazine of History* 35, no. 1 (Autumn 1951): 30–35.

Milwaukee Journal, 15–23 February, 13–20 May, 21 October–18 November 1934.

Mortenson, W. P. "Economic Considerations in Marketing Fluid Milk." *Wisconsin Research Bulletin* 125 (December 1934): 1–34.

Nesbit and Thompson, pp. 399–440, 453, 466–69.

Shover, John L. *Cornbelt Rebellion: The Farmers' Holiday Association,* 90–92, 130–31, 156. Urbana: University of Illinois Press, 1965.

Thelen, David P. *Robert M. La Follette and the Insurgent Spirit,* 1–125. Boston: Little, Brown, & Co., 1976.

THANKS to Jack Holzhueter and Jim Hansen (State Historical Society of Wisconsin), Peter Cannon and Richard Roe (Research Analysts, Wisconsin Legislative Reference Bureau).

INDUSTRIAL LABOR UNIONS pages 74–75 *Zoltán Grossman and Michael Gallagher*

Clark, James I. "The Wisconsin Labor Story." *Chronicles of Wisconsin,* 3–19. Madison: State Historical Society of Wisconsin, 1956.

Current, pp. 122, 186, 189, 386–88, 489.

Gavett, Thomas W. *Development of the Labor Movement in Milwaukee,* 5–13, 19, 23–25, 32–41, 49–54, 60, 83–88, 118, 121–23, 136–41, 155–57, 166–67, 182–83, 190–95, 207. Madison: University of Wisconsin Press, 1965.

Holter, Darryl, ed. *Workers and Unions in Wisconsin: A Labor History Anthology.* Madison: University of Wisconsin Press, 1999.

Glad, pp. 236, 244–46, 426.

Nesbit, pp.76–77.

Ozanne, Robert W. *The Labor Movement in Wisconsin: A History,* 1–102, 141–245. Madison: State Historical Society of Wisconsin, 1984.

South Central Federation of Labor AFL-CIO. "Madison Labor 1893–1993: Building a City, Building a Movement" (calendar). Madison: Wells Printing, 1992.

WEAC News and Views. Madison: Wisconsin Education Association Council (May 1992): 7.

Wyatt, Volume 1, secs. 8.1–8.6.

THANKS to Kenneth A. Germanson (Wisconsin Labor History Society, Milwaukee), James Cavanaugh (South Central Federation of Labor AFL-CIO), Joanna Ricca (Wisconsin State AFL-CIO, Milwaukee), Jim Lorence (University of Wisconsin–Marathon Center History Department), Mary Goulding (Green Bay Labor Council), Arlie Jaster (Wisconsin Education Association Council, Madison), Marily Crews-Nelson and Doug Crews-Nelson (Verona), Amelia Janes (Madison), Dexter Arnold (New Hampshire).

WOMEN'S INFLUENCE pages 76–77 *Marily Crews-Nelson*

Bletzinger, Andrea, and Anne Short, eds. *Wisconsin Women: A Gifted Heritage.* Amherst, Wis.: Palmer Publications, 1982.

Blue Book, 1913, pp. 270–71.

Bureau of the Census. *1980 Census of Population.* Vol. 1, "Characteristics of the Population." Chapter A, "Number of Inhabitants." Pt. 51, Wisconsin PC80–1-A51. Director, Bruce Chapman. Issued February 1982.

Bureau of the Census. *1980 Census of Population.* Vol. 1, "Characteristics of the Population." Chapter C, "General Social and Economic Characteristics." Part 51, Wisconsin PC80–1-A51. Director, Bruce Chapman. Issued August 1983.

Bureau of the Census. *1990 U.S. Census Database.* C90STF3A, Summary level: State-County, "Population." <venus.census.gov/cdrom/lookup> (10 February 1998).

Clark, James I. *Chronicles of Wisconsin.* Madison: State Historical Society of Wisconsin, 1956.

Clark, James I. *Wisconsin Women Fight for Suffrage.* Madison: State Historical Society of Wisconsin, 1956.

Current, pp. 528–34.

Famous Wisconsin Women. Madison: Women's Auxiliary, State Historical Society of Wisconsin, 1971.

Glad, pp. 104–9.

Kohler, Ruth Miriam De Young. *The Story of Wisconsin Women.* Committee on Wisconsin Women for the 1948 Wisconsin Centennial, 1948.

Maas, Jeffry. "The Role of Women in the Contemporary Agriculture of the United States" (unpublished report). University of Wisconsin–Eau Claire Geography Department, 1993.

McBride, Genevieve G. *On Wisconsin Women: Working for Their Rights from Settlement to Suffrage.* Madison: University of Wisconsin Press, 1993.

Nesbit, pp. 244–49, 446–73.

Neth, Mary. *Preserving the Family Farm: Women, Community, and the Foundations of Agribusiness in the Midwest, 1900–1940.* Baltimore: Johns Hopkins University Press, 1995.

Pederson, Jane Marie. *Between Memory and Reality: Family and Community in Rural Wisconsin, 1870–1970,* 157–85, 220. Madison: University of Wisconsin Press, 1992.

Risjord, pp. 32–33.

Thorn, John, and Pete Palmer, eds. *Total Baseball,* 2054. New York: Warner Books, 1989.

U.S. Department of Commerce. *Fifteenth Census of the United States: 1930.* Vol. 3, Pt. 2 "Population." Leon E. Truesdell, Chief Statistician for Population. Washington, D.C.: U.S. Government Printing Office, 1932.

THANKS to Margaret Beattie Bogue (University of Wisconsin–Madison history professor emerita), Doug Crews-Nelson, Sarah Davis (Madison), Joyce Westerman (Kenosha).

THE 1960S: TIME OF TURMOIL & CHANGE pages 78–79 *Zoltán Grossman*

Aukofer, Frank. *A City with a Chance*, 7–20, 41, 50–79, 97–136, 142–43. Milwaukee: Bruce Publishing Co., 1968.

Bates, Tom. *Rads: The 1970 Bombing of the Army Math Research Center at University of Wisconsin and Its Aftermath*, xix, 81–92, 103–21, 141–76, 195–206, 290–306. New York: HarperCollins, 1992.

Buhle, Paul, ed. *History and the New Left: Madison, Wisconsin, 1950–1970*. Philadelphia: Temple University Press, 1990.

Flaming, Karl Henshaw. "The 1967 Milwaukee Riot: A Historical and Comparative Analysis," 26–36. Ph.D. diss., University of Michigan–Ann Arbor, August 1970.

H. M. Gousha Company. *Street Map of Milwaukee*. 1995.

Milwaukee Journal, 3 September, 1967.

Milwaukee Sentinel, 4 June, 18 October (1965); 3 March, 9 August (1966); 3 March, 19 July, 28 August–8 September (1967).

Thompson, pp. 305–400.

Weber, Helen. *Summer Mockery: Civil Unrest Study 336*, 11, 15, 57–59, 84–87, 99–101. Milwaukee: Aestas Press, 1986.

THANKS to Clayborn Benson (Wisconsin Black Historical Museum, Milwaukee), Allen Ruff (Madison historian), David Newman (Madison).

FEDERAL ELECTIONS IN WISCONSIN pages 80–81 *Zoltán Grossman*

Blue Book, *1977*, pp. 904–5; *1981–1982*, pp. 906–7; *1985–1986*, pp. 916–17; *1989–1990*, p. 917; *1993–1994*, pp. 914–915; *1997–1998*, pp. 677–79, 700; *2001–2002*, p. 936.

Brye, David L. *Wisconsin Voting Patterns in the Twentieth Century, 1900 to 1950*, 163–85, 225–81, 295–335. New York: Garland Publishing, 1979.

Donoghue, James R. *How Wisconsin Voted, 1848–1972*. 3rd ed., 11–19, 25, 41–48, 63–67, 79–88. Madison: Institute for Governmental Affairs, University of Wisconsin–Extension, 1974.

Encyclopædia Britannica. Vol. 7. pp. 610–11. Chicago: Encyclopædia Britannica, 1993.

Risjord, pp. 153–208.

THANKS to Peter Cannon and Richard Roe (Research Analysts, Wisconsin Legislative Reference Bureau).

POPULATION & REPRESENTATION pages 82–83 *Jeffry Maas*

Blue Book, *1879*, p. 472; *1913*, p. 415; *1915*, pp. 480–83; *1933*, p. 445; *1935*, p. 442; *1937*, p. 450; *1997–1998*, pp. 8–9, 18, 697–99; *2001–2002*, pp. 739, 790.

Current, pp. 4–9, 11, 76–77, 426–27.

Forstall, Richard L. *Population of States and Counties of the United States: 1790–1990 from the Twenty-One Decennial Censuses*, 182–85. Washington, D.C.: U.S. Government Printing Office, 1996.

Nesbit, pp. 229, 275–79.

State Historical Society of Wisconsin and University of Wisconsin. *Origin and Legislative History of County Boundaries in Wisconsin*, 2–5, 8, 14–221. Madison, 1942.

Theobald, E. Rupert. *Equal Representation: A Study of Legislative Congressional Apportionment in Wisconsin*, 5–10, 57, 167–90. Madison: Wisconsin Legislative Reference Bureau, 1970.

U.S. Department of Commerce. *Congressional District Atlas*. Wisconsin sec. 7. Washington, D.C.: U.S. Government Printing Office, 1991.

White, William S. *Home Place: The Story of the U.S. House of Representatives*, 4, 20–21. Boston: Houghton Mifflin Co., 1965.

Wisconsin Legislative Reference Bureau. *Legislative Manual for the State of Wisconsin, 1877*, 441.

THANKS to Peter Cannon and Richard Roe (Research Analysts, Wisconsin Legislative Reference Bureau), Alice Hagen (University of Wisconsin–Madison Applied Population Laboratory), Bob Naylor (Demographic Service Center, Wisconsin Department of Administration).

STATE GOVERNMENT pages 84–85 *Amelia Janes and Zoltán Grossman*

Barnes, Almont. "General Jere. M. Rusk." *The American Farmer*. Washington, D.C., 1892.

Blue Book, *1892*, pp. 320–26; *1893*, pp. 320–26; *1935*, p. 254; *1958*, pp. 146, 147; *1987–1988*, pp. 874, 875, 878–81; *1995–1996*, pp 5, 22–98, 696–99; *1997–1998*, pp. 24–30, 48–63, 228–31, 661–68, 680–83; *2001–2002*, p. 709.

Brye, David L. *Wisconsin Voting Patterns in the Twentieth Century, 1900 to 1950*, 163–85, 225–81, 295–335. New York: Garland Publishing, 1979.

Current, pp. 599.

Donoghue, James R. *How Wisconsin Voted, 1848–1972*. 3rd ed., 20–24, 48–63, 99, 111, 112, 118. Madison: Institute for Governmental Affairs, University of Wisconsin–Extension, 1974.

Glad, p. 569.

Nesbit, p. 649.

Nesbit and Thompson, pp. 227, 230–31, 492, 486.

Risjord, pp. 146–200.

Roe, Richard L. "The Legislative Process in Wisconsin." In *State of Wisconsin Blue Book 1993–1994*, 103–5. Wisconsin Legislature, 1993.

Smith, p. 680.

Theobald, H. Rupert. *Equal Representation: A Study of Legislative and Congressional Apportionment in Wisconsin*. Madison: Wisconsin Legislative Reference Bureau, 1970.

Thompson, pp. 492, 739.

World Book Encyclopedia. Vol. 21, pp. 366–67. Chicago: World Book, 1997.

THANKS to Peter Cannon and Richard Roe (Research Analysts, Wisconsin Legislative Reference Bureau).

THE MILITARY IN WISCONSIN pages 86–87 *Michael Gallagher*

Blue Book, *1995–1996*, p. 759.

Houghton, Aimée, and Lenny Siegel. *Military Contamination and Cleanup Atlas for the United States, 1995*, 142–44. Pacific Studies Center and Career/Pro, San Francisco State University, 1995.

Klement, Frank L. *Wisconsin in the Civil War.* Madison: University of Wisconsin Press, 1997.

Naval Computer and Telecommunications Area Master Station Atlantic. Public Affairs Office packet, Norfolk, Virginia, 1998.

O'Laughlin, Terry. "Project ELF" (map). In *Threats to Wisconsin Communities*, 15. Madison: People United in Respect for the Earth and Wisconsin Action Group for Environmental Responsibility, 1981.

Wisconsin Department of Military Affairs. *Biennial Report 1995–1997*, 2, 12. Madison: Wisconsin Department of Military Affairs, 1997.

Wyatt, Volume 1, secs. 2.1– 5.5.

THANKS to Public Affairs Offices of the Wisconsin Department of Military Affairs (Fort McCoy and Volk Field), U.S. Army Military History Institute (Carlisle Barracks, Pennsylvania), Wisconsin Veterans' Museum (Madison), David Weingarden (Marquette Mining Journal, Michigan).

EDUCATIONAL SYSTEM pages 88–89 *Laura Exner*

Blue Book, *1997–1998*, pp. 625–43.

Current, pp. 161–69, 253–57, 399–401, 496–509.

Nesbit, pp. 359–64, 509–10.

Nesbit and Thompson, pp. 174–75, 229–31, 349, 354, 437–38, 480, 518–19, 523.

Raney, William Francis. Chapter 21 in *Wisconsin: A Story of Progress*, 423–54. Appleton, Wis.: Parin Press, 1970.

Thompson, pp. 494–506, 624–25.

Wyatt, Volume 1, secs. 1–4.

THANKS to Matt Blessing (State Historical Society of Wisconsin), Fran Sprain (Curator, Marquette County Historical Society).

Photograph & Illustration Credits

Index

Manchester, 17
Manifest Destiny, 68
Manitoba, 11, 21
Manitoulin Island, 13
Manitowoc, 21, 28–29, 31, 41, 56–57, 59, 69, 89
Manitowoc Co., 16, 18–21, 23, 28–31, 39, 43, 59, 69–72, 81
Manitowoc Rapids, 21
Manitowoc River, 7, 11–12
Mann, Sarah, 32
Manufacturing, 20, 52–56
Maple, 21
Maple Creek, 72
Maple syrup, 10, 42–43
Marathon Co., 16, 18–19, 21, 23, 28–29, 31, 39, 42–43, 59, 70–72, 81, 89
Marathon Electric, 75
March, Frederic, 33
Marengo, 21
Marian College, 89
Mariel (Cuba), 29
Marine Corps, 87
Marinette, 20–21, 26, 31, 41, 47, 56–57, 75, 89
Marinette Co., 19, 21, 23, 31, 43, 59, 71–72, 81
Marion, 30
Marquette, Fr. Jacques, 5
Marquette (Mich.), 11, 39, 57
Marquette Co., 16, 19, 21, 23, 28, 31, 39, 43, 58–59, 69–72, 81, 88
Marquette University, 89
Marshall, 17
Marshfield, 21, 41, 71, 89
Marten, 4
Maryland, 16, 64–65
Marytown, 30
Mascouten, 4–5
Mason, 21, 41, 71
Mason-Dixon Line, 78
Mass transit, 51
Massachusetts, 6–7, 16, 42, 64–66
Massey-Harris Company, 52
Mattawa River, 10
Maumee River, 4, 64–65
Mauston, 9, 77
Mayhew Manufacturing, 53
Mayland Cave, 2
Mayville, 39
Mazomanie, 17, 26, 29
Mazzuchelli, Samuel, 31
McCarthy, Charles, 73
McCarthy, Eugene J., 81
McCarthy, Joseph R., 80
McCarthyville, 17
McClaughry, 2
McClellan, George B., 81
McCord, 12–13
McFarland, William, 17
McFarland, 17
McGovern, Francis E., 73–74, 84–85
McGovern, George, 81
McKinley, William, 81
Mdewakanton Dakota, 8
Mears, Helen Farnsworth, 33
Measles, 4
Meat, 44
Meatpacking, 32, 52–54, 75
Mecan, 88
Mecklenburg, 18
Medford, 16, 30, 41, 59
Medical College of Wisconsin, 89
Medicine Lodge, 9
Medina, 16, 17, 21, 72
Meekers Grove, 38–39

Meir, Golda, 24
Mellen, 41, 71
Melrose, 17, 21
Meltwater, 37
Memorial Union, 79
Ménard, Fr. René, 5
Menasha, 41, 54–56, 59, 75
Mendota, Lake, 3, 59
Mendota State Hospital, 3
Menekaune, 47
Menominee, 4–7, 14–15, 41, 47, 54, 57, 64, 65
Menominee Co. and Reservation, 6–7, 19, 28, 43, 46, 59, 70–72, 81
Menominee March for Justice, 15
Menominee River, 5, 7, 11–12, 40–41
Menomonee Falls, 59, 77
Menomonee River, 24–25, 52–53, 78
Menomonie, 8, 13, 21, 29, 31, 41, 77, 89
Mequon, 29, 72, 89
Mercellon, 31
Merchants, 16, 24
Mero, 2
Merrick State Park, 60
Merrill, 21, 41, 46, 75
Merton, 17
Mesabi Range, 57
Meskwaki (Fox), 4–5, 14–15, 38, 42, 54, 64
Metals, 38, 50
Metalworking, 52, 74–75
Methodists, 30–31
Métis, 4, 10, 26
Metoxin, John, 6
Mexican Americans, 22, 25, 28–29
Mexican-American War, 68
Mexico, 4, 28–29, 53, 86
Miami, 4, 5, 64, 65
Michigan, 11–13, 38–39, 41, 47, 56–57, 67–68, 87
Michigan Island, 57
Michigan, Lake, 4–5, 7, 11–12, 23, 36, 38, 41, 43, 53–54, 56–57, 66–68, 82
Michigan Territory, 7, 66–67, 70
Michilimackinac, 4, 65
Michilimackinac Co., 70
Middle Mississippian culture, 3
Middle Sugar Bush, 47
Middle Village, 6
Middle Woodland culture, 2
Middleton, 16, 17, 31, 33, 59
Middleton Prairie, 17
Midewiwin, 10
Mifflin Street Block Party, 79
Migrant workers, 28–29
Military, 6, 30, 50, 53, 65, 77, 86–87
Military draft, 18, 20, 86
Military Ridge, 38
Military Road, 39, 69, 87
Militia, 18, 25, 65, 74, 86
Milk, 44–45, 47–49, 72
Milk strikes, 45, 72
Mill Bluff State Park, 60
Mill Pond, 2
Millard, 49
Mille Lacs (Minn.), 5, 11
Miller Brewing Company, 53
Millville, 2
Milprint, Inc., 52
Milton, 16, 26, 69
Milwaukee, 12–13, 16, 18–22, 24–26, 28–29, 31–33, 39, 41, 46, 51–53, 55–57, 59, 60, 67, 69, 72, 74–80, 82–83, 86–87, 89
Milwaukee and Mississippi Railroad. See Milwaukee Road
Milwaukee Athletic Club, 33

Milwaukee Chicks, 77
Milwaukee Co., 16, 18–19, 21–23, 28–29, 31, 39, 43, 52, 59, 69–72, 75, 80–81, 86
Milwaukee Garden, 74
Milwaukee Institute of Art and Design, 89
Milwaukee Iron Company, 52
Milwaukee Journal, 74–75
Milwaukee River, 5, 7, 12, 25, 46, 50, 52, 53
Milwaukee Road, 51, 53, 74
Milwaukee School of Engineering, 89
Milwaukee Sentinel, 75
Milwaukee United School Integration Committee (MUSIC), 78
Mineral Point, 38–39, 69, 70, 77
Minimum wage, 74
Mining, 8, 11, 17, 20, 22, 38–39, 50, 52–53, 59, 71, 86
Mink, 42
Minneapolis (Minn.), 60
Minneapolis, St. Paul and Sault Ste. Marie Railroad. See Soo Line
Minnesota, 7–8, 10–11, 20–21, 30, 38, 42, 44, 57
Minnesota River, 11
Minnesota Territory, 68–69
Minnesuing, Lake, 15
Minocqua, 15, 61, 83, 89
Minocqua Reservoir, 2
Minong, 71
Mint, 42–43
Miquelon Island, 64
Mirror Lake State Park, 60
Mishicot, 21
Mission, 5
Missionaries, 7
Mission Band, 13
Missions, 4, 30
Mississauga Band, 4, 10
Mississippi, 79
Mississippi River, 2, 4–5, 7–14, 16, 38, 41, 43, 46, 50, 54, 64–67, 69, 86
Mississippi River Band, 10
Mississippian culture, 2–3
Missouri, 16, 26, 38
Missouri Compromise, 68
Missouri River, 4, 8–9, 67
Missouri Synod, 31
Missouri Territory, 66
Mitchell, John L., 80
Mitchell Field, 86
Modena, 21
Modine Manufacturing Company, 52
Mohawk, 6
Mohawk River, 4
Mohawksin, Lake, 15
Mohican. See Stockbridge-Munsee
Molders, 75
Mole Lake (Sokaogon), 11, 14–15, 39
Mollica House, 33
Mondale, Walter, 81
Monico, 83
Monona, Lake, 3, 59
Monroe, 21, 30, 38–39, 69, 89
Monroe Co., 19, 21, 23, 28, 31, 42–43, 59, 70–72, 81
Montana, 11
Montello, 28
Montello River, 88
Monterey, 77
Monticello, 38
Montra's post, 5
Montreal, 4, 21, 39, 64–65, 71
Montreal River, 5, 11, 41
Montrose, 16, 17

Wisconsin Sesquicentennial Corporate Sponsors

This project has been funded in part by the Wisconsin Sesquicentennial Commission, with funds from the State of Wisconsin, and individual and corporate contributors.

A. T. & T.
Credit Unions of Wisconsin
S. C. Johnson Wax

Firstar Corporation
Harley-Davidson, Inc.
Marshall & Ilsley Corporation
Outdoor Advertising Association
Philip Morris Companies:
  Miller Brewing Company,
  Kraft Foods/Oscar Mayer Foods Corp.,
  Philip Morris USA
W. H. Brady Co.
Wisconsin Manufacturers & Commerce

ANR Pipeline Company
Blue Cross/Blue Shield United Wisconsin
Color Ink, Inc.
DEC International, Inc.
General Casualty
Home Savings
John Deere Horicon Works
Johnson Controls
Kikkoman Foods, Inc.
Kohler Co.
Marcus Theatres Corporation
Michael, Best & Friedrich
Midwest Express Airlines
Nicolet Minerals Company
Northwestern Mutual Life Foundation
Promega Corporation
Robert W. Baird & Co., Inc.
Snap-on Incorporated
Time Insurance

Weber-Stephen Company
Weyerhaeuser
Wisconsin Central Ltd.
Wisconsin Power & Light Foundation
Wisconsin Public Service Foundation
Wisconsin State Cranberry Growers Association

3M
Aid Association for Lutherans
Allen-Edmonds Shoe Corp.
A. O. Smith Corporation
Badger Mining Corporation
Briggs & Stratton Corporation
Case Corporation
Consolidated Papers, Inc.
Dairyland Power Cooperative
Edgewater Hotel
Eller Media Company
Fort James Corporation
Frazer Papers
Green Bay Packaging, Inc.
International Paper
Jockey International, Inc.
Jorgensen Conveyors, Inc.
Kimberly-Clark Corporation
Mann Bros., Inc.
Marathon Communications
Marcus Corporation
Marshfield Clinic
Modine Manufacturing Company
National Business Furniture, Inc.
Oscar J. Boldt Construction Co.
Pizza Pit, Ltd.
Rockwell Automation/Allen-Bradley
Rust Environment & Infrastructure
ShopKo
Stevens Point Brewery
Twin Disc, Incorporated
United States Cellular
Wausau and Mosinee Papers
Wisconsin Counties Association
Virchow, Krause & Company, LLP